Sustainable Program Management:
Hierarchical Causal Systems

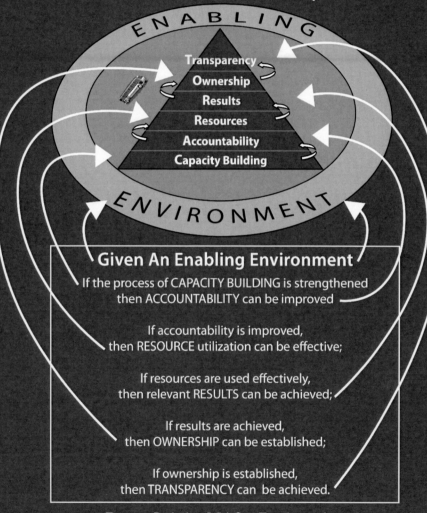

ENABLING

Transparency
Ownership
Results
Resources
Accountability
Capacity Building

ENVIRONMENT

Given An Enabling Environment

If the process of CAPACITY BUILDING is strengthened
then ACCOUNTABILITY can be improved

If accountability is improved,
then RESOURCE utilization can be effective;

If resources are used effectively,
then relevant RESULTS can be achieved;

If results are achieved,
then OWNERSHIP can be established;

If ownership is established,
then TRANSPARENCY can be achieved.

Bongs Lainjo, MASc, Engineering
Author of Monitoring and Evaluation: Data Management Systems
Former UN Senior Advisor

ISBN: 978-0-9909778-5-8 - Paperback
ISBN: 978-0-9909778-6-5 - Hardcover

Library of Congress Control Number: 2019904953

10 9 8 7 6 5 4 3 2   0 6 0 7 1 9

Printed in the United States of America

∞This paper meets the requirements of ANSI/NISO Z39.48-1992 (Permanence of Paper)

PYRAMID OF SUSTAINABLE PROGRAM MANAGEMENT

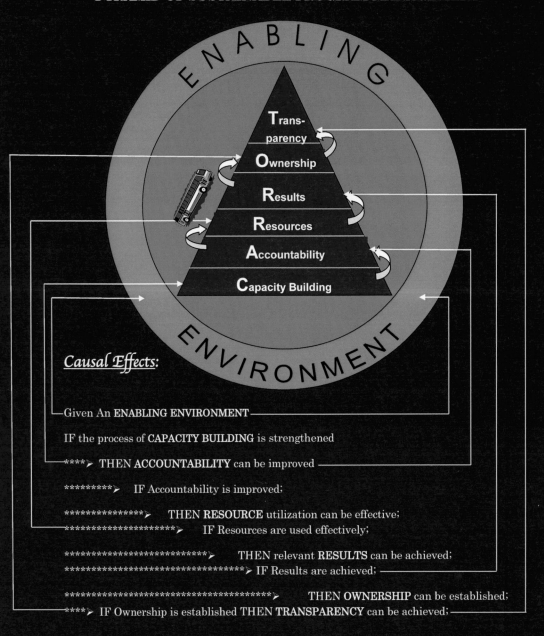

ENABLING

Transparency

Ownership

Results

Resources

Accountability

Capacity Building

ENVIRONMENT

Causal Effects:

Given An **ENABLING ENVIRONMENT**

IF the process of **CAPACITY BUILDING** is strengthened

****➤ THEN **ACCOUNTABILITY** can be improved

*********➤ IF Accountability is improved;

***************➤ THEN **RESOURCE** utilization can be effective;

********************➤ IF Resources are used effectively;

**************************➤ THEN relevant **RESULTS** can be achieved;

********************************➤ IF Results are achieved;

**************************************➤ THEN **OWNERSHIP** can be established;

****➤ IF Ownership is established THEN **TRANSPARENCY** can be achieved;

Table of Contents

Preface

After several decades of direct and indirect involvement in managing programs, I have come to think of international development as an invaluable duty to be expected from privileged communities by the underprivileged. It should never be perceived as a favour, and political motivations should be left entirely by the wayside. A willingness by Western countries to help vulnerable societies in improving their quality of life should always be an obligation that requires no second thought. All this can only be effectively achieved through mutual understanding, respect, and harmony.

I have also learned to appreciate the intricacies, complexities, and nuances that contribute to making effective interventions succeed. At this stage, I have no illusions that a one-size-fits-all solution exists. The field is diverse, the stakeholders and priorities are numerous, the needs are unquantifiable, and the dynamics as a whole are challenging and fluid. The natural human desire for standardized approaches versus the creative challenge of ambiguity, however, remains a major issue. A model that deals with fluidity while also providing some structure is clearly required. In order to address this very real challenge in program management, I have used a concept analogous to Abraham Maslow's hierarchy of needs pyramid in my proposed model — the hierarchy of causal systems (HOCS) — to define and describe every element of the ladder from base to apex. It is my sincere hope that such an approach will mitigate any shortfalls while serving as a tool to improve our current way of doing business.

My motivation for writing this primer was driven by several factors. The first was a professional urge to fill what I believed was an existing gap. The second was to use my many years of experience to contribute to this arena. The third was a personal challenge to produce an unbiased book based on reliable and verifiable anecdotal and scientific evidence to complement my own personal experience in the field. Finally, my goal is to use this opportunity to establish a common understating amongst potential readers by using a standardized approach, which every party will be able to identify with. As such, I have significantly limited the jargon and concentrated on documenting the essentials required in program management. Since the dialogue between book and reader will continue, readers should regard the methods described here as part of a process rather than an event, with the primer serving as a means to achieve meaningful outcomes on an ongoing basis. The pragmatic relevance of this book cannot be overemphasized; it becomes even more compelling since the extensive literature review has confirmed that no similar reference exists in the international program management arena.

In program management, achieving meaningful and intended (sometimes unintended) results remains a compelling element of any successful intervention. In light of this, I have highlighted the significance of one of the antecedents of the program management hierarchy framework in this manual.

My journey in producing this book has been long, tedious, frustrating, stressful, and sometimes controversial. The journey has also revealed a lack of the available, reliable, quality, and consistent data. To many of us who believe in data — both quantitative and qualitative — some limited progress continues to be made, though there remains room for significant improvement. As that old adage goes, "garbage in, garbage out" (GIGO), meaning results are only as good as the quality of data used in the decision-making process.

I have also discovered over the years that numbers are necessary, but not sufficient. While this primer is not focused on numbers, it does recognize both the importance and the limitations of quantitative data. We are all overwhelmed, for example, by the impressive indicators that tell us how far some countries have progressed developmentally. Indeed, some of these numbers do have a message; however, in several cases, these are overstated. A classic example is the development index. In some instances, numbers show outstanding success overall, while at the grassroots level, vulnerable communities are increasingly deprived of basic daily needs like access to clean water, health facilities, and an acceptable quality of life.

This book is organized into three handy sections. Part I serves as an introduction — or re-introduction — to the theory and background required to succeed in the program management of development projects. Part II provides the essential "filling" of the book — a set of case studies that show management practices in action. Part III looks at applications in program management and some specific frameworks, strategies, and tools to master the process, from operations research (OR) to specific software. Part IV contains personal anecdotes about projects from Africa to Asia, and part V highlights complementary program management strategies, with chapters ranging from monitoring and evaluation (M&E), to results-based management (RBM), to big data, cloud computing, and analytics (BDCA). A detailed table of contents will help guide the reader through the process and also provides a handy reference for returning to the material on an as-needed basis.

Acknowledgments

As with my previous book, I must acknowledge, with appreciation, the contributions of many parties to the success of this project. First, I would like to thank Jamila Kayastha for patiently and diligently working with me to finalize the image of the model. I also acknowledge, with gratitude, the help and constructive manuscript reviews of Philip "Jesse" Brandt and Alan Keller.

I dedicate this book to my mom and dad: the former for walking me through the multiplication table and the latter for teaching me the virtues of altruism and to stand up for what I truly believe in.

List of Abbreviations

AaaS – analytics-as-a-service

ADB – Asian Development Bank

AI – artificial intelligence

ANC – antenatal care

API – application programming interface

APP – Agriculture Perspective Plan

ASRH – adolescent sexual and reproductive health

BBUC – Bishop Barham University College.

BDCA – Big Data Clod Computing and Analytics

BSC – balanced scorecard

BUS – Bottom up strategy

CARROT – capacity, accountability, resources, results, ownership, and transparency

CB – capacity building

CU – Columbia University

CBS – cost breakdown structure

CGD – Center for Global Development

CIDA – Canadian International Development Agency

CIDA-INC – CIDA Industrial Cooperation Program

CMS – Centre for Medicare/Medicaid Services

CO – country office

COD – cash on delivery

CPM – critical path method

CRISP-DM – Cross Industry Standard Process for Data Mining

CRS – Catholic Relief Services

CSO – Civil Society Organization

CST – country support team

DA – development assistance

DAC – Development Assistance Committee

DAN – Dr. Ali Nawaz Foundation

DFAE – Département Fédéral des Affaires étrangères

DFATD – Foreign Affairs, Trade and Development Canada

DHT – district health team

DM – data management

DOHS – Division of Health Services

DoS – denial of service

DOS – disk operating system

EBRD – European Bank of Reconstruction and Development

EDC – Export Development Corporation

EH – electronic hacking

EHR – electronic health record

EHRS – electronic health record system

EIBC – Export Import Bank of China

EIGCM – Education and Income Generation for Conflict Mitigation

ELC – evaluation life cycle

EP – eligible practitioner

ESCO – energy saving company

EU – European Union

FAO – Food and Agricultural Organization

FH – Food for the Hungry

FP – family planning

G8 – Group of Eight

GAO – General Accounting Office

GDC – Grant Development Centre

GDP – gross domestic product

GIGO – Garbage In Garbage Out

GNI – gross national income

GOC – Government of Comoros

GOL – Government of Lesotho

GOS – Government of Swaziland

GOSL – Government of Sri Lanka

GOU – Government of Uganda

GTP – Growth and Transformation Plan

GTZ – German Agency for Technical Cooperation

HF – Health Facility

HIPC – heavily indebted poor country

HIV/AIDS – Human Immunodeficiency Virus/Acquired Immunodeficiency Syndrome

HPV – human papillomavirus

IATI – International Aid Transparency Initiative

ICPD – International Conference on Population and Development

ICSU – International Council for Science

IDA – International Development Association

IDB – Inter-American Development Bank

IFAD – International Fund for Agricultural Development

IFC – International Finance Corporation

ILAAP – International Legislative Audit Assistance Program

IMF – International Monetary Fund

INGO – International Non-Governmental Organization

IP – implementing partner

ISB – Islamic Development Bank

ISSC – International Social Science Council

IT – information technology

JICA – Japanese International Cooperation Agency

JVM – Java Virtual Machine

KPI – key performance indicator

LCU – Louisiana University College of Engineering

LFA – Logic Framework Approach

LDC – least developed country

LMIC – low- and middle-income country

LMS – learning management system

LMIS – logistics management information system

LOGFRAME – logic framework

M&E – monitoring and evaluation

MANOVA – model is multivariate analysis of covariance

MBO – management by objectives

MCH – maternal and child health

MDG – millennium development goal

MDRI – Multilateral Debt Relief Initiative

MfDR – managing for development results

MIC – middle-income country

MIGA – Multilateral Investment Guarantee Agency

MIS – management information system

MNCH – maternal and neonatal child health

MOA – memorandum of agreement

MOH – Ministry of Health

MOU – memorandum of understanding

MRS – medical records system

MTR – mid-term review

NSA – United States National Security Agency

NEHTA – National E-Health Transition Authority

NGO – non-governmental organization

NHS – National Health Service (UK)

NPfIT – National Program for IT

NYT – New York Times

ODI – Overseas Development Institute

OECD – Organisation for Economic Co-operation and Development

OR – operation research

ORT – oral rehydration therapy

PAA – predictive analytics algorithm

PAF – Poverty Alleviation Fund

PBA – program-based approach

PCA – principal component analysis

PCM – project cycle management

PDA – Personal Digital Assistant

PDF – Program design framework

PDM – precedence diagramming method

PERT – program evaluation and review technique

PIM – program implementing partners

PIN – personal identification number

PIP – project implementation plan

PISA – Program for International Student Assessments

PLC – program life cycle

PM – Program Manager

PMI – Project Management Institute

PNM – precision nitrogen management

POA – program of action

POE – panel of experts

PRISM – program indicator screening matrix

PSRP – Power Sector Rehabilitation Project

QA – quality assurance

QC – quantum computers

RC – results chain

RAM – responsibility assignment matrix

RAP – RHCS Action Plan

RAPSYS – RHCS Analysis And Planning System

RHCS – Reproductive Health Commodity Security

RBM – results-based management

REST – Relief Society of Tigray

RFE/RL – Radio Free Europe/Radio Liberty

RFID – radio-frequency identification device

RH – reproductive health

RHCS – Reproductive Health Commodity Security

RMAF – results-based management and accountability framework

RN – Registered Nurse

ROI – return on investment

SADC – Southern African Development Community

SAWA – South And West Asia

SD – sustainable development

SDC – Swiss Development Corporation

SDG – Sustainable Development Goals

SDPRP – Sustainable Development Poverty Reduction Program

SFW – strategic framework

SIDA – Swedish International Development Cooperation Agency

SIMI – Smallholder Irrigation Market Initiative

SIMPLE – Set expectations, Invite commitment, Measure progress, Provide feedback, Link to consequences, and Evaluate effectiveness

SMEs – small-and-medium enterprises

SQL – structured query language

SO – strategic objective

SP – service provider

SPP – sports performance platform

SSA – security supporting assistance

SWAp – sector-wide approach (to development)

SWOT – strengths, weaknesses, opportunities, threats

TALCO – Tajik Aluminum Company

TKP – turn-key program

ToC – theory of change

TOT – training of trainers

TQM – total quality management

UAT – user acceptance testing

UN – United Nations

UNDP – United Nations Development Program

UNFCCC – United Nations Framework Convention on Climate Change

UNFPA – United Nations Population Fund

UNICEF – United Nations Children's Fund

URL – uniform resource locator

U.S. – United States

USAID – U.S. Agency for International Development

WB – World Bank

WBI – World Bank Institute

WBS – Work Breakdown Structure

WFP – World Food Program

WHO – World Health Organization

WP – work plan

PART I: THEORY

CHAPTER 1: Introduction

In all management landscapes, and in development program management specifically, there is evidence that even with every effort and application of compelling strategies, outcomes are often disappointing. These often stem from unforeseen circumstances and uncontrolled, internal, and external factors. In some cases, poor budget oversight and inhibiting environments contribute substantially in derailing programs. As Murphy's Law states, "Anything that can go wrong, will go wrong." Program management is no exception.

Background

This literature review is intended to highlight the existing models, frameworks, or systems on program management with emphasis on similarities, differences, and scope compared to the CARROT-BUS model, detailed below. With regard to the available documentation, and as confirmed by evidence-based research, very few documents are available on program management framework. Most available frameworks are in project management with a particular focus on the corporate world. No literature is available on the CARROT-BUS model. The result of the review is, therefore, based on the available literature on project/program management.

Based on current literature, increasing efforts on "sustainability" in project management is promising. There are also some challenges because "sustainability" is difficult to define in concrete operational terms and is currently based on instinctive manifestations (Briassoulis, 2001). Silvius (2013) concludes that an overview is needed with insights and knowledge development. According to Silvius (2013), a structured review of the available literature on sustainability and project management will answer how sustainability is defined or considered in the context of program management. And how is program management impacted by considering sustainability?

In this book, a program is characterized as: Different thematic and complementary subsets or projects (micro) designed to effectively contribute in tandem to a common set (macro). And consistent with this characterization, a project and program can be used interchangeably where only one project is under implementation at a given point in time.

Population changes, climate changes, and energy resource constraints are the three driving forces that are undergoing major transitions in the world. It is essential to move toward "sustainability" in the implementation of projects and programs. Real "sustainability" exists where there is a global equilibrium (Haugan, 2013). Sustainable Program Management provides essential information on these three major driving forces of the coming decades for designing programs. Portfolio managers and senior planners are moving toward a sustainable future (Haugan, 2013).

A study was conducted by Mauro Luiz Martens, Fabien Brones, and Marly Monteiro de Carvalho (2013) in "A conceptual framework of sustainability in project management oriented to success" using systematic literature review. The paper highlighted a conceptual framework that contributes to the sustainability of economic, environmental, and social perspectives in project management oriented to success. The concept of corporate sustainability is linked with three dimensions: environmental, economic, and social (Gimenez, Sierra, & Rodon, 2012), i.e., sustainability based on the triple bottom line concept (Elkington 1998; Labuschagne, Brent, & Van Erck, 2005; Savitz 2006). Under this perspective, organizations that seek to achieve a standard of excellence must develop ways of reducing their negative social and environmental impacts.

Additionally, Carvalho and Rabechini (2011) claim the need for the environmental, social, and economic dimensions of sustainability to be combined into project management. This necessity has encouraged a discussion of how to upsurge sustainability in project management. According to Silvius (2013), the association between project management and sustainable development has been gaining consideration amongst professionals and scholars. According to studies by Martens et al. (2013), initiatives aiming at integrating these two themes are already underway (Anning, 2009; Bodea, Elmas, Tănăsescu, & Dascălu, 2010; Fernández-Sánchez, & Rodríguez-López, 2010; Jones, 2006; Mulder & Brent, 2006; Raven, Jolivet, Mourik, & Feenstra, 2009; Turlea, Roman, & Constantinescu, 2010; Vifell & Soneryd, 2012). More additional research is required to develop tools, techniques, and methodologies (Singh, Murty, Gupta, & Dikshit, 2012; El-Haram et al., 2007; Thomson, El-Haram, & Emmanuel, 2011) that can be applied in program management in order to analyze sustainability (Carvalho & Rabechini, 2011; Cole, 2005; Deakin, Huovila, Rao, Sunikkamand, 2002; Thomson et al., 2011).

Bebbington, Brown, and Frame (2007) highlight the significance of including variables of sustainability in activities related to project phases to improve the quality of the projects but, according to Shenhar and Dvir

(2007), Shenhar (2011), and Shenhar, Dvir, Levy, & Maltz (2001), this new look at the project management contributes to achieving success. In this new scenario, besides the demand for sustainability in project management, concepts of success in projects become relevant to the study. As mentioned by Wit (1988), the success in projects refers to the objectives and benefits of the project to the organization entirely. It is the effectiveness of a particular initiative linked to the compliance of its initial objective, enabling stakeholders to reap the benefits provided by the project. Moreover, the need for studies on the convergence of sustainability issues and project management, coupled with the increasing importance of both on the current business environment, as well as its relationship with success in projects, motivates this study, which seeks to contribute to the development of the sustainability issues in project management and success in projects (Martens, Brones, & Carvalho, 2013). Thus, this primer focuses on the alignment of these themes, with the aim of systematizing a theoretical framework to provide evidence constructs of sustainability in program management with an orientation to success in programs.

Over the last four decades, many funding agencies — both bilateral and multilateral — have invested heavily in assisting developing countries to improve their quality of life. An objective analysis of these initiatives shows that while some have achieved meaningful results, others have not. The need to create a "sustainable" development assistance management model as a gold standard in designing programs for foreign development aid has never been more pressing.

To create effective program management, both funding agencies and implementing partners (IPs) must first define the benchmarks for "success." Is "success" defined in terms of events, processes, or both? In the case of outcomes, is "success" achieved when the intended results cannot be precisely linked to a prescribed set of outputs but rather is influenced by situational responses that could not have been forecasted? For example, what about a critical change to an obstructive government policy or a change in political leadership? In the case or process, is "success" defined as a set of mechanisms and procedures that yielded positive outcomes as described in the original logical framework (logframe)? Despite unforeseen events that may have impeded progress, did the features and conditions established before, during, or after program implementation result in a stream of positive results, culminating in the desired outcome as stipulated in the logframe? Complex developmental undertakings require establishing a broad and binding consensus amongst different stakeholders; usually a complex task. Agreements with less than 100% buy-in from all stakeholders can directly affect outcomes. Therefore, planning and dialogue should focus not only on the process of identifying the desired outcomes but also on the progress of implementation and follow-up. In this manual, three cases of possible outcomes related to this hypothesis were carefully reviewed and described in detail.

Many foreign development aid programs have been created during the past few years. Often, these programs were neither coordinated nor integrated with one another. Despite some progress in the design and implementation of foreign developmental aid programs, most remain territorial in nature. Most of the time, these programs are predominantly vertical in terms of their implementation. Due to their complexity, it is never easy to identify specific factors that contribute to the success of the program, determine synergies that may have developed during implementation, or to assign attribution for both positive and negative results that occurred. To claim that a specific foreign development aid program is a "one-size-fits-all" model represents the viewpoint of specific proponents of specific models. More often than not, the events and processes needed for sustainability are not considered in their entirety.

Most foreign aid development experts agree that at the time of conceptualization and program design, significant responsibilities must be recognized as the preparation for the implementation occurs. Definitions of the expected or desired results, including the terms and conditions of the donor/lender, have to be carefully and conscientiously negotiated, and ideally, established in contractual form. Division of authority, roles and responsibilities of national or international paid staff and consultants, and the mechanisms of accountability for their actions and outputs should be established as unambiguously as possible at the offset.

Having acknowledged unique program features is not to say that a universally accepted procedure should not be considered when designing the program. As is stated in an Organisation for Economic Co-operation and Development (OECD) report on stakeholder participation, "Although there may have been broad and effective stakeholder participation at some stages of the development and implementation of national development strategies, none of the respondents identified ongoing, systematic, and unified mechanisms to support the continuous engagement of these stakeholders in the policy process." (OECD, 2011b, p. 32). Therefore, some questions or issues that need to be answered during the design phase are listed as follows:

- Who is deemed a stakeholder and in what sense?
- What is each of these stakeholder's vision of success? What specific

results or outcomes have been identified? And how can these be refined, so as to be said to contribute to the emergence of meaningful results for the direct beneficiaries, the donors, the host authorities, and, last but not least, those who will manage the program? Has sufficient research been done on the heterogeneous composition of the intended beneficiaries, their spoken languages, and the complexity of their societal structures?

- What degree of consultation (frequency, venue, and timing) with those deemed as immediate stakeholders (intended beneficiaries, implementing partners, government officials, program personnel) is considered adequate?
- How would consultations be done with all the identified and relevant stakeholders? By who?
- Who should take responsibility for flaws in program design that emerge later and were not visible/apparent in the design stages as risks and threats?
- What is the degree of active participation of/by/with the intended beneficiaries, target or other vulnerable groups (i.e., those expected to benefit either directly or indirectly from the intervention) that should take place during the design phase? During implementation? How should representatives of these groups be identified? What mechanism suits them best for their optimum participation?
- How can ownership, continuity, and transparency be defined for each stakeholder or stakeholder group?
- Are relevant and appropriate feedback mechanisms identified? How can these be put in place to monitor program dynamics, recognize, manage, and resolve conflicts, and adapt program processes and procedures to events that occur during implementation stage?

To achieve maximum potential progress and optimum growth, providers of development resources would most likely demand assurance of an acceptable level of success in all sponsored initiatives, as well as in financial and technical support they extend. At the same time, authorities of the beneficiary nations should be able to measure, sustain, and improve upon results from year to year. This is the bargain of foreign assistance: We, the donors/lenders will try to do something for you, as the host. Hopefully, this will be for/in your best interests. In return, we will mutually set the program on the road to success and achieve progress incrementally towards a realization of a sometimes fuzzily-defined goal, and hopefully a golden future.

<u>Current Practice</u>

Who are the stakeholders behind a foreign aid development program? Stakeholders of a foreign aid development program can be categorized as either international or domestic. Szent-Ivanyi and Lightfoot (2015, pp. 5–6) mentioned that international stakeholders include not only international organizations, such as the Organization for Economic Co-operation and Development (OECD), European Union (EU), Development Assistance Committee (DAC), and the United Nations Development Program (UNDP), as well as developed countries that support foreign aid projects. Additionally, stakeholders include host authorities along with the intended beneficiaries, the program managers, and all non-state and state actors in each underdeveloped or developing country who can affect the formulation of foreign aid policies. Oftentimes, international organizations such as the EU do not only influence the development of international foreign aid policies but also promote social learning and assist international donors such as the case of the Canadian International Development Agency (CIDA) and UNDP (Szent-Ivanyi & Lightfoot, 2015, p. 6).

The vision of success of the different stakeholders varies. For instance, the expected outcome of program managers is to make foreign aid projects successful. Aside from budgeting and risk management, it is the duty and responsibility of program managers to monitor and see to it that each team member is able to perform their assigned task within the expected timeframe. With this in mind, the program manager should always rely on the use of monitoring tools, such as the Gantt chart, and network diagrams to ensure that each of the identified deliverables will be completed on time. Aside from raising funds, the expected results of the host authorities and donors are to see to it that the intended beneficiaries are properly using the foreign aid fund for economic development activities. This ensures that donors continue supporting the funding of their development programs.

In relation to foreign aid development programs, previous studies show that there are similarities when it comes to the composition, language spoken, and societal structure of the intended beneficiaries. Oftentimes, intended beneficiaries are composed of disadvantaged people who are currently living in poverty and can be easily controlled by the rich and powerful within a given society (Platteau, 2003). Communication is the key to a successful foreign aid program. For that reason, determining the language spoken amongst the stakeholders is very important. In line with this, most of the foreign aid donors are English speaking countries and most of the intended beneficiaries are non-English speaking countries (e.g., Spanish, French, Portuguese, etc.) (Easterly, 2002). Aside from the differences in the language spoken, another characteristic amongst the intended beneficiaries is that most of them are found in rural communities (Platteau, 2003). Because of the socioeconomic inequalities within the social structure, the only way to mobilize the less fortunate individuals is to empower them through education and proper training. Therefore, poverty reduction policies should always be created in such a way that they can protect the interests of people living in poverty, rather than the sole interests of the powerful elites.

Social structures in developing countries can affect the success or failure of foreign aid development programs (Easterly, 2002). Even though the intended beneficiaries are able to access development funding from their donors, long-term effects may not be as promising as originally envisioned. Long-term benefits from infrastructure development programs in rural areas, for example, may not yield comparable results as those in urban areas. This argument is true because the majority of the people living in poor regions may not have the capital, knowledge, and skills needed to establish themselves as entrepreneurs. Due to lack of empowerment, people in rural areas are often unable to maximize the long-term socioeconomic benefits of investments in costly infrastructure projects.

Undergoing a consultation process is essential before a new foreign aid development project can be implemented. The consultation process amongst the donors normally includes the need to coordinate foreign aid programs and policies, as well as its priorities and strategies that could sustain long-term relationships between the donors and intended beneficiaries (OECD, 1998, p. 35). For instance, regarding U.S. government foreign aid assistance; it is common for the donors to seek consultation with the U.S. Agency for International Development (USAID) concerning projects related to "Development Assistance" (DA), "Security Supporting Assistance" (SSA), or "food aid" (Lancaster, 2007, p. 73). In the case of Canada, donors with similar questions will have to consult CIDA (now known as Global Affairs Canada) each time they intend to give food and/or non-food assistance to developing countries (OECD, 1998, p. 35). Before extending financial assistance to developing countries, CIDA normally consults with a wide range of civil society stakeholders regarding their "regional, sub-regional, and country policy frameworks" (OECD, 1998, p. 53). On the other hand, the consultation process amongst the domestic stakeholders is not limited to political leaders but also civil servants. As a result, the relatively long consultation process among the intended beneficiaries becomes a common complaint amongst the donors (Carlsson, Somolekae, & van de Walle, 1997).

Even though stakeholders would normally undergo a series of consultation processes, Carlsson et al. (1997) revealed that it is unlikely for any government bodies to consult with universities or academic institutions, or anyone from the civil society concerning the need to make any reforms of foreign aid policies. With this in mind, it is unlikely for the government sector to consult anyone from the private sector concerning issues related to foreign aid development reforms. Furthermore, it is also unlikely for the donors to consult their intended beneficiaries about the design and implementation of their proposed foreign development projects. Instead of talking directly to the intended beneficiaries, it is more common for the donors to consult with the local government bodies (Carlsson et al., 1997). Thus, the intended beneficiaries are often unaware of what they will receive from the donors. This further explains why most intended beneficiaries are unable to safeguard their own personal interests when it comes to the management and disbursement of foreign aid funds. Instead of the intended benefitting from foreign aid development programs, too often, the greedy and most powerful government officials are the ones who co-opt the available funds. Since the powerful government officials are the ones who receive foreign aid funds, it becomes very difficult to control and monitor where exactly the foreign aid funds go, and eventually to make the real recipients accountable for misusing the funds.

Considering the lapses or flaws in the entire program design and consultation process, both donors and the intended beneficiaries should be made responsible for the failure of foreign aid development projects. This is because both parties have roles and obligations to fulfill. Certainly, the issue on corruption and misuse of foreign aid funds is not new. Therefore, in the case of the donors, it becomes their responsibility not to release money to their intended beneficiaries without closely monitoring how they would use the foreign aid fund. This means that the donors should at least appoint their own people to oversee how the foreign aid funds will be used by the intended beneficiaries. It is the duty and responsibility of the intended beneficiaries to observe transparency when using the foreign aid funds. For example, assuming that the donors could not see any physical result from the foreign aid projects, the donors can easily arrange for appointed people be held legally accountable for their failure to deliver the expected outcomes.

One of the best ways to prevent corruption or misuse of foreign aid funds is to allow the intended beneficiaries to actively participate in the foreign aid development programs. However, given the fact that it is common for the donors to deal directly with the local government agencies of the intended beneficiaries, it is unfortunate that most intended, usually vulnerable beneficiaries do not have the opportunity to participate in the planning stage or the actual delivery of the foreign aid development programs. Because of their absence during the design, implementation, and monitoring phase of the project, the intended beneficiaries do not have the opportunity to voice their own concerns or provide feedback about the progress of the project. Likewise, the current arrangement between the donors and the local government agencies make the vulnerable groups unable to check or monitor whether the persons in charge of disbursing the funds are making the right decisions for the welfare and long-term interests of all the intended beneficiaries. Considering such a scenario, the best strategy or mechanism that could optimize the active participation of the intended beneficiaries is to encourage all donors to insist on their inclusion in all phases of project design and implementation, rather than dealing exclusively with local government agencies.

Each donor and its intended beneficiaries have unique ways of defining the concept of ownership, continuity, and transparency. For instance, CIDA identifies "ownership" and "local involvement" to be the main factors that could lead to sustainable results (DFATD, 2014). In the case of Ethiopia, for example, its strong commitment to anti-poverty programs and ownership regarding development planning and priorities make it a country that could benefit from long-term positive development results (DFATD, 2015). Aside from joining the International Aid Transparency Initiative (IATI), CIDA decided to launch its "open data portal" to promote the practice of transparency (DFATD, 2014). Likewise, CIDA also created report measures and set a committee that is composed of external partners to oversee its foreign aid development programs (i.e., International Legislative Audit Assistance Program [ILAAP]) (DFATD, 2014; CIDA, 2012b). Similar to the case of Ethiopia, Nepal also has a strong commitment to its poverty reduction campaign and human rights promotion, making this particular country become less dependent on foreign aid; from 53% in 2000 down to 34% in 2009 (Action Aid, 2011). Regarding transparency, Nepal has been active in practicing transparency when managing the usage of foreign aid funds and available supplies (Action Aid, 2011).

Appropriate feedback mechanisms play a significant role in the success of foreign aid development projects. By creating a feedback mechanism, foreign aid donors and their intended beneficiaries can conduct two-way communication, where both parties can freely ask questions about the foreign aid development goals, strategies, and expected timeframes, and file complaints or provide suggestions that can help increase the success rate of the project (Jean, 2012). As a way to assess, manage, monitor, and plan on foreign aid projects, Nepal managed to create a feedback mechanism at regional and national levels as a way to enable them to improve the accuracy and reliability of data used for foreign aid policy development and project planning purposes (UNICEF, 2011). CIDA (2007) reported that one of the weak points of CIDA-INC — the CIDA Industrial Cooperation Program that sought to get private firms involved in development projects — is that some private firms may not give much importance to feedback mechanisms.

The Bottom Up Strategy (BUS) and the CARROT Model

The processes of establishing an appropriate enabling environment require the development of one or more structured "gold standard" program management models. In my efforts to do that, the central approach was to create a management model based on a bottom up strategy (BUS). This particular proposed management model includes several important elements: 1) *capacity* building; 2) personal and institutional *accountability*; 3) effective utilization of *resources*; 4) the need to acknowledge both desired and undesired *results*; 5) group or community *ownership*; and 6) *transparency* of process (CARROT) (see Figure 1.1).

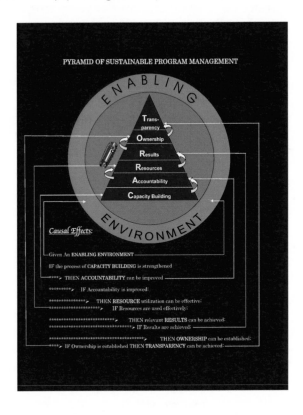

Figure 1.1: Proposed model illustrated in a pyramid form

Source: Lainjo, 2015

Shrewd readers will notice a close similarity between the CARROT model and Maslow's hierarchy of needs (see Figure 1.2), which is also illustrated by a pyramid, with bodily needs at the bottom of the pyramid and spiritual needs at the top. The Maslow model is so basic to social science that all readers must be familiar with it by now. However, it is familiar because it is so useful and an excellent reminder of why and how we do development work. It is well to remember that those higher up the pyramid owe a debt to those further down it, and it is the needs of those below the level of self-actualization that count the most. It would be wrong for donors, for example, to try to have their own needs for belonging and esteem met by development projects; our focus must be on our clients. Our job, essentially, is to make sure that all basic needs are met throughout the world so that all of humanity can make it to the top layer of the pyramid — self-actualization. Anything less perpetuates a state of injustice.

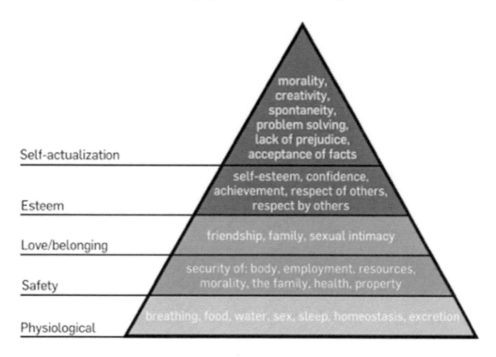

Figure 1.2: Abraham Maslow's hierarchy of needs
Source: <http://www.abraham-maslow.com/m_motivation/hierarchy_of_Needs.asp>

It is also well to remember, of course, that donors have needs as well. One of the self-actualization needs in the pyramid includes "generativity," or the ability to pass on wisdom, know-how, and even material possessions to the next generation. Looking at it from this angle, Western countries that have scaled the "development" pyramid cannot continue to focus on the need for "safety" exclusively and should not be gorging on over-satisfying their physiological needs when others are starving.

At the same time, the drive for development must come from below, hence the "bottom up strategy." The time for "trickle down" economics is long past. Donors must acknowledge and honour the urgency of their clients in order to forge relationships of mutual respect and trust; otherwise, nothing will be accomplished. This is why the CARROT elements — capacity, accountability, resources, results, ownership, and transparency — are so critical.

As one contribution in addressing some of these challenges, I have attempted to review current programs, life case studies, and strategies in order to provide possible and potential solutions that can be used by everyone interested or involved in program management. In light of the perpetual challenges in program management, I have produced what hopefully will prove to be a unique, practical, and compelling management model. This book uses a combination of systems including relevant strategies and case studies to demonstrate the CARROT-BUS tool that he hopes will contribute in mitigating many program weaknesses. It is now left to the reader to confirm if this is true or not.

With regard to the target audience, I tried to structure the subject matter to interest as many readers as possible. Groups that will find this document useful include staff of academic institutions — students and professors, government administrators, non-governmental organizations (NGOs) and staff of organizations nominated as implementing partners for multi- and bilateral-funded programs.

The CARROT-BUS model emerged from meetings and discussions amongst colleagues, stakeholders, national counterparts, and funding agencies. The model represents an accumulative combination of over three decades of development work. During these sessions with the different groups, I identified two areas of consensus. They generally agreed that the necessary components of a sustainable program outcome were "capacity building" as the baseline and "transparency" as the ultimate product. After several years of internalizing these opinions, I reached the conclusion that there had to be other factors connecting these two components. That is how the other intermediate components were established. The CARROT-BUS framework is not only neutral, it is also inclusive and applicable in as many program management landscapes as one can imagine.

This CARROT-BUS in some ways is really two major strategic frameworks — logic framework (logframe) and strategic framework. The former has been widely used by different proponents, ranging from the military (initially) to the different program management sectors today. Its ubiquity and level of acceptance continue unabated. The two frameworks together also serve as an invaluable tool that effectively complements results-based-management (RBM) interventions. In addition, the concepts operate around similar principles: the logframe with hierarchical antecedents begins with inputs at the bottom progressing to the goal at the top. CARROT starts with capacity building at the bottom rising to transparency at the top.

Graphically, the CARROT-BUS model is visually defined by three symbols. The first is a circle around the pyramid. This circle symbolizes the only crosscutting antecedent enabling environment — of the framework, while the second symbol, is the pyramid itself showing all the steps of the ladder with increasingly narrow spans representing the level of difficulty as one climbs from one step to the next. Details of all the levels of the ladder are presented elsewhere in the primer. And then there is the "BUS." The latter has two significant symbolic and practical implications. The first being that all participants will be ascending the ladder on a bus — an indication of the long "journey" involved and teamwork in moving from each level to the next. The other meaning is the strategy of the model bottom up strategy (BUS). The population dynamic of participants as it moves up the ladder of the systems is analogous to that of an open cohort in a longitudinal study. In light of the General Assembly's approval of the UN Sustainable Development Goals in September 2015, and their long-term timeline, this model could serve as a useful and appropriate framework during implementation and execution of activities to reach the seventeen goals.

Sustainable Development Goals (SDGs)

In the last decade and a half, development and funding agencies have concentrated on achieving the eight development goals — Millennium Development Goals (MDGs) approved by the UN in 2000. Various evaluation reports of the mammoth venture have demonstrated mixed outcomes. My belief is that while the MDGs were timely, necessary, appropriate, and inclusive, the goals with respect to intended targets were daunting in terms of realistically achieving them. The intensions may have been quite good but the intended outcomes were overly ambitious and unrealistic.

Many reports do indicate that some MDGs were achieved — a view that I believe requires further analyses of more critical and objective inputs. In that regard, I would like to believe that the jury is still out! It is indeed true

13

that some progress was made as indicated and that the quality of life in many parts of the world improved. There is every reason to believe that the reported data on the "impressive achievements" were substantially skewed by countries like China and India. Such skewing evidently can produce misleading and questionable conclusions. The reality is that in most parts of the world, especially in sub-Saharan Africa, significant levels of achievements were mixed and inconclusive in some cases. For example, in one UN report of two analyses of Maternal Health programs — one of them belonging to the UN — concluded that the outcomes were dismal with nothing to show for the initiatives. This has raised more questions about spending billions of dollars in these efforts with nothing to show for them.

Now, according to the UN, the world body has introduced another paradigm change — Sustainable Development Goals (SDGs) — as part of its development plan from 2016 to 2030. Graphic details of the seventeen global goals are presented in Figure 1.3. Based on the current updates on the MDGs, not much has been documented in terms of lessons learned; including the absence of relevant and appropriate mitigating factors aimed at minimizing potential risks and unforeseen challenges. The UN has promised to make details available at a letter date. The devil will be in the details!

Figure 1.3: The 17 global goals for sustainable development
Source: Jakob Trollbäck (http://www.weforum.org/agenda/2015/09/what-are-the-sustainable-development-goals)

One challenge that the SDGs will need to address (and that was prevalent with the MDGs), is the availability of adequate, reliable, and consistent data. Some of the problems encountered with the MDGs were caused by lack of good quality and consistent data. This is unlikely to change with the SDGs if significant efforts are not made to address these and some undocumented issues.

Development, unfortunately, generally takes place in unfavourable environments — a condition that makes strategic frameworks quite fluid and unpredictable. Therefore, it becomes critical to ask if these initiatives are yet another attempt by the UN to promote the world body's visibility and ubiquity. Multilateral and bilateral agencies have the good will but the resources continue to be dwindling, thin, and limited.

For instance, we all know that funding is becoming less and less available with donor agencies setting higher bars with an endless number of requirements. Above all, universal agreements by most donor countries are not even being respected. For example, in over five decades, most developed countries agreed on budgeting and allocating 0.07% of their respective gross domestic products (GDPs) to international aid. The reality today is that most countries have not come anywhere close to these targets.

With regard to the SDGs, the pathway remains rocky, and that will become more apparent when implementation starts. In the meantime, stakeholders and vulnerable communities can only start to grapple with 17 overarching goals and 169 subordinate targets that were approved by the UN general assembly in September of 2015. According to sources, the feelings of the International Council for Science (ICSU) in partnership with the International Social Science Council (ISSC) — involved in coordinating and analyzing these goals — the program remained uncoordinated, immeasurable and unrealistically ambitious (ICSU, ISSC, 2015). It is also my hope that given the uncharted way forward, the relevant parties will seriously look into the validity of using CARROT-BUS as an invaluable tool that will help in dealing with many implementation challenges.

CHAPTER 2: Models for Sustainable Development

According to John Morfaw, MBA, founder and CEO of Tanyimor Project LLC and Tanyimor Foundation Inc., and author of the book *A Comprehensive Guide to Project Sustainability, Systems and Organizations in a Competitive Marketplace,* most projects fail due to the absence of an "appropriate sustainable plan" (Morfaw, 2011, p. 1). To apply his perception of general foreign aid to developing countries and the way foreign assistance is currently being managed, it is necessary to consider all existing foreign development aid programs as something akin to the expression that the "glass is half empty." It means that there are still a lot of things to do and consider before these development assistance programs can work more efficiently and effectively over time and achieve a better sustainability record.

In developing countries, there are enormous complexities, some commonalities, and diverse challenges. Quite often, there is a need to solve some of these developmental challenges by addressing the symptoms. Many of the issues raised in the set of questions listed above have resulted due to designers' own ignorance, falsely rationalizing that the more intractable problems would simply fade away in time, and by falsely assuming that some events would take place along the way to change the context for the better. For example, after over half a century of development assistance in the 20th century, including budget subsidies to national governments or mechanisms such as the structural adjustment programs, only minor positive results were noted despite the large effort given to those in need (Boch-Isaacson, 2001, pp. 305–315). Debt forgiveness has become a mantra of sorts during the last decade or so (Balls, 2015). But debt forgiveness implies that the donors failed to assess the local environment properly, failed to perceive issues that might impede implementation, failed to design/modify appropriate interventions, and failed to control the input–output ratio and often could not precipitate (or cause) the intended outcomes. It also implies that recipients have failed to produce the expected results, perhaps due to a single event, perhaps due to a broader range of process-related reasons, or perhaps from a combination of both. In any case, it is a lose-lose outcome.[i]

The "lose-lose outcomes" may have resulted in the establishment of new "paradigms" of development partnerships such as the Paris Agreement and conferences known as the Agra Agenda for Action and the Busan Fourth High Level Forum on Aid Effectiveness Conference of 2011. In order to improve accountability, reduce corruption, and foster better transparency, program interventions are often channelled through implementation modalities used by various international non-governmental organizations

(INGOs), civil society organizations (CSOs), and NGOs (Funds for NGOs, 2008).

In retrospect, planning processes of NGOs, regardless of whether they are local, national, or international in composition, often have inadequate or inefficient strategic planning processes. Often one hears from representatives of donors or host governments alike that program control and authority are not appropriately exercised by NGO partners. Finger pointing by government representatives has always been a proxy mechanism for some who are power-hungry, corrupt or hope to gain control over the resource allocation processes. It is also true that some NGOs may not have accomplished their duty and responsibilities to ensure project success. Most of the time, NGOs were left on their own after being vetted and certified by the donor. Their hosts have little recourse to redress the grievances as NGOs were "locked in" by long-term contracts. Often, it remains unclear as to who actually monitors the program's success or failure.

When it comes to determining attribution for success or affixing blame for a project's failure, one has to look in-depth at some of the obstacles that may have hindered successful implementation (i.e., existing and past social, political, and economic environments). Recognizing all such factors can be quite daunting. The challenges not only include the identification of confounding factors but also the quantification of their impact on relevant outcomes. For instance, the World Bank reported that the number of international migrants[ii] doubled to 215 million in the last 25 years up to 2010, while remittances to developing countries more than quadrupled to over $300 billion (Sirkeci, Cohen, & Ratha, 2012, p. 440; World Bank, 2015a). These funds also represent three times the amount allocated for official development assistance by all developed nations with bilateral development programs and multilateral lending agencies such as the World Bank and the African Development Bank.

Democracy First, Development Second

One prevailing myth believed by some development authorities highlights the absence of a democratic setting as one of the key barriers to success. This can be a misguided assertion. When referring to democracy, what do analysts mean? Politically, democracy has often been viewed as a panacea for developing countries' perpetual problems (AbrefaBusia, 1961).

> Forty-plus years later, an African youth leader had this to say about democracy: "The right to vote has become the worst thing in the society. It has become the way to legitimizing a

small group of middle-class to take money from public coffers and go use it in private..." (Akugizibwe, 2012). As a result, the mindset of human beings became so influenced by such glib and naive pronouncements that any attempt to see things differently has a very limited chance of success. In fact, a more egregious tendency is to characterize an entire country or even a continent or way of life as a failure. Such dismissive and disingenuous assertions can be very misleading. Many of the root and underlying causes were (totally) ignored, sidelined, or carried forward from the colonial past of these countries with the hope that the problem could somehow just go away in time, preferably sooner rather than later. In my own opinion, I believe that democracy is an important aspect of society; it gives us the right and freedom of political will.

The Changing Development Paradigm

Cast in this light, pessimism arises regarding achieving successful development outcomes. In fact, many funding agencies have continuously changed their policies and procedures. These changes have included the need to re-establish development paradigms, as in the *Paris Declaration on AID Effectiveness of 2005* (OECD, 2005/2008, p. 14). More recently, these funding agencies have tried to channel program interventions through contracts with larger not-for-profit development entities (e.g., WINROCK, John Snow, Inc., BRAC, CHEMONICS, etc.) supposedly changing aid-giving practices for the better.

Forging their own national development strategies with the parliamentarians and elected officials, ownership has become the new norm for aid recipients. Other activities such as the need to encourage more donors to support these national strategies (alignment), streamlining the efforts in country (harmonization), creating clear goals and closely monitoring development results, and encouraging more donors and recipients to become more responsible in achieving these goals (mutual accountability) have also become a part of the new norm. Five years after the Paris Declaration and despite the summation of development principles as reflected in the Accra Agenda for Action, a review of the track record of success has produced some disappointing results.

In 2011, the outcome of the Busan Partnership for Effective Development Co-operation (Busan, Republic of Korea, 29 November–1 December 2011), recognized the fact that the process of successfully tackling poverty and inequality, as well as building a better world for all, means making joint efforts to address a wide range of challenges (OECD, 2011a). This can be done by leveraging and strengthening the impact of diverse sources of funds and knowledge. In effect, prior efforts such as the sector-wide approach (SWAp) to development was designed to focus more on strengthening its operating principles and practices within a narrow sector basis rather than focusing on policies and activities, politics, and institutional issues that may affect the public's welfare more broadly. In sum, the former approach was judged as not being able to address the complexities of development assistance fully or successfully (Cabral, 2010; Foster, 2000).[iii] To sum it up, the international development community has chosen to continue the search for more appropriate models that when deployed will more explicitly capture these complexities and produce more sustainable and valuable outcomes. To paraphrase the director of the OECD:

> The main achievement (of the former strategy) was that it appeared to have strengthened partner countries and to augment their sense of responsibility towards fulfilling the development expectations of their populations. A major paradigm change is now in place. Since Busan, the absence of suitable structures has ceased to be a valid justification for the direct implementation of development funds by the donor countries. On the contrary, where such institutions are not present, this is regarded as a deficiency on the part of the donor countries. This completely new approach was necessary because up to now, "we have been very conservative, understandably so, because we did not wish to put our taxpayers' money at risk. But in order to achieve results, we need to be ready to take risks." (DFAE, 2012)[iv]

There is a substantial number of evidence-based reports supporting the high levels of social inequality and unacceptable quality of life imbalance in LMICs. Geopolitically, there is also a significant number of compelling evidence-based and anecdotal reports with similar and some instances of dismal social inequality in many indigenous and vulnerable populations in some rich Western countries; typically, Australia, Canada, and the United States. Efforts made by these governments to improve the quality of life in these vulnerable and indigenous communities have been a colossal fiasco.

And in light of this documented evidence, while the CARROT-BUS model can "universally" be perceived as applicable to LMICs, a compelling analytical review of global thematic social indicator dynamics — life expectancy, infant mortality rates, risk of chronic diseases, school completion rates, suicide rates, alcoholism, access to meaningful jobs, household income, incarceration rates, child abuse, and domestic violence — confirms the appropriateness of this framework in Indigenous and other vulnerable populations.

Results of foreign aid and international development continue to be mixed. There is both compelling anecdotal and scientific evidence that foreign aid outcomes have ranged from dismal to reasonable. Many beneficiaries continue to live in squalid conditions. Poverty remains ubiquitous despite reports to the contrary, and improved quality of life in vulnerable populations remains a distant dream. Above all, the rich western countries have woefully failed to meet their own pledges to donate 0.7 % of their GDP to LMICs. Only a disappointing number of countries — seven —have achieved this objective (OECD, 2016 p.2). The Paris Declaration that was promulgated to address most developmental concerns has been quite disappointing too.

In cases where attempts to bridge these social gaps are being made, are the respective funding institutions getting their money's worth? Are effective and meaningful results being achieved?

For instance, in findings reported by the Canadian Auditor General (AG), the paper indicated that over an eight-year period (2010 to 2018), the Canadian government had spent a total of C$2.4 billion on job-training or capacity building — the lowest level of the CARROT-BUS pyramid — for the Indigenous peoples in Canada. An additional C$300 million per year was spent on the government's "Skills and Partnership Fund". In its review, the AG characterized the program's outcome as an "incomprehensible failure". The evaluation report further highlighted the government's unawareness in the program's success in helping Indigenous people find sustainable employment. This is one of copious examples bureaucratic inability to deliver meaningful results.

Readers, who have followed reports on our indigenous communities and their respective developmental challenges, will easily resonate with this and other related documented cases.

Statistic after statistic confirms the abominable and unacceptable levels of access to and utilization of social services in most of these communities.

Disjointed and lackluster efforts by the funding governments including the absence of effective participation by these vulnerable groups are part of the problem. LMICs suffer the same dilemma.

And that is why efforts including financial commitments by national governments continue to raise red flags, disapproval, and polarization. Bureaucrats at national and international levels need a significant paradigm shift. Current bureaucratic processes are too complex, convoluted, generally exclusive, and unproductive. An enhanced and more accountable approach needs to be their operating mantra. Tax dollars deserve more than what is being achieved.

A more effective, inclusive, and participatory oversight is an invaluable component of an effective, viable, and sustainable program management strategy.

Sustainability and Current Approaches to Strategic Planning

The bottom up strategy (BUS) has been described as a gold standard for development interventions. This is nothing more or less than a comprehensive strategic planning process wherein the intended beneficiaries convey their specific needs to the government representatives and development partners. Some of the elements mentioned by recipients include: 1) food scarcity, which must be eliminated; 2) access to household water, which must be safe to drink; 3) mother and infant mortality, which must be reduced, if not eliminated; 4) betterment of primary/secondary education for boys and girls, so that completion ratios are improved; 5) agricultural output, which must be increased, and at the same time, diversified; 6) employment rates, which must be increased; 7) numbers/percentages of people living in/at/below the poverty level, which must be reduced; and 8) HIV & AIDS, which must be prevented and that efforts to ensure that AIDS victims are well treated and cared for are initiated (Sustainable Development Knowledge Platform, 2009; also see Chapter 7).

The accomplishment of these goals obviously will be quite challenging. Oftentimes, country-specific development plans are being formulated under the aegis of the United Nations Development Program, where funding is usually available in the form of multilateral assistance, major development banks, and the IMF. Quite often, bilateral development assistance programs are formulated with the richest countries — the developed countries — in parallel to those of the United Nations (UN), as the individual donors and lenders have their own foreign policy objectives in mind. A good example is the emergence of China into the development assistance community, particularly in Africa. Neither multilateral nor bilateral programs have been completely effective in making development processes more sustainable. More often than not, the intended beneficiaries appear not to have been comprehensively consulted in the strategic planning process nor were they considered a vital part of the monitoring and feedback processes during implementation phases. In fact, the evidence reviewed indicates that intended beneficiaries were never actively involved in post-implementation evaluation and stocktaking exercises.

That key immunizations against common childhood disease can lower maternal and infant mortality rates and reduce the probability of contracting tetanus is well accepted. However, the United Nations Children's Fund (UNICEF), — the world's leading organization looking after the health and welfare of children and mothers — does not consult with families as to whether they will or will not receive childhood immunizations or tetanus vaccines. Instead, UNICEF enters an agreement with the appropriate state agency — usually the ministry of health — mounts a communication campaign, and then carries on business as usual. Concerning newer vaccines such as the human papillomavirus (HPV) designed to prevent uterine cancer in young females and genital warts in young men, it is only recently that some suspicions were raised about what these vaccinations can do to young people (NHS Choice, 2015; Battle, 2009, p. 373). Oftentimes, suspicion may arise since the administration of these vaccines confronts the societal norms about prevailing sexual norms and activities. HPV is a good case for re-examining the myth of an up-to-now near-perfect development paradigm in this area.

What would a viable bottom up strategy be in this instance? How would an adult constituency and associated caregiving institutions be convinced that the administration of HPV is a positive intervention and has nothing to do with whether younger generations are sexually active before marriage? Who will take ownership if desired results were either not known or doubtful in each stage of the development? In communities where satisfying basic daily needs is paramount, the explanation of an abstract long-term potential health consequence is not top of mind. People oppose HPV vaccination because they are uninformed or misinformed about why it is good for their kids to be vaccinated. Thus, the parents should be consulted about their beliefs regarding HPV (grassroots participation) and then a good health education program should be designed/implemented.

Concerning HPV vaccines, parents who allow their children to receive the vaccine are doing the right thing. In terms of satisfying their safety/security needs, children are not made accountable for the progress or difficulties generated by their decision to receive the vaccine. Their parents are made accountable in case a child feels ill soon after the vaccination is administered. If these issues were not anticipated by the program planner, there may be repercussions that could negate the whole intervention. Generally, the program and technical (health) experts and administrators must discuss the issues with the intended beneficiaries prior to the start of any intervention campaign. Right, all the actions you portray here would be part of a decent public health education program on the subject.

The fulfilment of basic needs is vital and essential before a person will be able to access, much less attain, higher levels of needs. What if one treats the development process like a person striving to satisfy one need after another in the Maslow hierarchy of needs model? This implies that the recipient country that values democratic principles should also strive to build up its capacity to become more responsible and accountable to each recipient resident in the state. In case the recipient is not a citizen, difficulties in building a sustainability environment are obviously more difficult and complex, but not impossible. Over the years, the world has witnessed what happened to people not incorporated into a state's development program. This is exactly what happened to the Muslim minority (Rohingyas) in southwestern Myanmar

In case specific ownership is not well established, it becomes more difficult to demand transparency from a recipient government. Ownership by the people assumes that a full range of human needs has already been achieved. Analogous to every step of the model ladder, here I am referring to evidence-based ownership. Applicable to each stage of the development intervention initiatives, all these issues bear on the question of who will take ownership if the desired results are unclear, unknown, or doubtful in the minds of the intended beneficiaries. Who will be accountable in case the use of resources allocated is not properly accounted for or remains unknown? Who will answer questions in case the outcome is unknown or misunderstood by the stakeholders?

In terms of specific results, program authorities can and often do point at each other for failures. For those results accomplished, many will claim to be the owners. It is a given that administrators wish to take credit for the success of the foreign aid development program but deny responsibility for failure. Credit for successes, however, should go to the intended beneficiaries. Blame for failure to produce the desired outcomes is also properly assigned to them but only in cases in which these people have been fully involved and their decisions were fully respected throughout the entire development process.

This scenario is similar to the hierarchy of needs. How can a person or family satisfy their needs for self-esteem and recognition if their social and personal security needs and sense of belongingness are not fully satisfied? There ought to be close parallels at all levels because the basic assumption is that the intended beneficiaries, such as individuals and families, have an innate capacity to progress.

The key elements of a gold-standard development model should include the following:

- capacity
- accountability
- resources
- results
- ownership
- transparency
- enabling environment

As an example, to build a community with efficient water supply, decisions made by the installation-planning group should include answering the following questions:

- What is the best way to exploit the water sources?
- Where should storage tanks be positioned considering the main source of water and its flow capacity?
- Where should water access taps be placed considering the location of the householders (stakeholders)?
- How should water usage be measured and regulated in each household?
- How should the investment made in building and maintaining the water system be recouped, such as through levying user fees?
- How should wastewater be managed and treated? For example, how could the energy potential of a strategic river basin such as the Mekong be developed?

In this model, the framework is an "enabling environment," which is defined as the availability of appropriate, relevant, and sustainable policies and laws; and political stability. It also includes advocacy for effective coordination mechanisms and adjunct strategies. A well-planned program must also give considerable thought to such issues as how to plan and manage the river for the following:

- commercial transportation
- hydroelectric energy exploitation
- the extraction of minerals from nearby deposits
- the conservation of fish populations
- a sustainable local/regional fishing industry
- tourism

All of these will likely require additional technical and financial support in order to realize successful outcomes, all of which eventually contribute to the overall (higher) goals.

> "Enabling environment" is the expression that encompasses government policies that focus on creating and maintaining an overall macroeconomic environment that brings together suppliers and consumers in an inter-firm co-operation manner... The purpose of the enabling environments... is to improve the effectiveness of the transfer of environmentally sound technologies by identifying and analyzing ways of facilitating the transfer... including the identification and removal of barriers at each stage of the process. (UNFCCC, 2015)

The Paris Declaration and the Managing for Development Results (MfDR) Conundrum

Originally called the "aid effectiveness pyramid" (2005), the Paris Declaration pyramid was supported by over 100 donors and developing countries (OECD, 2006, p. 49). The Paris Declaration was initially publicized as "changing behaviour" under the premise that it increases the flow of aid. In fact, it is unlikely this particular declaration can make any serious impact on global poverty if the donors do not change the way they go about providing foreign development aid. Most developing countries today still do not enhance the way they currently manage foreign development assistance received directly from the donors (OECD, 2006, p. 54). The donors and recipients at Paris agreed to adopt the use of a strategic framework known as "managing for development results" (MfDR), which consists of broad strategic planning and risk assessment/management exercises, a listing of progress monitoring objectives, and inclusion of (non-specific) outcome evaluation mechanisms (see Figure 2.1 and Table 2.1).

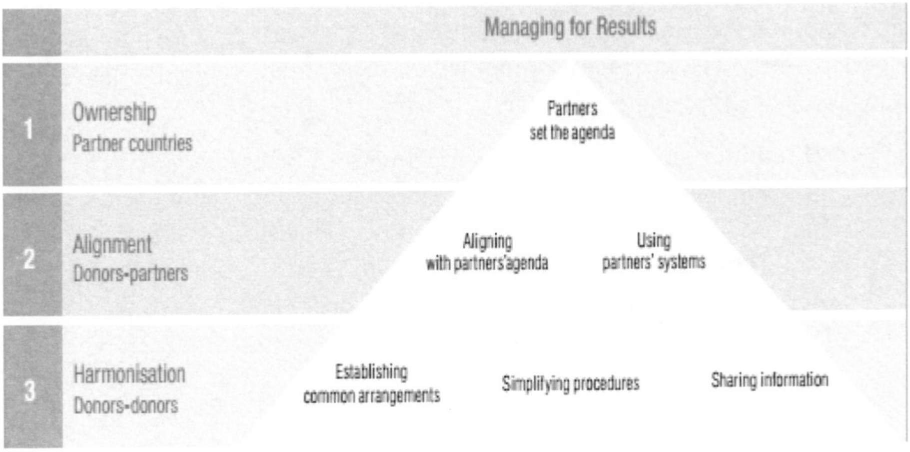

Figure 2.1: The Paris Declaration pyramid
Source: OECD, 2012, p. 18

Table 2.1: Indicators of the Paris Declaration

OWNERSHIP

1. Countries put in place national development strategies with clear strategic priorities.

ALIGNMENT

2. Countries develop reliable national fiduciary systems or reform programmes to achieve them.

3. Donors align their aid with national priorities and provide the information needed for it to be included in national budgets.

4. Co-ordinated programmes aligned with national development strategies provide support for capacity development.

5a. As their first option, donors use fiduciary systems that already exist in recipient countries.

5b. As their first option, donors use procurement systems that already exist in recipient countries.

6. Country structures are used to implement aid programmes rather than parallel structures created by donors.

7. Aid is released according to agreed schedules.

8. Bilateral aid is not tied to services supplied by the donor.

HARMONISATION

9. Aid is provided through harmonised programmes co-ordinated among donors.

10a. Donors conduct their field missions together with recipient countries.

10b. Donors conduct their country analytical work together with recipient countries

MANAGING FOR RESULTS

11. Countries have transparent, measurable assessment frameworks to measure progress and assess results.

MUTUAL ACCOUNTABILITY

12. Regular reviews assess progress in implementing aid commitments.

Source: OECD, n.d., p. 2.

Upon closer inspection, no implementing guidelines can be found that might show how a developing country could possibly be aligned with the MfDR model. It appears that the model was created to guide how the donors, but not the beneficiaries, would think. For example, concerning common arrangements, people might ask, "What is meant by "common arrangements" other than the existing development process that might not have been successful in the past. Furthermore, one might wonder whether there are specific "simplified procedures" to follow other than those each country is currently using. This issue may complicate the entire development process (see Table 2.2).

Table 2.2: Definition and principles of MfDR

<u>Definitions</u>

Managing for development results (MfDR) is a management strategy focused on development performance and on sustainable improvements in country outcomes. It provides a coherent framework for development effectiveness in which performance information is used for improved decision-making, and it includes practical tools for strategic planning, risk management, progress monitoring, and outcome evaluation.

<u>MfDR Core Principles</u>

1) Focus the dialogue on results at all phases.

2) Align actual programming, monitoring, and evaluation activities with the agreed expected results.

3) Keep the results reporting system as simple, cost-effective, and user-friendly as possible.

4) Manage *for*, not *by*, results.

5) Use results information for management learning and decision making, as well as for reporting and accountability.

Source: JICA, 2010, p. 2.

What happened to the Paris Declaration? Since 2005, the results of three subsequent surveys undertaken to understand the process and results of the implementation of MfDR showed that only one out of 12 goals was achieved (OECD, 2011b). This is the one wherein the donor country was found to have strengthened its capacity to align their programs with the national development strategies of developing countries, and by doing so, was able to support its overall capacity development (OECD, 2012, p. 199; ODI, 2011). While a single result might be disappointing in terms of the overall expectations, it is also important to review its achievement in light of the need to reshape the enabling environment critical to success.

Using Business Models and Life Case Studies for Development

The concept of total quality management (TQM) requires a total commitment by everyone in an organization to assuring quality and to a continuous process of innovation and improvement monitored and measured throughout the system (in all its procedures and practices), as well as assessing the quality of products and services provided to customers. TQM also requires the same commitment, controls, and measures by suppliers of products and services to the organization regardless of whether these are internal or external (Quality Assurance Solutions, n.d.).

Jeffrey Ridley, a visiting professor of auditing at London South Bank University, has observed that the "internal audit function does not need to be a bystander and wait to get on the quality bandwagon only when someone else in the organization sounds the quality horn..." (Ridley, n.d., p. 6). For example, there ought to be monthly progress reports that are checked against comprehensive monitoring plans with periodic onsite or visual inspection reports. These may be, and usually are, regular weekly or monthly reports that are founded on factual observations with little or no subjective opinion. By auditing the contents and ascertaining the veracity of information, potential fraud can be prevented. When it comes to ensuring compliance satisfactory to the funders/donors, concerned officials of least developed countries (LDCs) cannot be held responsible for the general lack of knowledge or education of its citizens. Individuals within the program's governing mechanism should accept responsibility for their actions. Therefore, there has to be some budget provision for training project operatives in a system of management such as TQM. Training in this regard is best considered a process and not an event.

ISO-based quality system standards have been around since 1987. In 2000, the ISO 9001 standard was extensively modified to include both product and service-provider organizations. ISO 9001:2008 is the label given to this worldwide standard for quality management systems. It can be learned by acquiring software, taking courses online, or by attending seminars. This implies that during the program/project development phase, it is imperative to assess what prospective managers and administrators know about implementing ISO 9000 as the international standard for quality management. Robert Broughton, a management consultant at the firm KPMG, defined its usefulness by saying that "ISO 9000 can help a company satisfy its customers, meet regulatory requirements and achieve continual improvements" (Broughton, 2011, p. 12). Linking ISO 9000 and 9001 to TQM, he opined that "Total Quality Management seeks to satisfy people and the organization over the long term by requiring all employees of the organization to improve... no matter who and what role he/she has in the chain of command: all staff are responsible for quality... the entire culture has to be involved in TQM." (Quality Assurance Solutions, n.d.).

In discussing a new development model, the involvement of project operatives in the development effort emphasizes that training in management systems is essential to both the capacity-building and accountability levels of the model. Whenever possible, intended beneficiaries ought to be involved in this aspect. This can be expected if joint effort follows the Paris Declaration model and MfDR core principles. Doing so would help meet such social needs as belongingness and involvement.

As part of any development initiative, this experimentation should be followed with great interest and responsibility. All stakeholders must understand each other's needs in order to enter into a partnership for development. In this model, the receiving agency on behalf of the people (stakeholders) they represent should be clear about the terms and conditions of the donors as well as the owners or providers of funds, technical assistance, and other resources. The joint communiqué assumes that all parties have clearly understood each other's terms and conditions before signing the joint agreement.

As explained earlier, there is the semblance of a sustainable oversight management system that values improvements in the output quality or results in all levels of the model. According to Besterfield et al. (2011, p. 1), "TQM is the art of managing the whole to achieve excellence." In the aspect of fighting graft and corruption, auditors and implementing authorities can be made accountable for failure to practice transparency. In case the use of regular compliance audits is agreed upon and well understood by the stakeholders, contracting parties who fail to pass this audit process can be terminated and replaced by more competent and honest people who agree to be more accountable for their own actions.

In a short appendix, the following nine different multilateral and bilateral assistance agencies were critiqued based on their statement of purpose and commitment to transparency:

1. International Monetary Fund (IMF)
2. Japanese International Cooperation Agency (JICA)
3. European Bank for Reconstruction and Development (EBRD)
4. United States Agency for International Development (USAID)
5. Export Import Bank of China (EIBC)
6. Asian Development Bank (ADB)
7. Islamic Development Bank (ISB)
8. Swiss Development Corporation (SDC)
9. Swedish International Cooperation Agency (SIDA)

The beneficiary countries of non-traditional systems of accountability and control over resources demanded that donors should virtually relinquish all control over the existing systems of recipient countries. As such, Nepal can be considered a contemporary case, since it emerged from a decade-long divisive and violent conflict period with no clear governance mandate vested in any of the major political parties currently vying for power. In addition, it is also recovering from a devastating earthquake that, according to UN estimates, caused its GDP to shrink by 1.5% (Sapkota, 2015). In an interview with the director of the OECD, the issue of control was clarified when he said:

> We wrote the report on the implementation of the Paris Declaration and in the framework of the global partnership for the effectiveness of development cooperation. In light of Busan, we will look very carefully at how these decisions are being implemented. Agreement was reached on half a dozen indicators that will be checked at international levels. But more importantly, from now on, the recipient countries will be setting the goals themselves. We will also be looking at the implementation of these goals. Thanks to this control system, pressure can be maintained, so that maximum effect can be achieved. The recipient countries themselves decide what development factors are important for them. That was their principal demand. But they want to maintain their control system. They were very impressed by the manner in which we checked the implementation of the Paris Declaration. Now, they want to see more surveys of this kind, partly because they want to put pressure on us. (Neuhaus, 2012)

The World Bank Conundrum

As of 2007, the World Bank pointed at the recipient government as the entity that "must have fiscal discipline" that needs "transparency on medium-term fiscal policy and targets…transparency on risks associated with the fiscal aggregates…transparency on the assumptions and models used to project revenues and expenditures…and transparency on assets and liabilities" (Folscher, 2007, pp. 79–103). In 2012, the World Bank redefined its commitment to sustainable development in terms of meeting the basic human needs for food, fibre, and fuel. Meeting these needs may heavily depend on the presence of natural resources such as "agricultural lands, forests, water, and fisheries" (World Bank, 2012a, p. 105). However, the bank is still apparently looking for a way to ensure its transparency (Folscher, 2007, pp. 79–103). To prevent corruption, the World Bank has posted a hotline telephone number for those who wish to report incidents of suspected fraud and corruption.

Based on UNDP reports, each year approximately US$1 trillion worth of bribes are paid from development funds (UNDP, 2011). Corruption is thought to have undermined democracy and impeded successful public development programs and is identified as a major barrier to sustainable development (UNDP, 2012). The World Bank's hotline is, for now, a reactive way to end the practice of corruption. The proactive and perhaps only legitimate way to prevent corruption is to utilize agreed-upon and well-communicated policies and procedures that serve as guidelines and rules. Perhaps there should be a sustainable management program expressly developed to conduct periodic exercises to ongoing programs. Examples include rigorous compliance audits of fiscal internal control systems. These need to be durable and capable of preventing fraud by senior managers. They also need to mitigate corrupting political influences and associated interventions such as firing whistleblowers.

CARROT-BUS: Hierarchical Causal Model

Extensive examination of the models for management of sustainable development programs led me to the realization that administrators of development funds for allocation to LDCs by multi- and bilateral agencies have been guided by universal goals and agreements. The proponents believe in taking collaborative initiatives intended to expedite social and economic development processes of vulnerable populations by extending both financial and technical support. These interventions are integrated with recipient government policies in order to achieve common goals. The mutual (recipient and donor) concerns would eventually extend to and encompass utilizing the inherent resources of intended beneficiaries as well. To create mutual agreements between donors and recipient countries, the governments of recipient countries should first strive to improve and coordinate their own development plans. Coordination by beneficiary governments remains inadequate and there is a strong and urgent need to significantly improve the current status quo. Good and effective coordination mechanisms serve as compelling catalysts to compelling potential ownership. Here is one of the many related recommendations that I frequently gave recipient governments:

"The government is encouraged to take a strong leadership position in coordinating expected increasing donor assistance to development programs. A database describing the national programs, including ongoing and potential donor support, needs to be created, utilized, frequently updated, and consulted to coordinate and brief visiting missions. The database could also be updated providing access to monitoring and evaluation results and financial data, including disbursement levels."

The seven components that facilitate the attainment of sustainable management of development programs are embodied in a conceptual framework called the "CARROT-BUS" model. The acronym CARROT stands for capacity, accountability, resources, results, ownership, and transparency. These factors are all essential to creating what is defined as an enabling environment. The acronym BUS stands for the bottom up strategy.

The concept of total quality management (TQM) has been included as a reliable and effective tool as it helps in streamlining and correcting potential gaps, weaknesses, and discrepancies during the implementation phase. It also serves as a quality control oversight. While other methods can be successful, contemporary evidence confirms that the CARROT-BUS model is an appropriate framework for development projects. A particular strength of this model, aside from its being simple and easy to follow, is its holistic and inclusive nature. For this reason, the CARROT-BUS model can be considered as one of the more recent practical approaches to increase the success rate of foreign aid projects.

Winrock International[v] is a non-profit organization that works with people in the United States and around the world. Despite the numerous successful foreign aid development projects handled by Winrock, this particular non-profit organization did not present any clear framework or useful model that could assist foreign aid personnel on how to increase the success rate of foreign aid developmental projects. In the process of promoting capacity building amongst the recipients of foreign aid funds, donors can become motivated in extending financial assistance to areas needing financial development support. This argument is true since the initiatives of the people living in developing areas can be considered as a reflection of their willingness to move away from poverty.

Through capacity building, the government of developing countries could empower the local residents to engage themselves in more fruitful livelihood projects. In the case of Nepal, more than 50,000 households were highly encouraged to participate in agricultural and vocational training, which eventually increased not only their annual income but also their available food supply. The case of the Ethiopian government was more focused on improving people's access to high-quality education as their way of capacity building. For instance, the Ethiopian government has tried to develop policies to align their classroom approaches regarding the learning needs of each community member, the needs of the educators and staff, and the support systems that should guide how the educators and staff are expected to function within the educational system (Sellamna & Gebremedhin, 2015). After completing the course requirements, the graduates of Ethiopia can have the option to engage in small and medium enterprises.

Accountability is one of the main problems of foreign aid development projects. Often, with poor accountability, donors of foreign aid may feel discouraged in extending their financial assistance to areas needing financial aid. In the process of imposing strict accountability, donors of foreign aid funds may feel more confident and more assured that the money they invest in foreign development projects could result in the increase in the quality of life of more people. Both Nepal and Ethiopia have been receiving foreign aid assistance. Nepal has been known for having successful foreign aid development projects, though in many cases, plausible achievements remain elusive. In the case of Ethiopia, there seem to be many donor-funded projects running. Despite continuous efforts to improve the lives of Ethiopians, the practice of corruption in this particular country has always been persistent (Plummer, 2012, p. 110). Therefore, in the absence of strict accountability, foreign aid donors may simply invest their money in other developing countries with less corrupt practices.

The availability of resources is crucial behind a successful foreign aid project. Therefore, the next important step is to ensure that all necessary resources will be available to increase the success rate of foreign aid projects. For instance, more than 50,000 households in Nepal attended some form of agricultural and vocational training. Assuming that these people will not be given access to land or planting equipment or materials such as seedlings and shovels amongst other resources needed in agricultural activities, those individuals without the financial capacity to purchase these items may not be able to practice what they have learned from the livelihood training. Therefore, within the enabling environment, the government of developing countries should pay more attention to how they can extend the necessary resources to local citizens. Obviously, without these resources, it is unlikely that foreign aid projects could create positive results.

Before demanding transparency from a recipient government, it is essential to create specific ownership in both parties (i.e., donor and recipient government). In almost all cases, economic and social development should be locally led before a country can produce and sustain meaningful results. This explains why CIDA supports all efforts that demonstrate the local country ownership of development (Tomlinson & Foster, 2004). For instance, it is necessary to identify specific needs and priorities through the development national policies and strategies. This way, foreign aid projects can be aligned with the national priorities and needs of their partner country (CIDA, 2012a). CIDA tends to support all countries that demonstrate clear local country ownership of development (Tomlinson & Foster, 2004). Likewise, CIDA expects all recipient governments to empower developing countries by forming leadership when it comes to defining, delivering, measuring results, and increasing ownership of development outcomes. In the process of being able to create strict national policies on foreign aid such as accountability and corruption, it will be easier for the recipient government to implement the practice of transparency.

CHAPTER 3: Sustainable Program Management Strategies

The first step in sustainable development program management is the identification of all contracting parties involved, as there may be more than one development partner classified as a donor. In the case of the Power Sector Rehabilitation Project (PSRP) in Kyrgyzstan, for example, the EBRD, EIBC, GDC, IDB, SADC, USAID, and the World Bank all acted as development partners in the energy sector, providing a good example of having to coordinate the interests of multiple stakeholders (ADB, 2011). All parties must understand each other's hierarchy of needs based on their mandates. As stated in the writ of governance for the PSRP, donors negotiate mandates for the distribution of development funds and other resources that must be fully understood by the Kyrgyz government. Kyrgyzstan has seen a tremendous political upheaval in the past several years and the PSRP has been tested in ways not anticipated at the commencement of negotiations.

All donors and beneficiaries must understand each other's terms and conditions before signing the agreement. If not, when program evaluation takes place, misunderstandings are likely to occur if all the details have not been enumerated at the outset. For instance, based on the World Bank's own evaluation, traumatic experiences caused its management to believe that there were flaws in their system of undertaking development. Partly because of this, the World Bank (2012b) aimed "to integrate governance issues more systematically" (p. 1) in order to ensure successful performance when managing development projects. Insufficiently systematic administration, in fact, may have contributed to corruption in some of the world's development projects. With this in mind, the World Bank's new focus, based on its 2012 mandate, is more focused on "governance and anti-corruption" (p. 7).

Before discussing the strategies related to sustainable program management, it is useful to define the term "sustainability" and stipulate how it can be linked to program management. Sustainable means that management is simply focused on satisfying the needs of the sponsoring organization and those of all of stakeholders, as the objective is to protect, enhance, and sustain both natural and human resources (D'Amato, Henderson, & Florence, 2009). A sustainable program or project should be acceptable to all people, economically viable, and environmentally friendly (Elkington, 1998). As such, the Kyrgyzstan gold mine (Case 1) serves to illustrate the wrong way of doing business.

Aside from having a good return on investment (ROI), a program is economically sustainable if it can address all factors that may affect its long-term feasibility (Silvius, 2010). It is environmentally sustainable if it focuses on minimizing such risks as water pollution and greenhouse gas emissions, reduces energy use, and promotes the reuse and recycling of waste products (Robichaud & Anantatmula, 2011; Silvius, 2010). The audit of the Tajikistan aluminum processing plant, for example, illustrates this quite clearly. In this case, the World Bank Group contracted a consortium of Norwegian, Ukrainian, and Tajik companies, led by Norsk Energi, to perform a plant-wide assessment of energy efficiency options of all major equipment and production lines at the Tajik Aluminum Company (TALCO), the largest aluminium manufacturing plant in Central Asia, headquartered in Tursunzade. The project team included Norsk Energi, SINTEF Materials and Chemistry, Energy saving company (ESCO) Energo Engineering, and Tajhydro (Solheim et al., 2012). The main purpose of the assignment was to quantify energy usage at the TALCO site and highlight any opportunities for potential energy savings. To achieve this, the study methodology comprised the following main tasks:

- Complete a comprehensive energy audit
- Identify energy and, in particular, electric power consumption related to all equipment, processes, and sub-processes in the plant
- Analyze and recommend opportunities to decrease energy use and costs, as well as estimate the associated investment needs
- Identify priorities for energy efficiency improvements in terms of the potential for electricity savings and cost-effectiveness

The consortium's final report provides an excellent example of how strategic programs directly related to environmental sustainability can incorporate the practice of energy conservation. Another example occurs with the emergence of "green building" in the construction business (Robichaud & Anantatmula, 2011).

The program life cycle (PLC) illustrates the basic flow in the program development process (see Figure 3.1). Based on this concept, it is possible to design the program, solicit funding, oversee the inception and implementation phases, expect a degree of sustainability, and evaluate the program in a manner consistent with the expectations of all those involved.

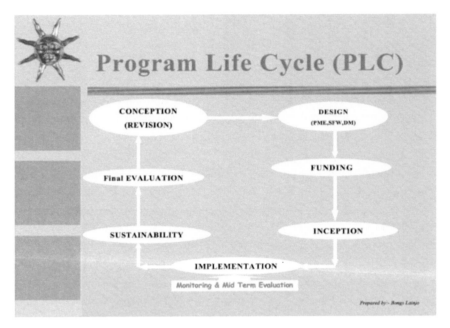

Figure 3.1: The program life cycle (PLC) model

A program can be socially sustainable, for example, if the sponsors respect human rights, avoid discrimination, provide essential support to the stakeholders involved, respect the customer's right to privacy, and eliminate corruption and bribery (United Nations, 2011; Silvius, 2010).

Why is it so important to ensure that the strategies used in the development of a sustainable program are effective? A closer look at the life cycle model provides the answer. Figure 3.2 shows the four basic stages of a project life cycle:

1. Initiating
2. Planning
3. Performing
4. Closing

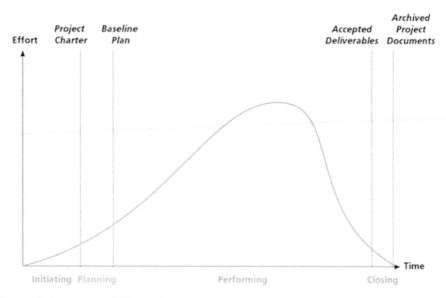

Figure 3.2: Image of life cycle model
Source: Gido & Clements, 2012, p. 10

During the initiating stage, sponsors should have a clear idea of what stakeholder expectations are. Management should communicate with stakeholders and provide details as to how the project will be completed. What processes, disruptions, and enduring changes may occur in the environment once the project commences and what the overall lasting impacts are likely to be should all be discussed. Doing so will enable sponsors and management to more easily win the support and trust of the people affected, directly or indirectly. At this stage, management should be able to complete a cost-benefit analysis, an accurate investment analysis, a value-benefit analysis, and a thorough risk analysis, including worst-case scenarios.

To avoid the risk of human error that inevitably results in public dissatisfaction, management should define the project scope, objectives, and goals in commonly understood language before proposing a fixed schedule, work plan, and deadlines. Failure to follow a transparent pathway could prove very costly; lack of transparency opens the door to budget overruns and economic non-viability.

In order to provide a more detailed model of the PLC, Archibald, Di Filippo, and Di Filippo (2012) modified the typical four stages into six: 1) concept, 2) definition, 3) implementation (including both designing and building), 4) handover and closeout 5) operations, and 6) termination (see Figure 3.3).

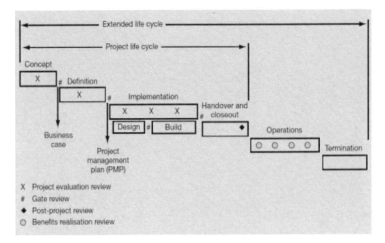

Figure 3.3: Modified project life cycle model
Source: Archibald, Di Fillipo & Di Fillipo, 2012

Features of Program Management

Creating effective strategies for the sustainable management of a program or project is a very complex task. Would-be program managers must be aware of the many considerations in arriving at a fully developed, definitive list of effective, tactical approaches. The first task is to differentiate between the terms "project" and "program."

Simply put, a project is a small part of a larger program. A program has an overall goal and several outcomes while a single project may simply be one of many program outputs. The outcome of each project should contribute to the overall goals of the program (Morris & Pinto, 2007, p. xii). In order to be successful, both programs and projects require clear visions, mission statements, and objectives. Both also require insightful management, comprehensive budgeting, and accurate scheduling.

Program managers are directly responsible for the development and implementation of strategies related to program sustainability (McKinlay, 2008). Before program managers can create an effective and sustainable strategy, they should first learn about the basic features of program management. As identified by the Project Management Institute (PMI) PMBOK, program management includes the following tasks or areas of expertise (Turner, 2014, pp. 6–7; Morris & Pinto, 2007, p. xii):

- Time
- Cost
- Human resources

- Communications
- Quality
- Risk
- Procurement
- Stakeholders
- Integration
- Scope

All these features should be carefully addressed to ensure that the program manager will be able to deliver the project within the specified scope, available budget, and agreed-upon timeframe (see Figure 3.4).

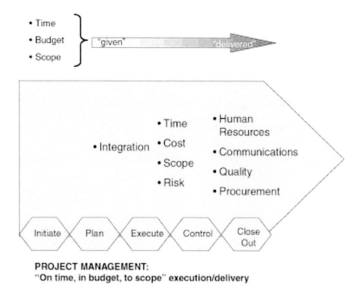

Figure 3.4: Significance of each of the 10 identified features in project delivery
Source: Morris & Pinto, 2001, p. xii

These specific features will be addressed in more detail in Part III: Practice. For instance, regarding time management or scheduling, the significance of using Gantt charts or bar charts as well as critical path analysis will be highlighted (Morris & Pinto, 2007). As well, Part III will discuss the significance of a work breakdown structure (WBS) and deliverables for the scope and the cost breakdown structure (CBS) for cost management purposes (Turner, 2014, p. 7). Many theories and tools are associated with each aspect of program management (see Table 3.1).

Table 3.1: Project management's main features and associated theories

Features	Related Theories and Tools
Time	• Gantt charts or bar charts • Network scheduling (i.e., the program evaluation and review technique (PERT), the critical path method (CPM), or the precedence diagramming method (PDM)) • Estimated duration • Time control
Cost	• Cost breakdown structure (CBS) • Cost estimates • Cost control
Human Resources	• Team contract • Responsibility assignment matrix (RAM) • Team building (i.e., Belbin's team roles, team role mapping, etc.)
Communications	• Verbal or written • Arises between the client and manager as well as manager and staff • Important in strengthening the project control measures
Quality	• Configuration management
Risk	• Risk management and control process • Identification and assessment of risks
Procurement	• Compliant to customer requirements and ISO 9000 standard
Stakeholders	• Stakeholder map or matrix • Stakeholder analysis • Resistance to change
Integration	• Integrated change control process
Scope	• Definition of the project or scope statement

	• Project charter
	• Work breakdown structure (WBS) and deliverables
	• Requirements management plan

Applying these basic principles of program management is essential to the success of any foreign aid development program. The following provides a basic introduction to these ten components:

Time management

Getting projects done on time is as important as getting them done within budget. Much has been written about time management, so many resources are available online and in print. However, those tend to focus on the day-to-day — as in how to get more done in a day — rather than on the larger project management scope.

There are many factors to consider, but the key element is very close consultation with stakeholders and beneficiaries in order to root out any potential factors that may inhibit the implementation of the project, such as hunting season, herd migration, weather, and so on. There may also be important deadlines to work towards, such as a key anniversary or celebration. For example, Canada celebrated its 150th anniversary in 2017, but Ottawa, the country's capital city and the epicentre of the celebrations, will still be mired in a massive transit construction project scheduled for completion in 2018. One can only imagine the goings on behind the scenes that resulted in such uncoordinated efforts.

Cost management

Cost management means managing the approved budget, including anticipating and providing for unexpected contingencies (Delaney, 2014, p. 4). It is a given that each project component within a program has a corresponding budget allocation exclusively meant for the specific project. It is the responsibility of program managers to allocate the funds authorized and make them available in such a way that they will be sufficient to pay for the actual cost of the projects authorized within the program.

Cost overruns are a constant source of stress for donors and recipients alike, and while every aspect of project management can play a part in these, the cost of time overruns alone can be staggering. The problem of unscrupulous contractors and corruption has also eaten up many millions of development dollars over the years.

Human resource management

Human resource management is the process of effectively managing and developing the skills and overall work performance of team members (Delaney, 2014, p. 4). The GTZ capacity building project in Kyrgyzstan (see Case 2), for example, included many sub-projects, including a business-training project with two project leaders assigned to facilitate two groups of participants. Several staff members prepared the training course materials and all other needed resources to deliver the actual training. A dedicated staff person coordinated scheduling, monitored the different tasks involved, and solved any problems during training (for example, if a participant had an emergency at home, become ill, or had other issues). Each team member received thorough training on how best to contribute to the success of the project. A clear project goal and objectives served as a common guide for each team. Since the goal was to deliver business training for the local people in Kyrgyzstan, the program manager took care to instruct the training team leaders to design a program suitable for those people in particular and avoid any examples and generalities alien to the region.

Communication management

Communication management means managing the inflow and outflow of information related to the program (Delaney, 2014, p. 4). Mistakes in giving instructions are often due to miscommunication amongst project staff. It is essential for both program managers and project team leaders to establish an organizational culture that practices open communication.

In some cases, communication management also means reporting on the entire project or program performance to a donor in order to maintain the donor's trust. Mishandled communication can also mean losing the trust of the donor, which can be fatal to the project.

Quality management

Quality management means ensuring that program execution accords with those indicators of quality delineated in the approved program narrative and associated logframe (Delaney, 2014, p. 4). Quality management includes the need to observe both quality assurance and quality control factors. In relation to quality assurance, program managers should evaluate staff performance by assessing pre- and post-knowledge of each participant who receives training. In relation to the quality of *business* training programs, quality control aims to determine how each staff person was able to comply with the indicators related to the quality of training (i.e., was the training staff able to train all participants based on the deliverables) (Schwalbe, 2010).

Risk management

Risk management pertains to the process of being able to identify, manage, and control risks while exploiting opportunities. Each time conflict arises, the program's project management team must implement immediate corrective measures to control the extent of damage as soon as it becomes known yet must also be extremely careful not to cover up the extent of that damage. The case of the gold mine accident in Kyrgyzstan (Case 1) serves as a reminder of failure to follow this exhortation.

For instance, as part of risk management plans, both program management and individual project team leaders must motivate staff to immediately report potential problems that could delay or irreparably harm the program. These may include, for example, issues related to internal staff conflict, budget allocation shortfalls, sub-standard training, delays in meeting task completion deadlines, staff absenteeism, and anything else that may not have been included in the training process. By being alert to and quickly determining problems and issues, both program management and project team leaders can immediately seek to rectify them.

Procurement management

Proper procurement management ensures that the program or project is able to acquire — on a timely basis — all necessary inputs, raw materials, and technical resources considered essential for its successful completion (Delaney, 2014, p. 4). The absence of any single resource could potentially impede the ability of the program team to complete their tasks successfully. Those charged with program management and implementation schedules, therefore, should ensure that the staff assigned to order raw materials, finished products, or services are enabled to alert authorized suppliers regarding delivery schedules and are able to continuously monitor and report on the procurement status. The importance of timely delivery of goods and services and of evaluating its assurance is a key managerial component likely to affect performance overall.

Stakeholder management

Stakeholder management requires understanding the key concerns of each stakeholder (Sanghera, 2008, pp. 45–46). Conflicts between or amongst stakeholders can emerge at any time during program management and can become exacerbated due to communication breakdowns or the lack of a suitable "referee" who can unemotionally objectively sort out the reasons behind the breakdown and resolve the conflict to the mutual satisfaction of all parties. The Melamchi household water supply project in Nepal is an excellent case study of such conflict (Melamchi, 2015). Considering the case of GTZ assistance in Kyrgyzstan (Case 2), the stakeholders include not only the staff members of GTZ but also those of the local implementing group and another 800 experts (Korf & Raeymaekers, 2013, p. 155; see Chapter 7).

To ensure good, durable stakeholder management, the management team must take into account the expectations of all the stakeholders. Integration management — a collection of processes required to ensure that the various elements of the projects are properly coordinated — is one way to accomplish this formidable task. It involves making trade-offs amongst competing objectives and alternatives to meet or exceed stakeholder needs and expectations.

Integration management

Foreign aid programs should always be closely controlled and monitored throughout their entire lifetimes, from initiating to closing down. Defined as the process of creating clear definition, identification, unification, and coordination of different program activities, integration management will always be key to the success of foreign aid projects (Sanghera, 2008, p. 82). Aside from deciding how to allocate the needed resources, integration management also considers the various trade-offs involved in managing the entire project, such as time versus budget (Thirty, 2010, p. 44).

Scope management

Of course, no project can begin without a clear scope, but scope management also refers to the process used in setting project boundaries within a complex program (Delaney, 2014, p. 3). The process of coming up with project scope statements can help define the expected work requirements for each team member (Heldman, 2005, p. 198). Based on these tasks, the project manager can better plan and schedule the use of budgeted funds and other resources (i.e., WBS, verifying scope, control scope, etc.) (Dinsmore & Cabanis-Brewin, 2011, pp. 79–82). Using an effective scope management technique, the program manager can set priorities and be more specific as to what has to be included or not included in the project and when.

PART II: LIFE CASE STUDIES

Case Study – Kyrgyzstan Kumtor Gold Mine

The Kyrgyzstan Kumtor Gold Mine lies in a rich agricultural valley in the Tian Shan Mountains near Lake Issyk-Kul, a popular tourist destination. At 1,600 meters above sea level, Lake Issyk-Kul is the world's second largest alpine lake, after Lake Titicaca in South America. Geologically, Lake Issyk-Kul, which never freezes, lies at the juncture of two tectonic plates, slowly moving apart. In a few centuries, the lake will be twice as deep as it is now. Deep under the lake's crystal clear water lies an ancient town from which divers have recovered artefacts, mainly household goods and ceramic pots.

Based on its size, the Kumtor gold deposit ranks amongst the top 10 largest in the world. Canada's Cameco Corporation was interested in exploiting this rich vein; it had exclusive rights to assess the deposit's feasibility for development and a right to a one-third interest if the feasibility study was positive. The capital costs were estimated by Kilborn Western Inc. at $US360 million. Ultimately, $452 million was required to develop the Kumtor Gold Project and operations began in 1997.

The Chase Manhattan Bank was chosen by Cameco to underwrite the commercial bank tranche of $155 million. Chase successfully syndicated the loan amongst a select group of North American and European Banks. Canada's Export Development Corporation (EDC) agreed to provide $50 million in the form of export credit. Both the European Bank of Reconstruction and Development (EBRD) and the International Finance Corporation (IFC) agreed to loans totalling $30 million each.

Cameco retained the voting majority for the first 10 years of operations, except for a limited number of issues requiring unanimous consent. The local government was to collect 2% of the profits during the loan repayment period and 4% thereafter. As Kyrgyz Republic balance of payments statistics indicate, in its first year of production, the mine contributed 30% of the total value of exports.

The production capacity of the processing facility is 14,500 tonnes/day. A portion of the open pit, which is 2 kilometers long and 1.2 kilometers wide, is covered by glacial ice. Glaciers generate considerable run-off during the warmer months so a water management program is required. In its first year of production, mining operations exceeded expectations with production topping 502,156 ounces, 25% over the forecast of 410,000 ounces. Mill throughput averaged 13,400 tons per day with a grade of 5.49 grams/troy compared to the forecasted 4.53 grams/troy. Operating costs averaged $185/ounce compared to the budget of $220/ounce. In 1998, the operation was expected to produce 600,000 ounces at an operating cost of less than $175/ounce.

On May 22, 1998, a convoy of five trucks carrying sodium cyanide left the railyard in Balykchy. The fourth truck in the convoy overturned at the Barskoon River Bridge, spilling 1.7 tons of highly toxic sodium cyanide into the river. The river, a source of water for drinking and irrigation, flows downstream into Lake Issyk-Kul.

According to reports, the spill led to approximately 2,600 people being treated with more than 1,000 of them hospitalized. Hospital officials attributed four deaths to cyanide poisoning. Radio Free Europe/Radio Liberty correspondents reported that tourists on the north shore received little if any information about the toxic spill and were still swimming in Lake Issyk-Kul. The full extent of the damage is still unknown.

UNDP was asked by the Kyrgyz government to assess the environmental damage caused by this breach and recommend an appropriate governmental response regarding regulating or shutting down the activities of the Kumtor mining operation (UNC, 2010).

The accident cost the mine $4.5 million in reparations and set the tone for years of discord between Kumtor's Canadian owners and the local Kyrgyz population who say the mine has not done enough to compensate for environmental damage (Radio Free Europe/Radio Liberty, 2013). Thousands of protesters have blocked roads and disrupted power supplies to the massive open-pit mine, demanding better ecological standards and free medical facilities. In response, Kyrgyz officials declared a state of emergency in the district surrounding the mine.

The protests erupted just days before Kyrgyz officials had hoped to persuade Canada's Centerra Gold to sign a new contract raising its preferential 14% tax rate and demanding a $467 million payment for environmental damage. The delay in these negotiations is certain to frustrate many ordinary Kyrgyz who see the Kumtor mine as an ecological time bomb. "Our women are giving birth prematurely. Our sheep and cows are suffering… Dear leaders, we're asking very kindly. We don't need gold. We don't need silver. We need clean water, healthy and good lives," said one protester (Radio Free Europe Radio Liberty, 2013).

Case Study – GTZ Assistance in Kyrgyzstan

GTZ, the German Agency for Technical Cooperation, is an international enterprise for sustainable development with worldwide operations. Established in 1975, GTZ was set up as a private company owned by the German government. It focuses on technical cooperation in the areas of political, economic, ecological, and social development with the aim of communicating knowledge that enables people to shape their present and future on their own, thus leading to sustainability. Any profits generated are re-invested exclusively for projects in international cooperation (Taking IT Global, 2015). Some 1,600 field-staff workers with 8,590 locally contracted personnel and another 800 "integrated experts" have been placed with employers in partner countries. Some 2,800 projects in 142 countries receive administrative and professional assistance from GTZ head office and more than 60 GTZ offices in partner countries. Experts are responsible for cooperation with individual countries to ensure that the technical solutions and management methods used in the projects match the sociocultural and economic conditions of their partner countries. Consulting firms, specialist institutions, and universities are also used as partners for projects where expertise on specialized issues is needed.

In the Kyrgyz Republic, the GTZ capacity-building project for food security, regional cooperation, and conflict mitigation is intended to develop capabilities for a better local government, more entrepreneurs, better IT support, improvements in election capabilities, business training, cooperative formation, energy source development in rural areas, and so on (Korf & Raeymaekers, 2013, p. 155; Baker, 2011). Its target areas were limited to the newest but restive Batken Province (area 17,000 km^2; population 40,000) and the agrarian province of Jalalabad (area 33,700 km^2; population 962,000). The headquarters of both are located in the Fergana Valley, which Kyrgyzstan shares with Uzbekistan. Most of the terrain of these two provinces is mountainous with 10 or 11 different ethnicities present, the majority (approx. 75%) being Kyrgyz. In total, the population affected by the GTZ project amounts to approximately 28% of the total population in the country.

GTZ works primarily in the area of technical cooperation. Activities include appraisal, technical planning, and control and supervision of projects commissioned by the Federal Republic of Germany or by other authorities. The agency is also responsible for the recruitment, selection, briefing, and assignment of expert personnel, assuring their welfare and technical backstopping during their period of assignment. Provision of materials and equipment for projects, planning work, selection, purchasing, and shipment to the developing countries is done by the organization. The GTZ also manages all financial obligations for the partner country. From the outset, negotiations between GTZ and Kyrgyzstan centered on a common understanding of the elements critical to success, as presented in Table 3.2.

Table 3.2: Elements critical to success

From the community:
- interest in helping oneself and readiness to seek help to help oneself
- positive use of traditions such as *ashar, kurultai, aksakal* courts
- unity of purpose at community level; few divisions and history of joint action
- openness to learn new things and to question old wisdoms
- trust between the people; history of transparent use of joint resources

From local implementation partners:
- commitment, transparency and honesty
- resistance to orders from powerful authorities lacking a legal basis
- refraining from accepting projects from donors because of funds only, despite the intervention being not convincingly promising for the target group

From the donor:
- professionalism congruent with job descriptions and the related levels of remuneration of international and national staff
- commitment of international staff and patriotism of national staff
- openness to new ideas and lessons learnt by others; listening skills beyond perfunctionary PRA exercises. Be driven by local demand rather than supply of funds and convictions
- willingness to cooperate with local stakeholders including state institutions and fellow donor financed projects
- market-based strategies: minimisation of grant component in favour of sustainable beneficiary funded cost-recovery

From government:
- develop and fund realistic development strategies
- arrange for donor coordination
- become a funding partner for activities jointly implemented by donors, and community
- facilitate or stand aside

Level 1, at the top of the chart, addresses the self-interest and readiness of the intended beneficiaries to help themselves and the positive use of their traditions to further their goals and objectives.

Level 2 consists of safety needs (security and protection) covered by the communities' pledge of unity of purpose, trust amongst themselves, commitment to openness to new ideas, and resistance to corrupting influences.

Level 3 deals with the social needs that depend upon an overriding sense of belonging and appreciation throughout the development process. This seems partly to be covered by the willingness of the beneficiaries to question the wisdom of old ways. It is also evident that the donor has considered its role by pledging professionalism and commitment from its agents of change, as well as pledges to retain openness, a willingness to listen, to co-operate with the local stakeholders, and to give priority to local demands rather than its own in terms of funding and convictions.

Level 4 would evolve naturally from a successful experience with the implementation process described above. If things went well then all involved would feel a sense of satisfaction, recognition of success, and a sense of self-esteem and status.

The enabling environment consists of three core principles set forth by the government and the endorsement of three others as expressed by the donors, namely 1) the use of market-based strategies, 2) professionalism and commitment in staffing project posts, and 3) minimizing the grant component in favour of sustainable cost-recovery.

The GTZ project funding was to be judged using a matrix of the following nine indices:

1. Target area
2. Donor human resources provided
3. Post-funding supervision requirement
4. Financial cost-benefit ratio
5. Pro-poor ratio
6. Organizational reliability
7. Bad governance risk
8. The minimum timeframe
9. Facilitate sustainability.

Overall, the key indicators used to measure success were as follows:

- Would institutions and models establish and operate at existing or increased levels in five years (i.e., by 2023)?
- Would institutions and models established be replicated and invested in by other parties, ideally national institutions, state organizations, and only secondly by donors?

In December 2007, at the end of five years of project implementation, the project staff believed that only active destruction from within would see the institutions and business models established fail to meet the requirements as set out under the first consideration. Unless technical assistance projects aimed at poverty reduction had proved successful, the provision of state funds or funds given by the international financial institutions can be deemed as wasted.

For example, during the initial stage, GTZ personnel and members of the management team first reviewed and reaffirmed the main purposes of extending foreign aid to Kyrgyzstan. The program goals included developing the capabilities of the local people to have a better local government, improvements in election capabilities, developing more entrepreneurs, better IT support, training in business practices, and cooperative formation and support of alternative energy sources in rural areas (Korf & Raeymaekers, 2013, p. 155). After reviewing the purposes and restating the overall goals and outcomes of the aid program, the program management team should carefully plan the next step. At this point, the program manager should consider the need to divide people into teams that must be assigned tasks.

For instance, to encourage and empower more people in becoming entrepreneurs, the program management needs a teamwork supervisor to manage a staff of 10. To strengthen Kyrgyzstan's IT infrastructure, the program manager needs a team leader to handle 15 IT experts (see Table 3.3 and Figure 3.5).

Table 3.3: Elements of project scope management: GTZ Capacity Building Project for Food Security, Regional Cooperation & Conflict Mitigation

Elements	Description
Vision/ Mission/ Objective	"…to improve people's living conditions on a sustainable basis" (Taking IT Global, 2015).
Goal	• To develop capabilities of the people to have a better local government, the development of more entrepreneurs, better IT support, improvements in election capabilities, the provision of more business training, cooperative formation, and support the development of energy sources in rural areas.
Strategy	• "Promote complex reforms and change processes under difficult conditions". (Taking IT Global, 2015)
Organizational Structure	See Figure 3.5

Roles	• "Provide viable, forward-looking solutions for political, economic, ecological, and social development worldwide" • "Strengthen individual initiative and capabilities of people and organizations". Source: Taking IT Global, 2015
Quality Standards	• Survey Measurement Standards (i.e., 5-point Likert scale) • Standards set on entrepreneurship promotion program • Standards set on IT development program • Standards set on energy development program • Standards set on business training program • Standards set on food security project
Metrics	• Response Rate on Surveys (i.e., response rate should be more than 50%). • Course evaluation must reach a minimum rate of 3.0 on a 5-point Likert scale (i.e., 1=poor, 2=fair, 3=average, 4=good, and 5=excellent).
Reporting	• Reporting includes stating the role and responsibility of each staff member (i.e., organizational chart).

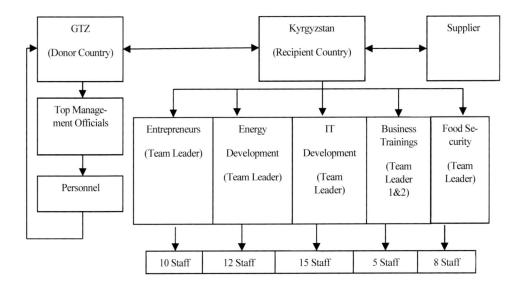

Figure 3.5: Organizational structure

In terms of integration management, the program management team assigned to handle the GTZ Capacity Building Project for Food Security, Regional Cooperation & Conflict Mitigation should not only closely monitor the disbursement of budgeted funds but also ensure that assigned project tasks are not redundant and may be completed within the expected deadlines.

Case Study – CIDA Assistance in Ethiopia

The Government of Canada is committed to making its international assistance more efficient, focused, and accountable. A key element of this aid effectiveness agenda is transparency. As such, Canadian International Development Authority (CIDA) states it is fully committed to making useful information public to enhance its transparency and accountability. Three priority themes are part of that agenda and guide CIDA's work including: 1) increasing food security, 2) securing the future of children and youth, and 3) stimulating sustainable economic growth (CIDA, 2011b). Moving forward, CIDA will place even greater emphasis on results and on empowering developing countries to take the lead in defining, delivering, measuring results and, thereby increasing ownership of development outcomes.

Often development must be locally led before a country can produce and sustain meaningful results. In line with this, CIDA supports efforts that demonstrate local country ownership of development (Tomlinson & Foster, 2004). This includes the identification of needs and priorities through national policies and strategies. CIDA programs and projects are aligned with the partner country's needs and national priorities outlined in such plans (CIDA, 2012a).

CIDA is using results-based management practices that combine strategy, people, resources, processes, and measurements to improve not only decision-making but also transparency and accountability (CIDA, 2009). CIDA conducts continuous evaluations on all of its programs in order to improve their design, delivery, and results. Aside from having an External Departmental Audit Committee that regularly performs audits of its programs to ensure effective, efficient, and prudent use of its resources, it also adheres to the proactive disclosure of financial and human-resources-related information for government departments and agencies. In some cases, CIDA publishes these reports on a monthly basis.

The goal is to make Canada's international assistance more focused, more effective, and more accountable. As part of its Aid Effectiveness Agenda, the Government of Canada announced, in 2009, that it would be directing 80% of its bilateral resources to 20 countries of focus. Several countries including Ethiopia were chosen based on their real needs, their capacity to benefit from aid, and their alignment with Canadian foreign policy priorities.

Aside from addressing the main causes of poverty within its population, the main challenge for Ethiopia is to continue and accelerate the progress made in recent years toward the Millennium Development Goals (MDGs). The government is already devoting a very large share of its budget to pro-poor programs and investments. Large-scale donor support is intended to continue to provide a vital contribution in the near-term to finance the levels of spending needed to meet these challenges. However, even if donor support had increased, the use of financial aid would require Ethiopia to improve its governance, empower the local authorities, and become more accountable to its citizens (see Chapter 7, Articles and Reports, Published Media Submissions, Will G8 Meet Its Aid Pledges?).

Over the past two decades, Ethiopia has made significant progress in key human development indicators. For instance, the primary school enrollment increased four times as compared to the 1990s, the child mortality has been cut in half, and the number of people with access to clean water has doubled. All these improvements are clear signs of poverty reduction. Based on a national survey, the poverty rate in Ethiopia was 44% in 1999/2000 and fell to 39% in 2004/05 and to 30% in 2010/11 (Plavgo et al., 2013). Food security, which affects as many as five million people annually, is one of the greatest barriers to sustainable development in Ethiopia. As of 2012, many Ethiopians were in need of food relief assistance (CARE, 2012). Therefore, being the core of poverty reduction, food security is the number one priority on Ethiopia's development agenda.

Canada supported Ethiopia's development vision and planned to deepen its engagement in foreign aid development programs. Because of its commitment to improve governance, reduce the rate of poverty, and make use of financial assistance effectively, Ethiopia was selected, in December 2012, as a country of focus for CIDA. The agency adopted a program-based coordinated approach that focused on Ethiopian priorities and harmonization of donor procedures. By implementing some of the aid effectiveness principles, the donor hoped to lessen the risk of reducing the impact of development assistance. Over time, the local ownership was expected to increase whereas the relative transaction cost was expected to decrease.

Ethiopia's Sustainable Development Poverty Reduction Program (SDPRP) was a three-year program implemented between 2002/03 to 2004/05. The SDPRP strategy was built on four pillars, or building blocks, including the following sectors: 1) agricultural development-led industrialization and food security, 2) the justice system and civil service reform, 3) good governance, decentralization, and empowerment, and 4) capacity building in public and private sectors (Embassy of Ethiopia, 2015). Recognizing the need to solve problems related to food scarcity in Ethiopia, its government started dealing with its development partners through a mechanism known as the New Coalition for Food Security. The work of the Coalition was an integral part of the SDPRP. It was considered as an unprecedented consultative effort that involved the government, non-governmental organizations, and donors like CIDA. Publishing CIDA's Poverty Reduction Strategy Paper called the "Sustainable Development Poverty Reduction Program (SDPRP)" was a sign of a strong country leadership that was used as a virtual work-plan by the international community (Embassy of Ethiopia, 2015).

Would the process of implementing the SDPRP strategies be effective in terms of reducing poverty from 44% down to 39%? Most of the comments regarding this particular question were published online in the article *The Experiences of Measuring and Monitoring Poverty in Ethiopia* (Woldehanna, 2004). This report concluded that a national survey strongly suggested that actual poverty, as measured by per capita income, remained the same. However, the Rural and Urban Household Surveys strongly suggest that the poverty rate in this country had decreased since 1989 (ODI, 2011). On the other hand, the result of the qualitative survey showed that the poverty rate and destitution in this country have increased over the past 10 years (ODI, 2011).

In 2003, the UN observed that despite the recent economic gains, the country's per capita gross national income (GNI) was less than US$100 per year and approximately 31% of Ethiopia's population was living on less than US$1each day (CIDA, 2004, p. 5). CIDA's own assessment was that in the process of promoting the local agricultural activities, it is possible to strengthen the effectiveness of foreign aid and significantly reduce the rate of poverty in Ethiopia as well as in poor countries all over the world (CIDA, 2004, p. 5). The effort to promote the local agricultural activities could also increase the trust placed on the leadership of Ethiopia's government. This idea was clearly reflected in the following statement:

> The international donor community, including Canada, anticipates that relief food aid needs will persist in Ethiopia for another three to five years at least, while the Government works to scale up agriculture production and improve access to food by vulnerable populations. Within 5 years, it is hoped that food security will improve for the 5 million Ethiopians who are chronically food insecure and significantly improve for another 10 million food insecure. This will occur if the Government is successful at implementing significant structural reforms in areas such as agricultural extension, land tenure security, and diversification of the rural economy. (CIDA, 2004, p. 3)

This multilateral program of food security assistance seems to be a laudable attempt to assist a significant proportion of Ethiopia's population (5–8%) to achieve basic physiological needs. For instance, in 2003–2004, the Productive Safety Nets Program was considered a significant achievement after implementing the program to as many as five million probable beneficiaries (IMF, 2006, p. 58). However, it was noted that even though the Government managed to allocate higher budget commitments, the fund given to the New Coalition of Food Security was much lower than expected (IMF, 2006, p. 27).

After the major drought in 2002/03 that resulted in GDP contraction, Ethiopia has been one of the fastest growing economies in Africa. Official statistics indicate an average real GDP growth of 11% over the last six consecutive years. Nevertheless, its robust growth performance and considerable development gains came under threat during 2008 and 2011 with the emergence of twin macroeconomic challenges of high inflation and a difficult balance of payments situation. The problem was exacerbated by high fuel and food prices in the global market (World Bank, 2015b). The inflation rate of food alone increased from 13% to 47%. In an effort to control inflation and stem the rising cost of living, the Government took various measures including imposing tight controls on government expenditures. The main challenge for Ethiopia remained to continue to accelerate the progress made in recent years toward the MDGs and to address the causes of poverty amongst its population. The Government is already devoting a very large share of its budget to pro-poor programs and investments. Large-scale donor support will continue to provide a vital contribution in the near-term to finance the levels of spending needed to meet these challenges. However, even if donor support increases, the effective use of aid will require Ethiopia to improve governance, empower local authorities, and become more accountable to its citizens (World Bank, 2015b).

Ethiopia's current five-year development plan (2010–11 to 2014–15), the Growth and Transformation Plan (GTP), has been geared towards fostering broad-based development in a sustainable manner to achieve the MDGs (Ababa, 2010). Agricultural production is to double to ensure food security in Ethiopia for the first time (Ababa, 2010, p. 14). Hence, it would appear that CIDA's optimism — as well as that of the other bilateral and multilateral participants in the SDPRP — was misplaced and the chief causes, leaving aside the drought, were a combination of inadequate donor support. Perhaps due to the 2008 global economic crisis, weak governance by the Ethiopian leadership at the time failed to empower local authorities sufficiently. This could indicate that efforts to apply the Paris Declaration model and implement the MfDR were insufficient and development aid was underutilized. From the statistics in these paragraphs, it is difficult to determine to what degree rapid economic growth is benefitting the majority of the population. Lower mortality rates along with growing education ratios sound promising. Hence, CIDA assistance may have helped a generally positive trend that began before their involvement.

Case Study – USAID Assistance in Nepal

During the late 90s, USAID reinvented and reengineered itself. In the early 2000s, continuous developments and reforms were observed in USAID and in the U.S. government's foreign assistance in general, particularly with regard to how the agency does its work. With the Afghanistan and Iraq wars in full swing, USAID was repositioned to help those two countries rebuild governance systems, infrastructure, civil society, and basic services such as healthcare and education (USAID, 2015b). The Agency started rebuilding using their five guiding principles:

1. Increase customer focus
2. Manage results effectively
3. Improve teamwork and overall participation of staff
4. Empower staff and increase their accountability
5. Promote diversity (GAO, 1997, p. 2)

It also began an aggressive campaign to reach out to new partner organizations — including the private sector and foundations — to extend the outreach of its foreign assistance. Eventually, its country-level sector offices were replaced by strategic objective (SO) teams.

Based on the Human Development Index, Nepal is a poor country that ranks 157th amongst 187 countries (USAID, 2014). By contrast, Ethiopia ranks 174th (Rural Poverty Portal, n.d.) and Kyrgyzstan ranks 126th (ADB, 2012). With a population of about 24 million, Nepal's agricultural base is considered as the most productive sector, yet it has been characterized by underemployment, antiquated practices, and low use of advanced technologies (Reed & McConnachie, 2002, p. vi). Based on the World Bank's assessment the central challenge for rural development in Nepal is to shift from subsistence to a commercial economy in an environment characterized by widespread and day-to-day insecurity and violence.

In poorer countries, agriculture is considered as the principal source of food, income, and employment for the majority of the population. Growth in agriculture therefore is crucial when it comes to reducing poverty. Based on the preliminary findings of the Nepal National Living Standards Survey, despite the insurgency, the agricultural sector has made a significant contribution to poverty reduction. With only 13% of its agricultural output traded in markets, agriculture is largely based on low-value cereals and subsistence production. Even though there is considerable scope to increase agricultural productivity, the country's agricultural sector share of GDP, which once was as much as 40%, has been declining. Despite increased reliance on remittances from labourers abroad, the absence of economic opportunities, outside of traditional subsistence agriculture, keeps most Nepalese poor. Until recently, the Maoist insurgency in rural areas has impeded improvements in the agricultural sector. Although this particular insurgency is now a legacy of the past, unrest and disruption continue as the country struggles to replace its constitution with a more inclusive and modern version.

Because of limited prospects for development, the poverty rate in this area has always been high (Agriculture Nepal, 2011).

For more than 60 years, USAID programs have been working closely with the Government of Nepal in order to address the effects of the country's meagre economic performance. By strengthening citizen participation, advancement can be made while Nepal transitions from a form of constitutional monarchy to a more republican democracy. As a result, it should be possible to improve the overall quality of life for many Nepalese despite lingering issues such as lack of universal education, caste, and ethnic and gender bias. Future development should also focus on strengthening the national health system, increasing income and employment rates in rural areas, and addressing the challenges related to food security and climate change. In each of these areas, special emphasis has been placed on disaster risk reduction, supporting Nepal's youth (55% of the population of the more than 31 million is under the age of 25), and addressing grievances of socially disadvantaged populations. These disadvantaged populations include members of so-called "scheduled" castes, victims of HIV/AIDS, and human trafficking, particularly of girls/women (the literacy rate amongst women is less than 50%) (Index Mundi, 2014). At present, there are five strategic objective teams in operation at the USAID mission in Nepal.

Nepal's decade-long insurgency ended in 2006. The country's leading political parties are now faced with the new challenge to focus more on reconciliation and making sustainable peace agreements to end conflicts, and to draft a new constitution. While a new constitution has recently been adopted by the interim constituent assembly, it has yet to be promulgated, and the country continues to experience violent turmoil in this process. While some political reform has been successful in terms of addressing critical development challenges, progress has been slow due to frequent changes in political leadership and to interest groups who continue struggling for power using tested tactics such as calling frequent nationwide general strikes and disrupting government functions often with violence.

Although Nepal has shown remarkable improvements in the past decades, it remains one of the poorest countries in the world. Between 2007 and 2011, 25% of Nepal's total population was living below the international poverty line of US$1.25 per day (UNICEF, 2013). Nepal's 1995 Agriculture Perspective Plan (APP) has been successful in increasing its agricultural productivity through irrigation and the use of fertilizer (Agriculture Projects Services Centre and John Mellor Associates, 1995). However, sustainable development in its infrastructure development and related technologies, which has been quite slow, was greatly affected by the April 2015 massive earthquake. To reform the APP, the National Agricultural Policy turned to promoting commercialization focusing on private sector development initiatives and on improving trade with India, Nepal's major trading partner. With this in mind, USAID entered into contractual agreements with Winrock International[vi] to help the government increase agricultural productivity and contribute to rural development through vocational training in this sector. On its official website, Winrock highlighted the need "to build a better world by increasing agricultural productivity and rural development while protecting the environment." Winrock Nepal currently conducts activities under three "multidimensional programs" amongst which is Education and Income Generation for Conflict Mitigation (EIGCM) (Winrock, 2015).

The inclusion of disadvantaged youth in relevant educational institutions, vocational training, and creating local employment opportunities are features of the EIGCM program — an approach designed to respond to the root cause of earlier conflict. This multifaceted program combines literacy and life skills education, technical and vocational training linked to employment, and training to increase agricultural productivity and raise rural incomes. Targeted scholarships are awarded to disadvantaged youth (i.e., internally displaced persons, lower caste groups, ethnic minorities, and girls) so as to increase access to primary, secondary, and higher-level education. A special emphasis on developing knowledge, attitudes, and skills for conflict resolution; peace building; and the promotion of human rights is a crosscutting theme throughout all of these activities, and an integral part of the process to achieve lasting peace and reconciliation. The primary beneficiaries of this program include the disadvantaged, conflict-affected people, and the internally displaced youth throughout mid-western Nepal.

To implement these various developmental programs Winrock created a team made up of mostly local Nepali organizations (Winrock, 2008). Through the Smallholder Irrigation Market Initiative (SIMI) project, this new project complemented Winrock's ongoing work in Nepal. For example, through the promotion of high-value crop production and micro-irrigation technologies, Winrock was substantially increasing the income of smallholder farmers in nine conflict-affected districts. The outcome of the EIGCM project resulted in more than 50,000 households benefitting from the increase in their annual income by more than 100%. The project has been very effective in demonstrating that increase in rural income, through improved agricultural and vocational training, can help decrease disaffection with traditional government policies and government-supported activities in this particular sector (Winrock, 2008). The question of ownership seems to have been answered through meeting the recipient's primary needs. By improving people's skills and know-how, Winrock managed to provide a more hopeful future for these 50,000 beneficiaries.

Other USAID programs are working with the Government of Nepal to address the effects of the country's poor economic performance and advance Nepal's political transition by strengthening citizen participation, improving the quality of life for Nepalese by improving its health systems, and addressing the challenges of food security and climate change. In each of these areas, special focus was made on disaster risk reduction and supporting Nepal's youth and socially disadvantaged populations. The World Bank has this to say about Nepal in the post-conflict period:

> Though it faces enormous challenges, Nepal is not without some significant assets. The evidence is compelling that the strength behind development in Nepal is highly concentrated at the community level. Success stories abound, from forestry user groups and women's groups to community-based programs in rural drinking water, rural roads, micro-hydropower generation, community management of schools, and the Poverty Alleviation Fund (PAF). Many of the truly community-owned efforts demonstrated great viability even during the height of the conflict. Where a supportive framework has been created for communities to undertake such activities, there have been impressive development successes. (World Bank, 2015c)

In Nepal, the World Bank Group includes the International Development Association (IDA), its concessionary lending arm; the International Finance Corporation (IFC), its private-sector arm; the Multilateral Investment Guarantee Agency (MIGA); and the World Bank Institute (WBI). These organizations provide Nepal with additional investment insurance and capacity-building services. The strategy was based on three pillars. The first was designed to increase productivity and connectivity for economic growth. The second focuses on the need to reduce weaknesses of local government and improve its flexibility. The third pillar aims to promote the right to improved quality services. "Governance, accountability, gender equality, and social inclusion" are important ideas that made up the three pillars (IMF, 2012). IDA is more focused on solving developmental problems related to road construction; increasing food supply; promoting the creation of more livelihood projects, access to health, education, and urban services; and improving the country's existing disaster management further. The IFC is more focused on improving people's access to finance and investment, trade facilities, lending to small and medium enterprises (SMEs), and support for trade finance facilities for local banks. IDA and IFC should support each other to improve not only climate change but also agriculture and creation of more power supply.

Subject to performance and economic management, Nepal was able to benefit from an allocation of approximately US$400 million from IDA between 2012 and 2013. These funds were used to finance four to five new operations each year. IFC can potentially commit to US$25–30 million on average, each year, depending on the availability of viable investments and improvements in the business climate (IMF, 2012). The main criteria for pledging additional financial support is stated as "building on programs with successful track records that are adapted to local conditions" such as that perfected by Winrock (IMF, 2012).

According to the World Food Program (WFP) in Nepal, "three and a half million people are considered moderately to severely food insecure" (CIDA, 2011a). This is about 10% of Nepal's present population. The task ahead is difficult. Under the food-and-cash-for-assets scheme, WFP, in partnership with the German development agency, GTZ, introduced the concept of community-based commercial farming villages "to improve the livelihoods of food-insecure people through effective long-term agricultural interventions" (World Food Program, 2015).

Case Study – A Modest and Successful Intervention in Uganda

I recently decided to support a community initiative in health or education. Before making this decision, I was aware of the potential challenges including such possible roadblocks as limited interest amongst certain groups, limited transparency, etc. In order to mitigate some of these challenges, I started contacting friends and former colleagues in countries where I had worked earlier. While the process was long and tedious, I personally find the outcome, in terms of agreeing on a possible intervention, satisfactory.

The consensus was a project in education. One of my philosophies has always been to help communities instead of individuals. Therefore, this project involves the need to sponsor the supply of computers to an educational institution that is in need of computers.

The next step was to identify an institution in need of such support. One of my associates, who served as a project coordinator, knew a college that her parents had given some books to in the past. The college's management was contacted and as it turned out, the college was in need of computers. During the discussion, we were told the exact number of computers the school currently needs.

In response to the requests made, I stated my terms before donating such equipment. These terms included: 1) the need to create a baseline report using my guidelines and outline and 2) the institution would have to pay the shipping cost of the computers from the U.S. to its campus as well as any customs fees and computer installation fees, and sending me a photo of one of the training sessions (see Figure 3.5a and Appendixes I–III).

The key lessons learned from this real-life case study are as follows:

- When finalizing any agreement, it is essential that commitment between the donor and the beneficiary be maintained throughout the entire duration, meaning, there should be a start and an end date to the process.
- To preserve trust between the two parties, the donor should avoid promising things he or she cannot deliver.
- Implementing the project is more of a process than an event.

Throughout the process, all transactions must be kept flowing smoothly if both donor and beneficiaries are to be satisfied that the intended outcome has been achieved. My personal experience is that both the donor and the intended beneficiaries are capable of satisfying terms and conditions associated with the project if the donor has stipulated clear terms and conditions. (see Chapter 7, My Published Media Submissions, Our Chance to Make a Difference and the International Development Fiasco).

Figure 3.5a: Student training session in progress (BBUC, 2015)

Case Study – Managing Unscrupulous Contractors

While the preceding case studies have helped in highlighting the different levels of "success" stories in Central and Southwest Asia and Africa, we should not lose sight of the reality that donors routinely face. The case study below is one example of how international aid went awry. It is an example of a situation where trust was met with distrust, loyalty was met with disloyalty, fair play was met with brutality, and empathy was taken as a sign of weakness.

During one of my evaluation assignments, I was invited by a multilateral agency to evaluate one of its programs. Part of this program was a project aimed at constructing and furnishing a health facility for a community. As part of the process, this multilateral agency recruited an international organization that had been registered to operate in the country. The motivation to recruit this company was strengthened by an earlier recruitment of the same contractor by a bilateral agency that was also operating and based in the same country.

After the vetting process, the multilateral agency awarded the contract as expected to this "local contractor." During my mission, I had meetings with different stakeholders including beneficiaries. As part of the assignment, I also visited the site of this "newly" constructed facility. What I observed was not only mind-boggling but also a situation where funds had been mismanaged, leaving the facility incomplete. The facility meant to serve as a maternity unit had uncompleted floors, no ceiling, no windowpanes, leaking roofs, no furnishings (as required in the contract), and neonatal-care women sleeping on uncompleted concrete floors. Through further investigation, I found out that this contractor had not only absconded, he had closed shop and left the country with no trace of his whereabouts. Interestingly, the multilateral agency all along had been left in complete darkness. Above all, during the construction process, no progress reports were presented, no supervision (by a third party) was conducted, and according to government sources, the recipient government was as isolated as all the other stakeholders.

It is not unusual for development agencies to be faced with challenges like this. What was unique in this case was the care, detail, and trust involved in the vetting process of this contract. The contractor obviously was reputable with convincing finished "poster projects" in the development arena. Moreover, the multilateral agency's experience of being "short-changed" was a significant disappointment — both expensive to the funder and adversely impacting the health of the clients who were the potential beneficiaries. Ironically, the multilateral agency had a standard policy of refraining from constructing health facilities — one strictly adhered to by every other program.

As I grapple with cases like this, several questions come to mind: What has happened to our sense of empathy? Have our ethical qualities been overtaken by greed? And what happened to our "Western" values? These and some general global concerns should highlight many of the unforeseen challenges faced by humanitarian agencies.

Obviously, this Western–based contractor's behaviour demonstrates a completely unacceptable level of insensitivity, irresponsibly, and a lack of compassion for vulnerable communities. This must be condemned in the strongest terms. There is every reason to believe that contractors like this put "the bottom line" ahead of human lives — an attitude that has no room in any society.

In one of its reports, Transparency International,[vii] an anti-corruption watchdog, characterizes corruption as follows:

> Corruption in humanitarian work is among the worst kind. It can mean the difference between life and death. It robs people of essential resources, destroying dignity and causing desperation. Emergency assistance pumps large amounts of money and goods into damaged economies. The risk of corruption is acute. Aid often flows through new, unmonitored channels. It faces the chaos of conflicts or natural disasters. So it's extremely hard to track where aid goes.
>
> Food, water and medical supplies can be stolen and sold on the black market. Companies can bribe procurement officials to win contracts. This can mean displaced families receive sub-standard housing or poor-quality food. Aid agencies feel the need for speed. Sometimes this makes them bypass standard anti-corruption measures. The result? Money or goods go missing. Aid can be used to buy votes or influence. Too often, powerful local groups and existing corrupt networks benefit. Those most needing help miss out.

Oftentimes agencies may be reluctant to tackle corruption head-on, fearing that it will make them look bad if they admit to being robbed. But Transparency International argues that corruption cannot be ignored. Like bullying, corruption only gets worse if not tackled head-on. Instead, they propose the following solution:

> Corruption in humanitarian aid is shocking. This often makes it a taboo subject. Aid agencies, governments, and communities fear for their reputations. But only by discussing it openly can we tackle it. This won't harm anyone if we

stress that addressing corruption doesn't mean condoning it. Nor does it mean anyone is especially vulnerable to it.

Aid agencies can do much to minimise corruption. They can analyse risks and local power structures as part of emergency preparations and staff training. Codes of conduct and strong financial controls will also protect them. Communities need to know who's entitled to aid and what they're entitled to. Then they can monitor whether any aid went missing. Confidential complaints systems are vital. These enable staff and recipients to report corruption freely. By working together, the humanitarian community can close loopholes against corruption. We must encourage them to share experiences and take joint action.

The original recommendation in my report then (and this possibly holds true now) was as follows:

because of the problems (managerial, technical, and administrative) plaguing this project, it is recommended that this project be terminated as soon as possible and that efforts be made to contact a designated contractor representative who will provide the final technical reports, including details of updated budget-related activities.

Essentially, there was nothing more we could do but cut our losses and start over. Taking all measures possible to avoid unscrupulous contractors in the first place is therefore essential.

Case Study – Enabling Environment

In this context, an "enabling environment" is defined as the availability of appropriate, relevant, and sustainable legislation (laws), government policies, internal political stability, effective coordination mechanisms, and strategies and tactics that will best support the successful realization of well-planned objectives. Often the presence of relevant sustainable policies and laws can help build a more stable political environment and contribute to development environments that facilitate effective coordination amongst the stakeholders in implementing useful tactics that lend themselves to the success of planned objectives.

When managing foreign aid projects, objectives that will help create an enabling environment include the development and implementation of government policies that aim to create and maintain sustainable macroeconomic environments, particularly ones that tend to bring together (unity of purpose) suppliers and consumers in a well-coordinated manner (UNFCCC, 2015). Another equally useful strategy that could promote the creation of an enabling environment is to remove all potential barriers that might be perceived as hindering the progress of foreign aid projects (UNFCCC, 2015). Likewise, it is also possible to make use of market-based strategies such as motivating and rewarding staff or stakeholders for staying committed to the success of foreign aid projects.

Aside from the use of market-based strategies, other useful strategies include the need to strengthen the sense of citizenship, improve people's knowledge concerning their rights and responsibilities as a citizen, and educate people about the importance of transparency and accountability when managing foreign aid projects. As such, one of the emergent "best" strategies is to strengthen a country's national and regional anti-corruption campaigns and associated initiatives. Thus, the presence of an enabling environment is an inclusive variable, possessing common elements of consistency that are now based on the UN charter of universal human rights. Too often, complacency with regard to the presence of and tolerance for corruption and corrupt practices only works against better and more effective and efficient management of development programs.

A majority of people in Ethiopia are highly dependent on international food assistance due to the presence of chronic food scarcity in rural areas (Action Against Hunger, 2015; USAID, 2015a). To create an enabling environment for foreign aid intervention, the government of Ethiopia fosters efforts to establish and maintain partnership agreements and ties with several foreign-based organizations such as the Catholic Relief Services (CRS), the Relief Society of Tigray (REST), Food for the Hungry (FH), Save the Children, and the World Food Program (WFP) (USAID, 2015a). In doing so, Ethiopia can receive "emergency food assistance" from these foreign organizations (USAID, 2015a). The use of this particular intervention can help the government save the lives of those facing dire health consequences caused by malnourishment.

The government of Ethiopia has tried to protect its people from hunger by creating the "social transformation" policy (Kissi, 2006, p. 25; Young, 2006, p. 132; de Waal, 1991, pp. 4–6). Based on Ethiopia's social protection model, social protection such as improvements in the availability of food supply in this particular country can be affected by three factors: those that are related to administrative functions, political intervention, and the availability of financial support (Rahmato, Pankhurst and van Uffelen, 2013, p. 7).

These are related to administrative functions, political intervention, and the availability of financial support (Rahmato, Pankhurst, & van Uffelen, 2013, p. 7). In the process of removing barriers related to these three factors that may affect the development of social transformation in this country, Ethiopia's food security strategies and production safety net programs can become more successful (Rahmato et al., 2013, p. 8). As of 2006, Ethiopia was still fighting to end its dependency on foreign food aid assistance (IRIN News, 2006).

The real-life experience of Rwanda is a good example of an effective enabling environment. Patterned after the social transformation model of Ethiopia, Rwanda's Economic Development and Poverty Reduction Strategy was implemented by Rwanda's government to reduce the country's poverty rate (Rahmato et al., 2013, p. 10). Rahmato et al. (2013, p. 10) explained that Rwanda's government created useful policies that promote local and international investments that would help create more job opportunities for local people. Ethiopia's government also provided strong support to local farmers. By increasing agricultural production, food scarcity can be eliminated in the long run (Rahmato et al., 2013, p. 10).

Case Study – Capacity Building

Education is obviously the main source of empowerment for all people. Development of knowledge and skills of individuals starts by encouraging more people to complete comprehensive education, meaning, going beyond the minimum standard established by the state (such as completing 12 years of primary and secondary education). Whether the furtherance of education is accomplished by training in a specific field, participating in various campaign activities, updating knowledge and skills through operations research, or working to create community awareness through community mobilization campaigns makes no difference to the desired outcome.

Since a government alone cannot execute foreign aid programs successfully without the active participation of enlightened citizens, upgrading knowledge and skills amongst citizens is a crucial part of this hypothesis regarding what ultimately makes for successful foreign aid-funded programs.

Presented in the lowest level of the CARROT-BUS model, the term "capacity building" can be defined as identifying strategies that can continuously develop the knowledge and skills of each person. The expectation is that if this process is applied on a massive scale, the citizens of the entire nation will be able to succeed in their unique roles and responsibilities essential in the economic progress and development of a country. The state of educational reform in the country of Finland is a prime example of how this hypothesis has been tested. Finland has changed its traditional education "into a model of a modern, publicly financed system with widespread equity, good quality, large participation—all of this at reasonable cost" (Sahlberg, 2009, p. 2). Finland now ranks first amongst all the OECD nations — the so-called "developed" nations — on the Program for International Student Assessments (PISA), an international test for 15-year-olds in language, math, and science literacy (Darling-Hammond, 2010).

The knowledge and skills of people in the development of foreign aid projects should be based on many years of experience, specifically in the design and implementation of capacity building initiatives. Often, the efficiency and effectiveness of capacity building can be improved by empowering the public and private institutions throughout a given country. In the process of meeting the basic needs of each citizen, a country's dependency on foreign aid can be reduced.

Regarding capacity development for managing foreign aid programs, the process should always begin within the context of the donor and recipient governments themselves. For instance, the government has the duty and responsibility to develop a strong environment that will encourage more people to participate in economic development such as sustainable agriculture. In doing so, the government can play a significant role in solving poverty problems related to the high market price of food products and food scarcity. Government should always support the basic needs and priorities of the local people, increase transparency and accountability, and ensure that all public and private sector players engaged in the manufacturing of food and non-food products stay committed to their roles in economic development.

The case of Finland's educational reform, however, needs to be taken in political context, as mere reform in one vital sector may not ensure that benefits follow on, inevitably to other sectors (Gotev, 2015; Ministry for Foreign Affairs of Finland, n.d.). The more recent developments in Finland have been very successful. Gotev (2015) and the Ministry for Foreign Affairs of Finland (n.d.) discussed in detail the success behind Finland's foreign aid development assistance. Therefore, the story of Finland should be required readings for any student of foreign assistance. It tends to focus upon the discussion central to this document—specifically on the lessons learned with respect to development assistance/cooperation.

Let us take the case of Ethiopia as an example. Ethiopia has been experiencing food scarcity for so many years. To solve this problem, people should understand that the process of producing adequate food supply is highly dependent on both individual and institutional capacity. Alternative livelihood activities, market development, control of the current population growth, ease on land tenure, and so much more are amongst the few possible solutions that could solve the problem in Ethiopia. In all areas, capacity development is fundamental to the development of sustainable environment and the empowerment of the community (FAO, 2014). For example, assuming that farmers in Ethiopia receive adequate knowledge on how to grow food crops properly, it is the government's job to support them with the required technological facilities. This support includes best practices in land preparation; necessary inputs such as non-toxic fertilizers, herbicides, and insecticides; selling the harvested food products through cooperatives; building farm-to-market roads; and constructing appropriate food storage facilities. There is a strong possibility that without consideration of these risks, and the devotion of considerable capital to address weaknesses in all these areas, it is highly doubtful that the country will be able to create a sustainable production of food supplies.

The same degree of government analysis and support should be given to avoid producing food crops that could not compete in the international marketplace without government price subsidies to the growers/producers. The current situation in Thailand serves as a reminder that populist agricultural policies may backfire on a political scale that leaves a once prosperous country in search of markets for its most important, and sought after agricultural exports. Indirectly related to a conundrum of fair pricing for producers and food scarcity amongst vulnerable segments of the population, governments may also need to address issues related to land tenure, corporate vs. individual farming, environmental protection, conservation, population growth rates, rural to urban migration, and gender equity. In Ethiopia, the physiological needs of people also relate to the number and quality of health facilities, staff, and costs of providing medical services to the most vulnerable population. Again, Thailand's case may be further researched in order to understand that dynamic in terms of political and social costs. Ideally, every community should have access to health facilities that provide quality services at affordable prices since maintaining physical health, by both curative and preventive means, improves the chances of all people to the right to a productive and healthy lifespan.

Case Study – Accountability

Accountability is all about being able to focus on whether the master program/project plan assures that stakeholders perform their defined/given responsibilities (Brown, 2008, p. 36). In carefully researching and planning the means of making all stakeholders accountable, there are higher chances management team members will be able to increase individual and group output and that foreign aid programs become more successful.

The term "accountability" can be defined as making people answerable for their own actions and/or decisions.

One of the best ways to provide safeguards to donor constituencies that foreign aid funds will be properly administered is to encourage the local citizens that are the "general" stakeholders, including intended beneficiaries, to participate in the process of monitoring the actual disbursement of those funds. The fact is that a large number of people who reside in developing countries, and are supposed to be the recipients of a stream of benefits brought about by the disbursement of foreign aid, lack the knowledge and skills on how they can effectively monitor the distribution of these funds (Birdsall, Savedoff, Mahgoub, & Vybomy, 2011, p. 8).

All of the foregoing postulations explain why the concept of capacity building is considered the founding principle of developing an enabling environment. The process of educating people about accountability, monitoring, and transparency should serve as the first step in preventing development programs/projects from being infected by corrupt practices.

One should be aware that accountability in foreign aid is not limited to the stakeholders' responsibility when managing the financial aspects of the endeavour. Accountability can also be applied to the ability of the stakeholders to comply with a set of rules and regulations imposed on them in order to see that the program/project gets off the ground. Stakeholders' commitments need to ensure all are involved in working towards the common goal, participate in the project through to its completion, ensure that the highest quality performance is delivered, and avoid abuse of authority (Griffiths, Maggs, & George, E., 2007; MCEC, n.d.). In this regard, Tobin Rick, an experienced development consultant from the Netherlands, created the acronym SIMPLE, which summarizes succinctly what accountability implies as it pertains to the process of setting expectations, inviting commitment, measuring progress, providing constructive feedback, linking personal accountability to consequences, and evaluating the project effectiveness (Rick, 2011; see Figure 3.6).

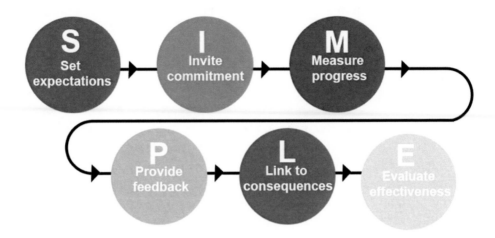

Figure 3.6: Model of accountability
Source: Rick 2011

To illustrate, CIDA programs and projects are aligned with the partner country's needs and national priorities outlined in national development plans (CIDA, 2012a). To make foreign aid projects successful, CIDA encourages stakeholders to support the program by letting them know that the agency strongly supports efforts that demonstrate local country ownership of development, including the identification of needs and priorities through national policies and strategies (Tomlinson & Foster, 2004). CIDA uses results-based management practices that combine strategy, people, resources, processes, and measurements of outcomes as a strategic means to improve not only decision-making but also transparency and accountability (CIDA, 2009).

To improve the design, delivery, and results of foreign aid projects continuously, CIDA sees to it that its staff and consultants conduct regular evaluations of program and project outcomes. Aside from the External Departmental Audit Committee that regularly performs audits, it also adheres to the proactive disclosure of financial and human resources-related information for government departments and agencies.

In some cases, CIDA publishes reports on a monthly basis. Unfortunately, even if the amount of donor support had increased over time, disbursement of financial aid funds in the case of Ethiopia remains weak in terms of the country's government commitment. The basic problem CIDA has encountered in Ethiopia is a lack of will by senior government officials to make the local authorities of Ethiopia more accountable to the intended beneficiaries when these authorities are caught and found guilty by local magistrates of the misuse of project funds. In this case study, the best way to improve the process of program design is to require the need to educate members of the Ministry and the local Department of Justice concerning the issue on transparency and accountability.

One has to be clear that accountability can either be classified as a "representative accountability," "principal-agent accountability," and "mutual accountability" (Brown, 2008, p. 37). In the case of foreign aid programs, all three types of accountability relationships should be carefully observed and delineated on a case-by-case basis. For example, given that NGOs sometimes act as the representative who will directly receive foreign aid funds, specific NGOs should be held liable for, as well as accountable, for any misuse of the funds (Edwards & Hulme, 2002, p. 41). Hence, there should be internal staff as well as appointed external auditors who will be in charge of monitoring the way the NGOs spend foreign aid. On the other hand, the principles of "principal-agent accountability" strongly suggest that the agents would at all times make important decisions based on the interests of principals and that the agents should at all costs yield their authority judiciously when handling foreign aid funds (Griffiths, Maggs, & George, E., 2007; MCEC, n.d.; see Figure 3.7).

	REPRESENTATIVE	PRINCIPAL-AGENT	MUTUAL
Status of Parties	Constituents most important	Principal most important	All parties important
Influence Relationship	Representative acts for constituent	Agent is subordinate to principal	Parties exert mutual influence
Desired Outcomes	Defined in general by constituents; specifics by representative	Defined primarily by principal; agent gets compensation	Defined by shared values and problem definitions
Transparency	Representative is open to constituents	Agent is open to principal	Parties are open to each other
Source of Incentives and Sanctions	Political support; media publicity; regulator oversight	Legal and economic sanctions; courts enforce contracts	Social and moral sanctions; peer networks enforce

Figure 3.7: Summary of accountability relationship
Source: Brown, 2008, p. 37

In practice, the actual transfer of foreign aid funds is not directly to the intended recipients. This is because of the weak enforcement capacity of government agencies as well as the presence of "rent-seeking behaviour" amongst the economically advantaged elites or some of the most powerful politicians in developing countries (Birdsall et al., 2011, p. 5). Because of the large sums of money involved in foreign aid projects, the incidence and scale of corruption can be quite high. In the absence of stringent accountability practices, there is a strong possibility foreign aid projects could be a fail based on this point alone (Birdsall et al., 2011, p. 6; Brown, 2008, p. 37). This explains why the issue of accountability remains as one of the most serious challenges to the issue of managing foreign aid projects[viii] (Birdsall et al., 2011, p. 8).

The case of CIDA in Ethiopia is another good example wherein the acronym SIMPLE can be applied to assess accountability and potentially make Canadian external assistance become more focused and efficient. In staying committed to its objectives, CIDA observes transparency by publishing reports concerning its foreign aid projects. To set expectations, CIDA reported that this particular organization aims to increase food security, secure the future of children and youth, and stimulate sustainable economic growth (CIDA, 2011b). Because of foreign aid intervention, CIDA expects to empower developing countries to develop leadership when it comes to defining, delivering, measuring results, and increasing ownership of development outcomes.

Case Study – Resources

To improve knowledge and skills of human resources, the provision of training is necessary to help ensure that the expected outcomes can be accomplished within the expected completion dates. As is widely known, different kinds of resources are essential for successful outcomes of foreign aid projects. Based on real-life experience, the timely delivery of essential resources remains a challenge. Other problems related to the management of resources include the risk of administrative red tape and the insidious prevalence of corrupt practices. Such corruption ranges from ignoring vital recommendations — such as structural weaknesses that reflect on preconditions to the release of aid, to procurement irregularities in bidding for and acquiring key technology and equipment, to the selection of consulting firms and specific individual consultants.

In relation to the practice of corruption, the United Nations Development Program (UNDP) reported that the cost of bribes, red tape, or illegal payments made when managing foreign development funds could reach up to

$1 trillion each year (UNDP, n.d.). For many years, the practice of corruption has been considered as one of the most serious barriers to successful sustainable development. In fact, unchecked corruption is claimed to have undermined the concept of democratic governance (Clark, 2012).

Applicable to this study, the term "resources" can be defined as material, technology, and human resources needed to make the operation and outcomes of foreign aid projects more likely to be successful.

Optimizing the use of the available resources is essential and is usually a major contributor to the success of foreign aid development programs. The only way to reduce the practice of corruption is to promote/increase the practices of transparency and accountability. Failure to improve accountability practices and transparency processes can cause donor constituencies to doubt the honesty and commitment of those close to the intended beneficiary groups. When this occurs, the host governments are seen to have hindered what are estimated to be sustainable projects from becoming more fruitful. Because of weak accountability, donors who once were willing to advocate for financial support to low and middle income countries (LMICs) may see public support falter, hence, negatively affecting the desire to participate in sustainable development projects. In 2015, Finland's domestic economic crisis prompted a 43% cut to the foreign assistance budget (De Vos, 2015; Shah, 2014; see Chapter 7, My Published Media Submissions, International development fiasco).

To ensure timely delivery of foreign aid, program managers are expected to design and practice the use of more flexible administrative systems. Using the most modern systems now available, a project manager can effectively monitor, manage, and control the movements of physical assets, non-physical assets, and technical resources. A significant gap often exists between the provision of essential resources and accountability for their value when delivered. For example, to improve resources in Ethiopia, its government strongly supported projects related to workforce development, enhancement of the existing information technology, research, and easy access to higher education. As such, the government of Ethiopia has tried to make use of some incentive strategies and policies that could encourage more local and international investors to support learning about the development process in this country (Sellamna & Gebremedhin, 2015).

In terms of educational development, the Ethiopian government has tried several strategies to improve access to quality education. For instance, there has been some effort to align classroom approaches with regard to the learning needs of each community member, the needs of the educators and staff, and the support systems that should serve as a guide on how the educators and staff are expected to function within the educational system (Sellamna & Gebremedhin, 2015). Sellamna and Gebremedhin (2015) reported that the government has tried to come up with a better "institutional structure" and the needed "incentives" in order to encourage more university staff to support the building of higher education through the development and implementation of more institutionalized values, practices, processes, and regulations. Enlightened policies were needed to improve higher education in Ethiopia. In line with this, the Ethiopian government decided to initiate the Higher Education Proclamation No. 650/2009, which aimed to form a political program and objectives for the future development of local universities (Sellamna & Gebremedhin, 2015, p. 3). Aside from promoting the development of research on areas related to the use of technology and technological transfer, the proclamation also supported the following:

- The need to design a more suitable framework for the developmental needs of Ethiopia
- The need to encourage and require all stakeholders to participate in institutional governance
- The need to ensure that each local university had sufficient institutional autonomy, especially when it focused on accountability (Sellamna & Gebremedhin, 2015, p. 3)

National education can be used to support and complement the presence of foreign aid development programs such as those offered by USAID. To promote participation, involvement, and commitment of each community member, this educational approach encouraged and motivated parents to participate in the development of building the capacity of the educational system (Method et al., 2010, p. 50; see Chapter 7, My Published Media Submissions).

Other strategies and recommendations made to improve the future education institutions include the need to modernize the political, economic, and social structure in Ethiopia. These approaches intend to develop a set of criteria that can be used in evaluating the quality of community service given by each educational staff member. In this respect, they intended to create sufficient suitable "space" that would enable educators and students to teach and to learn, thereby extending institutional and political support to all local and international universities in Ethiopia. One element was to offer incentives to people who would like to participate in the long-term development of education in Ethiopia, and to improve the knowledge and skills or capabilities of teaching staff (Sellamna & Gebremedhin, 2015, p. 6). Other equally important strategies included the following:

- Promoting gender equality in education
- Making education more accessible in hard-to-reach areas
- Improving teachers' skills through optional/mandatory training
- Offering better pay and other incentives to teaching staff in order to reduce high turnover rates
- Developing more relevant teaching materials for different educational environments and levels (Young Lives in Ethiopia, 2012; Method et al., 2010)

All of these interventions were offered in the context of persistent corruption within the educational system in Ethiopia, which was viewed as rampant, particularly regarding the management of funds, infecting the services provided to the students and their parents, and in the mismanagement of human resources, meaning the educational staff (Plummer, 2012, p. 110). The conclusion was that there was a dire need to improve the mechanism of accountability within the educational sector in Ethiopia (Plummer, 2012, p. 110). As such, social accountability should be applied to both the "supply-side" and the "demand-side" of educational institutions (Brennan, 2015, p. 81; Plummer, 2012, p. 110). Likewise, Sweeney, Despota, and Lindner (2013) highlighted the need to widely implement the practice of transparency in decision-making by managers.

Case Study – Results-Based Management (RBM)

To determine the extent to which a project's goals and objectives have been met, results should always be measurable and quantifiable (Wang, 2010, p. 40). However, concepts of ownership, accountability, and transparency taken together are difficult to measure. Assessment of results can also be considered in the form of *qualitative* evaluation (Rubin, 2006, p. 115). Observers and practitioners should understand the word "result" often implies an element of ambiguity.

Several factors may affect the results (outputs/outcomes) of a project. For instance, the availability of input resources such as careful budget preparation and distribution of allocated funds are but two of the most common factors that may increase the possibility of success or the risk of failure (European Commission, n.d.). In the case that the budget needed to execute the tasks assigned in the project is inadequately prepared, there is a strong possibility the project will quickly fail to produce the intended results. In any case wherein the project manager has failed to timely and accurately assess the progress (of assigned tasks), there is an exponentially higher risk the project team will be unable to complete the project's outcomes within the planned timeframe.

It seems appropriate to start the technical part of this manual with a brief look at results-based management (RBM) — its scope, applicability, and validity. RBM is quite broad, inclusive, and practical, as demonstrated by the many experts and different stakeholders.

The concept of RBM is not new. Indeed, it underlies all the effort that humans consciously undertake in order to achieve desired results such as these:

- Parents try to bring up their children with the goal of helping them become self-sufficient and successful
- Children go to school to learn and graduate
- Farmers plant crops and work the fields to ensure a good harvest
- People go to the gym to lose excess weight
- Businesses are established in order to make a profit

All these interventions have the common objective of transforming the inputs into intended and sometimes unintended results (outputs, outcomes, and goals) or strategic objectives (SOs).

The universality of this concept makes it a useful basis by which to streamline one's effort in order to optimize proposed interventions. From a program development perspective, definitions have generally limited RBM to the key results presented in a relevant program design framework (PDF). This approach, while correct, seems to limit the importance and the significance of the scope of RBM. Various organizations and groups have all developed different definitions. For example, OECD/DAC defines RBM as "A management strategy focusing on performance and achievement of outputs, outcomes and impact."

Here, the definition of RBM has intentionally been expanded. It has also been deliberately presented from a generic perspective. Such a strategy creates room for every stakeholder and facilitates the portability of lessons learned. It also enhances the versatility of this concept.

A "result" in logframe parlance is defined as a specific output, as a more general outcome or purpose, or as the achievement of a broader goal.

As an organization that provides bilateral and official assistance to developing countries, USAID publicly introduced performance-based (outcome) measurements as a prerequisite to awarding its approval to starting support for projects. Aside from stating a specific objective for each project, USAID measures and publishes the outcomes in its annual reports (GAO, 2007, p. 38). With regard to the concept of results-based management, it is possible to make use of a strong monitoring and evaluation (M&E) system to ensure that the progress of various activities authorized within the project is on schedule and properly documented. The expectations are that intended results will be significantly influenced by compelling and relevant inputs and related activities. Stipulated in the overall design are the outcomes that contribute to the realization of the goal (success). However, not all outcomes are intended, which is where the value of accurate risk and threat assessment in the planning process enters into the planning equation. As shown in Figure 3.8, IFAD (2002) came up with a system that illustrates how to plan for positive results.

Figure 3.8: Monitoring and evaluation system of the expected project result
Source: Crissman et al., 2013, p. 6

One of the most important aspects of a good data management framework is that it enables the researcher, as well as institutions, to meet their obligations to their funders and to make data available for sharing, for validation, and for reuse. To achieve this, the management of data derived from research should be carried out transparently from the onset by employing various stages, which include planning, collecting the data, analyzing the data, publishing study results, archiving the data, and enabling its later recall and reuse.

A good data management system requires the contribution of all those who are party to the exercise, which implies each player has a specific job description. The roles played by institutions include establishing, as well as promulgating, policies and procedures, the provision of the necessary and sufficient infrastructure, as well as service support. Primary researchers have the responsibility of managing their data within the institutional framework in line with the requirements not only of the funding agency, but also of the academic disciplinary expectations and standards.

Key principles underpinning data management frameworks are as follows:

- Data management is necessary to support the ever-evolving global research environment, which is data-intensive
- Data management is a necessary part of carrying out good research as well as supporting the wider global research community
- Data management enables each researcher to use his/her data efficiently
- Usually the data management framework of an individual institution falls within the existing external legal as well as regulatory frameworks, such as the Australian Code for the Responsible Conduct amongst others
- Institutions involved in research usually support all aspects of the life cycle of data such as collecting, storing, manipulating, sharing, collaboration, publishing, archiving and access for reuse
- Collaboration and teamwork amongst researchers, information specialists, research administrators, and technical support staff lead to achieving effective data management.

The Data Management Framework outlines some of the basic elements needed within an institutional context in order to support effective data management. The basic elements are set out in the following four separate categories:

1. Institutional policy and procedures
2. IT infrastructure: the software, hardware, and other facilities that support data-related activities
3. Support services: technical staff and other ways of providing training and advising, as well as other forms of support, e.g., web-pages
4. Metadata management: for the data records to be used for internal as well as external purposes.

A detailed and comprehensive model including graphs, descriptions, and case studies can be found in the primer, *Monitoring and Evaluation: Data Management Systems,* by Bongs Lainjo.

A helpful strategy for improving the likelihood of a project producing the desired results includes ensuring that the project manager is able to foster a culture that promotes the importance of results-based outcomes (Bester, 2016). In the process of creating such an enabling culture, stakeholders need to be trained to become more aware and sensitive to the nuances of the intended project outcomes (result). Another useful strategy is to train and educate stakeholders about the proper management of all possible risks/threats (barriers) that may influence whether a project/program is successful. The supposition behind this process of educating stakeholders about the importance of timely delivery of all needed resources hinges on the management team's need for continuous improvement in their own knowledge of the incremental progress of outputs, both qualitatively and quantitatively. The presence or absence of critical skills of staff employed in these activities affects the process as well. A continual process of capacity building in staff greatly improves the chances of successful outcomes by reducing the known risks and exposure to grave threats.

In the case of Ethiopia, mentioned earlier, the significant result of the first Sustainable Development Poverty Reduction Program (SDPRP) was the establishment of the New Coalition for Food Security. The Coalition reflects a new partnership with the government, the development partners, civil society, the private sector and those community members who chose to participate. Its mandate was to develop a new strategy and investment package in order to address, in a comprehensive and coordinated manner, the underlying causes of food insecurity including issues of recovery, asset protection, and the sustainable development of the affected areas.

The stated overall goal was to improve the food security of up to five million people who are chronically malnourished. A supplemental objective of the coalition was to have made the supply of foodstuff sustainable so the initiative could feed, through its extension, another 10 million people who were experiencing chronic problems with their assured food supply (CIDA, 2004, p. 11).

Certain foreign aid programs in Nepal have largely been judged as more successful when compared to those that were showcased in the Kyrgyz Republic. In Kyrgyzstan, the criteria that defined success of the program (desired outcome) was somewhat ambiguously stated by the lead (key) donor, GTZ: "unless successes of technical assistance projects aimed at poverty reduction are actually replicated utilizing the state's funds, or funds provided by international financial institutions, technical assistance projects aimed at poverty reduction in the Kyrgyz Republic are likely to be judged as wasted."

In the Nepal case (USAID-Winrock), more than 50,000 households benefited from the 100% increase in their annual incomes. By improving the local agriculture and vocational training, the project has also triggered a significant increase in rural incomes in general, due to a carryover or follow-on effect. Therefore, the case of Nepal was considered an example wherein the joint strategy to leverage IDA and IFC resources by setting an example through the efforts of USAID/Winrock became successful. Non-participating farmers saw the benefits others had achieved and adopted the methodologies demonstrated by those who participated formally in the effort.

Case Study – Ownership

Ownership must expand from merely the executive branch of whatever host government the donor is dealing with to wider segments of the country. Ideally, ownership of the development process should be from the conceptual to the end-of-project stage, regardless of the achieved outcome (see Figure 3.9).

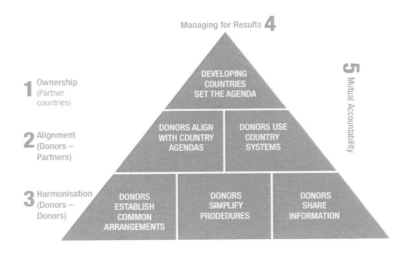

Figure 3.9: Top five principles of effective aid
Source: OECD, 2011

Ownership is another word full of ambiguity. Several OECD publications stress that ownership is key for "development to be sustainable over the long term," and that "developing country governments must exercise effective ownership over the development process, including over aid" (OECD, 2011c, p. 11). International dialogue is beginning to recognize the need for broader definitions of ownership.

In 2010, the U.S. government, as well as other aid donor countries, decided to increase efforts to ensure that recipient countries take more ownership and control over the planning and completion of foreign aid projects as well as the actual management of foreign aid funds (U.S. Department of State, 2010, p. 95). In effect, this decision "handed over" the responsibility for success/failure from donor countries to recipient countries (see Chapter 7, My Published Media Submissions).

Ownership is defined as the right to create and implement a set of developmental policies that will guide donors and recipient countries to accomplish their mutually arrived at socioeconomic and environmental goals. "By transferring ownership to partner governments, donors increasingly focus on ensuring that key local institutions—such as parliament, public financial management systems, civil service, ombudsmen and the judiciary—are functioning well" (OECD, 2011c, p. 14).

Ideally, ownership of the development process should be made clear from start to finish, whether there is success or failure at the end. To have achieved ownership at the offset would imply that all stakeholders, no matter how they are defined, had agreed at the offset as to what indicators or measurements constitute ownership. However, the Paris AID Consortium Declaration called for a better definition and for indicators or measurements of what ownership actually consists of (OECD, 2008, p. 33). Ownership actually means those identified as stakeholders (authorities) and who have consented to be held accountable in one way or another should agree to the stipulated terms and conditions — including defining the indicators — related to ownership prior to the signing of a memorandum of agreement or understanding (MOA/MOU).

To sum up, in prior decade's development plans initiated by the developing countries (although perhaps coordinated with the donors) were often devoid of sustainable management systems, particularly those concerned with internal control. Under the 2008 Paris Declaration, it was agreed by the current administrators of funds in the developed world to adopt the use of the existing systems of their clients in developing countries. The Paris Declaration is now encountering problems with this aspect of the development paradigm it proposed. Perhaps the most eloquent example of what ownership is, is the previously quoted finding by GTZ regarding its Kyrgyz project outcome relating to utilization of state funds. Ownership is achieved when and if the state government (Kyrgyzstan in this example) decides to carry out more projects embodying the principles, practices, and procedures applied to the management of funds allocated by the Kyrgyz parliament, or perhaps borrowed from the international lending community with the approval of the parliament. It is perhaps not coincidental that this process appears to reflect the current Paris Declaration indicators for ownership.

Among the few components that can strengthen ownership is the creation of a bottom-up community development strategy that has a team of *people-centered* staff (Allen, Bosch, Gibson, & Jopp, 1998). Another useful strategy is to educate people about the importance of good governance and ensure that the stakeholders are in consistent compliance with the practices of transparency (Carlsson et al., 1997, p. 96). Anyone found to be involved in graft and encouraging corruption should be subject to legal prosecution by the justice system of the recipient country. It is only through good governance that both donor country owners and recipient country owners can maintain sustainable long-term relationships and build trust.

A good example of donor ownership combined with recipient country ownership is the case of USAID and Nepal. For more than 60 years, USAID programs have been working closely with the Government of Nepal in order to address the effects of the country's poor economic performance. By strengthening the citizens' participation, advancement can be made in Nepal's political transition resulting in improvements in the overall quality of life for the Nepalese. As such, donor country ownership refers to rules, policies, and regulations set by USAID, inconsistent with the beneficiary government definition. The recipient country regards ownership as policies used by the local government of Nepal as relevant and contributing factors required in creating an enabling environment that will make foreign aid projects become successful.

Case Study – Transparency

It is common for funders/donors to demand that the recipients/beneficiaries will be transparent on government spending. As such, transparency demands full disclosure of all relevant government fiscal information on a timely basis and in such a way that the members of the public can check on accountabilities of government. What the Paris Declaration development paradigm (model) imparts is that the degree of transparency desired can be achieved once there are people who are capable, authorized, and (through these processes) made responsible to take ownership of foreign aid, often as proxies of the host government.

Ideally, transparency assumes that everybody is involved in development programs. If transparency is the outcome of ownership, whoever owns the project ought to be open about the facts pertaining to how development funds were utilized using the project implementation plan (PIP) as a road map. However, it is also true that transparency can be viewed differently depending on the interest of the recipient government and staff. For instance, in case the government and staff are selfless and want what is good for the majority, then, the practice of transparency can be seen as something positive. Assuming that the recipient government and staff of the recipient of foreign aid funds are corrupt, then, obligations to observe transparency can be seen as something spurious and even negative.

Applicable to foreign aid projects, transparency is defined as "a comprehensive availability and accessibility of aid flow information in a timely, systematic, and comparable manner that allows public participation in government accountability." It operates in such a way that it is easier for others to see what actions are being taken by the recipient country.

Several strategies can be made to improve transparency. For instance, recently SIDA has raised the level of its ambition to control and curtail corruption in terms of risk analysis, auditing, and reporting of results to strengthen anti-corruption work in project management. Often, regular monitoring of financial disbursement using both internal and external auditors and the creation of an open feedback channel available to all stakeholders (including the public) can help improve transparency. As such, feedback channels should at all times be open, active, and responsive.

Increasing the focus on controlling and managing identified risks and threat management is necessary. If it is found that a partner's corruption situation is too complex to be addressed only by applying more stringent internal controls, SIDA is prepared to terminate its assistance even though this course of action might jeopardize foreign policy objectives. SIDA also supports countries' own efforts to combat corruption. This can be perceived as part of efforts to strengthen human rights and democratic governance interventions that have a direct or indirect impact on the corruption situation. It supports endeavours aimed at increasing democratic participation, transparency, and accountability, which are all considered invaluable to changing corrupt environments. Furthermore, SIDA believes that civil society has a crucial role to play in this arena, and SIDA will help to strengthen institutions such as tax and audit authorities and systems for public financial management.

Consider the case of Ethiopia: 100% transparency requires hard work and some degree of trial and error. Regarding establishing the New Coalition for Food Security in Ethiopia, partnerships amongst the government, development partners, elements of civil society, elements of the private sector, and efforts to mobilize local communities were made in some instances successfully. The representatives of donor agencies should find this model useful in their efforts to prepare a more thorough sustainable management system that ensures transparency and better monitoring. They also need to understand that the best results are to be obtained through better participation by the intended beneficiaries including mobilized local community members. As such, donors can feel more comfortable with joint ownership and joint transparency, rather than being threatened and demoralized by the risks of corruption and project failure.

In the case of Nepal, the World Bank reported that the main reason the country's more recent development projects have been successful is the active participation of people within the communities involved themselves. The success of Nepal has also helped to validate the BUS approach and the CARROT model.

SIDA's website defined corruption as "the abuse of trust, power or position for improper gain. Corruption includes bribery — including bribery of a foreign official — extortion, conflict of interest and nepotism." Corruption is more than the opposite of transparency because it sabotages the very goal of transparency and destroys development. In fact, as Roy Cullen argues in his book *The Poverty of Corrupt Nations* (2008), it is not poverty that causes corruption but rather corruption that causes poverty. Therefore, any sustainable development effort must deal with the issue of corruption.

SIDA has articulated its mission to include ways and means to combat fraud and corruption in the aid effort it manages, and to support partner countries' anti-corruption efforts. Its anti-corruption work is carried out at four levels and may reflect other aid agencies' efforts or even offer a suitable model to be emulated. Key ingredients are: 1) promoting ethics and integrity in its own organization, 2) combating corruption in Swedish-funded project efforts. 3) supporting partner countries' efforts to combat corruption through strategic interventions, and 4) participating in international anti-corruption work.

CHAPTER 4: Creating a Dynamic Program Proposal

Familiarity with various theories related to project or program management is one thing, but being able to apply all these theories and models in real-life situations is quite another. It is essential to learn how to design a program proposal that uses different project management theories and models, choosing the ones most appropriate to the specific circumstances of the project. The secret to success is to minimize controllable risks and management errors caused by human negligence. Most of the time, this can be done by effective risk planning and the application of a suitable management theory. The case of GTZ assistance in Kyrgyzstan will help us to see what the theory looks like in practice.

Risks and Assumptions

Providing business training — including risk management strategies and assumptions as well as budget, timeline, and work plan — was one of the goals of the GTZ capacity building project in Kyrgyzstan. Several potential risks and assumptions lay behind the project.

Potential risks that could result in the team being unable to deliver the business-training program on time included both the failure to deliver the needed classroom resources and the failure of the project team to produce the training materials on time. To avoid such risks, program management must ensure that staff be held accountable, particularly if they fail. However, it is far better to put systems in place to ensure success.

For instance, in the GTZ case, project leaders A and B, the IT experts, and external training experts were all designated as responsible for the delivery of a quality business training program for the local people in Kyrgyzstan. Specifically, the IT experts and the external training experts were made responsible for the development of business training materials while project leaders A and B were assigned to select potential suppliers and identify and purchase all needed resources. To reinforce this expectation, each team member had to sign a contract outlining his or her particular project responsibilities (see Figure 4.1).

As an external training expert, I _____ (insert name) agree to extend my knowledge and skills in the planning and development of business program. For a short period of fourteen (14) days, a fixed amount of US$1,008 will be paid to _____ (insert name) given that he/she has delivered the training materials as agreed upon. _____ (insert name) is expected to work not only with the program manager but also with the rest of the team members (i.e., project leaders A and B and the IT expert). Any violation of this contract will mean an abrupt termination of the contract.

_____   _____
Signature over Printed Name   Signature over Printed Name

(Witness)   (Outside Training Expert)

_____   _____
Date Signed   Date Signed

Figure 4.1: Example of contract agreement

To ensure that a training program is as effective as possible, program management should ensure that any training materials are of high quality and compatible with the main objectives of the particular project. To do so, the program manager should compile a checklist (see Table 4.1) that details the required environment, equipment, facilities, and materials; share the checklist with staff; and then use it to monitor the staff responsible for the quality matrices (Schwalbe, 2010). The project training team leader should also have staff designated to assist with the delivery of the training and with specific tasks, including material preparation (such as sorting and binding handouts), and double checking everything on the checklist (Rose, 2005).

Table 4.1: Training setup checklist

Training Setup Checklist	Setup	Maintenance	Cleanup
Classroom setup (Name of person responsible)			
training course materials and handouts			
tables and chairs			
paper and pens			
name tags			

drinking water			
Teaching supplies (Name of person responsible)			
whiteboard			
markers			
overhead projector			
Technical setup (Name of person responsible)			
sound system/microphones			
electrical hook-ups			
computer terminals			
software			
Environmental setup (Name of person responsible)			
lighting			
fans			
air-conditioning			
Washroom setup (Name of person responsible)			
functional			
clean			
soap			
towels			
toilet paper			
Coffee break setup (Name of person responsible)			
coffee			
tea			
cream/milk			
sugar/sweetener			
cups			
spoons			
garbage/recycling			

Budget

GTZ allocated a budget of US$56,092 for the business-training program. Program management should be able to allocate the available funds as needed on the approved training schedule. The program manager must estimate the costs of all of the inputs of the training team members and other supplies, rental fees, food and beverages, etc. (see Figure 4.1).

	Resource Name	Cost
	+ Unassigned	₱0.00
1	+ Program Manager	₱19,656.00
2	+ Project Leader A	₱4,760.00
3	+ Project Leader B	₱4,760.00
4	+ IT Expert	₱4,608.00
5	+ Outside Training Expert	₱4,608.00
6	+ CD/ROM for Instructor-Led-Training	₱500.00
7	+ Procure Software	₱3,500.00
8	+ Procure Hardware	₱3,500.00
9	+ Tables and Chairs Rental	₱1,000.00
10	+ Whiteboard	₱150.00
11	+ Overhead Projector	₱2,000.00
12	+ Paper and Pen	₱150.00
13	+ Sound System & Microphone	₱1,250.00
14	+ Name Plates	₱50.00
15	+ Food and Beverages	₱2,000.00
16	+ Miscellaneous	₱2,300.00
17	+ Risk (Contingency)	₱1,300.00

Figure 4.1: Budget allocation for the business training program

All programs or projects must have specific budget allocations (see Table 4.1. Should actual expenditures exceed the allocated budget, program management must be able to access a contingency fund or face the project's failure. Project/program managers should, therefore, learn how to estimate the relevant costs as precisely as possible, identify and review the risks associated with the completion of the project, and ensure the contingency fund. To enable the program manager to present the budget, the designated risk manager should be fully acquainted with the cost breakdown structure (CBS). Using the CBS method, the risk manager should be able to itemize fixed costs and consider which other costs might arise in light of the risk factors. To ensure that the manager will not exceed the expected costs, it is the duty of the risk manager to monitor the schedule closely and report to the program management team on any threats to program delivery.

Contingencies such as illness, accidents, visa delays, strikes, political unrest, weather, and other factors are possible contributing factors to consider when planning for such projects.

Timeline

Scheduling is a vital part of project/program management. A dynamic program should make use of generic work planning spreadsheets such as Microsoft Project, not only to manage the costing of the proposed project but also to create useful Gantt charts or network diagrams to represent the expected date of completion of each identified task/activity. Use of such software will enable program managers to build elasticity into the project/program and make revisions quickly when needed.

Considering the proposed business-training program in Kyrgyzstan, Figure 4.2 is the network diagram representing the expected schedule of each project deliverable:

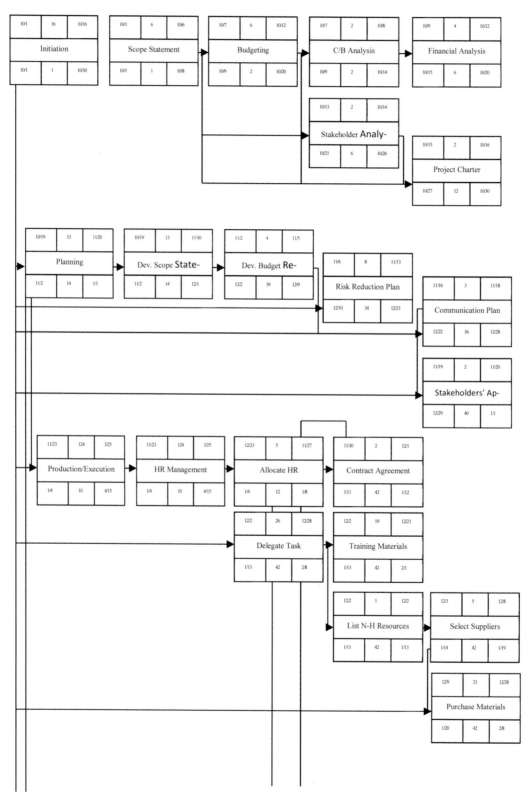

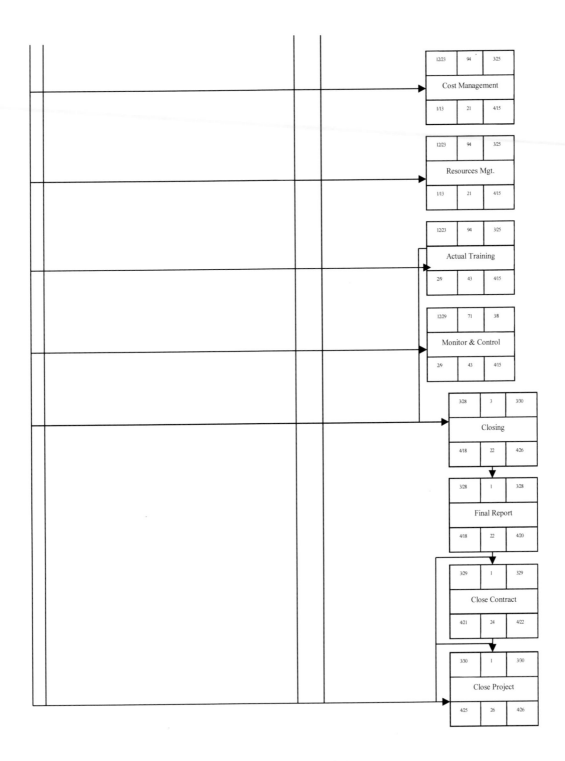

Figure 4.2: Network diagram of the business-training program

Work Plan

A work plan is essentially a timeline of the interlocking goals, objectives, and processes assigned to each team member. To serve as a guide, the program manager should first create the scope statement, WBS, and work-related scheduling (see Figure 4.3).

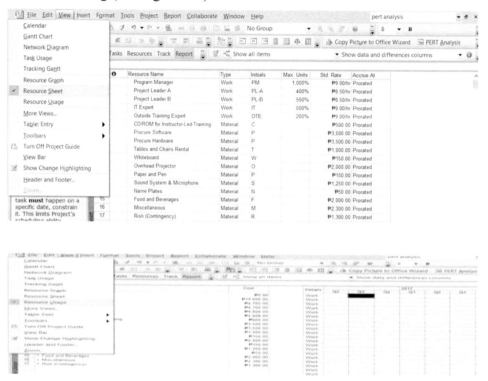

Figure 4.3: Resource sheet

Using software such as Microsoft Project, the program manager can automatically assign people to certain tasks without worrying about assigning conflicting jobs to the same staff person unless, of course, more than one person is needed to complete a complex activity. This particular software not only shows the precedence of each assigned task, it also increases the manager's capacity to effectively manage the project within the agreed-upon timeframe (see Figure 4.4).

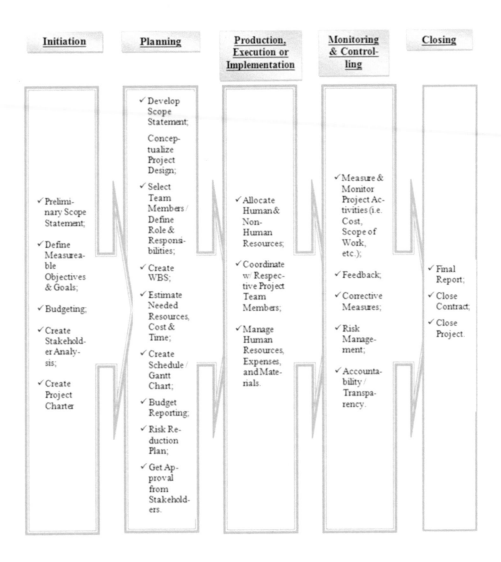

Figure 4.4: Summary of the proposed work plan structure

Strategic Frameworks in Proposal Development

The absence of a generally accepted "gold standard" complicates the design and development of proposals. There are, however, certain expectations and requirements established by funding agencies and donors. While the available guidelines serve as frameworks in developing proposals, they fall short of the standard with details and relevant specifications in certain cases. For example, while most of these agencies solicit proposals from both national and international organizations, there is a lack of comprehensive and universally accepted standards. Part of the problem arises from diversity in reporting, accountability, and loyalty. It is therefore incumbent on the proposal designer to adhere to these myriad different guidelines. Largely, donors seem to like what they get! There are, of course, several scenarios, the key factor being the delivery of a motivating and inclusive manuscript. Structured and inclusive frameworks are necessary and sufficient in magnifying results in strategic frameworks. There are currently two popular ones: the logic framework (logframe) – which is quite inclusive and is used by most donors – and the results framework, which is used exclusively by USAID.

A common pitfall that tends to undermine many strategic frameworks is an excess of project activities. It remains critical that activities and inputs be streamlined and refined in order to screen and eliminate redundancies. The second problem in that regard is an overemphasis on their importance. Activities must always be considered important and necessary but not sufficient by themselves in achieving the intended results. This highlights the importance of work plans (WPs) discussed elsewhere in the manual. WPs need to be concise, optimal, unambiguous, and achievable. They need to present activities with no duplication, specific timelines, responsible parties, costs and risks, and assumptions.

It is always important to remember that precise activities facilitate the achievement of outputs. As presented in Figure 4.5, indicators at the output level should contribute to one and only one indicator at the next (outcome) level. The converse, however, is not feasible and needs to be avoided. In the likely event that the latter case exists, the output or outcome indicators need to be re-formulated. The figure also represents a conditional logical flow of achievements from the performance to the impact level.

One other aspect of activity formulation that remains problematic is the involvement of implementing program managers (PMs) in the entire process. This unintentional omission has contributed to creating a gap between implementing agencies regarding the role and understanding of logframes, for example. PMs serve as catalysts and main actors in facilitating the achievement of intended results.

In one of my numerous assignments, I was attending a strategic planning session in Nigeria hosted by USAID. One of the very informed PMs (as I later learned) wanted to know why USAID kept changing its strategies. In my response, I explained the importance of effective strategies and how they are associated with the dynamics of the environment. I further indicated that as these environmental factors change, the corresponding strategies are also bound to change in order to reflect these changes. Strategies, I continued are dynamic, not static, and hence need to reflect the changing environment. A limited understanding by staff, especially at the program implementation level, continues to be a deterrent in effective project implementation. For instance, over the years I have encountered several PMs who confidently informed me that they had successfully and cost-effectively completed the work plans ahead of schedule. When I asked them if they knew how many of those activities actually contributed to the appropriate outputs, their responses frequently demonstrated their limited understanding of how strategic frameworks operate. As such, their understanding of project evaluation remains inadequate. For example, when informed that evaluations are guided by certain criteria developed by OECD/WG and used by most donors, they were in awe!

More details about these can be found in Chapter 9 and my book *Monitoring and Evaluation: Data Management Systems*.

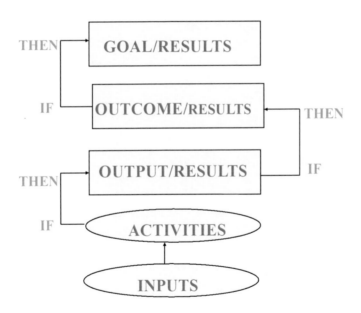

Figure 4.5: Logframe
Source: Lainjo, 2013

CHAPTER 5: Project Management Methodologies

Operations Research in Program Management

In relation to program management, operations research (OR) plays a crucial role in enabling managers to make the best possible decisions for project design (Chelst & Canbolat, 2012, p. 198; Tavares, 2002). Often, operations research is strongly connected to the task of risk management. For instance, using examples from available literature, program managers can gain better insights to help avoid making irrational decisions (Chelst & Canbolat, 2012, p. 384). Using operations research, program managers can be better equipped to respond when they face dilemmas or confounding situations. By deploying either mathematical or analytical tools, program managers can easily minimize making risky decisions based on traditional fault lines in those areas already identified (Tavares, 2002).

OR in program management generally pertains to the use of "quantitative analysis" (Kwak & Anbari, 2009, p. 439) or the use of mathematical models in analyzing business-related problems (Mole, 1987, p. 12). By integrating OR into program management, it is possible to improve resource allocation in each project (Mole, 1987, p. 10). Instead of making decisions based on intuition, OR makes project-related decisions more scientific. However, since it involves the use of complex algorithms and copious data observations, this tool may not always be appropriate in a fast-paced environment where decisions need to be made immediately (Mole, 1987, p. 11).

The history of operations research

Operations research began before World War II when Frederick W. Taylor promoted the importance of applying scientific analysis in production (Sharma, 2006, pp. 3–4). Henry L. Gantt also contributed by introducing the concept of Gantt charts that are now widely used in planning, scheduling, and controlling jobs or tasks (Sharma, 2006, p. 4). Over the years, various scientific methods have been used not only in the study of production but also in finance, marketing, R&D, quality control, procurement, and human resource management. For instance, the critical path method (CPM) or the Program Evaluation and Review Technique (PERT) can be used to monitor the time variations in different stages of tasks assigned in specific projects (Craven & Islam, 2006, p. 93). Frederick Winslow Taylor introduced the concept of work breakdown structure (WBS) and an associated method used in the allocation of project-associated resources (Tomar, 2009, p. 221).

The concept of OR in program management had already achieved widespread popularity by the 1990s. Many academic researchers then turned to emphasizing the importance of assessing issues related to risk management, realizing that this area had been neglected in the logical framework approach, and thus in the overall concept of program management (Gustafsson & Salo, 2005; Dillon, Pate-Cornell, & Guikema, 2003). Because of this shift in emphasis from traditional OR applications to the elements of organizational, behavioural, philosophical, and managerial elements (Kwak & Anbari, 2009), the focus and emphasis previously given to OR in program management started to decline early in the 21st century.

Strategic framework: classical, modern, and conventional

The traditional process of OR in project management has five different stages: 1) initiation, 2) planning, 3) production or execution, 4) monitoring and controlling, and 5) closing, as seen in Table 5.1.

Table 5.1: Traditional process of OR in project management

Stages	Tasks
Initiation	Preliminary scope statement
	Define measurable objectives and goals based on the project requirements
	Budgeting (i.e., cost and benefit analysis, financial analysis, investment analysis)
	Creating stakeholder analysis matrix
	Creating a project charter (i.e., specific tasks, schedule of deliverables, and detailed costs)
Planning	Developing a scope statement
	Conceptualizing a project design
	Selecting project team members and define their role and responsibilities
	Creating and finalizing deliverables and creating work breakdown structure (WBS)
	Identify project activities based on logical sequence
	Estimate needed resources
	Estimate the cost of resources and time or effort

	Create schedule using Gantt charts Develop budgeting reporting matrices Create risk reduction plan Communication planning Gather approval from the stakeholder to start the project (i.e., donor, government departmental heads)
Production, Execution, or Implementation	Allocate human and non-human resources Coordinate with respective project team leadership and members Manage human resources, expenses, and materials
Monitoring and Controlling	Measure and monitor project activities (i.e., cost, scope or work, quality of expected work performance, the use of key performance indicator (KPI) system, etc.) Feedback Apply corrective measures in case of problems Risk management Transparency
Closing	Final report Close contract Close project

Using algorithms, traditional or classical OR in program management created models to analyze complex operational problems and help managers achieve project objectives more efficiently (Chapagain, 2013, p. 4). Major steps in applying OR methods include the following:

- Articulate/formulate the problem
- Create the hypothetical model
- Gather data

- Devise solutions
- Validate outputs
- Scale up validated outputs to program level (Chapagain, 2013, p. 4)

Classical OR methods may be classified as either "hard" (mathematical/quantitative) or "soft" (qualitative), as shown in Table 5.2. In a comparative assessment, Chapagain (2013, p. 6) explained that the use of hard OR methods often provides project managers with better management tools that result in better control, better decision-making, better coordination, and better systems overall. Over the years, both hard and soft OR methods have continued to evolve. Since 1980, newer "softer" methods, known as neo-classical OR methods, such as cognitive mapping, robustness analysis, meta-game analysis, and hyper-game analysis, have become more widely used, as seen in Figure 5.1 (Chapagain, 2013, p. 11).

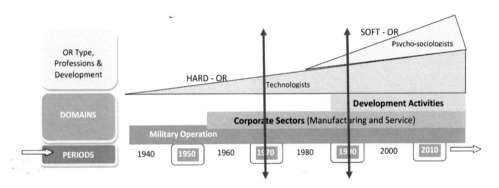

Figure 5.1: Historical trend behind the development of classical OR method
Source: Chapagain, 2013, p. 3

Table 5.2: Classification of OR methods

Widely-Used Classical OR Method	Hard/Mathematical OR Method
1. PERT/Critical path method	6. Linear programming
2. Network theories (i.e., flow analysis, spanning tree, shortest path problem)	7. Queuing theory
	8. Game theory
	9. Simulation
	10. Markov process
3. Dynamic programming	
4. Machine scheduling problems	
5. Inventory models	

Source: Chapagain, 2013, p. 5

Modern classical application of OR in program management, on the other hand, often attempts to integrate IT into operation research. The availability of advanced software has enabled more efficient number-crunching capacities if projects/programs have been structured to collect data about their dynamics (Alt, Fu, & Golden, 2006, p. 136).

MS-Project Software

Microsoft Project is a software program designed for the specific needs of project managers for assigning tasks, allocating resources, creating a project plan, managing the available budget, tracking progress, or analyzing specific tasks assigned to an individual. In program implementation, Microsoft Project can help managers create Gantt charts for budgeting and scheduling deliverables. It is also possible to estimate work duration by creating both WBS and Gantt charts. Microsoft Project software can also be used to create time-management models, such as determining when to schedule program evaluations, or to review the effectiveness of planning, such as PERT and CPM techniques.

Looking at the business training program in Kyrgyzstan (Case 2) as an example, let's follow step by step how Microsoft Project software would be used: the project budget was US$56,092 and the deadline was March 31, 2016.

Step 1: On a blank page, go to View then click on Task Usage. Fill out the task panel based on the different stages of the life cycle: initiation, planning, production or execution, monitoring and controlling, and closing.

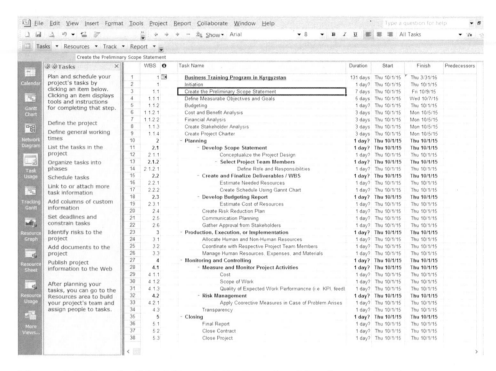

Figure 5.2: Step 1 of the Microsoft Project algorithm for creating time management models

Step 2: To create sub-tasks, click on the task to be indented then click on the green arrow, which points to the right, or simply press Alt+Shift+Right.

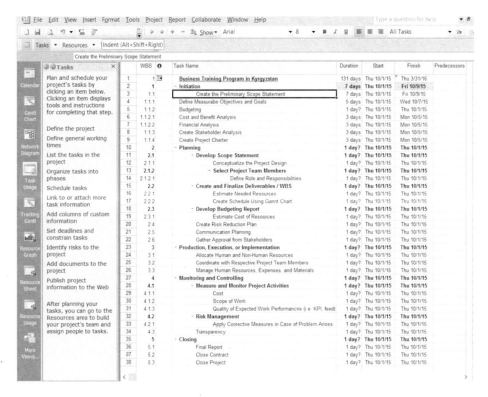

Figure 5.3: Step 2 of the Microsoft Project algorithm for creating time management models

Step 3: To add the WBS panel on the left-hand side, right click on the area where the WBS column will be inserted.

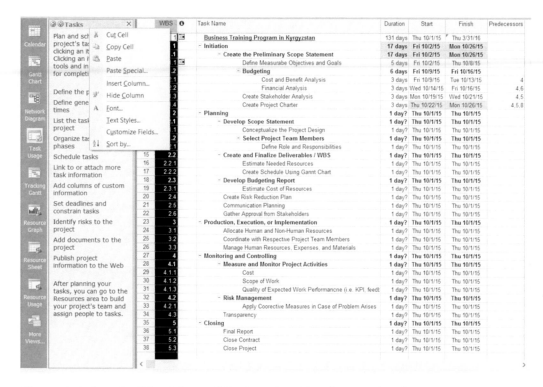

Figure 5.4: Step 3 of the Microsoft Project algorithm for creating time management models

Step 4: Click on Insert Column.

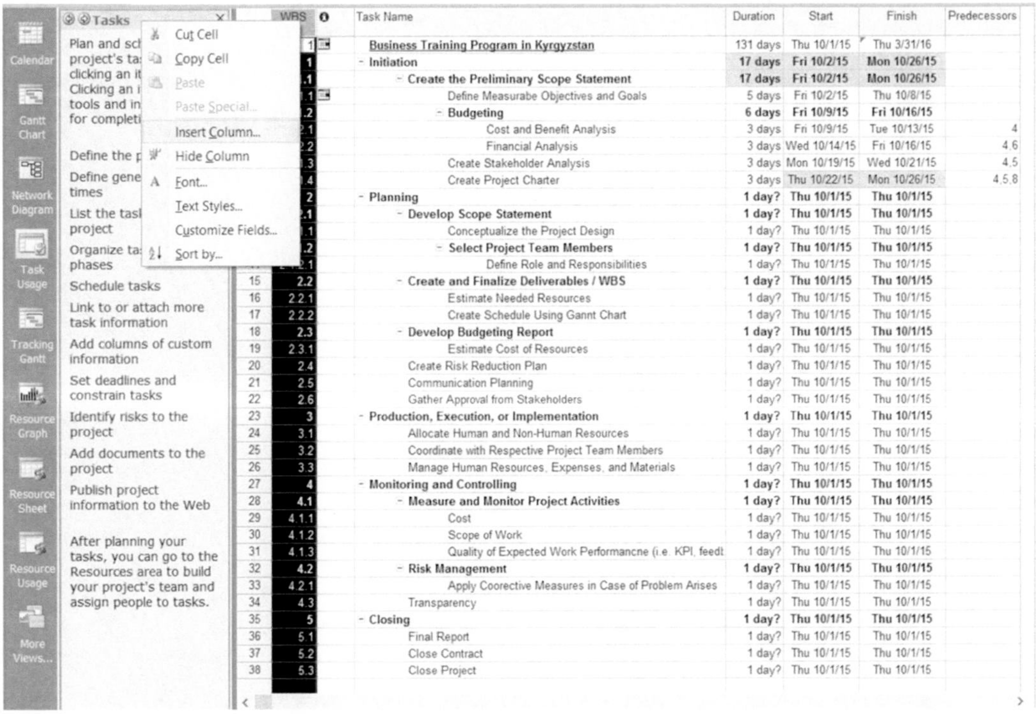

Figure 5.5: Step 4 of the Microsoft Project algorithm for creating time management models

Step 5: Create the Column Definition by selecting WBS, then click OK.

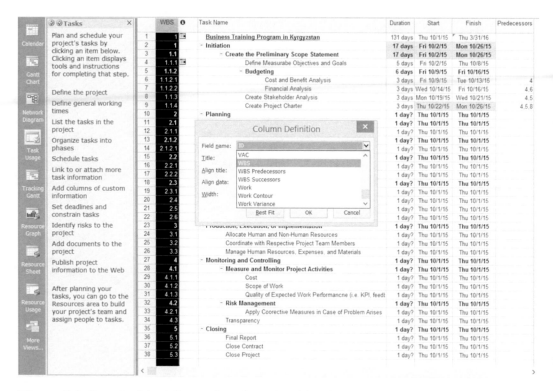

Figure 5.6: Step 5 of the Microsoft Project algorithm for creating time management models

Step 6: Schedule each task by setting the expected start and finish date, including the predecessors of each task. In this particular example, the start date is October 1, 2015, and the finish date is March 31, 2016. To set these dates, use the pop-up calendars. After entering the desired start and finish date, the exact duration — in this case, 131 days — will automatically be computed. Set the start and finish dates for the entire business-training program.

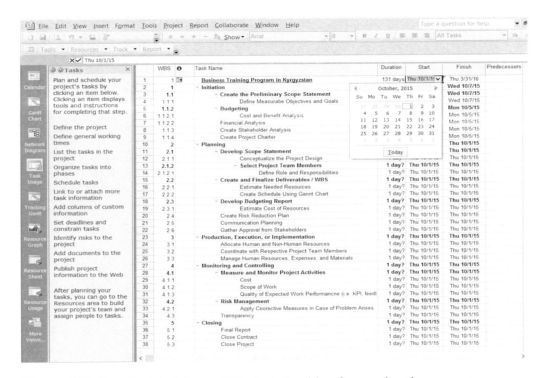

Figure 5.7: Step 6 of the Microsoft Project algorithm for creating time management models

Step 7: Set the predecessors (tasks that must precede) in each task and subtask so that the software can automatically adjust the start and finish dates. To set the predecessors, double-click on the cells that have predecessors. In this example, the predecessor being set is under the subtask Budgeting.

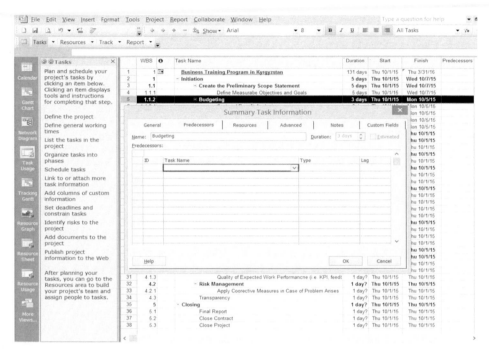

Figure 5.8: Step 7 of the Microsoft Project algorithm for creating time management models

Step 8: Click on the tab Task Name to select specific tasks that could affect the process of Budgeting. In this case, specific tasks are "Create the Preliminary Scope Statement" and "Define Measurable Objectives and Goals." Click on these two specific tasks (and subtasks) before clicking OK. Do the same procedure for the rest of the tasks and subtasks.

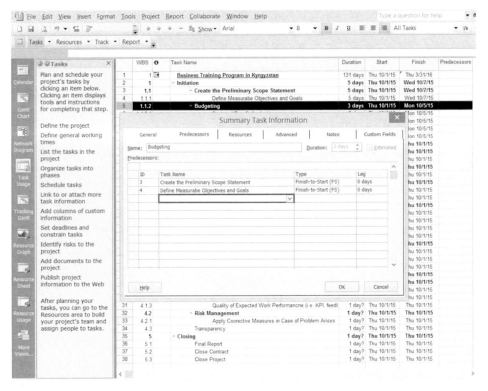

Figure 5.9: Step 8 of the Microsoft Project algorithm for creating time management models

Once the tasks are all interrelated in this way, the software automatically adjusts the start and finish dates in order to produce a timetable with no gaps or errors.

Budgeting

Using the Microsoft Project software, budgeting is made simple by first filling in the resource sheet (click View then click Resource Sheet). When the data are in place, clicking View and then Resource Usage will generate the cost of both human and non-human resources (see Figure 5.10).

	Resource Name	Cost	Details	2016 Q4	2016 Q1
	File Edit View Insert Format Tools Project Report Collaborate Window Help				
	No Group				
	Draw▼				Alig
	New Resource From▼ Security... Tasks ▼ Resources ▼ Track				
	Outside Training Expert				
	+ Unassigned	₱0.00	Work		
1	− Program Manager	₱19,656.00	Work	792h	1,392h
	Create the Preliminary Scope Statement	₱360.00	Work	40h	
	Define Measurabe Objectives and Goals	₱360.00	Work	40h	
	Cost and Benefit Analysis	₱216.00	Work	24h	
	Financial Analysis	₱216.00	Work	24h	
	Create Stakeholder Analysis	₱216.00	Work	24h	
	Create Project Charter	₱216.00	Work	24h	
	Conceptualize the Project Design	₱144.00	Work	16h	
	Select Project Team Members	₱288.00	Work	32h	
	Define Role and Responsibilities	₱216.00	Work	24h	
	Estimate Needed Resources	₱216.00	Work	24h	
	Create and Finalize Deliverables / WBS	₱144.00	Work	16h	
	Create Schedule Using Gannt Chart	₱144.00	Work	16h	
	Estimate Cost of Resources	₱360.00	Work	40h	
	Create Risk Reduction Plan	₱504.00	Work	56h	
	Communication Planning	₱288.00	Work	32h	
	Gather Approval from Stakeholders	₱216.00	Work	24h	
	Allocate Human Resources	₱360.00	Work	40h	
	Sign Contract Agreement	₱144.00	Work	16h	
	Cost Management	₱4,896.00	Work	56h	488h
	Resources Management	₱4,896.00	Work	56h	488h
	Final Report	₱144.00	Work		16h
	Close Contract	₱72.00	Work		8h
	Close Project	₱72.00	Work		8h
	Monitoring and Controlling (i.e. Risk Management, Apply Corrective Measures, Transparenct, Accountability, etc.)	₱3,456.00	Work		384h
	Develop Budgeting Report	₱360.00	Work	40h	
	Develop Scope Statement	₱1,152.00	Work	128h	
2	− Project Leader A	₱4,760.00	Work	72h	488h
	Sign Contract Agreement	₱136.00	Work	16h	
	List Down Needed Non-Human Resources	₱136.00	Work	16h	
	Select Potential Suppliers	₱272.00	Work	32h	
	Purchase Needed Non-Human Resources	₱952.00	Work	8h	104h
	Actual Business Training Program	₱3,264.00	Work		384h
3	− Project Leader B	₱4,760.00	Work	72h	488h
	Sign Contract Agreement	₱136.00	Work	16h	
	List Down Needed Non-Human Resources	₱136.00	Work	16h	
	Select Potential Suppliers	₱272.00	Work	32h	
	Purchase Needed Non-Human Resources	₱952.00	Work	8h	104h
	Actual Business Training Program	₱3,264.00	Work		384h

Figure 5.10: Cost breakdown structure

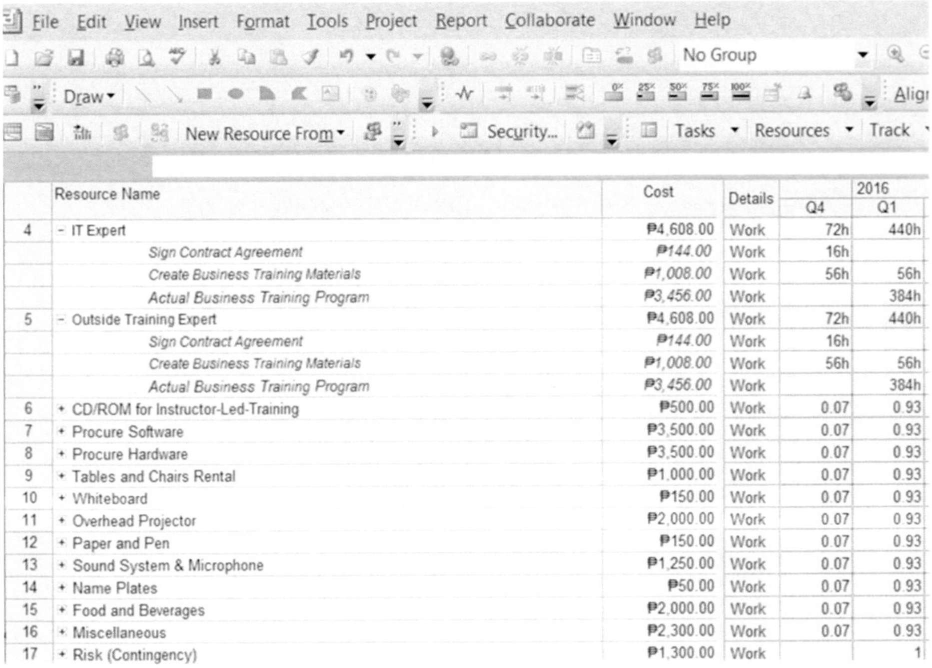

File Edit View Insert Format Tools Project Report Collaborate Window Help

Draw ▾ No Group

New Resource From ▾ Security... Tasks ▾ Resources ▾ Track

	Resource Name	Cost	Details	2016	
				Q4	Q1
4	– IT Expert	₱4,608.00	Work	72h	440h
	Sign Contract Agreement	₱144.00	Work	16h	
	Create Business Training Materials	₱1,008.00	Work	56h	56h
	Actual Business Training Program	₱3,456.00	Work		384h
5	– Outside Training Expert	₱4,608.00	Work	72h	440h
	Sign Contract Agreement	₱144.00	Work	16h	
	Create Business Training Materials	₱1,008.00	Work	56h	56h
	Actual Business Training Program	₱3,456.00	Work		384h
6	+ CD/ROM for Instructor-Led-Training	₱500.00	Work	0.07	0.93
7	+ Procure Software	₱3,500.00	Work	0.07	0.93
8	+ Procure Hardware	₱3,500.00	Work	0.07	0.93
9	+ Tables and Chairs Rental	₱1,000.00	Work	0.07	0.93
10	+ Whiteboard	₱150.00	Work	0.07	0.93
11	+ Overhead Projector	₱2,000.00	Work	0.07	0.93
12	+ Paper and Pen	₱150.00	Work	0.07	0.93
13	+ Sound System & Microphone	₱1,250.00	Work	0.07	0.93
14	+ Name Plates	₱50.00	Work	0.07	0.93
15	+ Food and Beverages	₱2,000.00	Work	0.07	0.93
16	+ Miscellaneous	₱2,300.00	Work	0.07	0.93
17	+ Risk (Contingency)	₱1,300.00	Work		1

Figure 5.10: Cost breakdown structure

WBS	Task Name	Duration	Start	Finish	Predecessors
1	Business Training Program in Kyrgyzstan	131 days	Thu 10/1/15	Thu 3/31/16	
1	- Initiation	17 days	Thu 10/1/15	Fri 10/23/15	
1.1	- Create the Preliminary Scope Statement	5 days	Thu 10/1/15	Wed 10/7/15	
1.1.1	Define Measurabe Objectives and Goals	5 days	Thu 10/1/15	Wed 10/7/15	
1.2	- Budgeting	6 days	Thu 10/8/15	Thu 10/15/15	3,4
1.2.1	Cost and Benefit Analysis	3 days	Thu 10/8/15	Mon 10/12/15	3,4
1.2.2	Financial Analysis	3 days	Tue 10/13/15	Thu 10/15/15	3,4,6
1.3	Create Stakeholder Analysis	3 days	Fri 10/16/15	Tue 10/20/15	3,4,5
1.4	Create Project Charter	3 days	Wed 10/21/15	Fri 10/23/15	3,4,5,8
2	- Planning	35 days	Mon 10/26/15	Fri 12/11/15	2
2.1	- Develop Scope Statement	16 days	Mon 10/26/15	Mon 11/16/15	2
2.1.1	Conceptualize the Project Design	2 days	Mon 10/26/15	Tue 10/27/15	2
2.1.2	Select Project Team Members	4 days	Wed 10/28/15	Mon 11/2/15	2,12
2.1.3	Define Role and Responsibilities	3 days	Tue 11/3/15	Thu 11/5/15	2,12,13
2.1.4	Estimate Needed Resources	3 days	Fri 11/6/15	Tue 11/10/15	2,12,13,14
2.1.5	Create and Finalize Deliverables / WBS	2 days	Wed 11/11/15	Thu 11/12/15	2,12,13,14,15
2.1.6	Create Schedule Using Gannt Chart	2 days	Fri 11/13/15	Mon 11/16/15	2,12,13,14,15,16
2.2	- Develop Budgeting Report	5 days	Tue 11/17/15	Mon 11/23/15	2,11
2.2.1	Estimate Cost of Resources	5 days	Tue 11/17/15	Mon 11/23/15	2,11
2.3	Create Risk Reduction Plan	7 days	Tue 11/24/15	Wed 12/2/15	2,11,18
2.4	Communication Planning	4 days	Thu 12/3/15	Tue 12/8/15	2,11,18,20
2.5	Gather Approval from Stakeholders	3 days	Wed 12/9/15	Fri 12/11/15	2,11,18,20,21
3	- Production, Execution, or Implementation	75 days	Mon 12/14/15	Fri 3/25/16	2,10
3.1	- Human Resources Management	75 days	Mon 12/14/15	Fri 3/25/16	2,10
3.1.1	Allocate Human Resources	5 days	Mon 12/14/15	Fri 12/18/15	2,10
3.1.2	Sign Contract Agreement	2 days	Mon 12/21/15	Tue 12/22/15	2,10,25
3.1.3	- Delegate Task to Each Member	20 days	Wed 12/23/15	Tue 1/19/16	
3.1.3.1	Create Business Training Materials	14 days	Wed 12/23/15	Mon 1/11/16	2,10,25,26
3.1.3.2	List Down Needed Non-Human Resources	2 days	Wed 12/23/15	Thu 12/24/15	2,10,25,26
3.1.3.3	Select Potential Suppliers	4 days	Fri 12/25/15	Wed 12/30/15	2,10,25,26,29
3.1.3.4	Purchase Needed Non-Human Resources	14 days	Thu 12/31/15	Tue 1/19/16	2,10,25,26,29,30
3.2	Coordinate with Respective Project Team Leaders	68 days	Wed 12/23/15	Fri 3/25/16	2,10,25,26
3.3	Cost Management	68 days	Wed 12/23/15	Fri 3/25/16	2,10,25,26
3.4	Resources Management	68 days	Wed 12/23/15	Fri 3/25/16	2,10,25,26
4	- Monitoring and Controlling	52 days	Wed 1/20/16	Thu 3/31/16	2,10,25,26,27
4.1	- Measure and Monitor Project Activities	48 days	Wed 1/20/16	Fri 3/25/16	2,10,25,26,27
4.1.1	Cost	48 days	Wed 1/20/16	Fri 3/25/16	2,10,25,26,27
4.1.2	Scope of Work	48 days	Wed 1/20/16	Fri 3/25/16	2,10,25,26,27
4.1.3	Quality of Expected Work Performancne (i.e. KPI, feedt	48 days	Wed 1/20/16	Fri 3/25/16	2,10,25,26,27
4.2	- Risk Management	52 days	Wed 1/20/16	Thu 3/31/16	2,10,25,26,27
4.2.1	Apply Coorective Measures in Case of Problem Arises	48 days	Wed 1/20/16	Fri 3/25/16	2,10,25,26,27
4.2.2	Transparency	52 days	Wed 1/20/16	Thu 3/31/16	2,10,25,26,27
4.2.3	Accountability	52 days	Wed 1/20/16	Thu 3/31/16	2,10,25,26,27
5	- Closing	4 days	Mon 3/28/16	Thu 3/31/16	2,10,25,26,27,32
5.1	Final Report	2 days	Mon 3/28/16	Tue 3/29/16	2,10,25,26,27,32
5.2	Close Contract	1 day	Wed 3/30/16	Wed 3/30/16	2,10,25,26,27,32,45
5.3	Close Project	1 day	Thu 3/31/16	Thu 3/31/16	2,10,25,26,27,32,45,46

Figure 5.11: Specific Tasks, WBS, and Duration of each task

115

Gantt charts

Gantt charts, one of the tracking tools available in Microsoft Project, are also commonly used in project management. These are flexible tools that can easily present the expected schedule and status of each task (Pritchard, 2014, p. 133). Aside from closely monitoring the progress of each project, Gantt charts provide project managers with better visual presentations of the proposed project schedule (Carpenter, 2004, p. 52). Using Gantt charts, the project manager can easily define the expected start and finish date for each project task.

Gantt charts can be used to present tasks in hours, days, weeks, months, or years. Figure 5.12 shows the Gantt chart used in the business-training program in Kyrgyzstan (Case 2). Since the length of the entire project duration is 131 days, the Gantt chart was created using months as the best unit. Compressing the chart into five months rather than 131 days easily allows the project manager to view the entire project schedule on a single page.

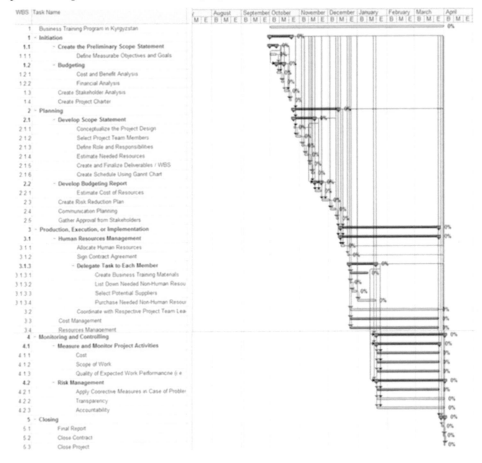

Figure 5.12: Gantt chart of the proposed business training program in Kyrgyzstan

Gantt charts can also be created for each team member assigned to perform specific tasks (Pritchard, 2014, p. 133). Before a program manager can assign the specific person for each task and sub-task, however, the human resource sheet must be completed, as seen in the following screenshot.

To add the staff member's name to a task, double-click on the task or sub-task, then fill in the blank by clicking on the resource sheet. The next two screenshots show how to add a staff member to a task and the finished sheet with tasks assigned.

Figure 5.13: How to add staff member for a task to resource sheet

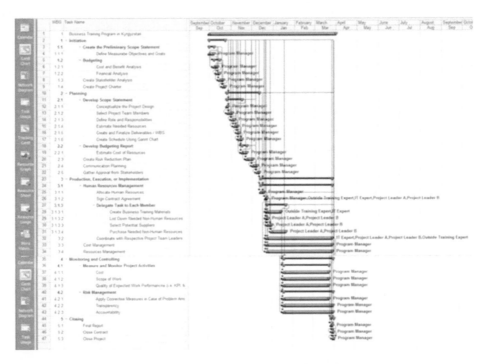

Figure 5.14: Finished resource sheet with tasks assigned

To clearly view the responsible party's name under each task and sub-task, go to View then click on Task Usage. This leads to the page that summarizes the names under each task and sub-task, the expected duration, start and finish dates, and the action that must precede the start of the task, as seen in the next screenshot.

File Edit View Insert Format Tools Project Report Collaborate Window Help

Calendar
Gantt Chart
Network Diagram
✓ Task Usage
Tracking Gantt
Resource Graph
Resource Sheet
Resource Usage
More Views...
Table: Usage ▸
Toolbars ▸
🔲 Turn Off Project Guide
✓ View Bar
☑ Hide Change Highlighting
Header and Footer...
Zoom...

Report ▾

				Duration	Start	Finish	Predecessors
			...ining Program in Kyrgyzstan	131 days	Thu 10/1/15	Thu 3/31/16	
				17 days	Thu 10/1/15	Fri 10/23/15	
			...gram Manager		Thu 10/1/15	Fri 10/23/15	
			...e the Preliminary Scope Statement	5 days	Thu 10/1/15	Wed 10/7/15	
			Program Manager		Thu 10/1/15	Wed 10/7/15	
			– Define Measurabe Objectives and Goals	5 days	Thu 10/1/15	Wed 10/7/15	
			Program Manager		Thu 10/1/15	Wed 10/7/15	
			...eting	6 days	Thu 10/8/15	Thu 10/15/15	3,4
			– Cost and Benefit Analysis	3 days	Thu 10/8/15	Mon 10/12/15	3,4
			Program Manager		Thu 10/8/15	Mon 10/12/15	
			– Financial Analysis	3 days	Tue 10/13/15	Thu 10/15/15	3,4,6
			Program Manager		Tue 10/13/15	Thu 10/15/15	
			...a Stakeholder Analysis	3 days	Fri 10/16/15	Tue 10/20/15	3,4,5
			Program Manager		Fri 10/16/15	Tue 10/20/15	
			...e Project Charter	3 days	Wed 10/21/15	Fri 10/23/15	3,4,5,8
			Program Manager		Wed 10/21/15	Fri 10/23/15	
				35 days	Mon 10/26/15	Fri 12/11/15	2
11	2.1		– Develop Scope Statement	16 days	Mon 10/26/15	Mon 11/16/15	2
12	2.1.1		– Conceptualize the Project Design	2 days	Mon 10/26/15	Tue 10/27/15	2
			Program Manager		Mon 10/26/15	Tue 10/27/15	
13	2.1.2		– Select Project Team Members	4 days	Wed 10/28/15	Mon 11/2/15	2.12
			Program Manager		Wed 10/28/15	Mon 11/2/15	
14	2.1.3		– Define Role and Responsibilities	3 days	Tue 11/3/15	Thu 11/5/15	2.12.13
			Program Manager		Tue 11/3/15	Thu 11/5/15	
15	2.1.4		– Estimate Needed Resources	3 days	Fri 11/6/15	Tue 11/10/15	2.12.13.14
			Program Manager		Fri 11/6/15	Tue 11/10/15	
16	2.1.5		– Create and Finalize Deliverables / WBS	2 days	Wed 11/11/15	Thu 11/12/15	2.12.13.14.15
			Program Manager		Wed 11/11/15	Thu 11/12/15	
17	2.1.6		– Create Schedule Using Gantt Chart	2 days	Fri 11/13/15	Mon 11/16/15	2.12.13.14.15.16
			Program Manager		Fri 11/13/15	Mon 11/16/15	
18	2.2		– Develop Budgeting Report	5 days	Tue 11/17/15	Mon 11/23/15	2,11
19	2.2.1		– Estimate Cost of Resources	5 days	Tue 11/17/15	Mon 11/23/15	2.11
			Program Manager		Tue 11/17/15	Mon 11/23/15	
20	2.3		– Create Risk Reduction Plan	7 days	Tue 11/24/15	Wed 12/2/15	2.11.18
			Program Manager		Tue 11/24/15	Wed 12/2/15	
21	2.4		– Communication Planning	4 days	Thu 12/3/15	Tue 12/8/15	2.11.18.20
			Program Manager		Thu 12/3/15	Tue 12/8/15	
22	2.5		– Gather Approval from Stakeholders	3 days	Wed 12/9/15	Fri 12/11/15	2.11.18.20.21
			Program Manager		Wed 12/9/15	Fri 12/11/15	
23	3	– Production, Execution, or Implementation		75 days	Mon 12/14/15	Fri 3/25/16	2,10
24	3.1	– Human Resources Management		75 days	Mon 12/14/15	Fri 3/25/16	2,10

Tracking Gantt
Resource Graph
Resource Sheet
Resource Usage
More Views...

Figure 5.15: Task Usage summary page

Network diagrams

Similar to Gantt charts, network diagrams can also be used for tracking progress against the project schedule and are another feature of the Microsoft Project software. One of the differences between a Gantt chart and a network diagram is that the Gantt chart resembles a bar graph whereas the network diagram looks more like a flow chart (Gambrel, 2012, p. 152). Why would program managers need to create both a network diagram and a Gantt chart? Network diagrams use activity-sequencing techniques to show the possible relationships of tasks to the overall schedule. By creating a network diagram, program managers can more easily visualize the rational links between tasks.

In Microsoft Project, go to the View tab, select Network Diagram and observe the result. The network diagram is easily created after entering the task and schedule information on the Gantt chart, as shown in the following screenshot.

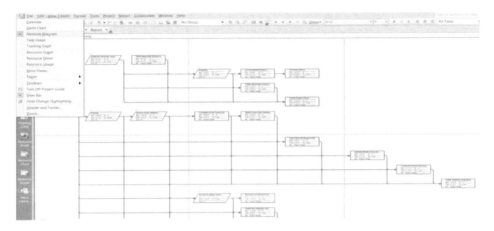

Figure 5.16: Network diagram created from task and schedule information on Gantt chart

A closer look at the resulting network diagram, shown in the next screenshot shows that the initiation state could last for as long as 17 days as its predecessor, the planning stage, could take as long as 35 days.

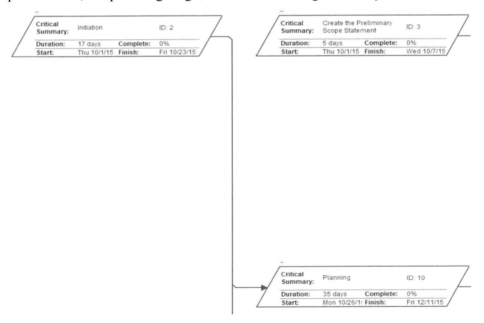

Figure 5.17: Network diagram created from task and schedule information on Gantt chart

PERT/CPM analysis

The CPM focuses on analyzing both the sequence and the length of activities. As such, the PERT/CPM analysis aims to create schedules based on the Optimistic Duration, Expected Duration, and Pessimistic Duration elasticities. Using the PERT/CPM analysis method, the program manager can produce more accurate cost estimates in case of uncertainties or identified risks that might arise in each stage of the project's life cycle (Kendrick, 2015, p. 182).

To create a PERT/CPM analysis, simply click on the View tab, then the Toolbars tab, and then the PERT Analysis tab. Next, click on the PERT Entry Sheet tab before adjusting the estimates according to Optimistic Duration, Expected Duration, and Pessimistic Duration. In the business-training program in Kyrgyzstan (Case 2), the Optimistic Duration was set one day ahead of the Expected Duration and the Pessimistic Duration was set one day behind the Expected Duration, as shown in the next screenshot.

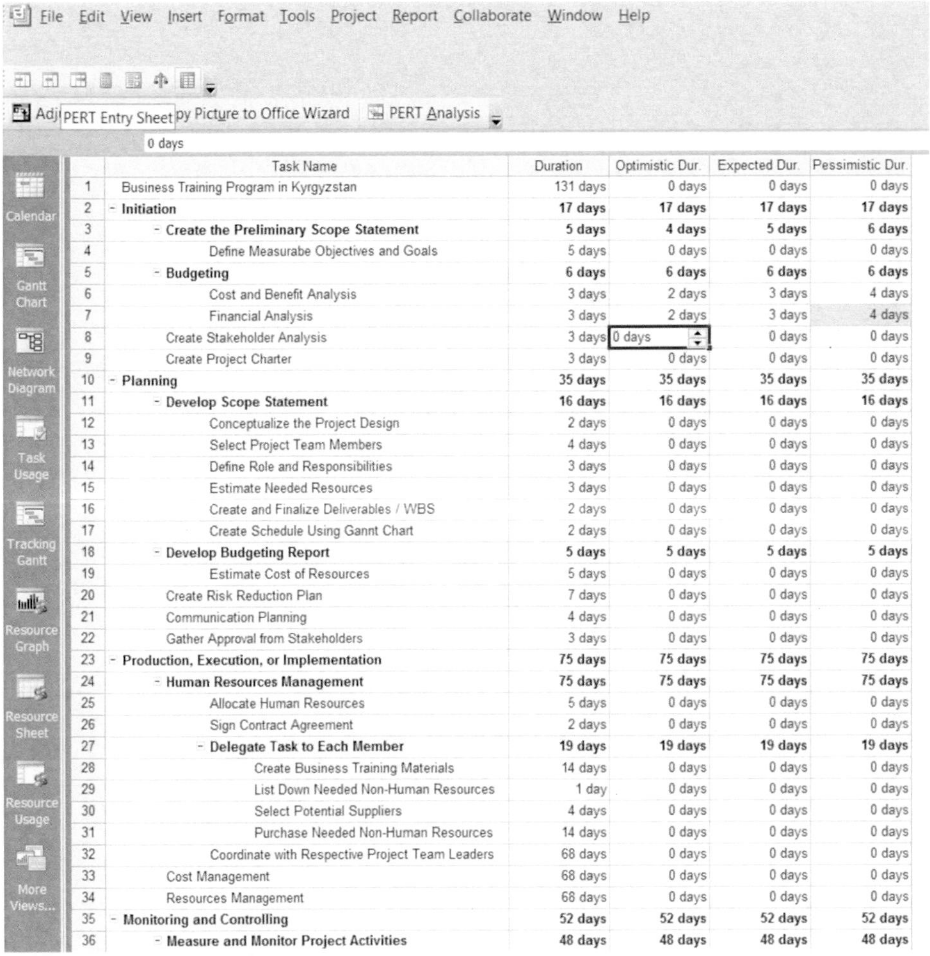

	Task Name	Duration	Optimistic Dur.	Expected Dur.	Pessimistic Dur.
1	Business Training Program in Kyrgyzstan	131 days	0 days	0 days	0 days
2	- **Initiation**	**17 days**	**17 days**	**17 days**	**17 days**
3	- **Create the Preliminary Scope Statement**	**5 days**	**4 days**	**5 days**	**6 days**
4	Define Measurabe Objectives and Goals	5 days	0 days	0 days	0 days
5	- **Budgeting**	**6 days**	**6 days**	**6 days**	**6 days**
6	Cost and Benefit Analysis	3 days	2 days	3 days	4 days
7	Financial Analysis	3 days	2 days	3 days	4 days
8	Create Stakeholder Analysis	3 days	0 days	0 days	0 days
9	Create Project Charter	3 days	0 days	0 days	0 days
10	- **Planning**	**35 days**	**35 days**	**35 days**	**35 days**
11	- **Develop Scope Statement**	**16 days**	**16 days**	**16 days**	**16 days**
12	Conceptualize the Project Design	2 days	0 days	0 days	0 days
13	Select Project Team Members	4 days	0 days	0 days	0 days
14	Define Role and Responsibilities	3 days	0 days	0 days	0 days
15	Estimate Needed Resources	3 days	0 days	0 days	0 days
16	Create and Finalize Deliverables / WBS	2 days	0 days	0 days	0 days
17	Create Schedule Using Gannt Chart	2 days	0 days	0 days	0 days
18	- **Develop Budgeting Report**	**5 days**	**5 days**	**5 days**	**5 days**
19	Estimate Cost of Resources	5 days	0 days	0 days	0 days
20	Create Risk Reduction Plan	7 days	0 days	0 days	0 days
21	Communication Planning	4 days	0 days	0 days	0 days
22	Gather Approval from Stakeholders	3 days	0 days	0 days	0 days
23	- **Production, Execution, or Implementation**	**75 days**	**75 days**	**75 days**	**75 days**
24	- **Human Resources Management**	**75 days**	**75 days**	**75 days**	**75 days**
25	Allocate Human Resources	5 days	0 days	0 days	0 days
26	Sign Contract Agreement	2 days	0 days	0 days	0 days
27	- **Delegate Task to Each Member**	**19 days**	**19 days**	**19 days**	**19 days**
28	Create Business Training Materials	14 days	0 days	0 days	0 days
29	List Down Needed Non-Human Resources	1 day	0 days	0 days	0 days
30	Select Potential Suppliers	4 days	0 days	0 days	0 days
31	Purchase Needed Non-Human Resources	14 days	0 days	0 days	0 days
32	Coordinate with Respective Project Team Leaders	68 days	0 days	0 days	0 days
33	Cost Management	68 days	0 days	0 days	0 days
34	Resources Management	68 days	0 days	0 days	0 days
35	- **Monitoring and Controlling**	**52 days**	**52 days**	**52 days**	**52 days**
36	- **Measure and Monitor Project Activities**	**48 days**	**48 days**	**48 days**	**48 days**

Figure 5.18: PERT Entry Sheet

Learning more about "slack time" is important so that project management can be aware of which tasks or sub-tasks are most critical in minimizing any delays. After entering the Optimistic Duration, Expected Duration, and Pessimistic Duration click on the Calculate PERT tab to compute the Free Slack and Total Slack times.

	Task Name	Start	Finish	Late Start	Late Finish	Free Slack	T
1	Business Training Program in Kyrgyzstan	Thu 10/1/15	Thu 3/31/16	Thu 10/1/15	Fri 4/1/16	0.33 days	
2	− Initiation	Thu 10/1/15	Fri 10/23/15	Thu 10/1/15	Fri 10/23/15	0 days	
3	+ Create the Preliminary Scope Statement	Thu 10/1/15	Wed 10/7/15	Thu 10/1/15	Wed 10/7/15	0 days	
5	+ Budgeting	Thu 10/8/15	Thu 10/15/15	Thu 10/8/15	Thu 10/15/15	0 days	
8	Create Stakeholder Analysis	Fri 10/16/15	Tue 10/20/15	Fri 10/16/15	Tue 10/20/15	0 days	
9	Create Project Charter	Wed 10/21/15	Fri 10/23/15	Wed 10/21/15	Fri 10/23/15	0 days	
10	− Planning	Mon 10/26/15	Fri 12/11/15	Mon 10/26/15	Fri 12/11/15	0 days	
11	+ Develop Scope Statement	Mon 10/26/15	Mon 11/16/15	Mon 10/26/15	Mon 11/16/15	0 days	
18	+ Develop Budgeting Report	Tue 11/17/15	Mon 11/23/15	Tue 11/17/15	Mon 11/23/15	0 days	
20	Create Risk Reduction Plan	Tue 11/24/15	Wed 12/2/15	Tue 11/24/15	Wed 12/2/15	0 days	
21	Communication Planning	Thu 12/3/15	Tue 12/8/15	Thu 12/3/15	Tue 12/8/15	0 days	
22	Gather Approval from Stakeholders	Wed 12/9/15	Fri 12/11/15	Wed 12/9/15	Fri 12/11/15	0 days	
23	− Production, Execution, or Implementation	Mon 12/14/15	Fri 3/25/16	Mon 12/14/15	Fri 4/1/16	0 days	
24	+ Human Resources Management	Mon 12/14/15	Fri 3/25/16	Mon 12/14/15	Fri 3/25/16	0 days	
33	Cost Management	Wed 12/23/15	Fri 3/25/16	Tue 12/29/15	Fri 4/1/16	4.33 days	
34	Resources Management	Wed 12/23/15	Fri 3/25/16	Tue 12/29/15	Fri 4/1/16	4.33 days	
35	− Monitoring and Controlling	Tue 1/19/16	Wed 3/30/16	Wed 1/20/16	Fri 4/1/16	1.33 days	
36	+ Measure and Monitor Project Activities	Tue 1/19/16	Thu 3/24/16	Tue 1/26/16	Fri 4/1/16	5.33 days	
40	+ Risk Management	Tue 1/19/16	Wed 3/30/16	Wed 1/20/16	Fri 4/1/16	1.33 days	
44	− Closing	Mon 3/28/16	Fri 4/1/16	Mon 3/28/16	Fri 4/1/16	0 days	
45	Final Report	Mon 3/28/16	Tue 3/29/16	Mon 3/28/16	Tue 3/29/16	0 days	
46	Close Contract	Wed 3/30/16	Thu 3/31/16	Wed 3/30/16	Thu 3/31/16	0 days	
47	Close Project	Thu 3/31/16	Fri 4/1/16	Thu 3/31/16	Fri 4/1/16	0 days	

Figure 5.19: Calculated Free Slack time

To view the Gantt charts using the Optimistic Duration, click on the Optimistic Gantt tab found under the PERT Analysis toolbar.

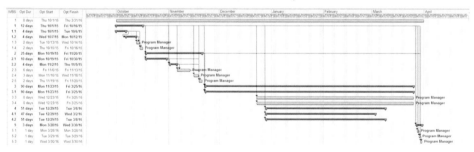

Figure 5.20: Calculated Free Slack time

To view the Gantt charts using the Pessimistic Duration, click on the Pessimistic Gantt tab found under the PERT Analysis toolbar.

123

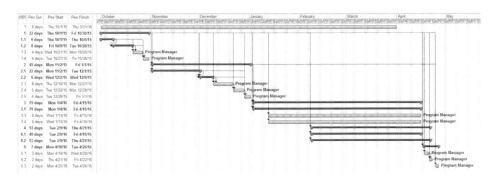

Figure 5.21: Gantt charts using the Pessimistic Duration

Based on the preceding two charts, the chart with the optimistic start and finish dates ends before the 31 March 2016 deadline whereas the chart with the pessimistic dates ends on 26 April 2016. Aside from such Gantt charts, a PERT analysis can also be represented by a network diagram composed of numbered nodes. Unlike the Gantt charts, the network diagram will not only make precedence relationships in each task more visible but will also more clearly identify the critical path.

A project will always be at risk of uncertainties. By showing the early start, late start, and slack time, it becomes easier to prepare and manage the entire group effort if the schedule slips. The network diagram is also composed of a series of Activity-On-Arc (AOA), presented in each arrow, and the Activity-On-Node (AON), represented by each node. Based on Figure 5.22, for example, it is clear that task A precedes task B, meaning that task B cannot be completed without completing task A (see Figure 5.10 and Figure 5.22).

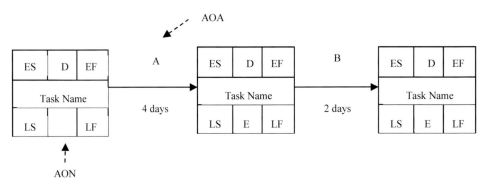

ES = Early Start; D = Duration; EF = Early Finish; LS = Late Start; E = Slack; LF = Late Finish.

Figure 5.22: Basic features of PERT/CPM network diagram

One popular theme that has not been described in the book is "strengths, weaknesses, opportunities, threats" (SWOT). Interested readers are encouraged to access and explore the internet for more details. There are several websites with a variety of in-depth coverage of helpful descriptions of the strategy. Among the available details are life case studies, methodologies including objectives, processes intended results, and more.

In this section, I have tried to limit my highlights to the possible extent in an attempt to entice potential and interested readers to be more focused, critical, and objective in their quest for pragmatic, relevant, and helpful sub-themes necessary during an effective implementation phase of SWOT. I am also hopeful that if such an approach is correctly and successfully applied, they stand a better chance of mitigating the myriads of copious websites made up of occasionally redundant, repetitive, and sometimes confusing contents.

While definitions and descriptions may sometime vary, SWOT in general is a planning strategy that serves both institutions and individuals. It is an antidote to addressing perpetual stakeholder problems including stream-lining different organizational and individual structural challenges, improving performance, and mitigating potential shortcomings — short, medium, and long term. It is considered very helpful and useful especially in cases where the relevant metrics or parameters — objectives, processes, intended outcomes etc. — are clearly and comprehensively defined.

From an implementation point of view, the sub-themes — strengths (S), weaknesses (W) — are characterized as internal factors. They are in most cases within the control of the stakeholder; comparatively easier to investigate, diagnose and revise. On the other hand, the sub-themes — opportunities (O) and threats (T) — are considered external factors. These are generally outside the stakeholder's control. And as such are more challenging to mange because of the level of fluidity, sometimes, complexity and unforeseen nuances. In summary, these challenges notwithstanding, the benefits significantly outweigh the risks as confirmed by the ubiquitous and inclusive global implementation by various users.

Wikipedia defines SWOT as: "… a strategic planning technique used to help a person or organization identify the *Strengths*, *Weaknesses*, *Opportunities*, and *Threats* related to business competition or project planning. It is intended to specify the objectives of the business venture or project and identify the internal and external factors that are favourable and unfavourable to achieving those objectives…"

As with many strategies, users implementing this plan need to be aware of potential pit falls. Risks and assumptions are an invaluable component of the entire process and cannot be adequately underscored. As Murphy's Law confirms, "Anything that can go wrong will go wrong," and SWOT is no exception. It is obviously not a one-size-fits all panacea. In that regard, caution, diligence, and astuteness are the key and guiding principles.

CHAPTER 6: Implementing the CARROT-BUS Model

Designing and implementing development programs remains a complex, convoluted and daring venture. Management systems presented in the abstract are obviously no panacea for addressing all these complications but they can help the systems serve as additional approaches aimed at controlling the overwhelming nuances that are an integral component of international development aid. Obviously, the systems are not a "one size fits all" solution. Each development institution has its own unique needs, and hence, corresponding plans and strategies.

While significant efforts have been made to highlight the added complexities contributed by corruption, it needs to be pointed out that this "cancer" remains a near-global challenge at all administrative levels of many development organizations. It would be unrealistic, misleading, and biased to attribute corrupt practices to only LDCs. It is universal!

It also needs to be recognized that the above systems do not necessarily have to be instantly implemented. Meaningful results will only be achieved in medium and long-term timeframes. There is need for adequate planning, recognition of certain limitations, relevance to specific development programs, and appropriateness. Every level of the hierarchy has its own unique challenges; each must be approached from both an objective and practical point of view. Each level has also been carefully defined with corresponding strategies supported by life case studies.

Over the last several years, I have continuously contributed articles and reports to mainstream news media. This has served as part of my advocacy in support of foreign and development aid; reminding our governments (especially Canadian) of their duty to unambivalently continue to help the underprivileged and vulnerable communities in the world. Highlights of some of these submissions are included in this primer in order to inform the reader about some of the challenges that come with international and development aid (see Chapter 7, My Published Media Submissions).

The systems and methods discussed here do not all necessarily have to be implemented. Meaningful results will only be easily achieved in medium- and long-term timeframes, often through trial and error. There is an obligation to anticipate pitfalls and thus a need for adequate planning, recognition of certain limitations, the relevance of prior past experience to development programs, and the appropriateness of each different methodology to the task. Each level of the hierarchy has its own unique challenges and each must be approached from both a relative and a practical point-of-view. Two major strategic frameworks — logic framework (logframe) and strategic framework — that were discussed earlier remain an important issue when developing planned "sustainable development goals" (SDGs) and the "cash on delivery" (COD) aid. In the former case, the Millennium Development Goals (MDGs) have come and almost gone. For those recipient governments that did not perform well on meeting the MDGs, along with the intended beneficiaries, it is a daunting task to choose amongst a new set of development initiatives when the prior ones are still unfulfilled. These new initiatives have advocates as well as detractors. As such, there remains much controversy and doubt about a new set being put forth. Various foreign-aid experts and important development assistance economists have expressed mixed reviews on the performance of all countries with respect to the MDGs and have yet to agree on the merits, attainability and rationale for new initiatives. In the end, the burden is on the LMICs and their constituencies of intended beneficiaries. Whatever the outcome, these stakeholders would need compelling arguments to confront the issues, such as corruption and accountability, to reflect comprehensive and relevant lessons learned from the MDGs experience.

Regarding COD, a recent article published by the Center for Development states: Cash on delivery (COD) is a new approach to foreign aid that focuses on results, encourages innovation, and strengthens government accountability to citizens rather than donors. Under COD Aid, donors would pay for measurable and verifiable progress on specific outcomes, such as US$100 dollars for every child above baseline expectations who completes primary school and passes the test. The Center for Global Development (CGD) is working with technical experts, potential donors, and partner countries to design COD Aid pilots and research programs (CGD, 2015). Looking at details of the COD framework, one is forced to ask difficult questions. For example, to contribute to this innovative model, where would recipient governments get the money needed for their long-term implementation? At present, development budgets in some, if not many, developing countries are still heavily subsidized by donor countries. Who will decide and what criteria will be used to establish these results or outcomes? Many foreign aid experts know intuitively that recipient governments still overwhelmingly emphasize processes as opposed to results. Current requirements of COD schemes necessitate higher-level results. Have these potential strategies been discussed mutually in forums wherein both donor and recipient countries have representation? What will be the role of contractors hired by donors to execute foreign aid programs such as Winrock in Nepal for example? Substantial amounts of funds are spent on covering contractor overheads and their technical expertise to realize effective outcomes — which would not be possible without donors' oversight bureaus, such as USAID.

Compelling anecdotal and scientific evidence shows that foreign aid outcomes have ranged from dismal to somewhat reasonable, i.e., results of foreign development assistance are mixed. For instance, the cases of foreign aid in Uganda and in Nepal have been successful but not in the case of Ethiopia, which seems to have more donor-aided projects, and Kyrgyzstan. However, in April 2015, Nepal was hit by a tragically damaging earthquake that has caused millions of dollars (if not a billion or more) worth of damage to its infrastructure and displaced hundreds of thousands of people. Does this mean foreign aid to this impoverished nation has failed, been irrevocably setback, been wasted, or irretrievably lost? Considering the case of Uganda, the project has been successful because the donor and the recipients of the computer package were able to maintain two-way communication that allowed them to maintain transparency and trust. In Nepal, because of the emphasis on transparency and accountability of the strategic approach and the quality of the technical assistance provided through a contract with Winrock, USAID was able to bring about a win-win situation over the long term despite long-standing distrust of the government by the donor and continuing chaos in the aftermath of a violent revolution.

The Paris Declaration that was promulgated to address most developmental concerns has been quite disappointing. In fact, over the years, only four countries worldwide were judged able to achieve the main objective of distributing foreign aid funds equitably and according to plan. Despite the willingness of donors to support the development in recipient countries, a majority of intended beneficiaries continue to live in squalid conditions. Today, poverty remains a challenge though middle classes are emerging in most developing countries, life expectancy is lengthening, education rates are rising, access to water grows, etc. However, one of the main reasons foreign aid projects are not successful overall is because of mistrust caused by corruption and misuse of funds. For this reason alone, donor countries can be said to have failed to improve the quality of life of those intended beneficiaries in recipient countries. Because of corrupt practices and squandering of funds by cronies within recipient governments, Western countries have little motivation to meet their own pledges to donate 0.7% of their GDP to LDCs unless transparency and accountability are universally honoured. There has been a failure to establish a common approach used by development agencies to achieve intended results. This observation is even more compelling in circumstances where agendas vary from one stakeholder to the next.

Many reviews of development interventions continue to be mixed, even though in general some progress seems to have been made. Obviously, the successes achieved cannot be generalized because they are skewed by the inclusion of India and China. There is compelling evidence that the standard of living and quality of life of many vulnerable groups around the developing world are still dire, and therefore, that more external assistance is desperately needed. For example, a UN report of two MDGs analyses of maternal health programs — one of them belonging to the organization — concluded that the outcomes were dismal with nothing to show for the initiatives. As expected, this raised more questions about spending billions of dollars in these efforts with nothing to show for them.

Therefore, there is every reason to believe that a framework like CARROT-BUS (in the absence of similar ones) remains an appropriate tool to help stakeholders streamline development initiatives. In light of the upcoming SDGs, I strongly believe that this framework can be an invaluable and compelling tool. It will help in avoiding duplication, facilitating coordination, maintaining meaningful timelines, optimizing resource utilization and setting medium and longer-term goals that are achievable and effective.

CARROT-BUS is presented as a simple and easy-to-implement strategy; the model seeks to clarify why the model prevails (in the absence of comparable and competitive tools) in beneficiary and vulnerable countries.

Given the observations above, it is clear that there is an urgent need to create a paradigm shift. In my opinion, the CARROT-BUS framework can be used successfully in an attempt to strengthen the existing foreign aid interventions through a paradigm shift. Aside from exerting more efforts to develop all the steps of the ladder, the application of operations research (OR) in project management, can assist program management teams to deliver better outcomes.

PART IV: PERSONAL ANECDOTES

CHAPTER 7: Introduction

All the life case studies presented in this book are meant to help the reader relate in a humanistic way with how successful and pragmatic interventions resonate in the real world. In one of my case studies — Uganda computer support — I looked at the challenges, problems, and logistics. I have included below, three other projects, that in collaboration with the beneficiaries, were successfully implemented. The remarks and observations in the Uganda intervention also apply here. One compelling observation amongst these projects is that given the impetus, community involvement, leadership, and continuous monitoring, the beneficiaries are capable of successfully executing and implementing these projects. It needs to be emphasized that community participation and contribution — mostly in kind — remain a good indication of ownership, and hence, a potential sustainable outcome. In every case, the communities were requested to sign an agreement demonstrating their willingness and how they were going to continue maintaining the project. It remains to be seen, however, what the future holds. The photos included tell the whole story — the school pupils, community members, etc.

For the most part, donor-funded programs continue to use the top-down approach. For example, the process is as follows: donor contacts national government, areas of support are identified (based on donor interest), proposals are solicited (from predominantly foreign contractors), a memorandum of agreement is signed and implementation is commissioned. And it also needs to be highlighted that political expediency amongst national governments is a significant driving force. With all my support below, I made it clear to all stakeholders that political involvement had to be brought to a minimum. Hence, do we need government participation? Yes, national governments are a "necessary evil" and are needed in order to create an invaluable enabling environment.

Following the CARROT-BUS approach for my projects, I started with the beneficiaries, identifying community development gaps and then tasking a national program coordinator who collaborated with the beneficiaries in developing a proposal. The rest was an outcome illustrated in the photos included. In some cases, expenses were below budgeted estimates. For example, with the Malawi team, some substantial amounts of funds were refunded. While in Bangladesh, a significant component was added to the initial plan — all for the same cost. There is no doubt that in many of these success stories, accountability was a key factor. And what are the prognoses? With current challenges notwithstanding, the different communities are capable of helping themselves, given appropriate and continuous relevant support.

Funding: Bangladesh – Safe Drinking Water Supply and Sanitation Project

The perennial shortage of a reliable source of water has impacted negatively on the smooth running of the Dr. Ali Nawaz (DAN) Foundation's Dr. Ali Nawaz Shishu Kanon School project. Management continues to be concerned due to the possible presence of arsenic-contaminated drinking water and sanitation. Competent and reliable staff is not willing to stay in the school as they find it difficult to walk long distances in search of arsenic-free drinking water and clean toilets when needed. No meaningful income-generating projects can be undertaken without a reliable source of clean water and sanitary latrines. Maintenance of the school ground is also proving to be difficult without any drinking water. Installation of an arsenic-controlled tube well and two sanitary latrines — one for boys and one for girls — at the institution will go a long way in solving this ongoing problem.

Acknowledgment

> The people of Shahebabad Village, including the DAN Foundation, NAWAZ Family, School Management Committee, the Teacher Parent Association, the union parishad Chairman, Upazilla Chairman, and the teachers and pupils of Dr. Ali Nawaz Shishu Kanon primary school would like to acknowledge and appreciate the contribution of Mr. Bongs Lainjo to transform the lives of the school children of Dr. Ali Nawaz Shishu Kanon Primary School and also the whole community. Mr. Bongs Lainjo's contribution through the funding of an arsenic-controlled tube well, 2 sanitary latrines and the building of a boundary wall behind the toilets has been very much valued. The community would like to sincerely thank Mr. Lainjo and will always remember this contribution.
>
> – *Dr. Zaman Ara, Project Coordinator, 2016*

The Principal of the school was very appreciative and said, "Now students do not need to go home for a natural call and our cleaner does not need to carry water from 2 kilometres away from school." The whole community was very thankful.

Figure 7.1: Bangladesh – Me flanked by project stakeholders & beneficiaries, the schoolchildren, in front of the new latrines
Photo courtesy of Adzem 2017

Figure 7.2: Bangladesh – Me and some of the schoolchildren

Figure 7.3: Bangladesh – Schoolchildren operating the newly installed water pump

Figure 7.4: Bangladesh – Project inauguration ceremony with the coordinator on the microphone and me to her left

Funding: Bindura, Zimbabwe – Muchaponwa Elementary School

The perennial shortage of a reliable source of water has impacted negatively on the smooth running of the school. The school administration is always in suspense, as it fears disease outbreak and closure of the school by health personnel, due to the acute shortage of clean drinking water. Competent and reliable staff is not willing to stay in the school as they find it difficult to walk long distances in search of drinking water. No meaningful income-generating projects can be undertaken without a reliable source of clean water. Maintenance of the school ground is proving difficult without adequate drinking water. Drilling of a borehole at the institution will go a long way in solving this ongoing problem.

I need to add that any similarities between the above narrative and the one from Bangladesh are solely due to chance and not by design! It is also interesting to note that two heterogeneous communities continents apart share the same perceptions about their respective and common access-to-water-related problems!

Acknowledgment

> Mr. Bongs Lainjo's financial assistance is well appreciated by the institution in particular and the community at large. We all look forward to a more productive, healthy and vibrant community.
>
> *– Mathias Kachiko, Project Coordinator, 2014*

Figure 7.5: Zimbabwe – Commissioning of new water pump with schoolchildren watching

Photo courtesy of Kachiko, 2014

Figure 7.6: Zimbabwe – Community leaders during the commissioning of the water supply project

Figure 7.7: Zimbabwe - Community members during the commissioning of the water supply project

Funding: Malawi – Nakhanda Elementary

Nakhanda Full Primary School, which is located in Dedza East, is being isolated as a good starting point in the endeavour to address the problems that are persisting in this constituency pertaining to primary school education. The upper classes of standard 6, 7, and 8 are the focus because these classes prepare and usher pupils into secondary school education. Nakhanda primary school is situated in the group village headman Chejelo, Senior Group Village Headman Kabulika II in Traditional Authority Kachindamoto, in Dedza district. There are three school zones in the area with Nakhanda belonging to Kapiri school zone. Table 1 highlights enrollment pattern in the zone, which provides an overall picture of education status within the area.

Currently, Nakhanda primary school has an enrollment of 868 pupils with 441 boys and 427 girls. The total number of standard 1 pupils is at 182 and in standard 8 it is at 39, demonstrating the huge dropout rate in the schools.

First, Nakhanda FP School is facing structural challenges. Currently, the primary school is only built with thatching grass and sticks, which undoubtedly renders it unsuitable for learning. The lack of basic infrastructure could affect students' desire to stay in school and the motivation of teachers. In addition, the school does not have proper and enough toilet facilities for the pupils attending this school.

Secondly, there is a dire lack of learning and teaching materials for both teachers and their pupils. Most students in the upper classes of standard 6, 7, and 8 have to share one textbook amongst three pupils. This situation is not conducive to their learning and preparation for national examinations.

Thirdly, the quality of the teachers at this learning institution leaves a lot to be desired and currently, there is a lack of professional support from the Ministry of Education. The untrained teachers are ill-equipped and ill-prepared to impart new knowledge to pupils and they have difficulty in finding their own ways of explaining new concepts. The handful of trained teachers has not had any refresher training sessions to receive the latest updates in the teaching field.

Lastly, the parents of the pupils attending the upper classes of standards 6, 7, and 8 are facing some socioeconomic challenges that threaten the continuation of their children's education. Poverty-stricken parents of pupils in the upper primary school classes are more likely to pull their children out of school instead of spending whatever little money they have on buying their school uniforms and other school supplies.

The poverty levels amongst the households further compound the many challenges in sexual and reproductive health, leading to decreased levels of women's empowerment. Hence, issues like early and unwanted pregnancies and child marriage continue to persist within the area.

Acknowledgement

> The people of Nakhanda Area including Group Village Head-woman Chenjero, The Teacher Parent Association, the chiefs, the teachers, and the pupils of Nakhanda Primary School would like to acknowledge and appreciate the contribution of Mr. Bongs Lainjo to transform the lives of the schoolchildren of Nakhanda Primary School and also the whole community. Mr. Bongs Lainjo's contribution through the funding of the school block consisting of two classrooms and toilets has been very much appreciated. The community would like to sincerely thank Mr. Lainjo and will always remember this contribution. This project has been very much appreciated and this is evidenced by the strong community contribution of bricks, sand, and water during the construction of the school block.

> *– Dorothy Lasaro, Project Coordinator, 2016*

The headmaster of the Nakhanda School was very appreciative and said, "This is the first time that I have received such a large number of books since I started my work as a teacher in Malawi." The whole community was very appreciative.

Figure 7.8: Malawi – Students, who are the project beneficiaries
Photo courtesy of Lazaro, 2017

Figure 7.9: Malawi – Students in class after receiving new desks with project coordinator standing in the back

Figure 7.10: Malawi – Community leaders (coordinator third from left) during commissioning session

Figure 7.11: Malawi – Book hand-over ceremony

Figure 7.12: Malawi – Section community members during project commissioning

My Published Media Submissions

Over the last several years, I have continuously contributed articles and reports to mainstream news media. This has served as part of my advocacy in support of foreign and development aid; reminding our governments (especially Canadian) of their duty to unambiguously continue to help the underprivileged and vulnerable communities in the world at large. Highlights of some of these submissions are included in this section in order to better inform the reader about some of the challenges that come with international development aid.

Source: Globe and Mail, May 12, 2010

Title: Africa's Promise

Re: With All Eyes on Africa, Canada Looks the Other Way, May 10

If the strategy in the mining industry includes partnership with African counterparts and significant national ownership, then Canada has done well (With All Eyes On Africa, Canada Looks The Other Way, May 10). Such an endeavour has the potential to help many vulnerable communities both socially and financially.

From a development funding point of view, Canada has not done well. With the current financial fallout, many donor countries are negating on previous commitments. For example, the US government has informed Uganda that its funding of HIV/AIDS drugs will dry up soon. In a case like this, where the number of recipients has jumped dramatically, there is cause for serious concern. Other countries, such as Nigeria and Swaziland, are faced with ubiquitous levels of drug shortages. Why? Because donor funding has run out and there is no likelihood of further funding.

What one might wish, though, is that with Canada's current foreign policy swing, there may be a better chance to demonstrate its willingness in helping Africa. This becomes even more compelling if the Tories carry through with their current maternal and child morbidity and mortality policy.

Source: Globe and Mail, May 24, 2010

Title: Stopping infant mortality

Re: Why Are Our Babies Dying? May 22, 2010

Canada's infant mortality rates are not only high, but also embarrassing and unacceptable.

Identification of vulnerable groups is essential in designing targeted and effective interventions. Aboriginal communities have significantly contributed in skewing these rates, and as such, any intervention strategy that is not targeted to them specifically is bound to fail.

We need to concentrate our efforts on improving the quality of life in our aboriginal communities, and the statistics around infant mortality rates are a wake-up call.

Source: Globe and Mail, Feb 21, 2011 Title: The sub-Saharan ladder

Re: The Staying Power Of Sub-Saharan Strongmen, Feb. 19, 2011

Many African communities are driven by what Abraham Maslow called the "hierarchy of needs." You move up the ladder as your needs are satisfied. These communities are preoccupied with surviving each day; political upheaval falls very low on the list of priorities. On the contrary, many North African and Arab countries have exceeded or satisfied many of the lower needs, as well as being more ethnically homogeneous.

It is only a matter of time before sub-Saharan countries start experiencing the type of "people power" movements currently seen in North Africa and the Arab world.

Source: Globe and Mail, Aug 30, 2012

Title: It Takes a Community

Re: Ottawa Rolls Out Maternal-Health Plan in Africa, August 28

Both critics of Canada's maternal-health plan and Minister Of International Co-operation, Bev Oda are correct. Access continues to limit the use of contraceptives in African countries, and cultural beliefs and practices remain a significant deterrent to the use of modern contraceptive methods (Ottawa Rolls Out Maternal-Health Plan In Africa - Aug. 28).

In countries like Mali, Niger and others, the influence of men in approving the use of contraceptives by their wives remains quite astounding. And even in cases where these services are available, the contraceptive prevalence rate (CPR) remains dismal. The CPR in these regions varies from 2 to 9%. And that is cause for global concern.

In addition to mitigating the effects of limited access to services, one area where Canada's plan can make a difference is community mobilization or organization. This additional intervention can give communities much-needed opportunities to participate and as such, address some of the current misperceptions about utilization of health services.

Source: Toronto Star, April 27, 2010

Title: PM's aid policy needs paradigm shift

Re: Will G8 meet its aid pledges? April 24, 2010

Your editorial does a great job in highlighting the crucial shortcomings of foreign aid in general and funding of Millennium Development Goals (MDG) specifically.

It is true that the current shortfall of between CAD$18 and $35 billion can be easily addressed if the political goodwill is there. And I'm hopeful that cooler minds will prevail in that regard.

Poverty remains ubiquitous and the overwhelming burden of developing country households remains mind-boggling. This deteriorating scenario has been exacerbated by widespread conflicts and instability in the vulnerable countries.

In Africa, for example, hunger remains prevalent in countries like Congo, Somalia, Sudan and Ethiopia: all of which face increasing instability and very poor infrastructure.

If Stephen Harper were to realign his foreign policy to conform with contemporary dynamics and conventional wisdom it would make a significant difference. Promoting the latest MCH morbidity and mortality policy is definitely a good first step. This initiative, however, should not be construed and implemented as a stand-alone and vertical initiative.

Significant efforts are still required to integrate this effort with current programs. This will only be effective if the appropriate strategy is developed and implemented. Any effective strategy developed by the Tories will require a paradigm shift from ideology to scientific based research evidence. There is no proof at this point that the Conservatives are doing any of that.

Significant efforts are also required to revamp the current MDG targets. In most cases, they remain too ambitious. And if the current performance by most countries is any indication, achieving these targets will continue to be an academic exercise. There is urgent need to act constructively now.

Source: National Post May 21, 2010

Title: Our Chance to make a difference

Re: Finishing what they started, May 18

Our chance to make a difference
National Post

[x] Re: Finishing What They Started, National Post, Brett House and Desiree McGraw, May 18.

The dilemma faced by developing countries with regard to continuous foreign aid policies is really nothing new. Donor willingness to assist developing countries is driven by the appearance of political expediency and a substantial degree of narcissistic agenda. This has ultimately created high levels of premature euphoria driven by high expectations among recipient governments.

In light of the above weakness among donors, during the coming G8 meeting the Canadian government should advocate for an institutionalized oversight committee. This team will be charged with agreeing with donor countries on the modus operandi of releasing funds. The committee will then use that to "remind" funding agencies of their commitments. If this can be accomplished during the deliberations of this G8 meeting, there will a better chance that many of these development programs will be accomplished. And Canada's role in addition to its current maternal and child morbidity and mortality policy will go down in history as the driving force behind this success.

Bongs Lainjo, former UN senior advisor, Montreal.

Source: National Post Sept 18, 2013

Title: International development fiasco

Re: Jeffrey Sachs meets Hayek, Sept 18, 2013

This comment on international development is not only timely, blunt, targeted, appropriate and relevant; it serves as a wakeup call to all development stakeholders.

For whatever reason, funding agencies were driven by Sachs' "portfolio" instead of his ability to deliver meaningful results. Sachs may be an achieved professor in Columbia; that does not automatically translate into an effective development guru. And that is why these donors poured millions of dollars, effectively giving Sachs a blank cheque to flaunt in Africa. Sachs understood the rules and played the game extremely well by doing an excellent job and doing it all wrong. This calls into question the reliability, validity and accuracy of program results given to these donors.

Development assistance and aid especially in Africa continue to represent the conundrum that aid agencies, developing partners and recipient national governments and beneficiaries constantly grapple with.

In over six decades of development assistance, effectiveness and sustainability remain elusive. Sachs' emotions and claims of success are not unique. The key issues that have hardly been addressed or solved are achievement of sustainable outcomes and attribution.

Indeed, every funding agency supports development initiatives because they expect meaningful outcomes. The millennium village project (MVP) is no exception. Sachs' refusal to establish an intervention and control arms makes his projects and outcomes less scientific and limits any chances of replication.

That's where the problem lies. The irony is that he is known to be a clinical economist. The other issue is the question of unintended outcomes. For example, the project convinced the community to move from planting "matoke" to planting corn in Ruhiira village in Uganda. What Sachs and his funding agencies failed to assess were the demand and potential market. And as we now know, things didn't work out as planned. I have every reason to suspect that the community members knew this was a "dead-on-arrival" venture; especially given their previous success across several generations.

One other aspect of this puzzle is the issue of attribution. The MVP may claim as much credit as it wants to; the reality is that because of the simultaneous developmental and economic synergies, no one agency (or project) can unilaterally claim for any potential success and the MVP is no exception.

Source: Maclean's, June 9, 2014

Title: Helping mothers to know best

Re: A matter of life and death, National, June 2, 2014

The Maternal, Newborn and Child Health (MNCH) meeting was meant to showcase the federal government's visibility as a champion of foreign aid in general, and maternal and child health specifically ("A matter of life and death," National, June 2). For this, the Conservatives deserve credit. But our government remains dogmatic and influenced by poor scientific evidence regarding family planning (FP) in its MNCH support.

FP is not only about population control, but also serves as an essential component of providing an improved quality of life for both the mother and the child. It serves significantly as an antidote to potential abortions and other childbirth-related complications. Also, we need to strengthen MNCH strategies amongst our Native communities, where the infant mortality rate remains unacceptably high. Governments attempting to help other countries need to recognize shortcomings at home.

Source: Wall Street Journal, August 2, 2014

Title: Aid for the World's Poor should Primarily Help the Poor

Re: Smart Aid for World's Poor, July 26, 2014

It is indeed true that some progress was made and the quality of life in many parts of the world improved. But the reality is that in most parts of the world, especially in sub-Saharan Africa, successful levels of achievements were disjointed, mixed and inconclusive in several cases.

Development unfortunately usually takes place in unfavorable environments—a condition that makes strategic frameworks quite volatile and fluid. It therefore becomes critical to ask whether these initiatives are yet another attempt by the U.N. to promote the world body's ego, visibility and ubiquity.

16   THE TIMES-TRANSCRIPT, JANUARY 31, 1983, MONDAY

THE COMPUTER AGE

READY OR NOT, HERE IT COMES

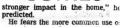

By Isabel MacLaggan
Correspondent

BATHURST (Special) — It appears the fast-developing computer style of living will sweep us off our feet unless we learn to swim with the tide.

Either that, or we'll be left stranded as today's fascinated and eager children leave us far behind.

"Computers are here to stay in our businesses, our homes and our education system," says a local Community College educator whose knowledge and observations lead to the above conclusions.

"There's something new every day," says Bongs Lainjo. "I limit my social life to keeping up to date. It's incredible."

Another obvious field of computer use and advancement is scientific research.

Lainjo, a former systems analyst in Montreal who does some consulting work, says 65 per cent of computer users are found in the business field, but the home, not education, comes next.

He suggested video games have helped to bring this about and now that the price of personal computers is dropping, more people are acquiring them. They even use them in their work.

The Community College professor, who teaches computer software,

mathematics and statistics courses at the Bathurst campus, said a leading company came out a year ago with the "office of the future".

No longer will messengers be needed to deliver papers and documents to other parts of the office. In another few years people will sit in different rooms and communicate with others by means of their own computers.

"Some computers can be carried like a briefcase," said Lainjo.

This could lead to more office work done at home and, for mothers with babies, the home could more often be the centre of gainful employment, he suggested.

He said shopping, banking, and the settling of bills will eventually be carried out without setting foot outside the door. All that is needed is a computer on the other end.

The computer will be used to balance books and even to tend meals when the cook isn't home.

Lainjo said all a person will need to do is dial the home computer, order that the oven be turned on at a certain time and that it be turned off again if the person's arrival time is delayed. The time will come when computerized robots will be programmed to answer door bells and give the message required.

"Computers are introducing a new life style and we're going to feel a

stronger impact in the home," he predicted.

He fears the more common use of computers may have an effect on family cohesiveness, especially if family members spend a lot of time using them for work or leisure time purposes.

"We could lose the human touch as we become more machine oriented," said Lainjo.

Turning to the education scene, he said teachers will be faced all the more with keeping a jump ahead of their pupils, even though computers are being introduced in the schools. The children will be referring to other computers and how they work, he noted.

Lainjo said another negative aspect is that pupils will become "too machine dependent" and will often give wrong answers "because the computer, says.

"Kids should still know the fundamentals and basics and then use the machines as tools," he insisted.

"Traditionally parents told the kids what to do to solve problems but now the parents and grandparents go to the children and ask how it's done on the computer," Lainjo mused.

"Whether we like it or not, computers are here to stay. Nuclear reactors and satellites are all controlled by computers. Lawyers and doctors are using them. The more sophisticated we become, the more we need computers," he maintained.

"But a computer is like a car. If there's no gas in a car it can't move."

That's where the software comes into the picture. A computer is essentially a machine that receives, stores, manipulates and communicate information. This calls for the ability to prepare and inject information through rather complex programming unless pre-prepared material is used.

Lainjo said computer courses are given at the Community College in both day and night classes. A night course through the continuing education program is being offered to the public commencing in February.

Lainjo gave an overview of the new and ever-changing computer world to members of the North Shore Amateur Radio Club at their last meeting last week.

In turn, he was invited to tour with his students the five computerized departments at the local Chaleur General Hospital by a club member who happens to be the hospital's medical director.

(Christie Photo)

Bongs Lainjo, right, discusses computers with Claude Vienneau, left, and Herb Shaw.

Professional Performance Compliments

Over the years working and during my stint with the UN as a senior program management, evaluation and logistics advisor, I received several positive and encouraging messages from both my supervisors and senior national government counterparts. Below is a sample of some of the unedited narratives.

Subject: Words of appreciation

Date: Thu, 27 Jan 2005 01:11:22 -0500

From: **obaid@unfpa.org**

To: ALL CST STAFF <allstaff.cst@unfpa.org>,ALL CO REPRESENTATIVES <allreps.co@unfpa.org>,HQ-ALL ICS STAFF <hq.ics@unfpa.org>

Dear colleagues,

It has been brought to my attention that three of our colleagues from CST/Katmandu have been working extremely hard in Sri Lanka to deal with the situation, as they responded rapidly to provide support to the Country Office:

Kiran Bhatia, Gender and Soc-Cultural Research Adviser, Bongs Lainjo, RH Logistics Adviser and Saramma Mathai, RH Adviser.

I would like to express my appreciation for their hard work and commitment and rapid response. I would also like to thank the team members who amended/cancelled leave plans to get to work as soon as necessary.

Best regards.

Country: Afghanistan

Dear Bongs

On behalf of the UNFPA CO Afghanistan – I too would like to extend my congratulations on a marvellous and effective support course well done!

Although I have been in post a short time and are not up-to-speed on many details – it is clear that the workshop hit on critical issues, which we are addressing as we move into the second year of a country programme in Afghanistan… and not least reprogramme for 2006-2008 with our country team colleagues.

Thank you for such a supportive and effective approach to building capacity we all look forward to applying these lessons to help make a difference in a country in which 56% are under the age of 18yrs, that lies in the bottom 5 of the NHDI and sees horrific mortality rates in much of the country.

I look forward to meeting up with you all sometime soon.

Best Wishes

David Saunders, Representative

UNFPA Afghanistan

4th May 2005

Country: Bhutan

Dear Jamila,

Thank you so much for making immediate follow-up. Two of us from Bhutan has just reached back on 3rd May 2005.

Today, we are reporting to Ministry and probably we will try to present and get their final comments. We will make sure that our plan reached in time.

Please convey our sincere thank and gratitude to Mr. Bond *(ed. Bongs)* and Mr. Gaisy *(ed. Jesse)* for sharing their valuable knowledge and experiences. This workshop is the best and we hope such type of workshop be continued in future.

Once again thanks and with best regards

Tobgyel

Bhutan

4th May 2005

Country: Iran

Dear Jamila,

Hello

First of all let me express my thanks from UNFPA headquarter for organizing such a workshop which had a lot of lessons of experience amongst region countries. Second thanks from Mr.Bongs for his commitment on running the workshop and also the other facilitators.

As I wrote before and also mentioned in the workshop, based on RHCS we omitted the central level warehouses at the country level, so we cannot complete the data which needed in the CCM. (We are eager to get the responses of the questions which we send to Abraham more than two months ago.) Of course we will write it in our finalized plan of action. I hope we can send our POA in the next week with all appendices to the specified persons. Please accept my apology for the delay, I was in another mission in the country immediately after Sri Lanka mission.

Best wishes

M.Eslami

Iran

7th May 2005

Country: Maldives

Dear Jamila,

Just to let you know that the Maldives team has also been having further discussions with MoH and DPH and today will be doing a presentation and discussion of the RHCS Action Plan in order to agree on next steps.

On behalf of the team our sincere thanks to CST, Mr. Bongs Lainjo, Jesse Brandt and the other facilitators as well as the Sri Lanka office for all the arrangements. The workshop was informative we look forward to further such initiatives to build our knowledge and motivate us.

Best regards,

Dunya

Maldives

5th May 2005

Country: Nepal

1.

Dear Bongs,

On behalf of the Nepal team and UNFPA CO, I would like to thank CST/UNFPA SAWA Nepal office UNFPA CO Sri Lanka and of course you very much for giving us the opportunity to attend the RHCS workshop and upgrade our knowledge in the given field. We would also like to thank Mr. Jayanti Tuladhar and other resource persons for the efforts they put in to make the workshop meaningful. Lastly but not the least, we thank Sri Lanka CO for their hospitality and for the excellent logistic arrangements.

On the follow up of the plan of action, Nepal team is meeting tomorrow at 10:15 am at DOHS to discuss the next steps for finalising the plans. We will definitely send it to the HQ before the deadline. We had a meeting after the workshop before we departed from Sri Lanka and have made some tentative plans. We are very pleased that Mr. Lamichchane & Mr. Shakya from our partner agency NFHP supported by USAID could participate in the workshop. We will be working as a team in fine tuning the plans with the narrative. I from the CO will do my best to facilitate/coordinate amongst the relevant partners and will consult you at CST as and when necessary for your assistance.

We look forward to receiving the certificate and the workshop report.

Best regards,

Peden

Nepal

4th May 2005

2.

Dear Jamilaji, namaste and thanks for the info.

Nepal group is meeting on Thursday May 5, for the follow up on the Sri-Lanka meeting. Please convey our gratitude to Mr.Bongs for whatever he has done to us. He is a perfect guru in RHCS and his effort to make the workshop a grand success is commendable. We all are benefited, so the country will.

With best regards,

Janardan

Nepal

3rd May 2005

3.

Ref: NEP/03/004

Dear Mr. Bongs,

Subject: Annual Meeting of UNFPA 5th Country Programme Team,
7-11 March 2005, Hotel Himalaya

I would like to express my sincere appreciation to you for facilitating the session on 11 March 2005 at Hotel Himalaya on the Results Based Management discussion between country team on results-based approach to programming and internal management in the context of the implementation of the Country Programme Output and UNFPA MYFF.

I am also pleased to share participants' evaluation of the session, which shows that the session was highly rated by participants and wanted more of such events to happen in future. I trust that the UNFPA staff have benefited from your session for programme and management effectiveness, efficiency and accountability by facilitating its application to RBM in improving performance for results.

On behalf of the UNFPA Country Office team in Nepal, I would also thank you once again for your support and cooperation.

With best regards,

Yours sincerely,

Dr. Hernando Agudelo
Deputy Representative

Junko Sazaki
UNFPA Representative

Mr. Lainjo Bongs
Advisor on Programme Management, Statistics and Evaluation
UNFPA CST
Sanepa

cc:
Mr. Wasim Zaman, Director, UNFPA CST, Sanepa

United Nations Population Fund, the UN House, Pulchowk, Lalitpur, Nepal, P.O. Box 107
Telephone 5523200, 5529197, 5527632, 5527304, Fax 977-1-5527385, Email: registry.np@unfpa.org.np

Country: Pakistan

Dear Jamila,

Thank you very much for forwarding Mr. Bongs' message. We enjoyed our stay at Colombo and we really appreciate the kind of support extended by UNFPA Country Office Sri Lanka. We are working on the plan with our other colleagues and hopefully it will be ready by the last week of May 2005. Please pay my best regards to Ms. Lubna, Ms. Malti and Ms. Tania.

Thanks,

Malik Ahmed Khan

Programme Officer

UNFPA, Pakistan

3rd May 2005

Country: Sri Lanka

1.

Dear Bongs,

I am sorry that I could not meet with you before you left. I went out of Colombo Saturday morning. Thank you, Bongs it was really a good workshop. And I can imagine how much under pressure you must have been. I want to know your secret of being cool under such circumstances.

Dr. Vidya said that you had sent a report to me to be given to him. But I did not receive it. I have been having quite a few problems with my email. Can I request you to send it again please. Thank you and best regards,

Malathi Weerasooriya

Sri Lanka

6th May 2005

2.

Dear Wasim,

I just wanted to drop you a line to express how pleased the participants were with the RHCS workshop. Although I was unable to attend the workshop (with the exception of the opening), I did meet the participants at the dinner we hosted and they were all very positive about this initiative. In my experience of attending such initiatives, I have rarely seen that the stake-holders adopt the process and output as their own. I think the credit must go to Bongs for taking pains to ensure that - and I know (from my colleagues in Sri Lanka MOH) that he has some tough clients. He is an excellent facil-itator - held the workshop together and participants in tow. You may share this email with him as you see fit. But I felt that it is important to give you this feedback. I actually never got a chance to officially record that he also did a remarkable job for us during the tsunami first month. And I want to thank you for being so flexible about his time during that period. We seri-ously could not have done it without him. I am not in the habit of writing thank you notes after missions as I feel that it is part and parcel of the job we do but I felt that it was warranted in this case including for the earlier mission in January. Sorry actually the feedback was so late - I am only get-ting back to some normalcy now. Actually I would like to catch up with you on other matters when you get back. Will try and call.

Regards.

Lubna Baqi

Representative

UNFPA

Sri Lanka

3rd May 2005

DISTRICT MEDICAL OFFICE
JINJA DISTRICT
P.O.BOX 558

16th April, 1998.

To

Mr. Bongs Lainjo,

Ref: A big thank you:

Many thanks for yours dated April 6th 1998 in which you informed us of your intention to leave DISH project at the end of this month.
Take it from me Jinja DHT and Health Unit staff at large will miss you greatly.
Thank you so much for the understanding you showed to all of us who worked closely with you.
I thank God for blessing you with ability to plan and get your programs going on as scheduled.
" We meet here there or in air ".

Yours Sincerely,

William Omase.
For District Medical Officer/Jinja.

Baseline Study – Electronic Health System Study (EHSS)

General Objective: To transform the current manual medical record system (MRS) into an electronic health record (EHR) system.

Specific Objective: To implement stage one of the Center for Medicaid and Medicare Service (CMS) Electronic Health Record incentive plan.

Background: The study was conducted in partial fulfillment of CMS's health records digitization program funding requirements. In 2007, the Federal Government introduced an incentive plan to encourage physicians to computerize as many of their activities as possible. This initiative, amongst others, was meant to enable doctors to provide their services with evidence-based support. There are also other advantages to automating health services. These include: more secure data, easy access, guaranteed reliability, improved efficiency, and better quality. While the initial level of acceptance was relatively low, the current trend does signal a potential uptake, increasing enthusiasm, momentum, and motivation. It is in light of this general interest and the need to improve service provision that Dr. Goddard's practice has decided to implement an electronic medical record system in his office.

Office Setting: This is an individual practice occupying a building with a square footage of 3,250. The layout is divided into a waiting room, a front reception area, nurses' office, three examination rooms, eligible professional's office, infusion room, closets, two general-purpose offices, and a kitchen.

The practice has been operating successfully for over two decades. During this period, all transactions have been done manually. Some exceptions include outsourced billing, occasional electronic prescription (e-Rx, supplied by Allscripts Healthcare Solutions), routine correspondence, and client check-in database.

The staff composition includes two medical secretaries, two registered nurses (RN), one receptionist, one professional organizer, and one medical assistant. They all report directly to the eligible professional (EP), Dr. Goddard Sighan.

Annual Service Statistics: Between 2008 and 2011, for which data is available, the total number of client visits peaked in 2009 with a drop in 2010. This drop is associated with extended vacation time taken by the EP for family reasons. The same observation applies to Table 2. Over that period of time, the mean number of patient visits was 6,027 with a corresponding mean number of new patients equal to 445. With respect to insurance claims between 2008 and 2011, there was an approximate average of 3,051 claims for Medicare and a mean of 3,434 for private insurance plans. Table 7.1 and Table 7.2 represent client load and insurance claim cases respectively. The number of cases and claims in both tables are quite consistent, as expected.

Table 7.1: Client load by year

Year	Repeat	New	Remarks
2008	4,524	400	
2009	6,684	544	
2010	6,121	420	
2011	6,778	417	

Source: EP's office.

Table 7.2: Number of insurance claims by year and type of insurance plan

Year	Medicare	Medicaid	Private	Other
2008	2,333	0	2,591	0
2009	3,401	0	3,877	0
2010	3,083	0	3,458	0
2011	3,385	0	3,810	0

Source: EP's office.

Morbidity Data: In its meaningful use strategy, the CMS has made availability and access to diagnosis-based data sets an important component of an efficient and functional EHR. In this regard, the CMS has developed a set of core impact indicators that will serve as a roadmap in its efforts to achieve meaningful results. Many EPs in return have also recognized the importance of these indicators and how they can significantly contribute to providing evidence-based reports, which can be used to make informed decisions. When produced reliably, these reports can also help EPs to strengthen their service provision.

In order for this system to succeed, substantial efforts will be required from both EPs and their respective EHR suppliers. Such efforts will make this initiative convincingly sustainable, user-friendly, and effective. While EPs are expected to use reports generated through the PQRS, suppliers will assume the key role of developing effective data quality control systems.

Dr. Goddard is a specialist in rheumatology. Table 7.3 indicates that between 2008 and 2011, the average number of arthritis-rheumatoid cases was 1,897; with a distant second of 841 cases with bursitis; followed by 596 cases with osteoarthrosis-low leg/knee; and 404 cases diagnosed with arthritis-gout. The remaining average number of cases was below 400.

On an annual basis, the highest mean number was achieved in 2009, with 671 cases. This was closely followed by 664 cases diagnosed in 2011.

In terms of morbidity differentials, about 40% of cases diagnosed between 2008 and 2011 were patients with arthritis-rheumatoid. The remaining cases ranged from 3% with Raynaud's syndrome to 18% with bursitis.

Table 7.3: Annual distribution of morbidity between 2008 and 2011

ICD9 Code	Description	2008	2009	2010	2011	Mean
714	Arthritis-rheumatoid	2,014	1,907	2,119	1,547	1,897
726.5	Bursitis	458	1,019	576	1,310	841
715.2	Osteoarthrosis-low leg/knee	300	990	412	684	596
74	Arthritis-gout	212	502	275	626	404
729	Fibromyalgia	261	393	438	489	395
715.1	Osteoarthritis	158	277	236	331	250
696	Arthritis-psoriatic	128	160	177	187	163

443	Raynaud's syndrome	211	123	157	137	157
	Average	468	671	549	664	

Source: EP's office

Current System: The automated office system includes desktops (procured in 2002 including Windows XP and MS Suite) with details presented in Table 7.4; a network system with description later; a WiFi system; two HP LaserJet 4500 series; two Canon 6500 series. The printers are all black and white and over three years old.

The network includes a server – HP ProLiant ML350, MS Window 2003 RS (OS), NETGEAR, technology G4, an APA battery backup (Smart-UPS 750, with 750 Watts, a system backup – Iomega (REV 70GB) used daily for designated tapes.

The internet setup includes an Intel PRO/100 VE network (provided by Time Warner Cable), RCA modem and router.

The wireless is a ZyAir (Zyxel), secured with model FS116 (NETGEAR Ethernet switch).

Table 7.4: Computer distribution and setup location

Location	Make	Processor	RAM	Use
EP's office	HP Compaq	2.80 GHz	2.49 GB	Professional
Infusion center	HP dx Microtower	2.2 GHz	.99 GB	Professional
Medical secretary (MS)	IBM	2.80 GHz	1.24 GB	Secretarial
MS	HP Compaq	3.00 GHz	199 GB	Secretarial
General office (three)	IBM	2.80 GHz	1.24 GB	General use
Front desk	HP dx2400	2.20 GHz	.99 GB	Check out

Front desk	HP dx7100	3.20 GHz	2.24 GB	Check in
Nurses' office	HP Compaq	2.80 GHz	2.49 GB	Professional
Server	HP Pro-Liant ML350	3.0 GHz	3.5 GB	Network

Source: EP's office

RFP Requirements: The proposals will be evaluated based on two key areas – technical and financial. Billing will be considered as either an integrated or a "standalone" part of the proposal.

Components to be addressed in detail in the technical section will include:

- Compliance with CMS requirements – PQRS, e-Rx, CQM), etc.
- Billing (insurance plans, quality control, security levels, backup, portability, ownership, etc.,)
- Training (manual, online, didactic, group, individual, etc.)
- Technical support (in-house, remote, etc.)
- System availability (web-based, standalone, etc.)
- Availability of Cloud computing (security, backup, etc.)
- Demonstration session (online, onsite etc.)
- Timeline (details to include task, responsible party, period, location and assumptions
- Copy of CMS accreditation
- A copy of company prospectus
- Provision for OCR services (include portability, hardware, software and license policy
- Computer system (software, two options with specs: desktops and laptops with 16+ inch screens)
- Data management (portability, security levels, quality control, input (screens), output (reports), etc.)
- Network specifications (manual, server, topology: network, Token Ring, Star, max nodes (simultaneous users), set up, configuration, S/W, OS, manufacturer etc.)
- WiFi (high speed, DSL, etc.)
- Voice recognition system (H/W, S/W, etc.)
- Three or more references

The costs will be detailed, categorized by groups of items. No hidden or "fine print" costs will be considered. In cases where figures are likely to change (hotel, car rentals, per diem, etc.), ongoing costs will be accepted.

Proposal Evaluation Criteria: The methodology that will be used to assess each proposal will be based on the following process:

RFP Score Formula:

- Total score = technical score + financial score
- Technical criteria weight; [70%], maximum 700 points
- Financial criteria weight; [30%], maximum 300 points

With this weighted scoring method, the award of the contract will be made to the individual supplier whose offer receives the **highest** score out of a pre-determined set of weighted technical and financial criteria:

- All the offers of individual suppliers who scored 490 (70% from 700) and more points will be included for financial evaluation. The lowest technically qualified proposal receives 300 points, and all the other technically qualified proposals receive points in inverse proportion according to the formula:

$P=Y*(L/Z)$, where, P=points for the financial proposal being evaluated.

Y=maximum number of points for the financial proposal.

L= price of the lowest price proposal.

Z=price of the proposal being evaluated.

Summary Table: Table 5 represents a summary of all items (technical and financial) to be considered. The table also serves as a reminder to potential suppliers. A completed copy is required with every proposal. Innovative ideas are encouraged and will be considered seriously. However, they will not be included in the evaluation process. The self-described table includes the following columns:

- Component (presented earlier)
- YES (Check if component has been addressed)
- NO (Check if component has not been addressed)
- Remarks (additional and relevant observations, e.g., when a component has been addressed and service is currently not available)

Table 7.5: Proposal summary table

Component	YES	NO	Remarks
Compliance with CMS requirements			
Billing			
Training			
Technical support			
System availability			
Availability of Cloud computing			
Demonstration session			
Timeline			
Copy of CMS accreditation			
Copy of company prospectus			
Provision of OCR			
Computer system specifications			
Data management			
Network specification			
WiFi			

specification			
Voice Recognition System (VRS)			
Three references			

CHAPTER 8: Capacity Building

In a given infrastructure, a solid, well-conceived, well-constructed foundation in general produces a sustainable, reliable, and dependable structure. This applies to buildings, roads, bridges, etc. These observations could also easily apply to the CARROT-BUS framework. Capacity building (CB), which serves as the foundation and invaluable component of the model needs to demonstrate the same or similar qualities. This is illustrated in the model by its size at the bottom of the pyramid. Like an infrastructure, capacity building should represent a process instead of being an event as is generally the practice. I remember during my high-school days when one of my professors would constantly remind us how he would continue to quiz the students until the skies fell down! The importance of CB cannot be over-emphasized.

In light of the above observations, I decided to include a chapter on my personal anecdotes with regard to strengthening capacity at the country or regional level. As a technical advisor working over a period of more than 20 years, I felt honoured and gratified to have served in several countries. In these circumstances, my assignments through multi and bilateral agencies gave me an opportunity to better understand and appreciate the daunting task of providing technical support to clients with variable, complex, and diversified needs. As satisfying as these missions were, they also came with unique and sometimes unavoidable circumstances. For example, due to the nature of my job, missions could only be conducted through requests from national and beneficiary governments. My stint in any region was for an average of about three years: a period of time that in many circumstances did not permit me to accomplish as much as I would have liked. This limitation made it generally and practically difficult to achieve many of the levels of CARROT-BUS ladder, though, in one country, we reached the results level. In this case, the result level was in reference to achieving the planned outcome during a three-year period. This was indeed exceptional from a strategic framework perspective. Being assigned to one country, as it happened on a few occasions, I was able to accomplish significantly more as that gave me an opportunity to plan, follow up, and revise programs. It needs to be emphasized here that whether at the country or regional level, substantial inputs from the beneficiary and requesting governments were the *modus operandi*: a policy that was very strictly adhered to.

In this section, I have subjectively selected some of the capacity strengthening assignments that I assessed, designed, and conducted in various regions and countries. The training sessions — "magisterial," working groups and practicums — lasted a period ranging from three to eight weeks depending on the needs and government requirements. Countries that have been included are Uganda, Swaziland, Comoros, and Lesotho. The Comoros is the only French-speaking country in the group. At the regional level, countries included Afghanistan, Iran, Pakistan, Bhutan, Nepal, Bangladesh, Sri Lanka, and the Maldives. In the latter case, one training session was conducted with participants from the identified countries. Because of the varying needs, one of my responsibilities was to help these countries and regions with identifying relevant thematic areas. As the case studies will illustrate, there were duplicates in some cases even though the outcomes were different. In the following narrative, I have tried to the extent possible to complement text with pictures. It is also important to note that in every workshop participants were qualified and competent professional in their own right.

District Computerization – Uganda

This was a one-month hands-on and participatory workshop conducted in 1997. The collaborative schedule was designed in such a way that morning sessions were, in general, reserved for magisterial and theoretical activities, while the afternoons and evenings were spent doing laboratory work. In the latter case, two participants were assigned to one computer. Laboratory assistants were always present and provided support when deemed necessary or required. Participants were also required to bring sample copies of their routine manual reports as part of the hands-on exercise.

The general objective of this project was to train district staff in applying selected and relevant software packages and applications.

In specific terms, the participants were expected to demonstrate competencies in:

- Using Microsoft Office with emphasis on Spreadsheet and Word
- Using a specialized logistic management application package
- Using a specially-designed accounting package
- Implementing and continuing the process after the workshop.

Immediate follow-up support by our team was conducted. During this phase, country offices were provided with the necessary assistance in implementing these packages with subsequent operationalization as part of the process. After this phase, our team provided the district offices with access to a direct helpline. This helped significantly in alleviating various degrees of stress, confusion, and frustration amongst most of the staff members. The final result was an overwhelming success (see Figure 8.1).

Figure 8.1: Participants at the Uganda district computerization workshop
Photo courtesy of GOU, 1997

Logistics Management Systems Survey – Lesotho

At the request of the Government of Lesotho (GOL), through the Ministry of Health (MOH), I was requested to assist the country in establishing the current status of its logistics management systems and identify potential strengths and weaknesses. As part of the assignment, the mission was required to come up with practical feasible recommendations to help the MOH in executing its duties and hence minimize stock outs with emphasis on improved quality of health and easy access, including timely and equitable distribution of commodities. Participants came from both NGOs and the MOH.

The assignment was broken down into two main phases. Phase one, which lasted from September 21 to October 11, 2000, included:

- Survey instrument design
- Survey team on-the-job training (plenary, working groups, and field/clinical work)

- Pilot-testing survey questionnaires
- Revising questionnaires
- Finalizing logistics plans for the survey activity.

Phase two, which took place between October 18 and November 5 included:

- Conducting the survey
- Collating and cleaning the data sets
- Producing a report of survey findings
- Presenting findings and recommendations to MOH senior officials.

The overall objective of the survey was to assess the state of the contraceptive logistics management information system in the Kingdom of Lesotho, specifically the following features and capacities of its facilities:

- Personnel profile
- Accessibility
- Monitoring and evaluation systems
- Outreach activities
- Supervision systems
- Personnel level and currency of training
- Data collection systems
- Reporting systems
- Contraceptive supplies and logistics
- Client profile
- Stock out levels
- Stock levels

The deliverable was to produce a report of findings and recommendations. An interesting scenario developed during the report-presentation session. One of the senior members of the MOH asked me (as many people would have done) to present the findings and recommendations. To everybody's pleasant surprise, and after thanking the GOL for inviting me, I handed over the control of the presentation to my national colleagues. The audience stood up and gave the presenting team a standing ovation! Why the standing ovation? By passing on the baton to the nationals and letting them conduct the debriefing session I had done something that was not only unusual but also unprecedented in Lesotho. This same dynamic was demonstrated in many of the countries I served. Technical advisors like me at the time traditionally conducted their respective debriefing sessions. And this time as in many other similar circumstances I let them run the show, hence, the euphoria and excitement from the audience. From a personal and professional perspective preparing and guiding the nationals in instances like this was not only building capacity, it was also empowering them to be more confident (yes, we can do it moment), accountable and pro-active. And as anticipated, the session went on glitch less as confirmed by the satisfactory feedback I received from the audience!

I also need to highlight the fact that the dynamics of this event were not a spur-of-the-moment occurrence. It was a long process that included training the national counterparts, guiding the through data collection, analyses and the presentation preparation activities. This effort included conducting "dry run" sessions during which continuous and participatory feedback was provided.

In summary, this and similar successful experiences served as one of many triangulation processes. They also helped significantly in discarding certain misconceptions about advisors and the good intentions. For example, during one of my missions to Niger, I indicated during my debriefing session that the implementation of the cost recovery system as alleged by the government was not national. This statement seems to have opened a can of warms. Cost recovery was a government policy that was very strictly monitored. So the feedback I received from the participating senior service audience was overwhelmingly in disagreement. What helped and ultimately made my day was a confirmation of my finding from my national counterpart with whom I conducted all field visits.

Figure 8.2: Lesotho – LMIS workshop participants
Photo courtesy of GOL, 2002

Figure 8.3: Lesotho – LMIS workshop working group in session

Figure 8.4: Lesotho – LMIS Workshop Session in progress

Figure 8.5: Lesotho – one national counterpart facilitating one session

<u>Logistics Management Systems – Comoros</u>

The terms of reference and methodology in the Comoros were similar. The differences of course included:

- The Comoros is French-speaking while the Kingdom of Lesotho has English as its official language
- Lesotho is primarily a hilly country while the Comoros is a combination of autonomous islands
- Lesotho is generally cooler while the Comoros is generally warmer and humid.

The cultural and landscape differences in both countries contributed substantially in making both training and survey activities very challenging. In the Comoros, every level of communication had to be in English—a challenge that I handled with ease given my bilingual capabilities. The mission was at the request of the Government of the Comoros (GOC). The pictures presented below are a sample of the participants trained and a cross-section of the public that participated in survey findings session.

Figure 8.6: Comoros – Cross section of LMIS workshop participants
Photo courtesy of GOC, 2001

Figure 8.7: Comoros - One national participant facilitating one of the LMIS workshop sessions

Figure 8.8: Comoros – LMIS training of trainers session in progress

Process Highlights

These were health facility (HF) surveys with nurses, midwives, and clinics as target groups. In both countries, Lesotho and Comoros, assistance included:

- Guiding the nationals on how to select health facilities
- Using sampling frames and randomly selecting appropriate HFs
- Designing and developing survey questionnaires
- Conducting training on how to implements surveys
- Training of trainers (TOT) on effective training protocols
- Pilot-testing survey instruments
- Revising pilot-tested questionnaires
- Conducting HF survey
- Analysing data
- Producing a survey report with findings and recommendations
- Using survey findings to design appropriate training program
- Implementing training program.

Maternal and Child/Family Planning Project Evaluation – Swaziland

Consistent with all technical aid missions, this one was at the request of the Government of Swaziland (GOS) through the ministry of health.

Objectives of the mission included the following:

- Assessing the effectiveness of the project outputs
- Providing baseline data for facility-based indicators of the next reproductive health (RH) component project currently under formulation
- Conduct training of nurses, midwives and other health personnel in interviewing techniques, in order to enable them to participate in the evaluation survey as interviewers.

Procedures

In order to accomplish the above objectives, a set of survey instruments developed by the Population Council was adapted to the Swaziland context. This set of tools was only implemented at the facility level since the unit of concern was the health unit. Data collected will enable the mission to establish the quality of services provided by the different health facilities. Data collected with the second set of tools will confirm contributions from the other key players. This could then be used to establish possible linkages of the successes and accomplishments achieved by the project and corresponding inputs from other agencies.

There was also a second set of questionnaires developed and administered amongst donors (including government, multilateral and bilateral agencies). The main thrust behind this second set was to establish the magnitude and contribution of other agency activities in the health sector and also to establish the levels of collaboration and coordination amongst these organizations.

Training

A three-day training workshop was conducted. The composition of the participants included matrons, nurse/midwives, and other medical staff drawn from the different regions and organizations. The total number trained was 22 (17 enumerators, 4 team leaders and 1 coordinator). Four interviewers were selected from each of the four regions. The broad objectives of the survey, including expectations, were explained to the team as part of the training. During the first day, participants were trained on different interviewing techniques using the questionnaires that were used in the training sessions. This process was also an opportunity for the team to adapt the questions to the Swaziland context. On the second day, the teams were sent to clinics (not sampled for evaluation) to conduct pilot tests of the questionnaires. The pre-test exercise was succeeded by further group review. At this stage, more modifications were made based on the pilot experience. Day three was dedicated to further reviews and group discussions of the field logistics including task distributions.

The following table represents details of the questionnaires used during the training and implementation sessions.

Table 8.1: Description of health facility questionnaires

Questionnaire	Description
INVENT	To collect data on health facility, including staff and level, services provided, levels of commodities and supplies, frequency of supervision, degree of training, adequacy of quality assurance, degree of integration and the quantity and quality of service statistics collected,

	processed and reported. Specific data are collected of key MCH/FP indicators, including maternity services.
STAFF	Data on staff training, experience, and types of services provided with emphasis on MCH, FP, and STD/HIV/AIDS counselling. Some demographic indicators were also collected.
OBSERV	Data on staff performance, including quality of service dispensed to FP clients involving some standard health delivery procedures.
FPEXIT	Data on FP clients (both new and revisits) on level of satisfaction, type of services received, associated costs, and client socio-demographic characteristics and magnitude of integration at the service-provider level.
MCHEXIT	Same as in FPEXIT above, excluding cost-related questions.

Field Work

Questionnaire implementation started soon after the training with a daily schedule. The group was divided into four teams, one team per region. Each team was assigned a team leader. No team member was assigned his/her region of origin in order to minimize possible biases. There was a focal person who operated as a coordinator. Supervisory visits were conducted daily in order to explain and clarify certain issues that came up during the interviewing process. All health facilities sampled were sent a copy of the interview schedule in order to facilitate the exercise and minimize possible disruptions during the team's visit. The teams had very long days starting very early and returning to their lodging sites very late. The day's final activity included a meeting with the different teams. During these sessions, the teams made a final review of all the questionnaires, correcting and updating the ones that required changes. It was the team leader's responsibility to check the individual tools both in the field and at the end of the day. As a result, quality control was performed both in the field and at home soon after the field trip. Every team member was given a copy of an operations guideline to serve as reminders during the fieldwork.

Lessons Learned

The following is a list of lessons learned compiled during the survey.

- There is a need to prepare all logistics for any survey before embarking on the survey itself to avoid confusion between the data collection and the coordinators.
- During the survey, we had learned about our mistakes and loopholes in our "dusty" stations.
- During the survey, we discovered that nurses in one region (Lubombo) were not attending to any clients during after-hours and weekends because they are not paid overtime. One nurse even said, "We let clients go back home and die," especially the maternity and malaria cases.
- visits after any training are essential for all health facilities to ensure the skills acquired during training are put into practice.
- Missed opportunities are still high because of poor integration of health services. In other clinics, health services are still conducted on special days.
- Most registers such as immunization, family planning (FP), and antenatal care (ANC) are incomplete, making it difficult to collect data.
- Ledger books for FP commodities and drugs are not available in a significant number of clinics. In other facilities, the ledger books are available but not complete.
- In most facilities, clients are few because of the distance and transport involved to purchase the required coupons before they can have services in the clinics.
- The survey instruments need to be developed in the country, involving relevant personnel in order to avoid mistakes.
- The number of personnel was not sufficient for the survey and there is a need to spend at least one day with one health facility to do proper observation. The survey time-frame was too short.
- Team leaders have much work to do. It would be appreciated if they are given more incentives.
- In the patient cards, dates of immigration are not written.
- Children under the age of five are not weighed and there is no charting of clients' health cards.

Figure 8.9: Swaziland – Cross section of evaluation survey team
Photo courtesy of GOS, 1999

Figure 8.10: Swaziland – Training session of evaluation survey
team participants

Figure 8.11: Part of the Swaziland evaluation survey team
Photo courtesy of GOS, 1999

Figure 8.12: More members of the Swaziland evaluation survey team
Photo courtesy of GOS, 1999

Reproductive Health Commodity Security (RHCS): Regional Workshop, Colombo, Sri Lanka

This was a regional workshop hosted by the Government of Sri Lanka (GOSL) and United Nations Population Fund (UNFPA). The extensive and demanding workshop was conducted in 2005 with participants actively working daily and nightly. Participating countries included Afghanistan, Iran, Pakistan, Bhutan, Nepal, Bangladesh, Sri Lanka, India, and the Maldives. A sample outcome of a case study produced by one of the participating countries during the workshop is included on page 353.

The sessions concentrated primarily on a model that I developed, titled "Reproductive Health Commodity Security Analysis and Planning System" (RAPSYS). The training processes of the pragmatic and inclusive model started with participatory and didactic sessions followed by working groups.

RAPSYS Highlights

General objective: to strengthen RHCS programming capacity.

Specific objectives:

- Weight RHCS determinants (composite indicator)
- Identifying relevant gaps
- Develop corresponding strategies
- Develop an RHCS action plan (RAP)

Background: Maternal and infant morbidity and mortality rates remain a global challenge. Based on latest reports, mitigation efforts have been discouraging. Unsustainable fertility rates continue to rise unabated especially in low and middle-income countries (LMICs) and based on the latest reports, vulnerability is not only limited to these countries. For example, in the U.S. about 40% of all pregnancies are unintended (NYT, 2016). Significant gaps in reproductive health and rights continue to escalate. According to a recent United Nations Population Fund (UNFPA, 2014) report, 225 million women do not have access to contraceptives. This shortfall is universal and only exacerbates an already dire situation. Inability to address these challenges has many implications, including ubiquitous poor quality of health for mother and child, unsustainable population dynamics, and fertility rates.

Efforts to improve reproductive health services (FP service specifically) are generally inconsistent. Challenges range from vulnerable countries' dependence on donor support/funding to inability to establish sustainable intervention strategies. The last six decades illustrate how programs have gone awry. This is by no means an attempt to marginalize achievements. Successes do exist and will continue to serve as "gold standards" and fodder for lessons learned.

Program Intervention: Reasons for some of these dismal performances include limited access to quality services, qualified staff, high attrition rates, inadequate supply chain and logistics management systems, limited funding mechanisms and poor infrastructure — all culminating to lack of required relevant and appropriate commodities.

These poor outcomes prompted me to develop the Reproductive Health Commodity Security Analysis and Planning System (RAPSYS) model, implemented by national experts using their different levels of thematic expertise and invaluable field experience. The final outcome is an action plan made up of different relevant components and factors that define reproductive health commodity security.

Methodology: The participatory model was pilot-tested and successfully implementation in ten Asian countries. It is based on qualitative expert assessments of pre-defined 12 key elements ranging from enabling environment to monitoring and evaluation (M&E).

The five-day workshop was conducted in Sri Lanka. During these sessions, participants were given background knowledge of commodity management. A significant amount of time was then spent describing the model, its applicability, and requirements. Participants were guided through the various elements. They were then given a demonstration using previously pilot-tested results.

The required qualitative assessment used is analogous with the Delphi methodology. In this case, participants use a Likert scale to measure country performance. The scales range from 1 (inadequate) to 5 (significant). The participants were then divided into thematic teams. Each group conducted the assessment individually and collectively. This was followed by an analysis of the intra- and inter-group concordance. A final outcome was then agreed on at the thematic and country levels. After these agreements, teams (lead by a coordinator and rapporteur) are then given an opportunity to present their country results. Questions from members of other groups and countries are used to improve the teamwork and ultimate report — an action plan.

Findings: There is adequate evidence that the conventional approach in program design and implementation continues to show different levels of understanding of the expected outcomes. This model has helped vulnerable countries in streamlining their interventions, making them more results-based, efficient, effective, sustainable, and accountable.

As confirmed by the pre- and post-tests, participants expressed a lot of appreciation. They also elaborated on their earlier understanding of what was expected. And the new exposure and experience gave them another perspective of their respective countries' limitations. They all demonstrated a high degree of satisfaction and self-fulfillment. Many thought an exercise like this was not within their reach and pleasantly surprised themselves on their level of achievement and success. They all voluntarily sent complimentary emails to me expressing both their individual gratitude and those from their respective governments. A sample of one of the emails received was from the Sri Lanka UNFP representative, which is presented in Chapter 7, Professional Compliments.

One key motivation of this workshop was a challenge open to various Asian countries by UNFPA. The fund promised to donate certain amounts of funding to the participating countries; especially those whom the Agency believed had a comprehensive and compelling plan. Many of them had compelling action plans, though not every country received funding.

A plausible case study developed by one of the participating countries is available upon request.

Lessons included:

- Panel selection (very critical)
- Role and level of coordinator (important)
- Panel composition should be relevant to determinants
- Level of responsibility of panel members (critical)
- Minimum of 2 days required for meeting
- Initial group of panelists represents RHCS ad hoc committee
- Selection process of group moderator and rapporteurs (critical)
- Rapporteurs are responsible for first draft report
- Media participation important
- Limit total number of participants to 25
- Leadership role of National government (very important factor)
- Panel members come from different levels
- Participatory nature of meeting is a strong motivating factor.
- Strong level of ownership amongst participants also a motivating factor

RAPSYS Methodology

Panel Selection

Panel of experts (POE)

Group Composition

Group members (5-9)

Rapporteur (1)

Moderators (1)

General rapporteur

Plenary

Inputs

Model

Outputs

Group Work

Assessment

Strategies

Action plan

M&E framework

Plenary

Group presentation

Peer review

Draft Committee

Rapporteurs

General rapporteur (1)

RAPSYS Highlights

- Practical
- Simple
- Participatory

- Synergistic
- Inclusive
- Multi-sectoral
- Adaptable
- Programmatic

Capacity Building Challenges

The diverse nature of strengthening capacity, like other areas of program management, remains daunting, fluid, and complex. At a personal level, I have to the extent possible, tried to explore and implement environment-driven strategies. These offer more flexibility, and at the same time, contribute in motivating participants in addition to avoiding an "every-size-fits-all" approach.

Countries vary with diversities ranging from cultural to social to ethnicity to degree of prioritizing. All these complexities need to be included in most interventions. These diversities notwithstanding, concentrated and compelling efforts to help remain the "modus operandi."

In every intervention, there is the need to recognize the significant effects of both internal and external factors. These do generally influence the success levels of any programs. While internal factors can generally be managed and addressed, the same cannot be said about external factors. For example, after nationals are trained, there is a tendency to look for better opportunities: an action that is beyond the control of any programs. The prevalence of these movements is astounding. I have always considered people moving to look for greener pastures as an inevitable quality of human dynamics. An internal factor that negatively affects many interventions is the perception of capacity building (CB) as an event. This observation reminds me again of my high school teacher and his continuous "quizzing" philosophy! CB is unique in several ways and should always be perceived as a process — a continuous skills update. As such, it can never be over-emphasized.

There is every reason to believe that, all these challenges notwithstanding and while successes could never be easily quantified, the benefits far outweigh the risks. Capacity building remains a building block that needs support and motivation from both suppliers and beneficiaries.

Figure 8.11: Asia - Participants of RHCS regional workshop in Sri Lanka
Photo courtesy of Jesse, 2005

Figure 8.12: Asia – (L–R): Me, MOH, UN rep, 2 senior government officials
and first secretary, MOH

Figure 8.13: Asia – RHCS regional workshop, Sri Lanka working group

Figure 8.14: Asia – Cross section of RHCS regional workshop participants

PART V: COMPLEMENTARY PROGRAM MANAGEMENT STRATEGIES

CHAPTER 9: Monitoring and Evaluation in Program Management

Introduction

This chapter is taken from my book, *Monitoring & Evaluation: Data Management Systems,* published in 2015. Over the past decades, international funding agencies, as well as recipient national governments in developing countries, have expended substantial amounts of money on developing and implementing programs. Both have increasingly been interested in putting in place sustainable and effective programs. This has made it necessary for all the players involved in a donor-funded program to understand the dynamics of these programs. This section is intended to help bridge the gap that currently exists between different players — donors as supply and beneficiaries as demand parties — who are both involved in program management. This is because program management has been globalized to include the different players with diverse experiences and varying levels of exposure. And during this period, monitoring and evaluation (M&E) has significantly evolved as a complementary and essential component of effective program management. The urge to achieve high-quality results has also been a strong motivating factor.

In the most recent past, and currently, M&E has included "lessons". Lessons learned effectively provide program management stakeholders with evidence-based documentation and an opportunity to identify, highlight, and address strengths and weaknesses of achievements made during the project life cycle. Lessons also serve as an invaluable, critical, and compelling input to informed decision-making processes. Some key questions that often need to be answered include: Are we doing the right thing? What can we replicate? What can we adjust? Does the intervention continue to be focused? The following sections provide some information that would help in addressing many M&E nuances.

My experience dealing with data of different types and categories spans over four decades. From attending a survey technician-training program after high school to engineering school, data management has played and continues to play a very significant role in my professional life. And the challenges encountered over this period of time continue to evolve exponentially! The most recent paradigm transformation in data management is the proliferation of analytics — a domain that has enabled businesses, industry, academia, banks, etc. to exhale and address competing forces with might and vitality.

With the increase in the number of fields relying on quality data management, the time has come for a comprehensive, easy to use, current manual that guides the reader through the data management process. The innumerable methods used for data collection and processing has created controversies in a variety of fields ranging from academic, business, organizations, and government to science. Demand to understand the transformation of data into meaningful results for decision-making is at an all-time high. In a variety of institutions: Hospitals, armed forces, space stations, small and large businesses, government and non-government organizations as well as in the public domain, processed data increases our knowledge (Pate and Fridell, 1994; Bennett, 2003; Daly and Bourke, 2000; Andrus, 2006; United States National Aeronautics and Space Administration, 1991). Data management handled by computers is here to stay. Its cross-sectional appeal to almost every field in very nearly every part of the world induces us to bid the question, "How does it all work?"

This background aims to evaluate the literature available on data management. The principal point is to ascertain whether, or not, a concise manual on the data management life cycle exists. If there is such a book, where does it need improvement? Books, periodicals, and university papers were amongst the types of literature reviewed from 45 countries around the world, representing 400 languages. The library catalogues used data from 1000 BC to present. What is apparent is that the current literature available is limited to information relating to input and output. Among all of the different components outlined in the framework, the focus is on the missing link in the literature that explains how data management works. The mystery begins after the raw data are collected.

If we weigh the pros and cons of using data in computers and in personal digital assistant devices (PDAs), it becomes very clear that their benefits outweigh their drawbacks. A power outage causes chaos in a world reliant on technical equipment to amass data, process, and create knowledge from them. This is slowly becoming less threatening with the increase of solar batteries and other reliable generators that are in even the smallest of handheld devices (Lee, 1973; American Society of Heating, Refrigerating and Air-conditioning Engineers, 1986). PDAs are continuously being adapted to suit the needs of real-time knowledge (Mekelburg, 2005). This change reduces the economic loss of power outages, making businesses even more anxious to digitally process data.

Expensive data storage warehouses that are bomb-resistant, temperature controlled secure facilities are essential to a society functioning through data. This drawback appears minimal. As evidenced by the United States army defence, reports by Rimikis (2008) and Bennett (2003), it is obvious that society continues to increase its reliance on real-time knowledge via data (Helal, 1999; Elahi, 2006; Fry, 1986).

Governments and other organizations are vulnerable to malicious manipulation of data, as are those who use devices for inputting data such as telephone and internet banking. Someone in sales could extract keywords from a popular online chat discussion or community group to use for increasing sales, either through learning essential target words, or advertising to those more likely to buy the product. The user of the PDA is vulnerable to malicious manipulation by others unless shielded by the knowledge of how the data life cycle should work. Without understanding the life cycle of data from conceptualization to the decision-making results, the product user is limited. Despite the risks, there is an ever-increasing preference for coded information, which suggests that the usefulness of data outweighs the risks involved. The number of people who want to understand what happens to the collected data is escalating.

The literature that currently exists generally highlights one or a few areas associated with data collection and input and these are often specific to a field (Bickman, 1998; Grover and Vriens, 2006; Box, 1978). There are guides to conducting sample survey research (Parker, 1992; Kalton, 1983; Kish, 1965) as well as guides that explain the basic concepts of statistical sampling (Cochran, 1977; Williams, 1978; Thompson, 1992) and theory books that explain sample survey theories (Hansen, Hurwits, Madow, 1953). In addition, numerous guides instruct as to how to interpret statistics (Miles and Huberman, 1994), spell out the principles of measurement, reliability, and variability (Portney and Watkins, 2000) and even offer a common-sense perspective on statistics (Henkel, 1976). An abundance of literature is available to educate one on data collection, input and output.

There are a limited number of books to educate those interested in statistical software packages. Statistical software packages widely used are Statistical Package for the Social Sciences (SPSS) — currently known as IBM SPSS Statistics — SAS and Stata. In some factions such as statisticians, Epi Info is also used, but little information is available on its pros and cons. What are their advantages and disadvantages and how does each software package affect the life cycle of a datum? Morgan, Orlando and Gloeckner (2000) provide instruction for use of SPSS at an introductory level, while Boslaugh (2005) provides an intermediate SPSS guide to programming. Field (2005) plays a role in unveiling the mystery behind statistical software by providing information on SPSS. However, to determine which software package is best for one's needs, these books would not help, as they do not include SAS or Stata information. A chemist, nuclear biologist (Engelhardt, 2001), or police force who might want to know the extent to which complaints of policy violations happen and how frequently officers use force (Pate and Friddell, 1994) would be better suited to using SAS. While those primarily interested in data analysis would thrive using Stata (Good, 2005).

A few books compare statistical software (Francis, 1979; Francis, 1981; Keeling, 2006). However, as they only compare statistical software, the books are merely another piece of the whole structure of data life cycle. Furthermore, the reviews of the statistical software packages are not current. What is required is an inclusive guide that explains how one establishes which software package is best to manage their data.

Presently, a person interested in learning what happens to data once keyed into a device would leave a bookstore with both arms full of highly technical texts, reference guides, and how-to books that are area specific. Learning how to input data and read the output becomes clear from the available literature either associated with the device, or in a technical manual, but an answer as to what happens to the data is vague. The overlapping of information makes the undertaking to ascertain the life cycle of data a wearying affair. There is no easy-to-follow manual that describes all of the basic concepts of a data management system. Such a manual should demonstrate, for example, how the process begins, what to set up, how to put in order an instrument type, an understanding of flow and skip patterns, and how to put the process through a preliminary check. It should also include a portrayal of an integrated data management system and its components. A clear understanding of how data cleaning works, how to write a report, and knowing how to chose appropriate software would complete the necessary list of elements of a manual that wholly explains how data works.

A concise, user-friendly manual that takes a person through data management process in its entirety does not exist. There are books, journals, and websites that touch upon various aspects of data management, yet they are either overly technical, only briefly mention a portion of the whole, or are heavily concentrated on a particular area of interest. To unravel the mystery of data management, a book written in clear language that appeals to all fields would be a positive addition to the narrative history of events that alter the world.

One adage that strongly and appropriately describes different forms of data is "garbage in garbage out" (GIGO). And interestingly, this adage is not only limited to conventional data as described above, it also includes a human dimension. For example, healthy eating habits correlate positively with an improved quality of life and health.

That is where Program Management Indicator Screening Matrix (PRISM) comes in. It is a model influenced by the gap between when data are collected and the outcomes they generate. In this manual, I have taken a holistic approach in an attempt to improve the quality of data; starting from when they are collected. PRISM screens every indicator using a multi-dimensional approach. The criteria defining this strategy are simple, direct, inclusive, and analytical. The model requires a good knowledge of how strategic frameworks like Logframe and Strategic Objective Model function. The process requires assessments conducted by experts using a set of pre-defined criteria. A composite score is then analyzed to decide if an indicator qualifies to be included in the program or not. Thematic working group exercises in the primer include, health, good governance, gender, population, and development, etc.

The manual covers topics that include amongst others, program life cycle, Logframe and Strategic Objective approach, program definition and corresponding algorithm, extensive complementary research and the model itself etc. In this era of the Sustainable Development Goals, nothing could be more compelling than such a primer. It has been used in Africa, Asia, Pacific Islands countries and was pilot-tested by a team of experts at a three-day partnership conference in NY. An abridged version of PRISM is a chapter in my book titled "Monitoring and Evaluation: Data Management Systems". It has also been presented at International conferences in Toronto, Canada and Bali, Indonesia.

Background

M&E is something people do in their daily lives (Ramboll, 2005). They observe what is happening or has happened around them; for example, they observe the amount of money they have in their bank account at a specific time of the month. They assess the current situation and then compare it to their expectations or goals. If there is a difference, they decide whether the difference is significant — did they save the amount they had planned towards their annual holiday, and if not, will that significantly affect their holiday plans. They then consider ways in which they can address these differences or shortcomings.

M&E can be considered as a practical management tool, used in reviewing performance (Ramboll, 2005). M&E helps in learning from experience, which can consequently be used to improve the designing as well as the functioning of projects. Quality assurance and accountability are integral components of M&E, which help to ensure that project objectives are met, in addition to achieving key outputs and impacts (Ramboll, 2005).

Diakonia developed a self-assessment tool in Cambodia in the early 2000s, which included eight capacity areas. Diakonia's tool uses a scoring system, similar to those used by USAID and Pact. M&E was one of the key capacity areas. The full list of the capacity areas include:

- Advocacy problem identification
- Research
- Goal setting
- Indicators
- Stakeholder analysis
- Action plan
- Coalition building
- Monitoring & evaluation

In order to make the strengths as well as the weaknesses of an organization's capacity easy to identify, a visual representation of the model is provided. It uses a spider chart as shown in Figure 9.1. According to Raynor (2009), a critic of such a model, it is too skills-oriented; although, it covers all the skill areas of interest.

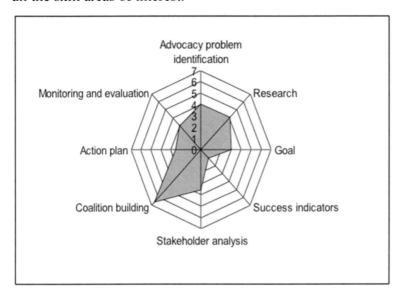

Figure 9.1: Self-assessment spider chart

According to de Mendoza (2010), all donors are expected to follow monitoring processes regularly. This, in some instances, includes a six-month review with both the stakeholders and beneficiaries. The aim is to help strengthen the self-assessments of progress, improve documentation of the implementation processes, and facilitate timely modifications as needed (de Mendoza, 2010).

Ramboll (2005) observed that it is necessary to specify the purpose as well as the scope of the M&E because it helps clarify what is to be expected of the M&E procedure, how comprehensive it ought to be, and what time and resources will be needed to implement it.

An M&E plan helps identify the report, which includes the M&E information and sets out the forums or meetings at which the information or the reports will be presented and discussed (WFP, 2014). Thus, the M&E plan sets out the important formal feedback opportunities, ensures that M&E reports are made available to all stakeholders, and the appropriate formal, as well as informal, discussions are held concerning indispensable findings (WFP, 2014).

According to WFP (2014), the following guidelines should be followed when writing an M&E report:

- There should be consistency with regard to the amount of information to be conveyed.
- The focus should be on the results achieved rather than on the expected results.
- A section must be included describing the reasons for the collection of data.
- A section must be included describing the sources of data and the methods used in collecting data for the findings to be objectively verifiable.
- It is essential to be clear on who the target audience is.
- The language used in writing should be understandable to the target audience.
- The progress reports should be submitted on time.
- A brief summary (approximately one page) that accurately captures the content, as well as the recommendations in the report, should be provided at the beginning.
- Technical terms or acronyms should be defined, and there should be consistency in the use of definitions and terminologies.
- Complex data should be presented with the help of summary tables, figures, graphs, maps, and photographs.

- Only the most significant words or key points should be highlighted using bold or italics.
- References for sources as well as authorities should be included.
- A table of contents should be included for reports with more than five pages.

Basic Principles of Monitoring and Evaluation (M&E)

The term "monitoring and evaluation" is sometimes misconstrued, as if they were a single thing. Yet monitoring and evaluation are, in reality, two different sets of organizational activities, which while related, are quite dissimilar.

Monitoring of a project/program is the methodical collection and analysis of information pertaining to or derived from observations of the work processes during the progress of a project.

The main aim of monitoring is to diagnose whether the work (work management plan) is working out as expected with the resources allocated, and/or to use the data gathered to improve, if necessary, the efficiency of those processes, as well as to perhaps positively affect the effectiveness of a work output/outcome project. Monitoring is often based on measuring achievement against set targets, as well as the successful completion activities that are planned and budgeted during the planning phases of work. It also helps keep the progress of work on schedule, or by proposing/making corrections to the work plan's budget or schedule to get it back on track by making management aware whenever things are going wrong.

If monitoring is done properly it lays down a useful foundation for the evaluation that will follow. Monitoring also enables a researcher to determine if the resources available (inputs) are sufficient and whether they are being optimally utilized if the project/program staff's capacity is appropriate and sufficient, and if the realization of both the project/program outputs and outcomes are progressing as planned.

Monitoring is an internal function in any organization or project and involves the establishment of indicators of efficiency, effectiveness, and impact. Monitoring includes the setting up of systems used in the collection of information related to the selected indicators, as well as collecting and recording the data/information, analyzing the data/information, deriving conclusions, formulating recommendations, and, lastly, in applying those recommendations selected and resourced to day-to-day operations and overall program management.

Evaluation of a research project involves the comparison between actual project/program impact and its agreed-upon strategic plans. Evaluation is also concerned with what is set out to be done, what has to be accomplished, and how it is to be accomplished. Evaluation can be formative, meaning that it can take place during the progress of the project/program with the main intention of improving/altering the strategic thrust of the project. It can also be summative, that is, it can draw lessons from a completed project/program, which may be used in subsequent program planning exercises.

The common aspect between monitoring and evaluation is that they are both geared to learning from what is being done and the manner in which it is being done, by focusing on efficiency, effectiveness, and impact. Efficiency helps to determine whether the input is appropriate when compared to output. The input can usually be valued in terms of time, money, staff/consultants deployed, and equipment and supplies allocated amongst others. The effectiveness of a research project measures the extent to which the specific objectives are achieved. Measuring the impact of a development program or project helps determine whether the factors such as policies and resources deployed made a difference to the problem being addressed; that is, was the strategy employed useful or vital to achieving the intended outcomes and the overall goal.

The following are the most commonly used terms under M&E:

Inputs: include the human, financial, technical, and material resources used in developing the intervention, and can be categorized as management structure, technical expertise, equipment, and funds.

Activities: include actions taken or work plans developed and work performed, such as training workshops conducted, coordination meetings organized, procurements made, quality of physical work undertaken, and monitoring conducted.

Outputs: include the capital goods, products, and services resulting from development intervention, such as the number of people trained, the number of workshops conducted, and the number of widgets constructed /manufactured.

Outcomes: changes observed/achieved pertaining to short-term as well as medium-term effects traceable to a project/program intervention's outputs, such as on productivity due to increased skills derived through training; additional demand for existing or new services experienced; sales or distribution of desired program products to intended beneficiaries, and new employment opportunities created.

Impact: the program's long-term consequences, which may have positive and/or negative effects such as an improved standard of living for a target population.

Monitoring and Evaluation Plan

The monitoring and evaluation plan (commonly abbreviated as the M&E plan) is a document, which is employed by the project team that can help plan and manage all monitoring and evaluation activities in the whole cycle of a particular project. It is necessary for it to be shared and used amongst all the stakeholders, in addition to being shared with program donors if so desired.

An M&E plan enables those responsible for program management to keep track of what indicators should be monitored, when to take measurements, where to monitor, and when to conduct evaluations. The M&E plan, which may take the form of a typical management by objectives (MBO) work plan that is specific to activities based on monitoring and evaluation, generally includes the following:

- Goals and objectives of the program and matrix of outputs and outcomes associated with these.
- Questions to be asked and methodologies to be employed in conducting and monitoring M&E.
- Work-plan or implementation plan.
- Matrix of monitoring indicators as well as their intended results
- Proposed timetable for all the activities related to monitoring and a separate indication of when evaluation(s) (baseline survey, mid-term or mid-cycle, final) will take place.
- Samples of pretested monitoring and evaluation instruments to be used in gathering data.

A good M&E plan should be rigid on one hand and flexible on the other. It should be rigid in the sense that it should be well planned and thought out, and flexible in the sense that it can account for any change, which could improve the monitoring and evaluation practice. Both rigidity and flexibility are equally important because of the ever-changing program environment and because of certain fast-moving conflict environments.

The M&E plan enables all stakeholders involved to have a common frame of reference that details all the M&E activities, which will occur as the project progresses. The M&E plan also helps signal and identify changes in data flows as the project/program progresses over a given period and helps funnel data into flows that contribute to the subsequent evaluation processes.

To sum up, an adequate M&E plan is very useful in management and its development is a "best practice". It should be employed as a reference tool throughout and should frequently be updated in order to incorporate unplanned interruptions or shortfalls of resources such as materials, manpower, and, money, and illustrate how such unplanned events might affect the production of outputs and the quality and timeliness of desired outcomes. The status of constant variables inherent to the management/operational work plan should be updated rigorously by specific staff and according to the schedule in the management plan. These updated monitoring indices should be presented in frequent biweekly or monthly staff meetings. The relevant audience should include the program management and the exact personnel specific for each activity or intervention. This group would then follow the approved methods and use preauthorized sources of data collected.

USAID requires that the program's official M&E plan should be completed one month after the signing of a program or project contract. Since an M&E plan is intended for use in an organized set of coordination meetings, its creators should be those involved in the program and should also include the strategic partners. This ensures that those who designed the M&E plan are also the users. The other advantage of this participatory approach is that it ensures the project team has the support of the major stakeholders and it also serves as a safeguard against arbitrary intervention by strategic partners and/or other stakeholders.

There is no particular standardized structure or template for an M&E plan, but an effective M&E should include the parts listed below:

- Executive Summary
- Project Background
- M&E Planning
- Monitoring and Evaluation Systems
- Project Risk Matrix
- M&E Information Map
- M&E Work Plan Matrix
- M&E Timetable
- References
- Annexes

The outline above can be modified with the consensus of the stakeholders to best fit the communication, program, and organizational needs of these stakeholders. Other documents may also be used as reference aids when writing the M&E plan. These include:

- Project/program proposal
- Logical framework
- Results framework
- Checklist for M&E plan

These supporting documents usually have information that is included in the M&E plan. They also make referencing much easier as well as ensure continuity between all project-related documents. The depth/detail of information included in the M&E plan should be more specific than that found in the supporting documents and some cases may, occasionally, call for some (contextual) revision to the goals and objectives as stated in the original documents.

It is important to carefully consider both resource and budget constraints when making an M&E plan. One of the greatest of these is the cost of data collection, which is usually divided into human resource expenditure and other financial costs such as computer time, printing, copying, etc. A program manager should be able to tell if the time proposed, as well as the resources made available, would be sufficient to cover all the described/planned M&E activities. A program manager should also model whether the value derived from the data collection process is worth the budgeted expenses of the data collection process.

A properly executed M&E plan is usually very helpful in the identification of problems, in the planning and the implementation, in reviewing the progress of the project in terms of intended outcomes, as well as in making any necessary adjustments within the project.

Most organizations consider M&E as more of an internal process requirement rather than as a strategic management tool. Although, it is the duty of management to provide stakeholder/donor reassurance that their money is being well spent, the primary purpose of an M&E plan should be to help the organization (or the project) monitor how it is progressing against the objectives, to show if it is having the intended impact, whether it is working efficiently, and if there is a need to improve the processes and then show ways and means of improving it. All these reasons make the M&E tools the key pillars of a strategic framework, which includes the vision, the problem analysis, and the project/program's strategic value.

Program Indicator Screening Matrix (PRISM)

Introduction

Historically, development program implementation has been plagued with a complex set of challenges, which vary from the program design stage to implementation plans and processes, to long-term sustainability. A key element of program design and implementation has been the selection of the relevant indicators and the capacity to optimize its robustness and mitigate the prevalence of bias. These challenges continue to influence effective program management initiatives. Attempts to address some of these issues vary from program to program. For example, what some program designers may identify as low-level indicators in practice, are sometimes higher-level indicators. Such a scenario could misrepresent or affect a program's potential results.

The PRISM tool is a table/matrix, which analyzes each indicator. It is an exercise executed by a team of experts who are selected and grouped based on their relevant expertise. An initial attempt is made to clearly describe the matrix, its limitations, and how it assists in addressing some of the challenges faced by program implementing partners in establishing meaningful indicators. The final outcome of this exercise is a consensus or high degree of concordance (as opposed to discordance) amongst the program leadership and staff (team) members.

The presentation outline of the PRISM is as shown:

- Introduction
- Objectives
- Relevance
- Target audience
- Evaluation life cycle (ELC)
- Program design framework (PDF)
- Themes
- PRISM: A Composite score framework
- Lessons learned

The PRISM should highlight the following points:

- Evaluation — demand-driven
- Participatory
- Inclusive
- Bottom-Up Strategy (BUS)

- Consensus-based
- Random thematic subgroups
- Intra-thematic group concordance
- Inter-thematic group concordance
- Bar (gold standard vs. effective)
- Binary outcome
- Delphi methodology
- Mapping
- Scope: Africa, Asia, and Pacific Island Countries

General objectives

To strengthen the knowledge of IPs, PMs, and other key stakeholders and emphasize sustainable engagement in program management and implementation processes.

This is in an attempt to address existing nuances, highlight the synergies that exist amongst the different result levels of the SFW, and hence facilitate a common ground between potential evaluators and different interested parties.

Specific objectives

- Streamline the monitoring plan by improving indicator causal links at all result levels
- Mitigate duplication of indicators
- Establish authentic contributions between different result levels
- Establish meaningful synergies amongst different result levels: no lower level result can contribute to more than one upper-level result
- Strengthen the program design
- Promote a common understanding amongst key actors
- Minimize cost and optimize the number of indicators included in the program.

Relevance of the PRISM

- Improve intended and unintended intervention results and make foreign aid more focused with evidence-based results
- Establish more effective, continuous and sustainable synergies amongst frontline forces, IPs, Funding agencies, stakeholders and beneficiaries.

Audience targeted by the PRISM

- Funding agencies
- IPs
- Program managers
- Relevant stakeholders
- Evaluators
- Development partners.

Evaluation of the Life Cycle (See Figure 9.2)

Demand recognition

The evaluation process demands that its attributes be identified and preserved by all the project's stakeholders.

Evaluation team identified

It is important to identify the best team to carry out the evaluation process. The team may either be drawn from the staff of the organization (self-evaluation) or have an external team carry out the evaluation process (external evaluation). In some instances, the project staff and the intended beneficiaries may be included in the team (participatory evaluation).

Inception report developed

An inception report that summarizes the review of the document undertaken by the evaluation team should contain approximately 20 to 25 pages. This report is used to set out the project's objectives, the suitable approach to be used, the methodology, the working program, and the study team for the present study.

Evaluation process implemented

The inception report should be revised where necessary and the implementation of the evaluation process should be carried out.

Draft report developed and presented

It is necessary to develop a draft evaluation report before submitting the final evaluation report. This report should be presented to the stakeholders, who should give their feedback after the presentation for further action (revision).

Final report developed and submitted

The final evaluation report should be developed and submitted after making the necessary revision to the draft evaluation report based on the feedback of the stakeholders.

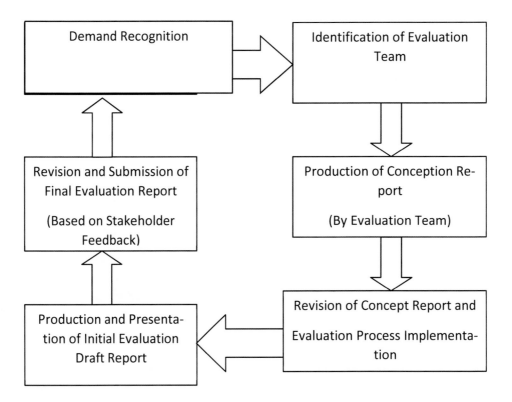

Figure 9.2: Evaluation life cycle
Source: Lainjo, 2013

Shapiro (2001) illustrated the effect of M&E using the cycle shown in Figure 9.3. It is worth noting that monitoring, as well as adjustments, should be carried out several times before one is ready to evaluate and re-plan.

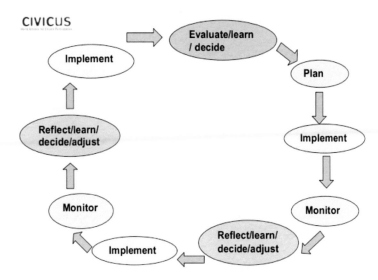

Figure 9.3: M&E data management cycle (Shapiro, 2001)

It is important to use M&E systematically because there is no guarantee that it will solve the problems without the relevant and interested parties undertaking the work necessary to formulate this evaluative process. Monitoring and evaluation can help identify the problems as well as their causes, suggest possible solutions to the problems, raise questions concerning the strategy and assumptions, provide and encourage action on information and insight, and increase the possibility of being able to make positive development difference. Various methods of carrying out evaluation exist. Some of the most common methods include:

Self-evaluation

An organization or a project management team assesses the program through the administration of structured questionnaires, or through self-criticism about how well it is doing; as a means of learning as well as improving practice. This calls for the staff of an organization or team to be very honest and self-reflective in order to effectively achieve this.

Participatory evaluation

This requires as many members of the project/program team as possible to participate. It is more of an internal evaluation, whereby project staff and sometimes the intended beneficiaries are called upon to work together on the evaluation. Outsiders may only be invited to act as process facilitators, but not as evaluators.

Rapid Participatory Appraisal

This is a qualitative method of evaluating, which involves a review of secondary data, semi-structured interviews, testimonies of key informants, direct observations by the evaluators, group interviews, diagrams, games, maps, and calendars. It was originally used in rural areas but has also extensively been applied in other communities as well.

External Evaluation

This involves the choosing of an outsider or an outsider team to carry out the evaluation.

Interactive Evaluation

This involves free flowing participation between the evaluation team or outside evaluator, and the organization or the project that is being evaluated. An insider may sometimes be included as part of the evaluation team.

Program Design Frameworks

Table 9.1 is a table showing program design frameworks:

Table 9.1: Program design frameworks

Type	Result Levels	Agencies
Logic Framework (Logframe)	• Impact • Output • Outcome	UN,CIDA,EU, Au-sAID, DfID, WB
Strategic Objective	▪ Strategic Objective ▪ Program Objectives ▪ Program Sub-objectives	USAID, UNDP

Source: Lainjo, 2013

Logframe

Figure 9.4 is a diagram showing IF-THEN chain results:

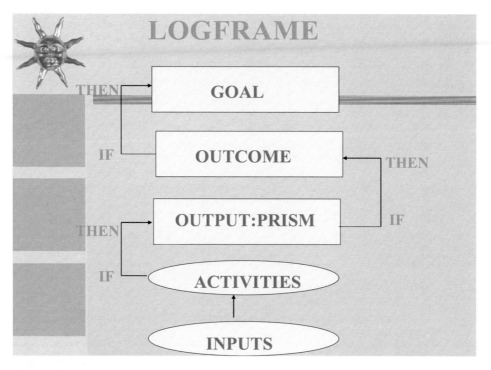

Figure 9.4: Logframe
Source: Lainjo, 2013

Testing internal and external logic: *If* the outputs are delivered through planned activities using the relevant inputs and the corresponding assumptions in the output, outcome and impact levels; they remain valid. So that the desired outcome will materialize; leading to the intended impact.

The goal of the logframe is described in terms of quality of life. The outcome of the logframe is determined by asking the question, "How will this goal be achieved?" and is described in terms of use, attitudinal change, and political commitment. For example, access to comprehensive reproductive health (RH) services increased. The other example is the utilization of age/sex-disaggregated data improved.

The Output refers to "deliverables"; time-bound strategies. For example:

- Increased availability of comprehensive RH services

- Improved quality of RH services
- Improved environment for addressing practices that are harmful to women's health
- National development plan and sectoral plans in line with ICPD/POA
- Increased availability of sex-disaggregated population-related data
- Increased information on gender issues

The inputs include resources such as staff, overhead costs, materials, equipment, and other project costs such as data processing, report writing, printing, and dissemination of results. (See Table 9.2)

Table 9.2: Strategic framework and M&E summary

Component	Description	Monitoring	Evaluation	Criteria* (See Table 9.3)
Goal	Described in terms of quality of life	No	Yes	Sustainability Impact
Outcome	Described in terms of use, attitudinal change, and political commitment	No	Yes	Effectiveness Relevance
Output	Concerned with "deliverables", time-bound strategies	Yes	Yes	Efficiency
Activities		Yes	Yes	Efficiency

Input	Include re-sources such as staff, over-head costs, materials, equipment	Yes	Yes	Efficiency

Table 9.3: OECD/DAC working group criteria definition

Criteria	Description
Sustainability	Measures the possibilities for the continuity of the benefits of aid activity, even after the funding by the donor has been withdrawn or terminated
Impact	Intended to cover/expose both positive and negative changes resulting from the development intervention
Effectiveness	Measures how well the aid activities attain their stated objectives
Relevance	Shows how well the aid activities are suited to the policies and the priorities of the donor, the recipients and the target group
Efficiency	Measures the outputs, both qualitative and quantitative, with respect to the inputs

M&E – Analysis Case Study

Background

In a typical evaluation term of reference, evaluators are often required to assess the extent to which inputs (human/financial resources, materials, etc.) contribute to the output during and after program implementation.

The case study (human resources) represents partial actual findings of an evaluation exercise conducted in a funding agency's office. In the office, there was also a consensus by many staff members that, with regard to workloads, while there was an increase in numbers of staff as a result of the restructuring exercise, the increase had not been proportionate to the workloads. Staff members continue to be faced with additional tasks that have cumulatively resulted in additional and higher stress levels. The reluctance of staff members to assist their colleagues in accomplishing certain tasks during high demand periods has only exacerbated an already dire situation.[ix] In Figure 9.5, an attempt has been made to establish a possible link or association between "absenteeism" and work performed from 2008 to 2010. In this context, the number of sick days will be considered a proxy for stress levels. This analysis will help explain some of the concerns raised by staff and help management introduce an informed decision strategy that will contribute to improving staff performance.

Analysis

Based on the average number of sick days taken by staff during the period 2008 to 2010, there is evidence, as illustrated in Figure 9.5, that there was an increasing trend during that interval.[x] The figure also shows that this trend peaked in 2010. While one might suspect that the increase in sick days might have been caused by other reasons, there is the likelihood that the significant increase of "absenteeism" in 2010 could have also been caused by higher stress levels possibly related to higher staff workloads as indicated earlier. The figures also suggest that during the last year, the mean number of absent days was also close to ten, which is the maximum payable number of sick leave days granted to staff. The figure also indicates that employees took over twice as many sick days in 2010 than in 2008. If these observations remain valid, then staff concerns about heavier workload are consistent with the distribution of the number of sick days taken.[xi]

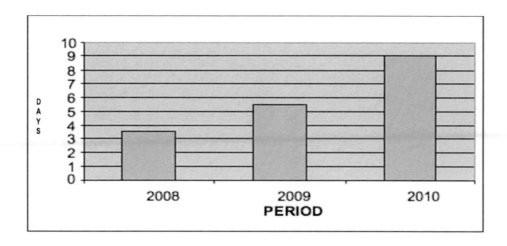

Figure 9.5: Mean distribution of staff sick leave from 2008 to 2010

The median has also consistently confirmed the trend by demonstrating that:

- Half the members of staff took four (median) or more days of sick leave in 2008.
- Half of Agency's staff took at least five (median) days of sick leave in 2009
- Half of the employees took eight (median) or more days of sick leave in 2010.

Conclusion

There is sufficient evidence here to suggest that staff stress levels (based on sick leave days) progressively increased during a three-year period. Further to this, there is an obvious inverse relationship between the level of effort and sick leave vacations. Hence, productivity was compromised in this circumstance; thereby, negatively affecting efficiency at the input level. Therefore, the likelihood exists to believe that this trend cumulatively and negatively affected staff performance. Senior management is thus requested to intervene with a more informed strategy in order to assist staff to improve their productivity. This strategy also needs to effectively be monitored to make sure that the appropriate results are achieved.

The Matrix

The table (see Table 9.4) that is used to establish the number of acceptable indicators is made up of as many rows as there are indicators and ten columns. The first row represents descriptions of each column. For example, in row one, column one, the relevant thematic area, result-level, and indicator are filled in. In the next eight columns (still on row one), the respective criterion is filled in that will be used in screening the indicators. In the row below and subsequently, a table of binary elements is shown, i.e., zeros and ones (0, 1). The former represents a corresponding indicator, which does not satisfy the criteria, whereas the latter is a corresponding indicator that fulfills the criteria. The same process applies to all the criterion and corresponding indicators. Column seven summarizes the scores in terms of the number of yeses (or 1). The seventh column is the final score attained by each indicator, which is represented as a percentage of positive responses in the row. The last column is the final outcome, which tells us if, based on the scores (1s), one should go ahead and recommend the indicator or not. The "gold standard" for this exercise is 100%. That would be an indicator that scores positive responses in all the criterion, so it qualifies for implementation automatically.

In short, the matrix should contain the following:

- An R by C Matrix where
- R = Number of thematic indicators and
- C = Six screening criteria.
- Each indicator is cross-tabulated with each criterion
- The intersecting cell is filled with either a "1" or a "0"
- The former, if the indicator satisfies the criterion, and the latter if it doesn't
- Exercise continues until all indicators are screened
- A corresponding final score (%) per indicator is established for each row. These are used to establish group concordance
- Thematic group and subgroups agree on effective %
- Each subgroup is made up of moderator, rapporteur and team.

Table 9.4: Program indicator screening matrix (PRISM)

Thematic Area: RH, PDS, GDR, Other Results, Level: Goal, Outcome, Output Indicator	1 Specificity	2 Reliability	3 Sensitivity	4 Simplicity	5 Utility	6 Affordability	7 Total # Yes	8 %S core	9 Implemented Yes/No

Source: Lainjo, 2013

Themes of the PRISM

- Health
- Education
- Environment
- Governance
- Poverty
- Judiciary
- Agriculture
- Social security and protection
- SDGs

Criteria of the PRISM

As this is a composite analysis, we need to remember that a final outcome is only valid when all these criteria are considered simultaneously. That is, the outcome identified in the last column. What happens if no indicator satisfies all these conditions? The answer is simple. Before all the subgroups begin their assignment, there must be a consensus established by the team with regard to an acceptable level. For example, the team could agree before the exercise starts that any indicator that scores 70% (total positive responses divided by sum of positive responses and negative responses) or another decision level will be considered acceptable. Sometimes, this bar can vary. For example, if the team recognizes that a certain threshold tends to admit too many redundant indicators, the bar can be raised higher in order to further refine the choices. See Appendix V and Appendix VI for group guidelines.

The following paragraphs attempt to define the meaning of each criterion as it applies to the matrix.

Specificity: This refers to the likelihood of the indicator measuring the relevant result. In other words, is there a possibility that the result the indicator represents does not represent exactly what we are looking for?

Reliability: This criterion is synonymous with replication. That is, does the indicator consistently produce the same result when measured over a certain period of time? For example, if two or more people calculated this indicator independently, would they come up with the same result? If the answer is yes, then the indicator has satisfied that condition and, hence, a "one" is entered in that cell, or else zero is entered.

Sensitivity: A test to assess the stability of an indicator. For example, does the indicator continue to deliver the same result with a small variation of either the numerator or denominator? How does the result change when assumptions are modified? Does the indicator actually contribute to the next higher level? For example, an indicator at the output level accounting for one at the outcome level will yield a misleading result. If the same indicator accounts for two or more result levels simultaneously it is not stable. As indicated earlier, any indicator that satisfies a criterion is given a one in the corresponding cell, or else a zero.

Simplicity: A convoluted indicator represents challenges at many levels. Hence, here, an indicator that is easy to collect, analyze, and disseminate is preferred. Any indicator that satisfies these conditions automatically qualifies for inclusion. The zero/one process is then followed as indicated above.

Utility: This refers to the degree to which information generated by this indicator will be used. The objective of this criterion is to assist in streamlining an indicator in an attempt to help the decision-making make an informed decision. This can be stipulated either during the planning process or during the re-alignment process. The latter represents occasions when an organization is evaluating the current status of its mandate.

Affordability: This is simply a cost-effective perspective of the indicator in question. Can the program/project afford to collect and report on the indicator? In general, it takes at least two comparable indicators to establish a more efficient and cost-effective one. The one that qualifies is included at that criterion level. Then, the same process as outlined above is followed.

Inclusion: Column eight simply represents the composite score. The total number of positive responses is divided by the total number of criterion (in this case, seven) and multiplied by 100 to produce the relevant score for each indicator. During this process, each indicator is then classified as either accepted (if it scores 70% or more in this example) or is otherwise rejected.

Implementation of the PRISM

- Theme identification
- Thematic group selection
- Random thematic subgroup selection
- Selection of subgroup moderator and rapporteur
- Individual thematic subgroup member scoring
- Establish intra-thematic-subgroup concordance
- Establish inter-thematic group concordance
- Conduct thematic group plenary
- Establish group consensus
- Select final set of indicators

Algorithm of the PRISM

Figure 9.6 is a graphic structure of the logic required to achieve the expected results—final indicator identification. Details of this algorithm are presented in the pseudo code in Figure 9.7. A copy of an oral presentation on PRISM, which was made at an international conference in Toronto, Canada, is available via the following link:

https://www.slideshare.net/CesToronto/prism-a-composite-score-model-by-bongs-lainjo-22859180

Figure 9.6: Algorithm of the PRISM

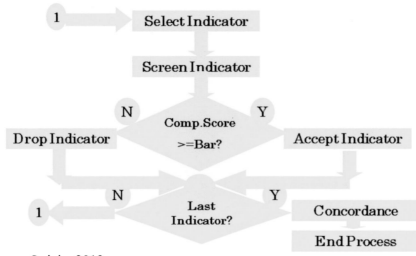

Source: Lainjo, 2013

Figure 9.7: Descriptive procedure of the PRISM algorithm

Descriptive Procedure of PRISM Algorithm

10 For Any Theme;

15 Are there any more themes? NO →→ Step 70

       20 Select thematic Indicator;

       25 Has the last thematic Indicator been Screened? YES→→ Step 70

       30 Screen thematic Indicator against Criterion; {Process continues through   every Criterion}

       35 Has Indicator been Screened against ALL criteria? YES>→→ Step 45

       40 →→ Step 30;

       45 Compute Indicator Composite Score {(Sum of "1"/(Sum of ("1" + "0"))};

       50 Compare Composite Score with pre-defined BAR;

       55 IF Composite Score >= BAR, ACCEPT Indicator >>>>>>Step 20;

       60 IF Not, DROP Indicator →→ Step 20;

       70 Calculate Group Concordance;

80   END PROCESS

A Logic Framework of SDG 3 Case Study is presented in Appendix VII

The following lessons can be learned from the PRISM:

- The importance of team composition homogeneity
- Consensus-building required
- No more than ten members per thematic subgroup
- Solid knowledge of theme essential
- The importance of time management
- Framework useful for pre-program implementation
- Also, essential during mid-term-review (MTR)
- Active involvement of top management critical
- Feedback provided to all active teams required
- Useful initial contact tool for evaluation team and relevant program key players.

CHAPTER 10: Results-Based Management – An Antidote To Program Management

Highlights: RBM and Theory of Change

The theory of change (ToC) is one of the most thorough approaches applicable in results-based management (RBM). It comprises three components that border on performance in the broader sense of RBM, performance measurements, and strategic planning. In the strategic planning, it identifies clear and measurable objectives, which are connected to precise indicators, and at explicit targets. The ToC approach in RBM develops a performance monitoring system linked to the assessment, analyses, and reporting of the actual results, that include outputs, outcomes, and impacts or goal. The ToC stipulates that the findings of the RBM are to be evaluated in order to facilitate organizational learning. Performance information is utilized by management for the purposes of accountability, resource allocation, learning, and other decision-making processes. Ideally, the ToC is a strategy for change that seeks to explore the main resources that need to be in place before change can occur through effective intervention.

Concept

In summary, this study has discussed the concept of results-based management as a management approach. Its target is improving results in a three-thronged model constituted of short-, medium-, and long-term types of results: outputs, outcomes, and impacts or goals. The concept is particularly prevalent in the public and not-for-profit organizations.

Scope

The analyses focus on the understanding of the results-based approach in program management and its application in a selected case study. The approach explored the application of RBM in the UN organizations such as UNESCO, UNDP, amongst others with a focus on the global, regional, and country-based implementation of RBM. The study critically reviews the advantages of RBM in strategic program management at the UN and the significant bottlenecks in the implementation process.

Limitations

The limitation of RBM as a strategic program management approach has been highlighted. Mainly, these limitations arise from the trade-offs between accountability and management of result in the management paradigm. In many cases, there is a lack of incorporation of performance indicators in the budgeting and management in public and not-for-profit organizations, constraining the successful implementation of RBM. Outputs are emphasized more than the outcomes and impacts in applying RBM. This leads to an increased focus on the organization's resources that will lead to short-term outputs creating imbalances at the three-results levels. Thus, performance assessment at the output level may be less challenging compared to assessment of outcome and higher levels.

Lessons

The study draws important lessons in the implementation of the results-based management model stemming from the introduction of changes in the RBM framework and the incentives for motivating the management to adopt this model. The study also notes the existence of RBM on policy papers with a minimal impetus to practically implement it despite its potential benefits in achieving organizational performance.

Life Case Study

The life case study focused on the UN and the modalities for the implementation of RBM. The study critically examines the successes and the challenges in the implementation process. It also focused on organizations such as UNDP, WHO, amongst others. The role of the managers in drawing objectives in tandem with the logical framework of RBM is highlighted.

Prognoses

The study recommends the removal of barriers to the implementation of RBM drawn from the UN case study. Such barriers include the incorporation of management as part of the budget process. The implementation of the framework has considerably been hindered by the parallelism of the budgetary programs and the management process. This implies that organizations are constrained to timely implement the RBM due to budgetary constraints. For RBM, including related, relevant, and complementary approaches to succeed, significant future mindset changes by key decision makers would be a compelling and necessary way forward. More participatory and inclusive strategies would also contribute to promoting and facilitating the implementation of this framework.

Introduction

The concept of RBM is not new. Indeed, it underlies all the efforts humans consciously undertake to achieve desired results. For example, countries go to war to win; parents bring up their children to be law-abiding citizens; children go to school (elementary, middle school, high school, community college, university) to successfully graduate; farmers plant crops in anticipation of good harvests; people go to gyms to lose excessive weight; businesses are established in order to make profits; and so on. All these interventions have in common the objective of transforming inputs into intended results (outputs, outcomes, and goals) or strategic objectives (SO).

The universality of this concept makes it a useful basis for efforts to streamline and optimize proposed interventions. From a program development perspective, definitions have limited RBM to the key results presented in a relevant program design framework (PDF). This approach, while correct seems to limit the importance and significant scope of RBM. In this book, the definition of RBM has intentionally been expanded. It has also been deliberately presented from a generic perspective. Such a strategy creates room for every stakeholder and facilitates portability—lessons learned. It also enhances the versatility of this concept.

Thus, I have attempted to define a more holistic meaning of RBM. RBM can be considered as a hierarchical framework of mutually complementary components (program design framework, monitoring, and evaluation (M&E), data management (DM) and management information system (MIS) with synergistic dynamics that collectively yield intended or unintended objectives. The beauty of RBM is that there is no absolute "goal standard". The unavailability of an acceptable "turn-key" system is a confirmation of the dicey nature of RBM.

Each intervention is different, and as such, RBM serves as a unique framework with a common potential of promoting efficiency and accountability (effectiveness). Effective and evidence-based performance monitoring contribute substantially to the achievement of RBM. It is my hope that such a document will serve a wide audience on the one hand and facilitate program design and implementation on the other.

While the target audience remains quite broad—bilateral and multilateral agencies, academic institutions, and program implementing partners (PIP)—it is my hope that this document can also be used by anyone interested in an improved understanding of the concept of RBM. To this end, I have tried to minimize utilization of technical jargon as much as possible.

Such an attempt will hopefully expand the target audience base and generate more interest, especially amongst the members of the program development communities. Finally, the current requirement for accountability and results by donors has provided compelling evidence of the need for information of this kind.

According to the Global Affairs Canada Results-Based Management Policy Statement (2008), RBM is an approach led by a life cycle that embeds strategic thinking with people, resources, different processes, and measurements meant to improve accountability, decision-making, and transparency (Farrell, 2009). It is important to emphasize that RBM is exercised with sound judgment in an attempt to comply with all government and organizational regulations and requirements that produce maximum potential and best accountability standards. The approach is focused on results, measuring performance, adapting and learning to a new environment, and reporting on these experiences about performance (Farrell, 2009). Therefore, RBM is meant to define realism, program identification, and progress monitoring that become linked to the overall success of the program, measured through results and utilized resources, and noted by indicators appropriate to the goal (OECD, 1997). Risks are managed under RBM, knowledge is attained, and new decisions made based on this methodology. Monitoring and evaluation, data management and management information system are invaluable components of a robust RBM (Kusek & Rist, 2004).

The goal of RBM is to maximize the results; the effectiveness of the method is based on the outcomes, and the outcomes vary depending on the setting of the program. Nevertheless, the overall goal is to attain the results planned before the commencement of the cycle. It is about change; changing assumptions, studying changed risks and identifying changing factors (internal and external) that may interfere with the development of the program (Kusek & Rist, 2004). Inherent in the program that utilizes RBM, is the idea that something must change to maximize potential or results. The design, then, is based on knowledge learned from experiences, that could lead to the design of a better, more effective management plan with new research, evaluative methods, practice policies, and learned lessons (Kusek & Rist, 2004). RBM entails the development of theories and ideas that reflect the process' overall goals, systemically mapping the sequence that would logically lead to the best outcome for the project (Kusek & Rist, 2004; Bester, 2016).

Otherwise defined as the results chain (RC), it is a visual manifestation of the relationships that must intertwine for a goal to be achieved, breaking it down into activities, inputs, outputs, and outcomes that will benefit the organization, project, program or company (Bester, 2016). Each organization will create its RC, unique and specific to its goals. For instance, the Global Affairs Canada organization has six different levels of its RC, i.e., inputs, activities, outputs, immediate outcomes (short-term), intermediate outcomes (medium-term), and outcome (long-term). In other organizations, such as the Organization for Economic Co-operation and Development (OECD), only five RC levels are defined, i.e., inputs, activities, outputs, outcomes, and impact (OECD, 1997).

Setting

Sustainable program management (SPM) is a complex, process-driven framework analogous to the CARROT-BUS model, where effective management produces useful and effective outcomes, intended or unintended. SPM has, over time, been linked to sustainability as observed in Silvius and Tharp (2013). Although defining the concept of sustainability is more challenging than expressing it, it has gained a foothold in program management in the recent past (Silvius & Tharp, 2013). This book adopts the definition of sustainability as a normative concept, which is delimited by values highlighting the attitudes and behaviour of individuals, where the focus is to minimize risks in program management (Eskerod & Huemann, 2013).

Where does RBM fit in the CARROT-BUS framework? RBM is an integrated component of every step of the ladder. It serves as a required, necessary, and sufficient revolving strategy that effectively establishes the causal links amongst the different levels of the CARROT-BUS pyramid. As already discussed in detail, in sustainable program management, the CARROT-BUS model seeks to create an enabling environment through a pyramid-structured model (Silvius & Tharp, 2013). The pyramid of sustainable program management consists of six elements, namely capacity building, accountability, resources, results, ownership, and transparency. These elements of the pyramid are executed in an ascending order up the pyramid. They include the strengthening of capacity, (C); building in organization management, improving accountability, (A); effective utilization of Resources, (R); so as to achieve relevant results, (R); establishment of ownership, (O); and the achievement of transparency, (T).

Sustainable program management fits into the pyramid model, where capacity development is at the base of the pyramid. Capacity development is related to human resource development in education and training. In Groot and Molen (2000), capacity development has been defined as the development of knowledge, skills, and attitude in either individuals or groups with the goal of improving management, as well as the maintenance of organization and operational infrastructures. It is the improvement of employees' ability to perform their duties and responsibilities within the organization (Groot & Molen, 2000).

The concept of results-based management is a management approach oriented towards results. The management approach has its roots in the public sector reforms of the 1990s, which responded to the results-driven approach as a result of economic, social, and political pressure (Pollitt, 2011). In program management, results are placed at the center of the cycle of the project from strategic planning, implementation, monitoring, and evaluations as well as reporting and the decision-making process. One of the prominent aspects of RBM is performance measurement.

As highlighted in Binnedjik (2000), performance measurement seeks to assess how a firm meets its primary aims. Performance measurement seeks to improve management through learning, and at the same time leverage it with improved decision-making and planning. To implement performance assessment, RBM relies on an external and internal pool of accountability to the firm's results (Vahamaki *et al.*, 20011). Results in RBM are classified into three distinct phases—immediate outputs, intermediate outcomes, and finally, the long-term impacts. The existence of results in three different levels raises the challenge of assessment as observed by Binnedjik (2000).

In brief, results-based management is a management tool, which is based on performance management. It defines the expected results from key stakeholders in the program management process. It is a results chain (RC) focusing on human and financial resources to generate both short-term and long-term outputs for the organizations. RBM is a philosophy that focuses on achieving tangible changes (Aly, 2015). It is a set of tools employed in program management that seeks to summarize organizational core objectives. Program management is focused on the achievement of defined results. In the strategic systems approach, RBM is a results-focused approach. RBM focuses on performance and achievements, which are weighed regarding impacts, outcomes or outputs (Aly, 2015, p.1).

RBM Background

Results-based management logical framework

The logical framework of RBM resides on the structured, logical model, which identifies the expected outputs and consequently the inputs as well as activities required to accomplish the outcomes (Aly, 2015). The logical framework is structured around five items; assess, think, plan, do, and review.

Logical framework in RBM assess the current situation; what causes it or what is involved and what is going to be achieved; the plan on what to do and when and the resources involved; how it is going to be done and what are the adaptation plans; and finally reviews what was done well and what requires revision in the next period (Aly, 2015). The process of RBM is an iterative undertaking that relies on two concepts — strategy, and expected results. The process is composed of at most 12 phases, where the first seven phases are linked to result-oriented planning.

The first phase is the analysis of the problem to be addressed and its causes and effects. The second phase is the identification of principal stakeholders and beneficiaries. This stage also involves the identification of objectives and the design of interventions to meet the expected needs (Diamond, 2005). Thirdly, the expected measurable results are formulated. The performance indicators for the expected results are specified in the fourth phase. The fifth step is the setting of targets and benchmarking each indicator with the specified results to be achieved.

The sixth phase of organizational RBM is the strategy development, where a conceptual framework is drawn from the expected results. It is at this stage where the main modalities of actions involving the constraints and opportunities are identified (Diamond, 2005). The seventh phase is the balancing of the expected results and strategy with the available resources in the program management. The eighth phase entails management and monitoring the progress of RBM, with appropriate performance monitoring systems.

The last four phases of the application of RBM entail reporting and self-evaluation, where results are compared to the targets and the actual results achieved. Also, there is the integration of the lessons drawn and the self-evaluation, where information emanating from the monitoring system is interpreted for possible inferences and discrepancies between the expected and the achieved (Diamond, 2005). The dissemination and discussion of results and lessons are performed in a transparent and iterative manner (Diamond, 2005). The performance information from the monitoring and evaluation systems is then applied in the internal program management learning and decision-making process.

The significance of RBM in an organization rests in its ability to change the organization's culture by keeping track of outcomes such as financial performance and market share. One of the principles of RBM is the results chain, shown below.

Resources/inputs → activities → outputs → outcomes → impact

Result chain is composed of inputs, activities, outputs, outcomes, and impact. Positive or even negative effects of an intervention lead to tangible results, which are grouped into three levels as outputs, outcomes, and impacts. Outputs are the direct product and services arising from an intervention. They are the immediate effects of an intervention where one has the highest level of control (Flint, 2002).

Outcomes are the medium-term effects of intervention outputs. In program management, there is lesser control of this second level of results compared to the first level, outputs. They represent the tangible changes being brought into the program management dynamics. The third level of results is the impact, which can be categorized as primary and secondary effects and can either be negative or positive (Flint, 2002). This is a sum of some precise activities and other compounding factors. This level of results has the lowest level of control. Inputs are used to perform activities; activities produce precise outputs, outputs produce outcomes, and the resultant outcomes contribute to impacts. In the RBM logic, interventions are in the form of hierarchies, which are a set of inputs and activities leading to results in the form of outputs, outcomes, and impacts (Flint, 2002).

Firstly, the implementation of RBM is dependent on the extent to which the key performance measures are connected to the existing strategic or policy framework. According to OECD (1997), successful implementation of RBM takes the time to develop its core indicators and streamline the management systems before collecting any performance data. Poate (1997) insists that organizations need to be persistent and patient because building consensus and maintaining the momentum is crucial to success.

Although it may be tempting to rush the implementation, firms must come to terms that rushing implementation only serves to decrease the likelihood of having a useful measurement system (Hatch & Cunliffe, 2006). It is worth noting that organizations are often limited in their use of indicators in several cases until they acquire sufficient measurement experience. In this regard, Itell (1998) concludes that outcome-oriented measures should be allocated sufficient time to develop them. This is bound to occur when relevant departments gain enough experience to identify both the cause and the effect. Diamond (2005) has reported that unrealistic projections of what RBM can accomplish in an organization only serve to undermine the RBM initiative. Therefore, it is the responsibility of senior managers to set and manage these expectations in their organizations.

The experiences of some major multinationals suggest some key guidelines for defining performance indicators and measures. For instance, Gibson and Boisvert (1997) argue that it is important to start with the end in mind, and this means going back to the broad objectives and vision that defined the long-term effects that the program, policy or service was intended to achieve (Downey, 1998). From this point, it becomes easy to identify both the short-term and the medium-term results that can contribute to the achievement of the anticipated effects. It also becomes possible to identify the indicators that reflect the short-term and long-term results (Kettl, 1997).

When it comes to the importance of management culture in RBM, Price-waterhouseCoopers (1999) argue that RBM requires more than just the adoption of new operational and administrative systems. Rather, there should also be an emphasis on outcomes that need a performance-oriented management culture that can support and encourage the utilization of the new management approaches. These observations echo previous findings by Epstein and Olsen (1996), who had argued that the successful implementation of RBM depends on the organization's ability to establish and maintain a management culture whose sole focus is in results.

Still, on culture, senior managers should be visibly seen propelling the RBM regime. According to Golinelli (2010), experimentation and innovation need to be supported, and both managers and staff should be given the opportunity to demonstrate their proven RBM practices, as well as the programs they are accomplishing using those practices. For new organizations introducing RBM, senior management staff will more often say the right things to be seen as supportive (Kusek & Rist, 2004). However, the actual actions could suggest otherwise. In this regard, there is likely to be an inconsistency about RBM, and this can undermine the organization's success.

While reviewing the New Zealand experience, Norman (2002) notes that RBM systems only influence the organizational behaviour when the top managers opt to use the available information throughout the organization. A Canadian delegate making a presentation at the World Bank roundtable (2006) emphasized on the need for managers to "walk the talk" in delivering on the RBM approaches. This involves senior management staff respecting their managerial freedom as part of an RBM culture, and supporting other subordinate managers who may be experimenting with new RBM approaches.

RBM systems are mainly motivated by two fundamental principles that include performance reporting or accountability and performance learning or improvement regarding efficiency and effectiveness (Binnendijk, 2002). It is these two pillars that have transformed RBM into a critical tool that assist policymakers and decision-makers in tracking organizational success (Meier, 2003). As a basic principle, organizational learning serves as the major motivation behind the successful adoption of the RBM approach in the most effective organizations (Eriksson & Kovalainen, 2008). RBM facilitates organizational learning by channelling performance information to policymakers through feedback loops from continuous performance evaluation and audit activities (Farrell, 2009). This process creates ideal opportunities for learning at the individual, group, and system-wide levels, thus continuously transforming the organization in a direction that increasingly satisfies its shareholders (UNESCO Bureau of Strategic Planning, 2010).

When it comes to performance reporting, simplicity has been identified as a fundamental tool for successful RBM implementation (Kvint, 2015) Instead of focusing on the core set of expected results, most successful organizations have a tendency to design complex results chains with finely differentiated outcomes, outputs, and impacts. This approach increases the number of performance measures and indicators needed to produce reliable performance data by an exponential factor. However, a study by UNDP (2007) revealed that the best approach is to keep the indicators and results for the vital few who can continuously monitor the entire results chain and transform the internal audits and evaluation into possible learning opportunities.

Theory of change in RBM

The theory of change (ToC) is one of the most thorough approaches applicable in the implementation of RBM. Holistically, RBM is composed of three components that border on performance in the broader sense, performance measurements, and strategic planning. In the strategic planning, the organization identifies clear and measurable objectives, which are connected to precise indicators. The objective is to target specific milestones. The fourth aspect of holistic RBM is to develop a performance monitoring system that is in turn connected to the reviewing, analyzing, and reporting of the actual results (outputs, outcomes & impacts) which correspond to the set targets. The findings are then evaluated to facilitate organizational learning.

Management uses performance information collected to improve accountability, resource allocation, learning, and other decision-making processes. In strategic system approach in RBM, ToC can be perceived as the strategy for change that seeks to explore the major items/resources that need to be installed for developmental change to occur (Thornton *et al.*, 2009). It involves the contribution of partners in the program management such as the partnership between donors and aid recipient countries. It outlines the role of the partners and non-partners in executing change in an organization. ToC approach in RBM draws the intervention methods necessary to cause change (Nigel, 2011).

One of the models that seek to explain ToC is the value, support, and capacity model. In the value component, it seeks the specific benefit of solving a problem, i.e., the benefit to a country or region for executing relevant changes through intervention. The second component is the support required for carrying out the particular intervention. The support, for instance, can be in the form of government or non-governmental organization (NGO). Support can also be from within the organization such as the support from the board of directors. The third component of the model is the capacity and comparative advantage. This component queries the capacity and comparative advantage gained by carrying out the interventions (Thornton *et al.*, 2009).

Limitation in the implementation of RBM

The challenges derived in the implementation of RBM stem from the tensions and trade-offs between accountability and management of results as required in the management paradigm (Giani, 2014). RBM is the prevalent management model in the public sector and NGOs (Moynihan, 2006). In these organizations, performance information is not part of the budgeting, constraining the effectiveness of RBM in its implementation. In the initial stages of the application of RBM, the results are based on the actual goods and services produced, rather than the outcomes (Binnedjik, 2000). Currently, there has been an increased focus on the outcome of the RBM results; the challenges are more complex than in the initial stages of implementation where the outputs were the major focus (Binnedjik, 2000). The performance assessment at the output information may be less challenging compared to assessment of outcome information (Moynihan, 2006).

It requires fundamental changes in the organization to integrate performance information in the management and budgeting (Moynihan, 2006). This requires evidence-based outcome focus that will, in most cases, lead to significant and fundamental changes in the way organizations are managed (Moynihan, 2006). The implementation of RBM will need organizational behavioural changes in the delivery of programs and services. As noted by Behn (2000), reorientation of the organization to adapt to RBM will change the operational management and personnel assessment down even to the strategic planning and budgeting in the organization. This will be a cultural change where performance information becomes essential in the management of the organization (Behn, 2000).

The successful implementation of RBM may take relatively slow progress fuelled by consistent effort. The long period of implementation can be disrupted by changing priorities — as key people along the path of implementation move on, and there is an alteration of governance structure in the organization. This will lead to relearning that will further extend the time required for full implementation of RBM (Behn, 2000). Apart from the temporal resources invested in the implementation of RBM, there are also additional costs that hinder its RBM implementation, especially in small organizations with comparative low returns (Behn, 2000).

Best practices in RBM implementation

To successfully implement results-based management in an organization, it is imperative to identify RBM's best practices. Ideally, the best practices are based on six principles. These include promotion and support of a results culture in the organization, fostering senior-level leadership in the RBM, building results frameworks within the ownership at all levels, assessing and developing a sensible user-friendly RBM information system (Mayne, 2007).

Other principles include building an adaptive RBM framework, where there are regular assessments and updates as well as using the results information in the learning and management of the organization to instill a reporting and accountability culture in the organization. In fostering senior-level leadership in the organization, the senior managers are supposed to consistently lead and support RBM through their policies and actions (Mayne, 2007). This should include but is not limited to, supporting RBM in resource allocations, fostering RBM champions and managing the expectation of RBM (Mayne, 2007).

Promotion of an RBM culture may include the provision of formal and informal incentives, which seek to support RBM practices (Mayne, 2007). This calls for more autonomy for the managers to manage the results and accountability programs under their leadership. The accountability framework should put into consideration the challenges of managing the outcomes and impacts of RBM (Mayne, 2007).

Best practices involve instilling a result culture that encourages learning from past performances and adjusting accordingly after identifying various modalities such as regular forums and results in information sharing (Mayne, 2007). This can help in the identification of areas of improvements through an in-house RBM capacity. In-house professional RBM capacity can foster continued training of staff and even managers on the best practices in the adoption of RBM (Mayne, 2007).

A culture of results is also supported by in-house professional RBM capacity and through ongoing training of managers and staff in RBM thinking and practices. Ultimately, the underlying culture of results is a clear and shared vision of the value of results information and the role it should play in managing the organization, and of the roles and responsibilities of the various stakeholders in RBM. In establishing a results orientation, any firm will need to develop and agree on a strategic results framework, outlining the organizational key objectives and the strategic system approach in meeting the objectives.

The second layer of the RBM framework structure is developing results frameworks for the programs. This involves outlining the expected specific activities and how they will lead to the achievement of the intended results for each program (Mayne, 2007). There is considerable guidance available on developing such results frameworks and the sequence of results underlying them. At both the organization and program levels, it is good practice to address the risk faced in meeting objectives. Results, which are focused on planning, imply that realistic and clear objectives for programs are identified and that there are performance expectations set out for each program (Mayne, 2007).

Best practices emphasize the need to get insights into the types of expectations/targets being set — predictive or stretch targets. In addition, it is important to consider a multi-year strategy for establishing expectations as experience in assessing RBM is gained (Mayne, 2007). Expectations for RBM are thus based on established baselines, past trends, and available resources; and involving all those engaged in the managing and delivery of programs (Flint, 2002). Setting indicators to track performance completes the RBM framework structure. It is important to set a manageable number of indicators, which can easily be measured, without missing critical performance indicators. This is to ensure there are no unintended distortions in program delivery

Lastly, it is important to build ownership for the various results frameworks established in an organization (Flint, 2002). Without ownership, there will likely be little use made of the information gathered from the results. Best practices include building a buy-in, through the involvement of those using the framework and linking the frameworks with work plans. In addition, ownership of RBM framework can be done through the building of a solid base for RBM using champions and pilots; and ensuring that the RBM regime is relevant and useful to managers. It should also be flexible enough to accommodate various types of programs (Flint, 2002).

Setting up well thought-out results frameworks is a good base, but without them actually measuring and analyzing the results being achieved, the RBM regime will not deliver much (Flint, 2002). There is an extensive experience available in measuring results and best practices. It is necessary to make use of this experience. Measurement and analysis of "fit for purpose" and the appropriate use of evaluations to complement ongoing performance measurement, are viewed as best practices (Mayne, 2007). In addition, steps should be taken to control the quality of the data being gathered. Both results and the costs of achieving the results need to be measured. There is also the need to assess, as best as possible, the extent to which a given program has contributed to the results being observed (Mayne, 2007). The results data and information gathered as part of the RBM regime will be part of the information system of the organization. The need to customize the results information within the IT system and to make the RBM system user-friendly is underlined as a best practice (Mayne, 2007).

Using the results information to help manage the organization and its programs are the aims of RBM implementation. There is a tendency for results information to be mainly focused on reporting. Thus, best practices are geared towards perceiving results as information rather than for determining the decision-making process. This leads to the balancing of the managerial requirements and the needs of the corporation in the RBM practice (Flint, 2002).

Most organizations apply results information for reporting on how well they are doing, especially to external audiences such as regulatory bodies. This is usually aimed at having a credible performance story about the accomplishments and to even point out underachievements. Finally, results information can play a useful role in the accountability processes in an organization, informing on the results achieved through the use mechanisms such as results-based performance agreements and balanced scorecards (Mayne, 2007).

The last principle speaks to the need to regularly review and update the RBM system (Mayne, 2007). Best practices include annual reviews and the willingness to change the RBM system, keeping track of problems within the RBM system by getting feedback from users of the system, and after few years, undertaking an evaluation of the RBM regime (Flint, 2002). Firms working to enhance their RBM capacity should be able to find a few specific suggestions for improvement in the report. For a particular organization, the prominent best practices depend on the robustness of its RBM and its limitations (Flint, 2002).

The process of monitoring and evaluating the RBM requires the evaluator to take a written assessment of the gaps and successes in the program management. This results in the involvement of the evaluator in the learning, decision-making, and accountability process of the RBM. The reliance on the evaluator makes the process of results-based management evaluation non-standardized since each evaluator has a unique perspective on the program management. It is difficult to have two evaluators with the similar views on the RBM. Therefore, the actions taken after the assessment of the RMB model will differ depending on the individuals assessing the program management (Flint, 2002).

There is a dearth of understanding of RBM as a results-focused approach in its implementation in the organization. As a consequence, and in some cases, institutions are unable to identify and differentiate outputs from outcomes strategically. The reporting of outputs and outcomes, therefore remain an area of weakness in the implementation of RBM since the field managers, project managers or the logistical personnel lack the capacity to identify outputs from outcomes (Golinelli, 2010). The project manager may, at times, not emphasize the significance of results since they perceive outputs to be out of the scope of the results-focused strategy of management, thereby ignoring the assessment of results early in the program management. Most focus is placed on the final outcomes, which are tangible to the program managers.

Effective RBM implementation may not occur without the inclusion of partners and stakeholders who understand the objectives of the organization. Effective RBM application is fostered by an explicit commitment of existing partners (UNESCO Bureau of Strategic Planning, 2010). The partners in RBM should be involved in the planning and reporting of the RBM process. Effective RBM practice, especially in the not-for-profit organization, will not occur in the absence of the developing partner. The presence of a developing partner increases the commitment to the plan in the program management. RBM monitoring and reporting involving only one side of the partnership may not bear substantial and relevant results, since the outputs and outcomes are valued differently by the partners (Cross, 2011).

Another challenge in the RBM practice is the identification of realistic and unexpected results. The identified and targeted results should be realistic so that there is a successful results-based strategy in the program management (Itell, 1998). Results projections should be based on achievability rather than the ambitiousness of the results, which in the end, will be unsustainable from a management perspective. The identification of unexpected results is achieved through precise definition of expected outcomes, outputs, and impacts (Kvint, 2015).

When a donor requires targeted results to be part of a proposal, it is important for those results to be evaluated on how achievable they are, not simply their ambitiousness. Executing agencies and their implementing partners on the ground also regularly ignore the identification of unexpected results. The need to define expected outputs and outcomes and impacts at the planning stage can catalyze the focus of those implementing a project into achieving those specific results. Unexpected results, which may be very significant, end up being ignored or downplayed if they do not neatly fit into the original results framework (Kvint, 2015).

Meaningful stakeholder participation

RBM cannot be effectively managed without key stakeholders — beneficiaries, development partners, and donor agencies — involvement. Stakeholder participation must be relevant so that realistic assessments can be achieved without significant challenges. Some proponents push for equal partnerships or equal participation. This is impossible to measure and even the word "meaningful" is open to discourse Grappling with the challenges of defining, implementing, and ascertaining meaningful stakeholder participation is vital to RBM, but it is also one of the hardest things to operationalize effectively.

Appropriate and effective indicators

Appropriate and effective indicators are critical for measuring success and feeding project learning. Constraints on time and resources often lead to the selection of simplified, easily gathered quantitative indicators that do not measure results as deeply as they could, especially at the outcome level. For example, the mainstreaming of gender equality has made the inclusion of gender issues and accompanying indicators mandatory in many projects. It is common for projects to select indicators that measure nothing more than the percentage of project staff and participants who are women. While this is important, does it measure the change in gender relations or power imbalances in any meaningful sense? Simplified indicators make it much more difficult to measure meaningful relationships between inputs and results.

Managing risks

All project partners need to be able to take informed and timely action to manage risks. Projects must be nimble and flexible enough to adapt to changing conditions over their duration. Are the executing agency, the partner or partners, and the donor agency entrepreneurial enough to make changes in project design and capacity as needs and the environment change over a multi-year period? If not, RBM risks being thwarted, leading to results that are inappropriate, irrelevant or both. This should not be confused with manipulating project ends to meet the capacity or interests of the executing agency or beneficiary.

Limited focus on evaluation

In many cases, there is a limited focus on external evaluation within project and program activity, despite the critical role of evaluation in measuring results and generating learning. Some projects and programs are evaluated annually, but many others are not. An end-of-project evaluation has no influence on project or program delivery. An external evaluation at the 60% point of a project is also hard-pressed to make a mark. Furthermore, there is often a challenge in maintaining consistency in evaluation. For example, a five-year project or program could have three different donor-agency project officers and two different monitors over that period. Maintaining evaluation consistency in such a context is a considerable challenge. Performance incentives and consequences include: Does an executing agency that reports poorly, with little apparent commitment to or knowledge of RBM, compromise significant potential results? Often the results of not being committed to RBM are not disastrous enough to modify behaviour in advance, and maybe not even so problematic as to affect behaviour significantly after the fact. Similarly, are projects rewarded appropriately for results that have been defined, achieved, and reported through the participation of all stakeholders? Without real incentives for achieving results or consequences for poor reporting and management, the potential of a results-focused strategy is greatly diminished.

Opportunities for learning

Results-based management training is focused on employee enhancement processes during which every employee undergoes training by their respective supervisor or the management team of the human resources department of the organization. Pompa (2012) indicated that training is one of the most effective responses to enhance the skill and knowledge of employees and stakeholders responsible for infusing new roles and responsibilities for any tasks being rendered. The purpose of training, as established by results-based management, is to promote the productivity of the company as well as to reach its targeted goals on a regular basis. This approach seeks to increase the level of competitiveness of the vulnerable target as they are going to be trained by their respective managers on a regular basis. Training can be incorporated with seminar workshops so that participants will be given the chance to demonstrate all the learned procedures essential for the productivity of the operating organization.

The results-based management training will enhance participant ability to be more analytical, curious, and motivated. The goal of training is to improve the level of performance and knowledge of participants. After the training, the impact enables participants to become more productive, reliable, and functional. Indeed, a good reflection of the model.

One of the key roles of RBM reporting is to provide information that can be acted upon. Managing performance requires ongoing learning. The connection between data collection and reporting on the one hand and the incorporation of learning arising from these data on the other is often not made. The demands of day-to-day operations frequently rob organizations of time to reflect on information gathered through monitoring and evaluation, to draw lessons from these reflections, and to incorporate this learning into project management. The result is lost opportunities. The best projects incorporate learning throughout their lifespan, leading to effective, efficient, and relevant results for beneficiaries. Many projects simply cannot find the time to do this.

Conceptual framework in the RBM approach

This management strategy facilitates the achievement of strategic goals. In particular, program managers can utilize this model to map out the goals, set deliverables and boundaries, and produce the intended outcome. While the unwanted outcome is at times part of the RBM process, it is within the results-based management plan to accommodate crisis intervention and risk management to tackle or prevent any unintended outcomes in the process. To facilitate the achievement, the RBM method employs several steps that lead towards the intended goal. The method includes assessing the situation at hand, defining the possible causes for the current situation, envisioning a new scenario, planning it, and initiating the project with a change management plan in hand. The retrospective stage includes lessons learned and future goals. While in several circumstances unintended results cannot be avoided, they, for the most part, serve as compelling and frequently invaluable contributions to lessons learned.

Results-based management is a strategy that primarily anchors its logic on feedback to achieve the goals at hand. Those who contribute to the results, be it management or other organizational actors, are doing so indirectly or directly and, as a result, there is a process created that facilitates an outcome. The outcome may be in the form of a new product/service, a change, or an impact/contribution towards the goal at hand. The information gathered from these strategies is then used to account for future needs within the program. RBM is a strategy-based control mechanism similar to third-generation balanced scorecards (Lawrie, Kalff & Andersen, 2005).

RBM is often used by organizations such as the UN and the International Committee of the Red Cross (United Nations, 2016). It is used for commercial-based organizations as well, including the Asian Development Bank. It will also be useful to include utilization of RMB by other establishments. For instance, the U.S. government uses management by objective (MBO) — similar to RBM — in its government departments. The results approach is also used in program development, and it has been implemented since

2000 (ICRC, 2008). All program cycles began with the use of RBM, and it has not proven to be an efficient way to continue the development and acceleration of program management and non-commercial management programs. If that approach failed as indicated here, what alternatives did they use? And, how did that solve their problem?

To apply RBM, the program manager must assess the current situation and decipher the best possible attainment for the betterment of the program or project. The next step is to think about its causal and relational effects, followed by the vision of what is required to achieve the purpose. The planning stage includes the assignment of roles and responsibilities, as well as resources. The execution stage involves the need to adapt to external and internal circumstances to attain the goal. The last stage in the RBM framework involves the retrospective lessons learned, accumulation of organizational assets, and the enterprise environmental factors that will allow for future similar endeavours to be a success.

Definitions

Results-based management: RBM is the form of management that is tailored for results (Bester, 2016).

Results oriented: The design and management of a project in a way that will assure the continuous focus on outcomes and their achievements (Bester, 2016).

Results-based monitoring and evaluation: This encompasses the constant focus on collecting and analyzing the data available to better predict outcomes and measure the progress of the expected issue.

Continuous adjustment: This involves the collection of data and its subsequent assessment throughout the life cycle of the project and the adjustment of its operational standards, implementing the strategies to maximize the probability of the result (Bester, 2016).

Managing risk: Risk management in RBM entails the identification of risks about the expected outcomes and attaining the necessary resources to overcome them (Mayne, 2007).

Participatory approach: This is the constant and active participation of stakeholders, which includes beneficiaries as well as intermediaries, donors, and implementers.

Crosscutting theme integration: During the results-based management cycle of planning, design, and implementation, issues such as equality, sustainability, and governance are considered crucial parts of the process (Bester, 2016).

RBM methodology

The methodology seeks to explain how the research will be performed and the data collection process implemented for a given study. Theoretical consideration and the theory-building process that will be undertaken in a potential study is provided.

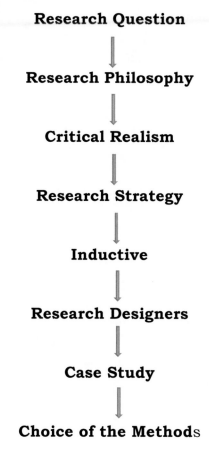

Research Question

Research Philosophy

Critical Realism

Research Strategy

Inductive

Research Designers

Case Study

Choice of the Methods

Figure 10.1: Results-based management methodology

The philosophical assumptions underlying this study are based on critical realism. This study seeks to establish the mechanisms applied in results-based management and the structures that are required via a life case study of the UN organizations, presented later. In critical realism ontology, three aspects are considered, the real, the actual, and the empirical. To understand the application of RBM in the case study, this study combines all the three aspects of an insightful analysis.

The study also applies abstraction and concretization, including an induction approach where the analysis progresses from the actual level to the empirical implementation of RBM in the case study.

Theoretical consideration

Theoretical consideration seeks to reinforce the choice of theory in any research. For RBM, monitoring and evaluation is applied to explore the case study. Systems and a variety of theoretical perspectives could be applied.

Theory building

This study will seek to build theory through triangulation by engaging multiple paradigms in understanding the implementation process of results-based management in an organization (Birger, 2011). Designing a "state of the art" RBM system is not only difficult to achieve but also complicated by the lack of a universally accepted "gold standard". Reasons for these complications vary. Some include the inadequate effectiveness, limited quality assurance, and overall oversight mechanisms. There are also other exacerbating factors like the inability of program designers to effectively manage the unreliable and incomplete availability of required data sets. Another challenge faced by designers is the ability to produce a program document within an unrealistic timeline. An attempt to overcome this deadline crunch exposes the team to myriads of vulnerabilities.

Team concordance, harmony, and complementarity are also other compelling issues that must be addressed by the team. In some cases, the program designers spend a significant amount of time trying to establish consensus; sometimes on trivial issues. For example, during one assignment, I remarked several instances where the team could not agree on where to incorporate some performance indicators in a strategic framework. And this is just the tip of the iceberg. In light of some of these shortfalls, I am proposing in Figure 10.2 a "road map" that I believe will serve in mitigating some of the system deficiencies that continue to erode attempts to produce a useful and effective RBM system.

Research design

This life case study explores a case study of how results-based management has been used by UN organizations in project and program interventions. The study investigates the different frameworks that have been utilized in the successful implementation of RBM. The case study allows for the use of multiple data collection methods to explore the case (Creswell, 2014). The choice of these methods relates to the nature of the case and the research objective. In exploring the life case study, this work seeks to answer the "how" and "why" in RBM implementation through an explanatory type of research.

In explanatory research, the aim is to uncover the causal-effect-linkage, and in this context, the effective contribution of RBM implementation in enhancing the effectiveness of UN organizations. Descriptive research has been used to identify and collect information regarding the implementation of RBM. Selected UN organizations have been used due to the rigorous implementation of RBM in a variety of projects within the organization over the years.

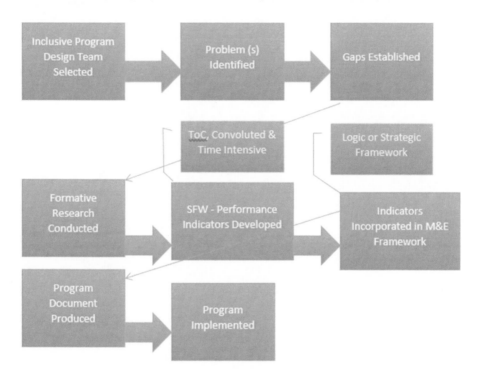

Figure 10.2: Proposed RBM system methodology algorithm
Source: Lainjo, 2017

In a related World Bank article, Roberts and Khatti (2012) highlight some of the salient and crucial elements to be considered and included in an effective and useful RBM approach (p. 20-22). The authors also emphasize the role and importance of theory of change (ToC) and how the strategy helps in improving program results. And using the concept of ToC, the authors further elaborate on how it helps in establishing the necessary and relevant pathways required in effectively and genuinely mapping the

hierarchical causal links amongst the different result levels of a strategic
framework. They also included a modified sample case study (Figure 10.3)
as an illustration of a "success" story.

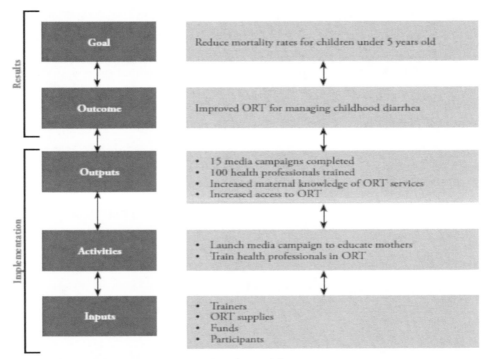

Sources: Kusek and Rist 2004; also adapted from Binnendijk 2000.
Note: ORT = Oral rehydration therapy.

Figure 10.3: Sample program logic to reduce childhood morbidity through the
use of oral rehydration therapy

Scope and significance of RBM frameworks

The vital role of a results-based management (RBM) system could never be
adequately emphasized. RBM systems are universally acceptable strategies.
They give program managers and different stakeholders a better sense of direction, an evidence-based management approach, a consensus-driven decision-
making process, an opportunity to make informed and effective decisions, and
ultimately, an invaluable, necessary, and sufficient pathway to success.

A better sense of direction

The concept of RBM is not new. Indeed, it underlies all the efforts humans consciously undertake to achieve desired results. For example, countries go to war to win, parents bring up their children to be law-abiding citizens, children go to school (elementary, middle school, high school, community college, university) to successfully graduate, farmers plant crops in anticipation of good harvests, people go to gyms to lose excessive weight, businesses are established in order to make profits, and so on. All these interventions have in common the objective of transforming inputs into intended results (outputs, outcomes, and goals) or strategic objectives (SO).

The universality of this concept makes it a useful basis for efforts to streamline and optimize proposed interventions. From a program development perspective, definitions have limited RBM to the key results presented in a relevant program design framework (PDF). This approach (while correct) seems to limit the importance and significant scope of RBM. In this document, the definition of RBM has intentionally been expanded. It has also been deliberately presented from a generic perspective. Such a strategy creates room for every stakeholder and facilitates portability — lessons learned. It also enhances the versatility of this concept.

Thus, I have attempted to define a more holistic meaning of RBM. RBM can be considered as a hierarchical framework of mutually complementary components (PDF, M&E, data management (DM)) and management information system (MIS) with synergistic dynamics that collectively yield intended objectives. The beauty of RBM is that there is no absolute "goal standard". The unavailability of an acceptable "turn-key" system is a confirmation of the dicey nature of RBM. Each intervention is different, and as such RBM serves as a unique framework with a common potential of promoting efficiency and accountability (effectiveness). Effective and evidence-based performance monitoring contribute substantially to the achievement of RBM. It is my hope that such a document will serve a wide audience on the one hand and facilitate program design and implementation on the other.

While the target audience remains quite broad — bilateral and multilateral agencies, academic institutions, program implementing partners (PIM), and academic institutions — it is also my hope that this document can be used by anyone interested in an improved understanding of the concept of RBM. To this end, I have tried to minimize utilization of technical jargon to the extent possible. Such an attempt will hopefully expand the target audience base and generate more interest, especially amongst the members of the program development communities. Finally, the current requirement for accountability and results by donors has provided compelling evidence of the need for information of this kind.

Life case study – RBM implementation in the United Nations organizations

The United Nations applies the results-based paradigm in a different perspective, where different terms and terminologies are used to represent the results-based approach in the management of institutions related to the UN (Bester, 2016). Also and more specifically, in the UN system, there remain significant differences in the thematic application and implementation of RBM amongst the various agencies. For instance, in the United Nations Children's Fund (UNICEF), planning and management replaces a results-based approach while the UNDP uses results-based budgeting. In the Food and Agricultural Organization (FAO), the results-based approach is substituted by the strategic framework, or even enhanced monitoring and evaluation regime.

The existence of different conceptual frameworks in the UN describing the results-based approach complicates the communication across the organizations. It points to the different views, of RBM in the organization structure usually aligned with the agency's mandate and objectives. While some organizations perceive RBM as management practices, others perceive it as budgetary practice and others may objectify it as a bureaucratic requirement of the organization. In all, the organizations operating under the UN funds and programs, such as UNFPA, WFP, and UNDP, have been found to have a systematic and methodical implementation of RBM (Bester, 2016).

These organizations have approached RBM as a management practice and have also learned from the experiences of other organizations. This has made it possible for them to build an effective and solid system of management. It is important to note the significance of conceptual frameworks in the proper implementation of RBM. This has been a major challenge in the perspective of RBM in the different UN organizations and the eventual application of the management practice (UNESCO Bureau of Strategic Planning, 2010). Conceptual frameworks lay the ground for the tools and terminology for harmonizing RBM within the organization. The conceptual framework seeks to link RBM to the business and operation of an organization.

A conceptual framework is a time-bound coherent strategy for implementing RBM. In the context of the UN, there is the lack of a coherent and holistic approach to RBM as a pure management practice (Bester, 2016). The advancing of RBM has mainly concentrated on the format and vision without much regard to the effective translation of RBM to improved work process to support the administrative, financial, and information system within the organization (Bester, 2016). Many of the bottlenecks in the application of RBM in the UN have been found to reside in the understanding of conceptual issues amongst the managers (Mayne, 2007). Where there is a clear conceptual framework of RBM, the organization is committed to the implementation and institutionalization of the RBM process. In conclusion, the presence of a clear conceptual framework illustrates a broad management strategy of the organizations.

Another important facet of RBM in the implementation process at the UN is the respective responsibilities of the partners in the RBM. Effective implementation of RBM calls for a shift in the operational modalities of an organization. This presents a significant challenge for the member states of the UN to adapt to an outcome-driven programming and budget from the input-driven process of program management in an effective an efficient manner (Bester, 2016).

Being a new form of management practice, RBM adoption has been slow in most of the organizations under the UN as stakeholders simply adapt to the system management to avoid setbacks and work efficiently (Bester, 2016). The culture of RBM can only be consistently harnessed when the ownership of the programs is fostered and the accountability in the organization is promoted (Bester, 2016). The RBM at the UN promotes a culture of trust and understanding between the member countries (ownership,) and the UN Secretariat (managers) under an environment of trust in micro level management in the RBM settings.

The UN also adopts a key principle in RBM practice, which is vested in the long-term objectives of an organization. The UN system has acknowledged and recognized the need for strategic frameworks that provide the vision and overall direction of the organization. This is based on both short-term and long-term results in RBM. The sum of the long-term organizational objectives contributes to the overall organizational goals such as the UN Millennium Declaration (Mayne, 2007). This helps the organizations to identify its priorities in the implementation of its programs.

The goals and sub-goals, which contribute to the priority goals, are defined, and in the RBM, they constitute the critical results to be achieved or assessed in the organization. Therefore, the objectives of the UN organizations are precise, clear, and verifiable, so that the performance assessment process is effective in the long-term (Bester, 2016). Essentially, the desirable traits of the statement of objectives in RBM entail a statement of results, which is devoid of actions or means, with precise, simple, measurable and logically consistent objectives, across all levels of the organizations that reflect the causal-effect-linkage.

Alignment of the programs with the organizational goal is a principal component of program management at the UN organizations. This helps in combining results so that they can constitute a major medium-term outcome of the organization. The alignment of programs with the organization objectives is through a cascading process that seeks to set the sub-objectives at the operational levels of the organization. For example, the World Health Organization (WHO) programs are grouped into three levels, global, regional, and country, and the specific objectives are lumped together to form the overall objectives of the organization (Bester, 2016).

The UN implementation of RBM demonstrates the flexibility of the RBM approach to management. Resources are aligned to the long-term objectives of the UN organizations. This gives birth to the results-based budgeting as a variation of RBM, which harnesses organizations resources to meet the desired objectives by demonstrating the link between results and resources in an effective RBM approach (Bester, 2016). The RBM framework allows for the shifting of resources from underperforming and obsolete programs, to more efficient and relevant programs considered high priority. In RBM in the UN, effective cost accounting is linked to the resources, which are then tied to the organizational goals. Performance assessment is thus, performed in tandem with the budget cycle of the UN organizations. The predictability of available resources in the UN system acts as an important tool in aligning strategic planning with the results. It helps in integrating the multi-year funding frameworks to the programs objectives, resources, budgets, and expected outcomes (Bester, 2016).

RBM and the Accountability Framework

The results-based management and accountability framework (RMAF) is intended to serve as a blueprint for managers to help them focus on measuring and reporting on outcomes throughout the life cycle of policy, program or initiative. Managing for results is not completely new to businesses organizations but what makes the current approach different is the determination to make RBM the driving force behind the organization's institutional culture and practice — and to develop and apply a corporate methodology for this purpose. When it comes to results-based management, balance is key to prevent the process of defining and monitoring indicators from becoming a major workload.

In this regard, balance requires that the definition and use of indicators have to be taken seriously for credible and effective assessment, learning, and accountability. On the other hand, care must be taken not to overinvest in results measurement and indicators. If the measurement is emphasized too much there is a risk that managers will be motivated to undertake certain activities simply because measurable results can be achieved. In the process, they may be diverted from less measurable, but ultimately more fruitful, development interventions.

It is noteworthy that the outcomes and outputs furnished within the strategic results framework by operating units should reflect the key results against which managers wish to be assessed. However, because outcomes are not the result of one single actor's intervention, enforcing individual and personal accountability with respect to the substantive attainment of outcomes would be unreasonable. In this regard, the measurement of results is not an isolated activity. Rather, the process of measuring results begins with the design of policy, program or initiative, and its evolutions. Different results-measurement activities occur at different points in time, but always as part of the ongoing management of policy, program or initiative. This continuum runs from the initial consideration of performance measurement, through performance monitoring, to formative and summative evaluation.

While managers can be held accountable for ascertaining that outcomes are monitored, their full accountability can be applied only to outputs. In a situation of shared accountability, it is important that responsibilities and performance expectations be defined. Managers, while not being held accountable for the achievement of outcomes, are expected to report on progress against intended outcomes.

RBM and Development vs. Management Results

As a critical step in the evolution of logical framework approaches, RBM attempts to respond to some issues of the project cycle management (PCM) and logic framework approach (LFA) methods. People often ask what the difference is between PCM or LFA and RBM. In a sense, it can be said that RBM is PCM done right. It provides more tools and directives on what should be done to ensure that project design is performed in an inclusive and participatory way, and to make sure that one takes into consideration any assumptions and risks. The latter being defined as internal and external factors that are likely to influence project implementation and outcomes.

RBM is also critical of many donors' focus on inputs (funds and resources) and activities, and promotes a shift towards the results of the project: its tangible outputs, its effects, and its impact — that is the 'results' part of RBM. As for the "management" aspect, RBM provides some tools to monitor the performance of the project. In many projects, there continues to be a tendency to emphasize work plan achievements with little regard for how these achievements contribute towards intended results. Some of the salient questions that need to be answered include: Are you getting the results you wanted? How can you be sure? How many resources do you use? RBM can provide an answer to these questions.

Compared to its predecessors, RBM also makes sure that the context or environment in which one is working is dynamic, relevant, and influences the project — in positive ways but also in negative ways. RBM stimulates the project manager and other relevant stakeholders to think about assumptions and risks, not just at the project design stage, but also over the whole course of the project life cycle.

Conclusion

This work has discussed the approaches for effective strategic systems implementation including the CARROT-BUS strategy, theory of change (ToC) and the results-based management. The ToC contains three components that border on performance in the broader sense of RBM, performance measurements, and strategic planning. In the strategic planning, it identifies clear and measurable objectives, which are connected to precise indicators; a process that is accomplished through the identification and establishment of relevant, reliable, valid, and compelling pathways leading to intended and sometimes unintended results.

The ToC approach in RBM includes developing a performance monitoring system that is linked to the assessment, analyses, and reporting of the actual results, which include outputs, outcomes & impacts. The ToC stipulates that the findings of the RBM are to be evaluated to facilitate organizational learning. Management uses performance indicators to manage accountability, resource allocation, learning, and other decision-making processes. Ideally, the ToC is a strategy for change that seeks to explore the main resources that need to be in place before change can occur through effective interventions.

In conclusion, this chapter has explored the concept of results-based management as a management approach intended to improve results in a three-thronged model: Short-, medium-, and long-term; types of results — outputs, outcomes, and impacts. The concept is particularly prevalent in public and not-for-profit organizations. The analysis has focused on getting an insight on the results-based approach in program management and its application in a selected case study. The UN study explored the application of RBM in UN organizations such as UNESCO and UNDP amongst others, with a focus on the global, regional, and country-based implementation of RBM. The chapter critically reviews the advantages of RBM in strategic program management at the UN organization and the significant bottlenecks in the implementation process.

The limitation of RBM as a strategic program management approach has also been highlighted, identifying the challenges and possible opportunities for improvement in the implementation process. The limitations arise from the trade-offs between accountability and management of result in the management paradigm. In most cases, there is a lack of incorporation of performance parameters in the budgeting and management of public and not-for-profit organizations, constraining the successful implementation of RBM. Processes are emphasized more than the output, outcomes, and impacts in applying RBM. This leads to an increased focus on the organization's resources that will lead to short-term outputs, creating imbalances in the three result levels. Thus, performance assessment at the output level may be less challenging compared to assessment of outcome level. Fundamental changes are required in the organization to integrate performance interventions in management and budgeting.

The chapter draws important lessons in the implementation of the results-based management model stemming from the introduction of changes in the RBM framework and the incentives for motivating the management to adopt results-based management. Research findings note the existence of RBM on policy papers, with no minimal impetus to practically implement it, despite its potential benefits in improving the organizational performance. The life case study focused on the UN and the modalities for the implementation of RBM. The report (Bester, 2016) critically examines the successes and the challenges in the implementation process. The section focused on select UN organizations. The role of the managers in drawing objectives in tandem with the logical framework of RBM is highlighted.

Research findings recommend the removal of barriers for the implementation of RBM drawn from the UN organizations case study. Such barriers include the incorporation of project management as part of the budget process. The implementation of RBM has considerably been hindered by the parallelism of the budgetary programs and the management process. This implies that organizations are constrained to timely implement the RBM due to budgetary constraints. And finally, for RBM to succeed, significant paradigm shifts by key decision-makers would be a compelling, appropriate, and necessary way forward. More participatory and inclusive strategies would also contribute substantially to promoting and facilitating the implementation of this framework.

CHAPTER 11: Using Big Data, Cloud Computing, and Analytics (BDCA) in Program Management

The integration of big data analytics, cloud computing, and analytics (BDCA) encourages innovation and provides timely and cost-effective data management aimed at increasing efficiency and effectiveness. Big data analytics and cloud computing have not only revolutionized information technology departments around the world, its impacts have been witnessed in almost every sector of society, from healthcare and education to science, technology, and finance. Besides being used in all sorts of work and professional settings, people are also able to share information through social networks and stream live events. Overall, increased information sharing means increased efficiency, and thus, increased economic growth.

The successful implementation of programs with medium- and long-term objectives depends on access to high quality and reliable data, amongst other critical factors. If applied efficiently, this can subsequently transform into high-quality information to help make informed program management decisions. Every level of the hierarchical model calls for sound and plausible decision-making pathways. Informed decisions are compelling, evidence-based, and sustainable, and BDCA is an integral part of this process. While current findings locate low- and middle-income countries (LMICs) behind the curve, it is only a matter of time before they become an integral part of this contemporary data management wave.

Big data represents digital information coming from sensors, digitizers, mobile devices, the internet, videos, email, social networks, and more (Singh, Uddin, & Pinto, 2015, p. 529). Technology evolution means that data has grown in volume, velocity, variety, value, and veracity. "Volume" is the word most associated with big data, with its velocity growing explosively beyond our ability to handle these massive data sets without new techniques (Stanoevska-Slabeva, Wozniak, & Ristol, 2009, p. 29). "Variety" is seen in the many different data forms of data while "veracity" represents the quality, accuracy, and trustworthiness of data. All of this is what gives data its value as never before.

Data are valuable, with many firms looking for ways to unlock the potential of hidden data to ensure competitiveness. Business data grew by over 800% between 2011 and 2015, with about 80% of this growth coming from unstructured data (Bruns & Liang, 2012, p. 39). E-mail alone accounted for nearly 30% of unstructured data, with videos, social media content, images, and documents making up the remaining 70%. As far as overall data growth, the remaining 20% represent structured data, such as contact information and credit card activities. North America and Europe have been the biggest generators and consumers of big data, with Africa so far being the lowest consumer and producer.

Over a few short decades, people have advanced from trying to understand disk operating system (DOS) to handling data in numerous formats — texts, documents, data volumes, and videos — on smartphones, sensors from RFID (radio-frequency identification device), e-readers, etc. Real data are determined by the insight they produce during analysis, including usage patterns, derived meaning, and decision-making indicators (Friess, 2013, p. 43). Big data uses enhanced technologies to collaborate with huge volumes of heterogeneous data, as well as sophisticated quantitative approaches (Gao, Li, Li, Janowicz, & Zhang, 2014, p. 90). Quantitative methodologies include machine learning, robotics, artificial intelligence, and neural networks to explore data and identify interrelationships. Cloud computing has made it possible for data to provide insights that encourage competitiveness, helping firms to discover new methodologies to process, manage, and analyze data (Dobre, 2014, p. 49). Today the scope of data analytics has expanded to include intelligent applications like in-vehicle infotainment, internet kiosks, and device sensors with "smart home" technologies on the rise.

Amazon.com, for example, is a global leader in e-commerce that has unlocked big data potential. The online retailer collects anonymous usage data from customers and analyzes usage patterns to derive meaningful trends. By deriving usage trends, the company can predict shopping patterns and user preferences. This information is used to improve Amazon's operating efficiency as well as the customer experience.

One of the most compelling and comprehensive frameworks of BDCA is shown in Figure 11.1, a pragmatic layout of how big data, cloud computing, and analytics work together. The cloud connects supply (big data and hardware) to demand (human ware and software).

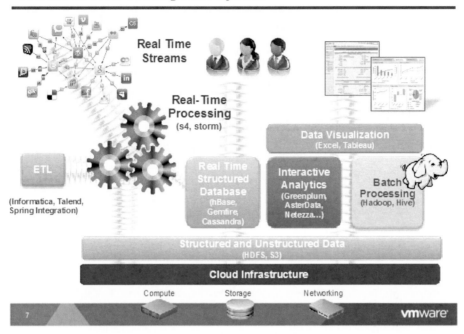

Figure 11.1: Ecosystem of BDCA
Source: vFabric Team, 2012

Cloud Computing and Big Data

Cloud computing has become vital for numerous businesses, with service providers deploying private clouds. Cloud technology has matured to improve security and data integration, prompting increased trust in various cloud delivery methods. Firms store more data in the cloud, representing immense and valuable information to support data mining. Cloud delivery platforms provide exceptional flexibility, allowing the efficient utilization of resources and proper data analysis in private or external cloud centres in client devices (Singh et al., 2015, p. 532). It is critical to have data services in order to obtain value from big data. Depending on need and usage, firms utilize their IT budgets on an analytics-as-a-service (AaaS) basis.

Google is the world leader in the provision of AaaS. With the company's consumer database consisting of billions of records, the organization can harvest useful information from people who use any of its services, such as Google Search, Google Maps, or Google Scholar. Through big data analytics, the company can derive data patterns that other businesses will pay for.

Such data patterns may include regional preferences for certain goods and services. Most businesses do not have the capacity to collect and process data of such magnitude so they procure the AaaS services they need from Google or similar companies. It is possible to meet a wide range of analytics needs with AaaS services.

When a company develops a comprehensive cloud-based big data analysis, it is possible to define a framework to optimize the data's value (Lu et al., 2011, p. 620). The framework includes key abilities, such as the ability to capture and extract both structured and unstructured data from trustworthy sources (Percivall, 2010, p. 19; Khalil, Khreishah, & Azeem, 2014, p. 14). AaaS can also prioritize most relevant data and examine what to retain and for how long. With an AaaS framework, an organization can perform data integration, analysis, visualization, and transformation to provide the required information to the right place and location (Oza, Karppinen, & Savola, 2010, p. 621).

Utilization by Sector

Any sector, organization, or business can use big data, cloud computing, and analysis in order to improve its decision-making and delivery of goods or services. Let's look at two sectors — health and education — that have particular bearing on development issues.

Health

When compared to other industries, the health sector has underutilized technology in enhancing health service delivery (Michener & Jones, 2012, p. 89). Most healthcare operations still use manual medical reports and records. The digital enhancements are typical in nature, and lack of portability inhibits information sharing amongst many health sectors. Using technology to support collaboration and coordinate care between patients and health providers, as well as the entire health community, has been limited. Around the globe, healthcare reforms have embraced "healthcare information technology" to modernize their processes, hence cloud computing initiatives to enhance transformations (Roche, 2014, p. 709). The health sector has shifted to a service and care delivery mode that is information-centric, supported by open standards that encourage cooperation, collaborative teamwork and workflows, and seamless information sharing (Li & Narayanan, 2004, p. 682).

Cloud computing supports hospitals, large medical practices, insurance firms, as well as research institutions to help enhance computing resources at a low initial capital structure (Khalil et al., 2014, p. 21). Moreover, cloud computing supports major technological needs in the health industry by enabling on-demand accessibility to computing and data storage. The convergence also ensures big data sets in electronic health records (EHR), radiology images, as well as genomic data offloading into simple tasks (Loveland et al., 2000, p. 1310).

In the context of EHR management, health professionals can collect massive volumes of patient data and use big data analytics to discover patterns, such as the period that a patient waits before a nurse attends to them. In health provision, such information is extremely useful in improving service delivery to patients. Accordingly, through convergence, it is easier to share EHRs amongst authorized health providers in different geographical locations, allowing timely access to life-saving data, and eliminating duplicate testing. It also becomes easy to track information on treatment. The health sector demands stringent security, confidentiality, and access only by authorized users, hence the need for cloud providers to conform to government and industry regulations (Loveland et al., 2001, p. 1310).

According to Fernandez-Aleman et al. (2013), the main difference between the U.S. and other high electronic health record systems (EHRSs) adopter countries is the level of government involvement. Other developed countries received intensive support from federal and state governments. An example includes the UK, whose population equals 20% of the U.S.'s, investing over US$17 billion through their National Program for IT (NPfIT). On the other hand, Australia has given physicians adopting EHRs subsidies managed through the National E-Health Transition Authority (NEHTA) (Charles, Gabriel & Furukawa, 2013). Additionally, Germany has established a public-private partnership to promote interoperability standards and certification of EHR systems, known as Gematik. The same applies to Denmark, which is currently the international leader in adopting IT into its healthcare systems. Denmark has the highest EHR adoption rate, with the most interoperable ones globally. Despite the impressive figures, countries such as the UK have been facing increased challenges, which forced the nation to dismantle their $17 billion Health IT development projects. The UK categorically stated that their main vendor, Computer Sciences Corporation, had wasted over $10 billion because it never provided the expected software. To help it catch up with countries such as Denmark, the U.S. has adopted a HITECH Act (209) that provides EHR incentive programs.

Figure 11.2 summarizes the EHRS ecosystem by graphically presenting global digitization rates amongst select industrialized and middle-income countries (MICs).

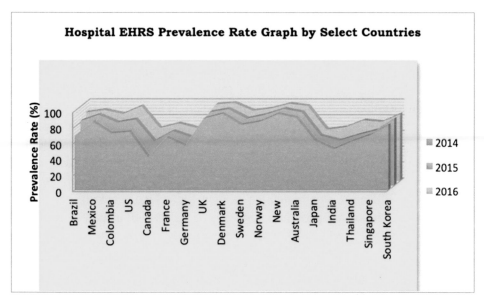

Figure 11.2: The trend of EHRS implementation amongst select countries between 2014 and 2016 inclusive. According to the trend, every country included in the graph increased its digital manual transformation rate during this period. Australia, Denmark, and the UK maintained EHRS conversion rates of above 90% each. Canada, on the other hand, demonstrated a lacklustre performance in 2014 and 2015, occupying the last position amongst these countries. In 2016, Japan took over the bottom of the list amongst industrialized countries. Other very strong performing countries include Mexico, Colombia, the U.S., Sweden, Singapore, and South Korea with 70% or more conversion rates. In 2014, Thailand, India, Japan, Germany, and France all scored below 70%. The same trend continued the following year. While in 2016, Thailand achieved a significant improvement — increasing its digitization rate from 64% to 77% between 2015 and 2016. Japan remained unchanged between 2014 and 2016 with a marginal increase in 2016.

Current Global Geopolitical Dynamics

Until recently, U.S. EHR adoption rates were lower compared to other developed countries. According to Chiasson et al. (2007), in 2006, the U.S. lagged behind other industrialized countries in adopting EHRSs. Even in 2009, the country still lagged behind, particularly amongst primary care doctors (Shachak & Rei, 2009). The adoption rate was still low in other developed countries globally. However, things began to change in 2012 all over the world with the U.S. experiencing an increase from 46% to 69%, while Canada recorded an increase from 37% to 56%. Nevertheless, most of the adoptions were mainly basic, with multi-functional adoption still lower, specifically amongst small medical institutions (Vanek et al. 2016).

Education

In most cases, government institutions handle the education sector, and have been inhibited from using big data by poor infrastructure (Michener & Jones, 2012, p. 90). Cloud computing offers a solution, allowing for the sharing of information by enhancing an education framework (Percivall, 2010, p. 16). The cloud ensures that students, teachers, employees, guardians, and education facilitators can access important data using available gadgets and apps. Public and private institutions can use a cloud to support better administration, even with few assets (Percivall, 2010, p. 16). Some types of data generated and stored by the education sector include student record data, alumni data, staff data, financial data, application and admission data, as well as course data.

Learning management systems (LMSs) make it possible for institutions to offer online material as part of the teaching process. In turn, the LMS captures vast amounts of data about each student, and about the course materials themselves, such as which resources are used most and when. Each class exists in its own online space where students can log in to access announcements, class notes, assignments, readings, and so on. Such systems also enable students to submit work online in various formats — uploaded essays, blogs, discussion groups, etc. On a large scale, such systems also enable universities to teach many more students at one time than would be possible in the classroom. Such massive open online courses, or MOOCs, allow education to be shared around the world.

Utilization by Region

Many policymakers and regulators globally support cloud computing because of its benefits to states, firms, service providers, and the research sector (Ozaet al., 2010, p. 626). Let's look at the state of this technological development region by region.

Africa

In Africa, the success of converging big data and cloud computing requires coherent regulatory frameworks that support transparency, data safety, and adherence to data integrity (Percivall, 2010, p. 16). Despite much progress, advances in big data face issues such as data quality, poor cost-effectiveness, and increased maintenance costs. Additionally, poor internet infrastructure, unsound software, and hardware applications that require virtualization have also inhibited the adoption of big data. Africa faces the biggest challenge as it is significantly affected by low internet penetration and lack of bandwidth to support big data operations.

It has also become hard to trust the security systems in the region, thereby reducing privacy, accessibility, reliability, and compliance (Lu et al. 2011, p. 5). The continent has a long way to go, including launching a reflection process on a well-collaborated and coherent approach to adopting cloud computing, making use of available opportunities while minimizing the risks. It is essential to adopt guidelines that include a transition process to cloud computing, capacity-building procedures, as well as the harmonization of legislative and regulatory frameworks. Other steps include adopting data-centre selection procedures to attract investment and take advantage of business opportunities (Percivall, 2010, p. 16).

Europe

When it comes to the convergence of big data and cloud computing, Europe has managed to conform to proper management performance and assessment procedures, adopting the rules of responsibility sharing (Loveland, Merchant, Brown, & Ohlen, 1991, p. 1454). The firms in Europe have also developed infrastructures that identify incidents associated with system administration failures, providing rapid solutions to existing internal process controls. The main area of improvement, however, includes the need to maintain good relations and open communication channels between all cloud-computing participants and regulators (Oza et al., 2010, p. 626).

South America

Available evidence shows the positive impacts that big data analytics and cloud computing have on South America's IT industry. For many years, traditional computing services in South America have been facing reliability issues and infrastructure inadequacy (Frost & Sullivan, 2016). As a result, stakeholders have been actively embracing the use of big data analytics and cloud computing to address the challenges facing traditional computing practices. One of the main drivers has been the urge by both governments and non-governmental organizations to increase revenue. For instance, total revenue generated in 2015 was US$6.46 billion with a projected increase to $7.7 billion by 2016, attributed to the increasing awareness and deployment of cloud computing software. The region has been registering increasing deployment of infrastructure and software as a service. Also, many companies have been emphasizing cloud computing and big data analytics in their IT projects.

North America

North America has the best infrastructure to support big data operations (Chen, Mao, & Liu, 2014, p. 175). The excellent system in North America has influenced most local governments to embrace technology in streamlining processes and solving operational problems. The need by local governments to provide transparent services by engaging citizens in running government institutions has resulted in the increased use of cloud computing and big data analytics. The approach has enabled local governments and businesses in North America to modernize their IT infrastructure, leading to the present growth of the industry (Chen et al., 2014, p. 178). For instance, increased sharing of data amongst government departments has increased the effectiveness and efficiency of service delivery (Chen et al., 2014, p. 181). Also, data sharing policies have been enacted in most parts of North America to guide the practice of big data analytics and cloud computing. In addition, increased emphasis on data sharing between government agencies and the private sector aims to improve service delivery to citizens.

Asia

Despite big data analytics and cloud computing gaining relevance across the globe, state agencies and businesses in Asia have been reluctant to integrate technological advances into their IT departments. One issue has been uncertainty about data security due to the lack of control over websites and servers (Asprey, 2012, p. 4). Other concerns include inadequate IT staff to ensure efficiency in computing services and the challenges of data integration.

These challenges have influenced both private and government agencies to handle the issue of cloud computing on four fronts: 1) increasing integration of data and analytics into business decisions; 2) making cloud services accessible and secure; 3) embracing the use of social internet services to converse with their customers; 4) leveraging different cloud platforms, both public and private (Asprey, 2012, p. 2). Cloud computing and big data analytics are projected to increase business revenues by US$1.1 trillion in a year. However, growth will not be equal; Japan registered a growth of 155% between 2012 and 2015 while India registered 99% within the same period (Asprey, 2012, p. 2).

Hacking Trends and Big Data

Users expect a safe and secure online experience, for both business and personal purposes. However, increased data breaches, espionage, and cybercrimes have created big challenges. Reports indicate that 178 million records were stolen in 2015, with security breaches highest in Asia and the Pacific region while Europe and North America reported the lowest (Cisco,

2016). In this regard, cloud management is a major, increasingly expensive challenge as shown in Figure 11.3.

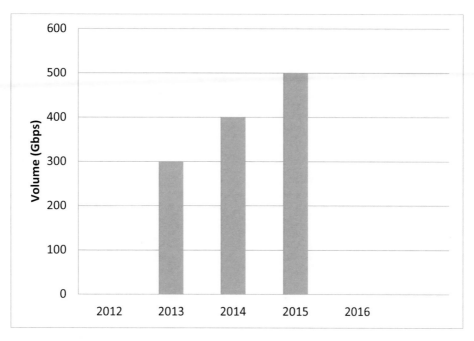

Figure 11.3: Security: hacking trends and big data

Generally, cybercrime damage is expected to cost the world more than US$6 trillion yearly in the next five years, up from $3 billion reported in 2016. Costs include stolen money, destruction of data, loss of productivity, post-attack disruption of normal operations, embezzlement, and theft of intellectual property. The costs also include reputational harm, forensic investigation, and restoration of hacked data.

With cloud-based enterprise workloads projected to increase by 29% in the next five years, security remains one of the biggest challenges.

Case Study – The Ubiquity of Electronic Hacking: My True Cybercrime Story

In the past year alone, large, high-profile companies, including Bell Canada, Deloitte, and Equifax were victims of cyber attacks, failing to protect their systems and their customers' private information. If titans of industry with a small army of people working to protect those systems are vulnerable, what makes us mere mortals still believe it can't happen to us?

I too used to think that only careless and complacent neophytes were likely to fall victim to electronic crime. Boy, was I wrong. So wrong that I ended up with the leading role in my own true cybercrime story.

As I do every year, I contacted my telephone service provider (SP) in December to suspend my services for a period of time. And as always, I tried to contact the SP electronically via a chat session. The process of logging in to my account to do so became impossible. I tried every username and password combination to no avail. Based on the excessive number of login procedures that many of us have to perform for bank accounts, emails, telephones, etc., I concluded that I may have forgotten the login parameters. Wrong again.

I begrudgingly contacted my SP by phone, got comfortable, waited for the endless loop of "muzak" to begin, and proceeded to hold until what felt like the end of time. Someone finally picked up and delivered the dreaded two words: "You can't!"

That's the immediate response I got from the SP representative for wanting to suspend my services. When I asked why the SP told me I had a contract plan and holders of such plans are NOT eligible for any service suspension. I smelled a rat and knew the worst was yet to come.

Fast forward one week: My telephone bills have been automated for the last decade. Every month, I receive an electronic statement from the SP. Unbeknownst to me, and partially because I trust my SP, I realized that I had not received my September and October 2017 statements — even though automatic deductions continued to be made from my account.

During my earlier phone call to the SP, I listened to an automated message detailing my payments and deductions for the month of October. The payment amount was more than twice my regular payment. The drama only escalated when I eventually spoke to a real person at the other end of the line. When the SP told me about the ineligibility of suspending my services, I reminded the provider that I wasn't doing anything out of the ordinary, and that, in fact, I did this every year. She reiterated that because I was on a "service" contract, I couldn't suspend my services. I retorted that I wasn't on a service contract. The SP insisted — even telling me the brand of phone I had, which was provided as part of the contract. I told the SP that during the last decade, I had always used my own phone and that contracts were not desirable to me. We agreed that I needed to verify my automatic deductions. Once I did, I found out that monthly overpayments had been deducted from my account more than twice. I also verified my electronic monthly bills, and low and behold, I had not received any bills for September and

October. The SP confirmed that the bills were sent to my "new" email address and that was the reason no red flags were raised.

The SP immediately initiated an investigation, and all the extra charges to my account were reversed. It turned out the perpetrator hacked my SP account and modified my details, including changing my email address, to syphon payments from my account to pay for their costly new phone and services.

So what can we take away from this? Even with painstaking care taken by some users and providers, hackers are generally always ahead of the curve. With all the sophisticated and advanced technological strategies available and implemented by some small and large organizations, the challenges continue to evolve with limited green light on the other side of the Rubicon. This situation becomes even more distressing when trusted "insiders" are found to be complicit in some of these criminal practices.

According to current research findings, electronic theft is yet to peak and the tipping point will surely be a wake-up call for all of us!

At a personal level, my experience as a user of many services reminded me how vulnerable we are, especially in circumstances beyond our control. Even when precautions are taken, the reality is that even the most diligent and adept institutions remain at risk. So stay vigilant my friends, and try to make peace with "musak" and being put on hold.

Summary Statistics

Based on the most current and available data from various sources, an effort is made to analyze available and current statistics in an attempt to better resonate the dynamics of BDCA in the last several years.

In one survey (IDC, 2012), there is a distribution and estimates of capacity utilization rates. The projected data indicate that by 2020, the amount of data created every second per person will be about 1.7 megabytes. Retrospectively, between 2013 and 2015, Facebook recorded more than one billion users daily — a significant utilization of big data. Over the same period (See Figure 11.4), there was an increase of 31% performing analysis on operations-related data, 29% analyzing consumer behaviour on online platforms, 21% on transaction-related data, 19% on service innovations, 17% on machine data analysis, and 11% on workloads not related to analytics.

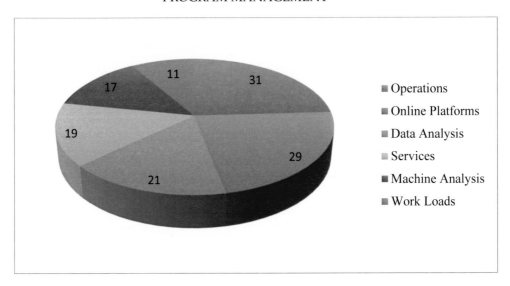

Figure11.4: Thematic rate (%) of data utilization
Source: IDC, 2012

A global distribution (www.statista.com, 2016) of cloud utilization rates by volume was also reviewed. These figures range from 1,971 in 2012 to 5,074 exabytes (one billion gigabytes) in 2016, with a corresponding rate from 19% between 2012 and 2013 to 41.5% in 2016.

A thematic (health) distribution of cloud utilization by costs indicates a volume of data-related funding of $2.4 billion dollars. There were annual increases of 25% and 133% in 2013 and 2014 respectively. In 2014, there was an unexplainable decrease of 14%.

With regard to the thematic (social media) distribution (Sara & Todd, 2016, p. 4) of cloud utilization rate by category of users, the following was also reported: Between 2012 and 2016, there were progressive increases ranging from 1.6 to 2.3 billion users. This represented an increase of 13% in 2013, 10% in 2014, and 2015 and 9% in 2016.

In the business thematic area (www.cisco.com, 2016), data were not available for 2012 and 2013. In 2015 and 2016, the distribution of cloud utilization by volume was 167,784 and 196,788 petabytes (one million gigabytes) respectively; an increase of 17.7% between both years.

From a regional perspective, no data were available for Europe between 2012 and 2014 inclusive. In 2015 and 2016, the cloud utilization rate by volume was 198,048 and 240,780 petabytes respectively; yielding an increase of 21.6% between both years.

In North America, no data were available between 2012 and 2014 inclusive. During the subsequent two years — 2015 and 2016 — cloud utilization volume was 297,108 and 363,804 petabytes respectively; with a rate increase of 22.4%.

In Asia, no figures were available for 2012 to 2014 inclusive. There was a cloud-utilization by volume of 45,864 and 64,560 petabytes respectively, an increase of 21.4% between the two years, 2015 and 2016.

Africa had no data between 2012 and 2014. The corresponding figures for 2015 and 2016 were 23,160 and 32,376 petabytes respectively with an annual increase of 21.6%.

South America also had no data from 2012 to 2014. The utilization between 2015 and 2016 was 54,000 and 65,892 petabytes respectively with an annual increase of 22%.

Conclusion

The evidence shows the numerous benefits resulting from the application of BDCA. The technology has increased information availability and promoted economic growth by optimizing the efficiency of services delivered to the society. The challenges, however still exist. These range from data security to data quality to ubiquitous vulnerability of individual privacy. On the whole, the benefits do outweigh the risks and the future looks brighter than ever. While the technology continues to be driven by industrialized countries, there is every reason to believe the universal implementation of BDCA is a matter of time. BDCA has revolutionized the way we do business. It has transformed megabytes of data, as we know it, into petabytes of information. And if current trends are any indication, no region will be left behind. It's significant contribution to improved productivity, optimizing costs, facilitating information sharing and access including the ubiquitous capability of analyses of latent data cannot be adequately emphasized. Its ecosystem is adequately comprehensive, inclusive (human beings, hardware, and software), complementary and pragmatic. Based on research findings, in summary, the BDCA challenges and achievements are profound. And what about the prognoses? The best is yet to come.

A longer version of this chapter titled *"How big data, cloud computing and analytics (BDCCA)"* by Lainjo, B. is published in *"Humanities and Social Sciences Review (HSSR)"*, Volume 8, No. 2, http://universitypublications.net/hssr/0802/index.html.

CHAPTER 12: Cybercrime – Implications On Program Operation Management

Introduction

The internet (also known as World Wide Web) has enabled people to do almost everything, from playing games online to carrying out bank transactions, to shopping, and so on. However, according to Amoroso (2012), with all these advantages the internet has also brought new forms of crime. These crimes are done virtually and may include sabotage and/or theft (Bossler & Burruss, 2011). Furnell & Warren (1999) cited that these crimes are usually hard to combat. According to Brenner (2010), this is mainly because as internet and personal computer technologies become more sophisticated, new forms of cybercrime emerge to exploit the vulnerabilities and opportunities that these new technologies offer. This means that today's cybercrime has gone high tech and has become even harder to fight (Holt & Lampke, 2010).

The question is have we now become victims of our own strategies? To a large extent, the answer is a resounding and unequivocal yes. Innovations come with both intended and unintended outcomes. Automations or electronic transitions are no exception. At the individual and institutional levels, the vulnerabilities remain daunting, compelling, and challenging. The complexities of electronic hacking have, for the most part, remained an enigma. The difficulties faced by the service providers in establishing stable trends have also limited their ability to effectively pre-empt many of these attacks.

The cybercrime ecosystem is also very diversified. It ranges from bank accounts, emails, phone services, education and political party databases, just to mention a few. There have even been cases where perpetrators have held victims as hostages and requested ransoms.

Program operation computerization or electronic transition is driven by convenience; it guarantees universal access to services by users, it facilitates competitiveness and the management of large amounts of data, it improves productivity, and when used effectively, updates and the execution of routine processes are optimized. However, each and every one of these outcomes comes with risks, anxiety, and in some cases, a significant amount of uncertainty. To the suppliers or service providers, concerns like the following become the order of the day: How vulnerable is my system? How can I be ahead of the curve and protect my system from potential cybercriminals? Are there any fool-proof security systems? How can confidentiality be continuously assured?

Suppliers and users of electronic services are often at the mercy of hackers. And if currently reported achievements by these perpetrators are any indication the mysteries and challenges continue to be ubiquitous. Pro-activity and the ability to pre-empt these reprehensible crimes should be the focus of any strategy. The inclusion of an information officer as an information technology team member would also help in mitigating the magnitude of these concerns and vulnerabilities. Also, current laws in different countries need to be revised and updated in order to better address cybersecurity weaknesses.

Ways in which cybercrime may be executed

Applegate (2015) notes that currently there are three main ways in which cybercrime may be executed; through hacking, through malware, and through "distributed denial of service attacks." According to Morris (2010), hacking is gaining unauthorized access to online data or on an interconnected system. Hacking is usually carried out by hackers. However, Cashell, Jackson, Jickling, & Webel (2004) argue that not all hackers are actually criminals. Some of them are law-abiding hackers who gain access to systems only in order to test their vulnerability to external attacks (criminal hacking) (Gandhi, et al., 2011). Big companies like Google, Facebook, and Microsoft employ such hackers (Allen, 2015).

Vulnerability of the corporate world to electronic hacking

According to Gal-Or & Ghose (2004), a number of companies have suffered as a result of electronic hacking. For example, according to Bloomberg (Walters, 2014), in 2014, South Korea alone reported that more than 140 million accounts stemming from a number of retailers, gas stations, and e-commerce websites were compromised (Walters, 2014). In the United States (U.S.), according to Allen (2015), in December 2013, Target (a departmental store based in Minneapolis) reported that information from more than 110 million credit and debit card payments by its customers were accessed illegally. The hackers stole personal identification numbers (PINs) from the cards, and as a result, Target lost more than $3.5 billion (Jarvis, Macdonald, & Nouri, 2014). Hutchings (2014) cited that Neiman Marcus (a Dallas based retail store) also reported that the information from 1.1 million credit and debit card payments was hacked in 2013. In 2008, data in more than 130 million credit and debit cards belonging to Heartland Payment Systems (a U.S.-based payment processing and technology service provider) customers were breached by electronic hackers (Poulsen & Summerer, 2015).

Why hack?

According to Snail (2009), criminal hackers do not hack systems for pleasure, fun, or sport. They search the internet for vulnerable systems to steal information they deem they can benefit from financially. According to Orr (2008), such types of information may include Social Security numbers; insurance identification numbers; passport numbers; bank credit and debit card numbers; usernames, PINs, and passwords; driver's license numbers; utility bill account numbers; student and employment identification numbers; etc.

McGuire & Dowling (2013) cite that hackers tend to use this information to commit fraud. They may use credit and debit card numbers to make purchases or sell the information to third parties. Moore (2010) noted that a single credit card number may be sold for $10 dollars. Moore (2010) further notes that elite cards with no limit may be sold for hundreds of dollars. This means that a hacker who successfully accesses such information from a big company and steals thousands or even millions of such information may make huge sums of money.

Implications of cybercrime on program operation management

The aim of every company, regardless of it being non-profit oriented, profit-oriented, government-owned, or privately owned, is to ensure that its operations such as supply chain, contracts, production processes, management, etc., are running smoothly. Any interference to such operations may have dire consequences. With computerizations and the advent of the internet, management of such operations has not only become easy but efficient. However, the adoption of computers and the internet in the program operation management has exposed companies to electronic hacking.

According to Iovan & Iovan (2017), in 2014, a number of supply chains of companies located in the U.S. and Europe were attacked by cybercriminals. Since these hackers were unable to attack the main companies directly, they targeted their contractors who were located in Japan, China, and South Korea (Iovan & Iovan, 2017). One such group of attackers was known as "Icefog." According to Iovan & Iovan (2017), these attackers were so focused, that after getting the information they wanted from the supply chain agent, they would disappear within a very short period.

According to Iovan & Iovan (2017), some specialized electronic hacking programs, such as Trojan, are able to track online banking operations and either sabotage the system or steal money from the banks — or even both. Hackers are also capable of compromising company websites and redirect visitors to other sites with the intention of damaging the company's reputation or interfering with its supply chain (Iovan & Iovan, 2017).

Prognosis of hacking

With the current threat of electronic hacking in the corporate world, the social world, and the political word, what does the future hold? This might be the question lingering in the minds of many people. What is certain is that as internet and personal computer technologies become more sophisticated, new forms of electronic hacking will emerge to exploit the vulnerabilities and opportunities that these new technologies will offer (Taylor, Fritsch, & Liederbach, 2014). This means that in the future, hacking will be high tech and even harder to combat. For example, as the automobile and aviation industries continue to take advantages of computer technology to develop technologically advanced cars and airplanes, new threats that target these technologies are coming up. An example of this would be the case in which two professional hackers hacked into the Toyota Prius' computer system and were able to accelerate the car, stop the car, and jam its steering wheel. They were able to do all these activities remotely (Allen, 2015).

Background

What is cyberattack or electronic hacking?

Cyberattack, or simply, electronic hacking, is an attack that is launched from one or more computers against another computer, computer network, or a group of computers, with the aim of accessing information without the owner's or admin's authorization or knowledge (Loukas, 2015).

The aim of cyberattack

The aims of these attacks may be categorized into two. One, to disable the targeted network, computer or groups of computers, and knock them offline. Two, to gain unauthorized access to information or data in the target computer and steal the admin's privileges on the data and use them to commit fraud (Kim *et al.*, 2012).

Techniques used by electronic hackers to achieve their goals

There are a number of techniques used by electronic hackers to achieve their goals. These include malware, hacking, phishing, man-in-the-middle attacks, and denial of services.

Malware

These are software that are downloaded and installed on the target's computer or computer network system (McLaughlin, 2011). The software may launch itself by exploiting the vulnerabilities in the target's computer operating system or compel the owner to install it by enticing them with some kind of false information. After successful installation, the malware can then do anything on the host computer or network, from stealing sensitive information or data to encrypting the data and demanding ransom. A ransom is usually demanded for the victim to be able to regain access to the encrypted data (Savage, Coogan and Lau, 2015). A good example of software that can download and launch itself into the victim's computer is Trojan. This malware is capable of tracking victims' operations such as online banking activities, shopping activities, etc., with the aim of stealing information or sabotaging systems. Another example of this malware is ransomware. As explained earlier, this malware encrypts victims' data and demands ransom in exchange for re-access.

Many types of malware exist, including spyware, crimeware, computer virus, scareware, and adware. In order to spread this malware, the hackers may create malicious websites and lure victims to them. They may also exploit vulnerabilities in software applications used on a website or the vulnerability of a web server.

Phishing

Phishing involves sending potential victims fake emails that appear to have come from reputable and legitimate companies, such as a person's credit union or bank (Chu *et al.*, 2013). These fake emails have a uniform resource locator (URL) that redirects the victim to a malicious web page where they will be asked to enter private information such as credit card numbers, bank account information, passwords, etc. (Chu *et al.*, 2013). The hackers may then use this information to commit fraud. The phishing sites are normally hosted on legitimate websites, which have been attacked as a result of poor internet security (Alsharnouby, Alaca and Chiasson, 2015).

There are different types of phishing, including clone phishing, spear phishing, and whale phishing. Whale phishing normally targets high-profile business people, such as executives (Chu *et al.*, 2013). Spear phishing is aimed at specific departments or people. It collects personal information about its victims (Chu *et al.*, 2013). Clone phishing, on the other hand, duplicates a legitimate email that someone has sent and resends it (Chu *et al.*, 2013). However, it replaces the original email attachments or links with malicious ones.

Hacking

Hacking generally involves accessing a computer network or computer by exploiting its weakness (Loukas, 2015). Hacking is usually carried out to access the personal data of the victim. There are a number of hacking techniques including keyloggers, rootkit, vulnerability scanners, packet sniffers, Trojan horses, password crackers, structured query language (SQL) injections, etc. SQL injection is a code that takes advantage of security vulnerabilities that exist in the database of a software application (Loukas, 2015). Generally, it targets software and applications that require user input information, such as username and password, to access the system or database. This method has been used to gain access into a number of financial institution systems, global payment processor systems, and retail enterprise systems. Applications such as ModSecurity may help prevent these types of attacks (Kim *et al.*, 2012).

Denial of service

Another form of electronic hacking (cyberattack) is denial of service (DoS) (McDowell, 2009). This type of attack works differently compared to how other cyberattack techniques work. While other types of electronic hacking are looking for ways of gaining access into the victim's website, network, database, or computer, the denial of service technique allows hackers to sabotage a computer network system, or a computer itself, without actually gaining internal access (Feng and Tesi, 2017). The attackers overload the system's routers with large quantities of fake traffic until it fails. It is usually very difficult to prevent these types of attacks. However, an attempt at reducing the consequences of such attacks employs services or software that can differentiate between malicious traffic and legitimate traffic.

The threat of electronic hacking

More and more individuals, companies, government agencies, and non-governmental agencies (NGOs) have become either vulnerable to, or the victims of electronic hacking. According to Iovan and Iovan (2016), a big proportion of organizations throughout the world have experienced some form of electronic hacking. Of the companies that have experienced these cybercrimes, a good proportion of them have either lost important data or money. These attacks are often carefully planned in advance in order to successfully access the network infrastructure of a target company. The current ubiquity of electronic hacking is a result of the widespread use of digital technologies businesses use to enhance operations. This has also made it relatively easy for cyber espionage malware to steal company data.

It is important to note that cybercrime (through computer fraud) is not necessarily carried out online. Some of these computer frauds may also be carried out offline (Kim *et al.*, 2012). However, an online platform provides a perfect environment for a wide variety of cybercrime: stealing of debit and credit card information, identity fraud, phishing, advance fee fraud, internet auction fraud, etc. (Iovan and Iovan, 2016). These types of cybercrime may be conducted via a number of media, such as social networking sites, emails, online shopping sites, company websites, etc. This means that companies whose operations have gone digital (online) are highly vulnerable to electronic hacking. Company operations that may be carried out online may include submission of tender and contract documents, supply information, monitoring of employee performance, monitoring of the manufacturing or production process, carrying out online payments, conducting job interviews and employee selections, etc. (McLaughlin, 2011). Once these operations are online, a company becomes vulnerable to electronic hacking since the information tied to these activities can then be accessed (Iovan and Iovan, 2016). Therefore, proper actions should be taken to prevent illegal access to the company's network infrastructure. Any successful access to the company's system may have both legal and financial consequences.

Current Dynamics in Cybercrime

Cyberattacks have become a reality since the advent of the internet and computer technologies. In an attempt to deal with this threat posed to companies and individuals, computer and internet technologies have become highly sophisticated. However, this sophistication also helps to create highly sophisticated cyber threats, as hackers also upgrade their systems to exploit vulnerabilities in these new systems. Therefore, it is harder to fight electronic hackers today compared to many years back. For example, it is estimated that in 2017 alone, electronic hackers caused more than $5 billion in damages in the U.S. (Smyth, 2017). This is a more than a 15-time increase in damages compared to the two years previous to that. The estimates for losses that resulted from cybercrime are shown in Figure 12.1. At this rate, it is estimated that within the next three years, spending on cybersecurity could exceed US$1 trillion (Smyth, 2017). It is also estimated that, given current trends, by the year 2022, damages inflicted by cyberattacks could exceed $6 trillion per year (Smyth, 2017). This is because even more complicated and sophisticated threats will emerge in the future

Recently, a new crop of cyber threats has emerged. These attacks, which are harder to fight and highly sophisticated, include: Wannacry, Ethereum attack, NotPetya, Yahoo (revised), Equifax attack, etc.

WannaCry

This was a ransomware cyberattack that occurred and spread around May 2017 (Fruhlinger, 2017). It infected the victims' computers and encrypted the contents of their hard drives. It then demanded payments in Bitcoin in order to decrypt the files (Fruhlinger, 2017). One of the biggest victims of Wannacry was the NHS (National Health Service), the national healthcare system in the United Kingdom (Fruhlinger, 2017). The malware (Wannacry), infected computers at NHS facilities by taking advantage of a weakness in Microsoft Windows using an algorithm that was developed by the United States National Security Agency (NSA) (Fruhlinger, 2017). This code was developed secretly and without the knowledge of Microsoft. The code (algorithm), called "EternalBlue," was stolen from the NSA's systems by a group of hackers who call themselves "Shadow Brokers" (Fruhlinger, 2017). This is just one glimpse of what modern-day cybercrime is capable of.

NotPetya

Another recent cyberattack was NotPetya. This is also another form of ransomware, which started spreading in 2016 as a phishing spam (Smyth, 2017). It encrypted "master boot record" (files in a computer operating system responsible for booting up the computer) of the victims' computers, making it difficult to gain computer access. In 2017, a more dangerous and sophisticated version of the malware popped up and started spreading quickly, causing just under US$1,000 in damages (Smyth, 2017). This version also spread via EternalBlue, just like the WannaCry attack.

Ethereum attack

This attack occurred in 2017, and huge amounts of money were stolen by an unknown hacker in the form of Ether, a cryptocurrency similar to Bitcoin (Karl and Gervais, 2016). The hacker took advantage of a weakness that existed within "Parity multi-signature wallet" on Ethereum (the cryptocurrency's platform) (Fruhlinger, 2017). The attacker first stole $7.4 million from the platform (Fruhlinger, 2017). Two weeks later, the system was hacked again, and the hacker managed to steal more than US$31 million within a few minutes before they were stopped (Fruhlinger, 2017). Given they had more time, it is estimated that more than $180 million could have been stolen (Fruhlinger, 2017). Since the stolen money could not be recovered, and the system could not be protected, a group of computer security specialists drained all the funds before the attackers could do any more damage. The estimate for the total amount of money that has been lost by cybercrime victims between 2013 and 2016 as a result of electronic hacking is shown in Figure 12.3.

Equifax attack

In 2017, Equifax, a credit rating agency, reported that cybercriminals exploited the vulnerability of their U.S. website and accessed a number of files. These files contained the personal information of close to 150 million people (Perlroth, 2017). The scale of this single attack is proof of just how successful modern hackers can be (Perlroth, 2017).

Yahoo attack

Technology giants like Yahoo are not spared when it comes to these high-tech criminals. Although Yahoo systems were hacked in 2013, the potential severity of this type of attack was not realized until 2017, when more than 3 billion Yahoo email addresses were hacked (Goel and Perlroth, 2016). The hackers stole backup email addresses, encrypted data (data encrypted through outdated techniques), and passwords (Thielman, 2016). This attack proved the secrecy of anything stored online can never be guaranteed.

Evolution

Where did this cybercrime menace come from? It is understood that cyber-related crimes were committed even before the arrival of the internet (Le VPN, 2017). To answer this question, we need to ask more still. Why were computers invented? Why was the internet invented? Why were computer networks created? All these technologies were invented mainly to create, store, and distribute information. That information may be personal, corporate information or government information. The desire to access this information for personal gain has bred cybercrime.

Generally, the evolution and history of cybercrime coincide with the evolution of the World Wide Web (the internet). Initially, cybercrimes didn't even require the internet to be executed (Le VPN, 2017). They involved stealing information from a local computer network. With the invention and advancements in internet technology, cybercrime also became advanced. While cybercrime has been in existence for a long time, major cybercrimes started to occur in the 1980s, with the invention and spread of the use of emails (Le VPN, 2017). In these early hackings, the hacker would create malware or/and scams and send them to the victim's mailbox. A good example of this kind of scam was "Nigerian Prince," where an email was sent to someone's mailbox by someone pretending to be a prince from Nigerian (Le VPN, 2017). The email purported that the prince wanted to send millions of dollars out of their country but could not do so for one reason or another (Le VPN, 2017).

The second wave of cybercrime came in the later part of the 20th century (1990s), with the invention and advancement of web browsers. It is understood that most web browsers that were in use during the 90s were vulnerable to viruses (Le VPN, 2017). The virus would be delivered to people's computers whenever they visited malicious websites. Some of these viruses made computers operate slowly, others would create some pop-up advertisements that tended to crowd the victim's computer screen, and some would redirect the victim to websites such as pornography sites (Le VPN, 2017).

Cybercrime started becoming a more serious threat in the early 2000s when social networks were invented (Le VPN, 2017). This was propagated by the desire to put personal information on social networks. This essentially created a database of personal and identifying information. This availability of personal information gave rise to cybercriminals, who then targeted this identifying information for theft. This information was used for a number of purposes, namely: to set up credit cards, access victims' bank accounts, etc.

The latest cybercrimes involve highly sophisticated electronic hackers who target anything on the internet that they may deem beneficial to them. Cybercrime is a global industry, responsible for damages worth trillions of dollars annually (Le VPN, 2017).

Review of Cyber Security Data Breach in U.S.

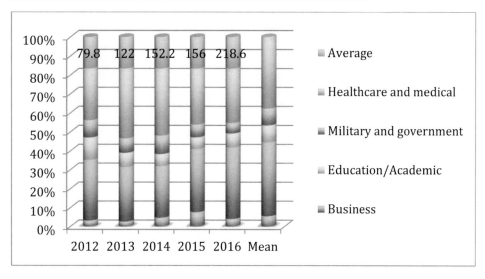

Figure 12.1: Reported annual thematic cybersecurity breaches in the U.S.
Source: ITRC 2013-2017

In Figure 12.1, between 2012 and 2016, there was an increasing trend in banking and finance, business, and healthcare institutions. The trend in education/academic and combined military and government was mixed.

Business had the most number of cases reported in 2012, 2015, and 2016. The healthcare and medical institutions took the lead in 2013, 2014, and 2016. The banking finance and credit institutions had the least number of cases reported between 2012 and 2016. This may be either due to the conservative nature of the institutions or compelling successful rates of biometric data utilization to mitigate cybercrime.

On the average during this period, business institutions had the most number of cases closely followed by the health and medical establishments. Banking, credit and finance were at the bottom with military and government with education and academic setups in between with an equal number of cases.

With regard to the annual performance, there is an increasing trend amongst these select institutions between 2012 and 2016; with the highest mean reported in 2016 and the least in 2012.

In summary, the thematic of reported electronic hacking cases maintained an upward trend between 2012 and 2016.

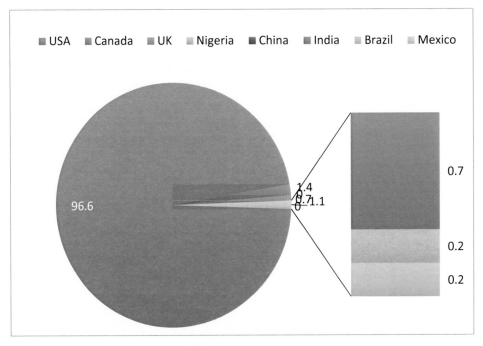

Figure 12.2: Percentage of annual regional EH reported cases in select countries,
Source: FBI Internet Crime Complain, 2012-2016 excluding 2015

The results in Figure 12.2 do not include 2015 because of incomplete data. Hence the period under consideration was from 2012 to 2014 and 2016.

The select count from N America, S America, Europe, and Asia. The highest proportion of reported case was from the U.S. with 96.6% or 298,728 cases. China and Nigeria had the least percentages, which were both not significant. The UK and India had 0.7% each while Brazil and Mexico came up 0.7% each.

Periodically, the number of reported cases peaked in 2016 and bottomed in 2013 with 38,498 and 34,025 respectively.

Implications of Cybercrime on Program Operation Management

Why cybercriminals target companies

As a result of efficiencies associated with digital technology, companies are now employing the technology in their day-to-day operations. Today, almost all operations in companies are controlled by computers through automation. Businesses can award tenders by just a click of a button, tenders can be requested without physically visiting the company, manufacturing can be done entirely by automated robots, meetings can be held through teleconferencing, every production stage in manufacturing can be monitored in real time, a nuclear power plant can be switched on or off, etc. These operations are so important that interfering with any of them can bring down an entire company. Today's crop of cybercriminals is targeting such operations, with the main goal of sabotaging them. Cybercrime is on the rise with each passing day and is costing companies dearly. Cybercriminals break into company databases to steal customer or financial information. They may also deny customers access to a company's website. The hackers may also install a virus that is capable of monitoring company operations both online and offline, so long as the operations are carried out or monitored by a computer or computer network system (Iovan & Iovan, 2017).

As mentioned earlier, companies or businesses that operate online are highly vulnerable to cybercrime and have to deal with a number of possible ways that cybercrime may affect program operation. These include loss in sales, cost of protection, and changing modes of doing business.

Impact of Cybercrime on PoM

Given the current trends and the escalating negative impact of electronic hacking, one is led to believe that the service providers and users will develop different ways of defeating this potentially ubiquitous crime. The burden will, however, be more daunting on the latter. They will need to be more polyvalent in addressing these dynamic and complex landscapes. Mindsets will change (hopefully for the better); more effective and inclusive strategies will be developed and enhanced; the level of resilience will be strengthened; more enabling environments and effective mechanisms will be developed, established and implemented; and level of awareness will be significantly improved. Other implications of cybercrime on program operations management will include the following:

- Increased global demand for services will alter the playing field.
- Level of vulnerability amongst SPs and users will continue to escalate.
- Need for industrialized countries to be ahead of the curve will increase. They will also need to maintain leadership roles in mitigating electronic hacking-related challenges.
- Social media will dominate the level of vulnerability.
- Demands on SPs will be more complex and unstructured.
- Cybercriminals will have more opportunities to invade systems.
- Electronic hacking (EH) will motivate more countries to update and revise cybercrime laws reflecting the reality on the ground.
- Escalating cybercrimes will dramatically increase the cost of Big Data Cloud Computing Analytics.
- SPs will be more interested in participating in cybercrime mitigation partnerships.
- There will be more and more cybercrime litigations.

Loss in sales

Over the past five years, a new crop of cybercriminals called cyberactivists has emerged. These electronic hackers target a company's online operation programs. Their main intention is to shut down the operations and steal information regarding a company's business practices, which they give or sell to third parties (Cavusoglu, Mishra and Raghunathan, 2004). Examples of companies that have been attacked in this way are MasterCard and PayPal.

In 2010, PayPal's website was hacked by a group claiming to be part of "Anonymous" (responsible for a number of cyberattacks) (Hintz, 2013). The hackers tried to access a "denial of service" system, which PayPal had imposed on WikiLeaks. The motive of the attack was revenge on PayPal against its decision to shut down services provided to WikiLeaks (Hintz, 2013). A number of hackers were arrested and charged. Even though PayPal was not entirely shut down by this attack, there were a number of companies that were not as lucky (Hintz, 2013). As a result of the "denial of service" attack, customers were not able to access online stores for a number of companies. If such a denial continues for a lengthy period of time, the victim company may lose some of its customers, and consequently, company revenues go down.

Changing modes of doing business

As a result of cybercrimes, companies normally think of new ways of collecting and storing data to ensure these data are not vulnerable to electronic hacking (Iovan & Iovan, 2017). Due to the vulnerability of online platforms, a number of companies no longer store their customers' personal and financial information such as birth dates, Social Security numbers, and credit card numbers on their platforms (Iovan & Iovan, 2017). Other companies have completely shut down online operations they cannot adequately secure. These changes in operations may cost businesses a lot of money since they will not enjoy the competitive advantage that comes through the use of digital technology.

Protection cost

Because electronic hacking can have dire consequences, companies normally protect their systems against such threats. However, this protection does not come cheap. The costs involved in detecting threats, buying cybersecurity hardware and software, and developing safer operation processes are usually high (Hintz, 2013). Regardless of the high cost, businesses that are highly complex or store sensitive information, or whose operations are controlled digitally, often hire cybersecurity consultants in order to develop a system that is safe and customized to suit their needs (Hintz, 2013). But this also does not come cheap. The upfront fees normally paid to these consultants are usually very high (Hintz, 2013). In addition, the developed systems must be continuously monitored and tested to ensure that they still function effectively. (Hintz, 2013).

The Impacts Of Blockchain Technology

Current data access protocols

The success of modern business is determined in part by access to information. However, the access to such information and data is currently controlled by a few individuals or entities. These individuals or entities are commonly referred to as gatekeepers. Examples of such gatekeepers are Facebook and Google. These entities have managed to effectively monopolize on the business-driven data and consequently, information dynamics. This gives them a competitive advantage over new entrants and their competitors thus maintaining a status quo.

With the emergence of social media and internet technology, things are now changing. Social media has enabled individuals to have great control over their personal information. People can now share their information with whom they want. This means that people now play a greater role in information sharing.

Blockchain protocol

Even though blockchain technology is still in its infancy, the technology is able to break the transactional barriers put up by the gatekeepers. Through blockchain technologies users in a network can effectively share information in a format that is credible and safe from electronic hackers. That is, the blockchain protocol enhances the open data access where data is made available for those who need it. This is opposed to the current protocol in which data is kept and controlled by the gatekeepers.

Blockchain technology and cybersecurity

The emerging blockchain technology may offer some hope to companies in terms of security for their online data. The technology enables users to create a permanent history of transactions carried out amongst themselves. The transaction history can only be changed with the agreement of all the parties involved, and even after information is changed, the previous information is still saved and interlinked with the current information. According to experts, the system cannot be hacked. In order to corrupt or destroy data, a hacker will have to destroy data in each user's computer in the global network. These computers could range in the millions, with each computer storing a copy of the data.

Even though few companies have adopted the technology, a number of industries have adopted or tested its application in program operations. For example, in 2017 Maersk (a global shipping company), partnered with IBM to digitize its supply chain using blockchain technology. The company expects to start using blockchain ledger to track and manage the movements of its shipping containers later in 2018. Another company that is already using blockchain technology is Guardtime (a software security company).

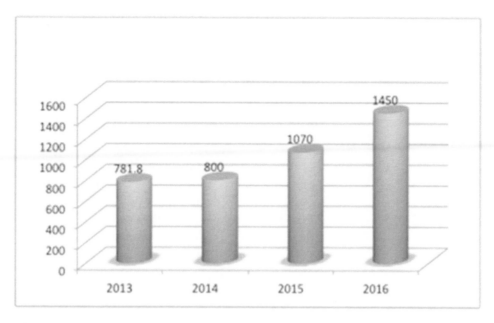

Figure 12.3: Annual cybercrime costs (million $) in the U.S.
Source: FBI Internet Crime Center, 2017

Figure 12.3 illustrates a cybercrime positive rate increase from 2013 to 2016, inclusive. The annual rate increase between 2013 and 2014 was about 2.3%. Between 2014 and 2015, there was a positive increase rate of 3.4%. This positive trend continued with an increased rate of about 3.6% between 2015 and 2016.

From Figure 12.3, it is observed that there is a positive trend in the number of successful cybersecurity breaches in the U.S. in almost all industries from 2012 to 2016. There was an exception for the education sector and military and government agencies, which recorded staggered trends in the same period. Regardless of this, there is a general positive trend in the total number of successful cybersecurity breaches per year for the same period (2012–2016). The successful breaches were as follows: 399, 614, 761, 760, and 1,093 for the years 2012, 2013, 2014, 2015, and 2016 respectively. It is also observed that the most vulnerable sectors are businesses, and healthcare and medicine. These two sectors account for more than 70% of the total data breaches in all the years considered. In 2012, they accounted for 79.7% of the total breaches. In the years 2013, 2014, 2015, and 2016, they accounted for 70.9%, 78.2%, 75.3%, and 75.4%, respectively, of the total data breaches as a result of electronic hacking.

From Figure 12.2, it is observed that the U.S. accounts for a larger number of reported cases of electronic hacking. In all the years, it accounted for more than 90% of the total reported cases — except for the year 2015, where it accounted for 80.2% of the cases. The U.S. was followed by Canada, which accounted for less 3% for the years considered. Recorded countries in other regions such as Nigeria (Africa), China (Asia), Brazil (South America), etc., accounted for less than 1% of the reported cases.

Discussion

The results show that there is a general increase in almost every aspect of electronic hacking. The cost of cybercrime in the U.S. is on the rise, and the number of successful cybercrime breaches is also on the rise. There is obviously a cause for serious concern when one looks at these positive trends. These results are just a glimpse of the actual figures, as many businesses do not report cases of cybercrime for fear of negative outcomes, such as losing credibility, client confidence, and potential revenues.

The results also show that the most vulnerable sectors to cybercrime are businesses and healthcare institutions. This means that program operations in these sectors are at high risk of being attacked by cybercriminals. Therefore, every company, NGO, government, and other institution (especially the ones under the above sectors) need to stay on alert and seriously consider the possible ramifications if this trend were to continue. In that case, the future remains bleak and enigmatic. But the advancement of technology such as blockchain technology offers some hope in the future. According to experts, a system that is developed using blockchain technology cannot be hacked (at least for now). This is currently being tested by a number of companies. However, it is important to remember that as technology continues to advance, the knowledge and skills of electronic hackers will also continue to advance. It is, therefore, hard to predict the effectiveness of future cybersecurity technologies, like blockchain.

Conclusion

Computer and internet technological advancements have enabled companies, government institutions, NGOs, etc., to carry out their daily program operations efficiently through automation. In many companies, almost every aspect is automated. However, the enjoyment of the full potential of these technologies is being hampered by cybercrime. The more a company digitizes its operation through online platforms, the more vulnerable it is to electronic hacking. Companies and individuals have lost billions of dollars worth of data due to electronic hacking. In recent times, companies, as well as individuals have faced very complicated cyber threats such as Wannacry,

Ransomware, Notpetya, etc. These threats can sabotage the operations of a company, such as preventing its customers from accessing the company's website or redirecting customers to malware websites, or even stopping a company's production machine remotely.

The trend of increasing cyberattacks is expected to continue as internet and computer technologies become more advanced. This is because as technologies in internet and computer become more sophisticated, new forms of electronic hacking techniques emerge to exploit the vulnerabilities and opportunities offered by the new technologies. The levels of vulnerability are global and inclusive with very high thematic risks of large-scale negative effects on productivity. Long-term, effective, and sustainable strategies are urgently required. These need to include more innovative national laws and policies. The current levels of vulnerabilities are, as expected, skewed towards big data, cloud computing and analytics service providers — primarily from industrialized and high-income countries, with the U.S. significantly most affected.

CHAPTER 13: Enhancing Program Management with Predictive Analytics Algorithms

Introduction

This chapter examines the current knowledge and scholarly information about predictive analytics algorithms (PAAs) by focusing on the concept of working principles on which they are used to predict future events and the procedures followed in creating them. The PAAs have been used extensively in predicting future events in healthcare practice, manufacturing companies, businesses, education, sports, and agriculture. The main programming languages used to create PAAs are Java, C, and Python amongst others. The forms of algorithms that are commonly used are brute force algorithm, simple recursive algorithm, backtracking algorithm, randomized algorithm, and dynamic programming algorithms.

Background

Over the years, the concept and principles of data management have remained mostly unchanged. What has changed, however, includes the introduction of a complex, state-of-the-art, sophisticated, and integrated technological ecosystem: big data, cloud computing, and analytics (Khan et al., 2014). The dynamics of this system have moved the way data are managed to a higher level, and institutions (public, private, sports, healthcare, and more) have capitalized on this! They have maximized their respective productivity levels using these systems with no reservations. As expected, these innovative developments come with significant risks from reliability to privacy and security concerns. Data are only as good and useful as their level of validity and reliability. Analytics, mentioned earlier, is one of the major components of the ecosystem that is used in transforming data into information. It is a sub-system that is also as useful as the reliability of the data used in performing different analytical interventions. At the conceptual level, analytics is an algorithm-driven strategy (Purcell, 2014). It facilitates the transformation of complex (generally) historical data sets into meaningful outcomes used for predicting future events. Its effectiveness has transformed and refined different sets of intended results. Institutions have used its predictive capabilities to optimize resources, streamline activities and increase productivity—ultimately becoming more competitive. The key players involved in the management and utilization of these ecosystems are the service providers (SPs) and their clients (users) (Assunção et al., 2015).

It has been difficult for equipment manufacturers to develop innovative products using hardware alone. Those involved in product development have been able to add capabilities by applying solutions that improve customer satisfaction and value creation. Predictive analytics programs and equipment have been effective in promoting the anticipation of failures and provide forecasts for energy requirements while reducing the cost of operations. Predictive analytic models are used by companies in developing forecasts and creating plans for better utilization of resources. Before PAAs are used, the developer must review the available data and create/test mathematical models that incorporate computational processes in predicting future outcomes. The models provide forecasts of future outcomes based on a particular metric such as the associated parameter changes.

This chapter looks at the scope, thematic applicability, challenges, and prognoses of predictive analytics with life case studies from different institutions. It also highlights limitations, implications, and potential vulnerabilities. In this study, a select number of key institutions are included. These serve as examples of classical life case studies meant to help readers resonate with their own different and unique challenges. The various organizations are reviewed and analyzed on multi-dimensional thematic platforms. These include problem statements, strategic approaches, relevant processes, algorithmic layouts, programming descriptions, pilot testing, process reviews, initial implementation, and challenges and lessons learned. The relevant contents of these themes are only limited by the inability to access reliable, valid, evidence-based, useful, and compelling sources of information. Every attempt is made to address these limitations, and at the same time, prioritize available sources based on their pragmatic perspectives, simplicity, and authenticity. The select institutions include business (e-commerce, banking, finance, marketing, and more), health, education, government, sports, agriculture, social media, and so on. One invaluable approach applied in developing this narrative is an extensive review of available and contemporary literature. While the topic remains new and evolving, available documentation does indicate an inclusive degree of participation by different stakeholders. Key limitations like technical inability to develop and implement the various models have not been a significant deterrent. Readers need to consider this chapter as an evidence-based, knowledge-sharing cursory or soft-core and easy to understand demonstration of the strength, scope, and application of PAAs in optimizing program management challenges.

Quality of Data (QOD)

My experience dealing with data of different types and categories spans over four decades. From attending a survey technician-training program after high school to studying in an engineering school, data management has played and continues to play a very significant role in my professional life. As well, the challenges encountered over this period of time continue to evolve exponentially! The most recent paradigm transformation in data management is in the proliferation of analytics — a domain that has enabled businesses, industry, academia, banks, etc. to exhale and address competing forces with might and vitality.

One adage that strongly and appropriately describes different forms of data is "garbage in garbage out" (GIGO). Interestingly, this adage is not just limited to conventional data as described in the previous paragraph—it also includes a human dimension. For example, healthy eating habits correlate positively with an improved quality of life and health.

The importance and significance of good data cannot be adequately emphasized in general, and more specifically and critically in data-intensive methodologies like analytics.

Here is a personal and professional life case study example. In 1992, I was recruited as a Senior Data Management Advisor by Columbia University (CU). My very first assignment was to recalculate the incidence rate of HIV/AIDS.

Four years earlier, CU had launched a project that was primarily managing an open HIV/AIDS cohort. That is a population of interest that recruited new members as the study progressed.

The project's focus was to manage a cohort of over 13,000 participants and produce periodic reports (in this case every six months) on the dynamics of the epidemic. The milestones were morbidity rates — incidence and prevalence.

The week when my assignment began coincided with a scientific conference in Holland where Dr. Maria Wawer (my boss) and other colleagues were presenting papers on the project findings. During that first week of the conference, Dr. Wawer contacted me to inquire about what incidence rates I had come up with.

In the meantime, because of my limited knowledge of the data set, I recruited two experts who had been with the project as consultants during and since its interception. I identified what I believed were the most critical issues to be addressed before starting the computations and subsequent analysis.

The team was then assigned specific tasks. These included cleaning the relevant data set: generating frequency tables; identifying outliers; triangulating with both source data (original questionnaires), laboratory technicians (serology test results), and survey team members.

After completing this cleaning and validation process (including correcting the numerous inconsistencies), we proceeded to perform the calculations using the statistical package — Statistical Package for Social Sciences (SPSS).

This phase of the assignment went very well. After compiling the results, I then submitted the findings (as earlier agreed) to Dr. Wawer who was still at the conference in Holland. The recalculated rates this time were one infected case lower than what was being presented at the conference. And that, as it turned out, was a big deal! I received immediate feedback as anticipated, highlighting the fact that I was new to the project team with a limited understanding of the data sets.

During one of our weekly team meetings (post-conference), primarily to review what had gone wrong with our incidence rate, one of my colleagues was so embarrassed and distraught that he started shedding tears. Since no amount of consolation could calm him the meeting was immediately adjourned.

In the meantime, members of a similar and "competing" project were constantly and consistently asking us what the real incidence rate was. What should they quote in their papers? As the message continued to spread, our team agreed on a consensus response, which was that the team was still in the review and validation process after which the final and latest incidence rates would be disclosed. This resolution served very well in mitigating further concerns.

During this process, our team went back to the drawing board to confirm what the real rates were. After our earlier computations and part of the triangulation process, we had actually conducted a recount of the new infections. The numbers were consistent with our findings. This recounting exercise was again conducted in addition to further calculations. And this time every degree of verification confirmed our results: there was one infected case too many!

And what is the message? PAAs and other quantitative methods are only as valid, reliable, and useful as the quality of data used.

Objectives

The objectives of this chapter are to examine:

- the current literature on PAAs with the focus on methods in which they are used to enable prediction of future events.

- case studies of the use of PAAs in industrial applications
- the conceptual framework on which PAAs are used to develop a machine language that enables prediction of future outcomes.

Theoretical frameworks

Descriptive highlights on which this framework's algorithm is based are as follows:

- A collection of literature materials explaining the concept of PAAs
- Relevant and applicable models used are reviewed;
- And simultaneously analysing available literature material;
- An outcome report is compiled and;
- Findings are presented to relevant parties
- The required theoretical framework is as illustrated in Figure 13.1.

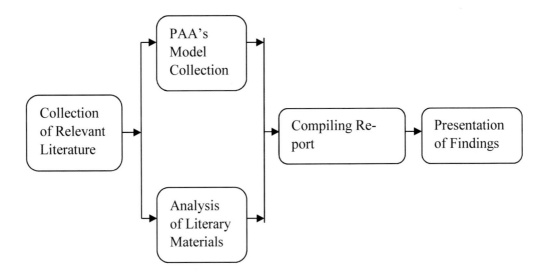

Figure 13.1: Theoretical framework
Source: Bastos, Lopes & Pires (2014)

Scorecard

Description of the conceptual framework

A scorecard is a technique of measuring the performance of an organization in its entirety rather than focusing on a particular process or component of activities, tasks, and operations (Zizlavsky, 2014). A balanced scorecard can be used to test the effectiveness of a program such as the ability of the program to be achieved at a reduced cost, increased efficiency, reduced efforts, and a high accuracy in producing the required outcomes. Previously, a balanced scorecard was designed to enable the assessment of the performance of companies and the extent to which its strategic decisions can be made to achieve the desired operational outcomes. It has been a relevant tool for companies in the assessment of the performance of internal processes and providing opportunities for learning and growth (El Deen & Solayman, 2015). In spite of the perception that a balanced scorecard is used as a tool for measuring performance, it can be used in the measurement of other activities such as operational efficiency, effective time utilization, and the level of competitiveness of an organization in a particular industry.

How it works

A balanced scorecard (BSC) is used in deciding what a business is trying to achieve, to align resources in a manner that the regular activities of a business are achieved, and to create priorities for the provision of products and services to customers. It is composed of small boxes containing elements of mission, vision, core values of an organization, strategic areas of focus, and the activities in which a business will undertake to achieve continuous improvement (Chitra & Subashini, 2013).

BSC is primarily used by businesses, government agencies, and non-profit institutions. The working principle of a BSC is that an organization can be viewed from a number of perspectives, which can be used to create objectives, targets, and actions in relation to various points of views. The main perspectives of a BSC are listed below.

- **Financial performance:** The performance of an organization is viewed in terms of the effectiveness of its use of financial services.
- **Customers/stakeholder needs:** The BSC measures performance in terms of the ability to meet customer expectations.
- **Internal procedures:** The performance of an organization is viewed based on the quality and efficiency of production of a particular product, service, or major business processes.

- **Capacity of an organization:** From this perspective, an organizational performance is viewed based on its ability to utilize resources, technology, human capital, and other capabilities that create an environment for the achievement of a high performance.

When it is used to create PAAs

BSC can be used during the creation of PAAs by enabling the formulation of the performance features of the algorithms. The algorithms for analyzing an organization's performance can be analyzed using a BSC composed of capacity components such as the ability to be produced at low cost, ease of operation by the users, reduced likelihood of breakdown, and the ability to provide accurate forecast of an organization's performance (Gera & Goel, 2015).

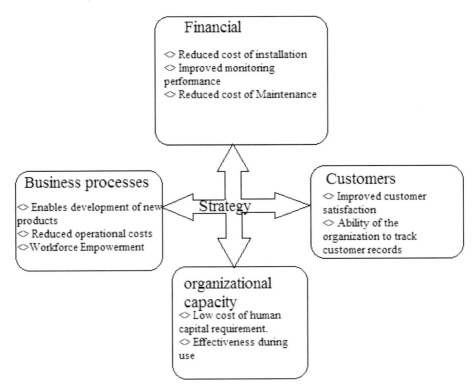

Figure 13.2: Balanced scorecard for the implementation of PAAs
Source: Gera & Goel (2015)

Strengths and weaknesses of the model

The strength of a balanced scorecard is that it provides the opportunity for putting all the operations of a business into consideration. It also accounts for the impacts of different components on each other rather than examining the manner in which a particular component operates or achieves its intended goals (Awadallah & Allam, 2015). When a BSC has been integrated into the functions of an organization, it can be used as a tool for monitoring the achievement of goals and objectives.

The disadvantage of a BSC is that it focuses on the impacts in general, which neglects the performance of an individual or a particular process within a set of processes. There is the possibility of perverting a scorecard by using it as a tool for monitoring employees rather than the performance of a business (Stefanovska & Soklevski, 2014). It also takes into account a large number of variables to constitute a practicable scorecard, making it challenging to manage.

In Louisiana University College (LCU) of Engineering, a ClearPoint Strategic balanced scorecard software is used to align the activities such as enrollment, assessment of students, and improvement of the infrastructure of the department according to its vision, mission, and goals. The outcomes of the balanced scorecard enabled members of the institution to understand their performances in relation to the target outcomes that need to be achieved (Soumya & Deepika, 2016). Due to this strategic plan, there has been increased enrollment in the college and it is considered to be the fifth fastest growing college of engineering in the U.S.

Current Models of Designing PAAs

Forecasting and PAAs

Forecasting and analytics algorithms are used to create a model of a future event. An example of a common future event forecasted in many businesses is sales volumes. PAAs are used by sales managers to compare the outputs of the algorithms with achieved results, and to discuss the variations with their representatives who examine them and make estimates (Mishra & Silakari, 2012). Forecasting algorithms also provide salespeople with the opportunities to know when they need to communicate prospects based on changes in algorithms, which have an impact on the buying decisions of customers.

Statistical models

Time series algorithm is a common statistical model of PAAs and is categorized into frequency-based algorithms and time-domain algorithms. Frequency-domain algorithms consist of spectral and wavelength analyses, while time-domain methods include algorithms used during auto-correlation and cross-correlation analyses (Padhy & Panigrahi, 2012). Another commonly used statistical algorithm is the market segmentation algorithm that is extensively used in customer profiling depending on particular characteristics or priorities of a business.

Linear regression models

In simplistic terms, linear regression algorithms are used in modelling relationships between observed (dependent) and design (independent) variables. It is based on the least squares method that fits the best line and results into the minimal sum of squared errors between the expected and actual data points. Linear regression algorithms are used to make decisions such as the most suitable marketing mix to achieve optimized sales when particular investment channels are used. An example of a case where linear regression is used is at Cable Company X in the United States, where a program is used to determine the effect of variables that predict truck rolls within seven days. The variables used are downstream power, upstream power, and downstream signal-to-noise ratio (Mandal, 2017). The results that are statistically significant provide an insight on the interventions that need to be made to prevent truck roll.

Multiple regression models

Multiple regression analyses are used when product pricing is required across an industry such as real estate pricing and marketing organizations in order to establish the impact of a campaign. It is a broader category of regressions that incorporates both linear and nonlinear regressions and uses explanatory variables to perform an analysis (Hassani & Silva, 2015). The main application of multiple regression algorithms in practical situations is social science research, the analysis of the behaviour of a device, or in the insurance industry to estimate the worthiness of a claim. Multiple regression analysis was used to examine the factors that affected the outcome of a referendum in which the United Kingdom opted to leave the European Union. The research involved the application of multivariate regression analysis in which the Logistic (Logit) Model was combined with real data to determine the statistically significant factors that have an impact on the voting preference in a simultaneous manner, in addition to the odds ratio that supports

Leave or Remain (Razali et al., 2017). The results of the multiple regressions showed that the gender of voters, age, and level of education were statistically significant factors, while country of birth was a statistically insignificant factor.

Multivariate regression model

In multivariate regression models, the value of a single variable is predicted using a number of independent variables. It is also used in the estimation of the relationship between predictors and responses. Predictors constitute continuous, categorical, or a combination of both. Multivariate analysis measures multivariate probability distributions in the context of their impacts on the observed data (Soumya & Deepika, 2016). An example of such a model is multivariate analysis of covariance (MANOVA), which performs the analysis of variance that covers instances where more than one variable is analyzed simultaneously. Principal component analysis (PCA) is a multivariate analysis that enables the creation of a new set of orthogonal variables containing similar data as the original set. Multivariate regression analysis has been used by DHL, a global delivery company to predict future status of global trade, in its Global Trade Barometer program. A machine-learning language is used to input collected data related to different intermediate commodities that range from clothes, bumpers, or mobile devices (Pippal et al., 2014). The program leverages artificial intelligence and multivariate analysis PAAs to create a single data that enables understanding of the effects of a number of variables on a single variable. The output can be used by stakeholders to make decisions such as planning the capacity for future demands of their services and benchmarking on the forecasts to understand the industry's competitiveness.

Decision tree

Decision-tree algorithms are classified into supervised learning algorithms. They are used to create models for solving regression and classification problems. The goal of creating a decision tree is to generate values that can be used to predict the outcomes of a particular class or target variables by applying learning decision rules derived from past data (Thomas & Galambos, 2004). The concept of tree representation of algorithms is used to solve a problem. Corresponding attributes are used in various internal nodes of the decision tree while class label is made at the leaf node. Pouch, a British plugin company developed an artificial intelligence (AI) chatbot, which informs customers of Black Friday discounts. The bot is available to users on Facebook Messenger and uses decision-tree logic to understand people's preferences (Semenov et al., 2016). The decision tree enables users to search the directory according to codes such as departments and their products, brands, and voucher codes of their preferences.

Milwaukee-based Aurora Health Care uses the technique of decision tree in the design of a "digital concierge," which operates on the principle of AI. The organization has cooperated with developers from Microsoft's arm of healthcare innovation in the development of a tool that simplifies decision-making in relation to patient care. The concept of decision tree is applied through a chatbot program, which can be accessed via a web browser (Anderson, 2018). This computer code enables mapping out symptoms and the common descriptions used by people to describe their health issues.

The input is provided through answers to a set of questions regarding the symptoms presented. The bot adapts to the answers and outputs possible causes and treatment plan suggestions. The algorithm enables the creation of a command for making a decision on whether the patient may need further clinical care by the patient clicking a section that reserves his or her place in a line at an Aurora urgent care center. The conceptual framework of the chatbot is illustrated in Figure 13.3.

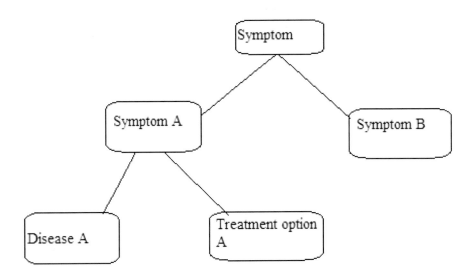

Figure 13.3: Framework of decision tree used by Aurora Health Care
Source: Anderson (2018)

Data Management

Testing data quality using predictive analytics algorithm takes place through the creation of a computer model for validity and reliability of data. The resulting computer model is usually a Pearson correlation that explains the relationship between response and design variables (Bhargava, Sharma, Bhargava & Mathuria, 2013). In measurement of reliability, the objective is to measure the extent to which the measured value is likely to change when the research is replicated. Some computer algorithms measure reliability by performing random and systematic error analyses. Eco-Absorber is a panel acoustics commercializing company that uses reliability and validity algorithms to get accurate outcomes of its surveys (Obermeyer & Emanuel, 2016). The outcomes are used to determine the suitability of the survey findings to recommend a change in practice that addresses the 4Ps of marketing in an effective manner.

Program Management Implications of PAAs

A number of considerations must be made when applying PAAs in program management. Good prediction can be achieved only if there are good data such as past records, which can be used to predict future outcomes of a process or an activity. For instance, prediction of sales of an organization in the next six months is subject to the availability of historical data that, when analyzed, provide a better understanding of the trend of changes in sales (Perry, 2013). Before data analysis is conducted, they must be organized to reduce redundancy and unnecessary fields must be discarded. In order to deploy the insights from predictive analysis into the systems, it is recommended that software applications should be used to integrate them into predicting performances of businesses (Danjuma & Osofisan, 2015). Some of the software that can be used includes API calls, predictive markup language, and web services. The reliability of PAAs algorithms is subject to the use of original data that have been prepared effectively through calculation of aggregate fields, identifying missing data, and merging a number of sources. Each component of data analysis should be analyzed independently. In case of advanced requirements, more advanced algorithms may be required (Ganas, 2009).

Stages of PAA Development

This section explains a more streamlined and contextual version of cross industry standard process for data mining (CRISP-DM). It is a neutral framework that addresses data analytics from two perspectives: application and technical. It is commonly used in predictive data analytics. As we focus on these details, it needs to be pointed out here that conducting (PDA) should never be diploid simply for the sake of expressing curiosity or flaunting one's knowledge of an existing problem-solving strategy. PDA is meant to solve problems. And in order to solve these problems, significant efforts are required to justify its application. One important component of such an exercise is the identification of a relevant management challenge. Hard questions need to be asked. What specifically is the issue? What are some of the interventions that have been made? How have the intervention outcomes improved or addressed the problem? And how have these interventions contributed in mitigating these problems. A combination of these questions will help significantly in redirecting and focusing intervention strategies.

Problem statement

In this stage, the business problem that needs to be addressed should be identified. The objective can be to perform a forecast of the future needs or to establish the likelihood of occurrence of a particular defect. The resulting predictive algorithm should be one that promotes the attainment of the goals and objectives that have been identified (Mandal, 2017). Problem statement identification also involves the definition of performance metrics that a business needs to achieve. A plan should be devised that enables the measurement of the metrics when data are input into the algorithm.

Intervention strategies

The intervention strategy involves making a decision about the right software or application to use in creating algorithms for resolving a particular operational procedure in a business. The intervention strategy may be to design an algorithm that enables understanding of the breakage of devices being manufactured, the likelihood of reduction in the number of purchases, or overall change in customer satisfaction.

Processes

The process of algorithm development will be determined by the goals to be achieved and the data to be analyzed. Algorithm development is achieved by the use of machine learning and data mining methods composed of relevant analytic platforms. The process of developing an algorithm can take different shapes according to the purpose to be achieved (Vijayan & Ravikumar, 2014). Some of the commonly used methods in creating algorithms are the creation of computer programs that enable processing of data input to perform a number of tasks such as regression analyses or estimation of variances. The relationships between an organization's data sets can be amassed by the use of unsupervised clustering algorithms. The processes to be followed during the design of algorithms can be illustrated using flow charts (Yadav & Pal, 2012). These are charts composed of activities to be performed, decisions to be made, the arrows which show the direction of a program, and conditions that must be satisfied before a program progresses to the next stage.

Algorithm design

During algorithm design, the designer creates mathematical processes that can be used to solve problems. The concept used to develop algorithms is coding engineering. Algorithm design and implementation are achieved by the use of design patterns or template patterns and involve the use of data structures to create programs and subprograms that can be used to derive the mathematical output from a particular data input (Kinkade, Jolla & Lim, 2015). In order to develop an algorithm, mainframe programming languages that are recommended include ALGOL, FORTRAN, PL/I, and SNOBOL. The developer of an algorithm can create hand-written processes and a set of mechanical activities to be performed by hand before creating a corresponding algorithm using a computer program.

Program development

During the program development stage, a code is written in the form of pseudocode and logic requirements to be followed in a particular programming language. Various coding language choices can be made in relation to a programming task depending on its characteristics and usability (Semenov et al., 2016). A relevant coding language is selected and syntax rules are followed with little deviation to improve the accuracy of the program.

Pilot testing

In this stage, the written program undergoes a debugging stage in which the programmer identifies errors in the program. The identified errors can be syntactic or logic. In addition, the programmer explores other areas that are likely to make the program not run in a proper manner or not run completely (Obermeyer & Emanuel, 2016). The pilot testing stage is usually lengthy and tedious and often constitutes more than 50% of the program development process. However, when there is greater attention to program design and coding, it is possible to reduce the amount of time spent in the debugging stage. Syntax errors result in difficulty of executing a program and constitute simple errors such as misspelling or failure to comply with the syntax rules to be followed in a particular programming language (Padhy & Panigrahi, 2012).

Pre-implementation testing

In this testing, test data is added to the program to determine its usability in providing the required outputs. Agile testing can also be performed by following the principle of testing from the customer's perspectives (Danjuma & Osofisan, 2015). This testing should be performed by the quality assurance (QA) team. User acceptance testing (UAT) is performed on the program to determine whether it is usable in the intended system when released. This is due to the fact that changes in software characteristics undergo changes as it is developed. The resulting changes can be misunderstood in a fashion that is not according to the objectives of users. When UAT is completed, if all requirements are met, the program is moved to production and made available to the users.

Final implementation

The final implementation stage is where a program is used to conduct an analysis of a particular data to provide an output that can be used to predict future activities of an organization (Hassani & Silva, 2015). In the implementation stage, the data mined from an organization's database are input into the written computer program, processed (machine learning) and the resulting output is recorded and analyzed to enable prediction of a future characteristic of a program.

Lessons learned

The programmer conducts an assessment of a written program to establish whether the expected output has been achieved. A program that results in a desired output such as the number of customers who purchase products in a particular time period and considered useful should be retained by the organization.

Challenges

A major challenge that is likely to be encountered during any programming activity is that some programmers may not use algorithms that produce the expected output. Some problems are difficult to solve because they do not have parallel codes that can be used to write their corresponding programs. Some parallel algorithms have complex features that make execution of programs difficult. Debugging is an important skill but most people do not have the ability to identify and correct errors due to the frustrations and difficulties encountered during this process. The design phase of a computer program can be challenging in terms of the need to think about the program requirements that need to be put together in a manner that would facilitate future updates. When program design is not effective, the resulting program can be difficult to modify in the future.

Life Case Studies of the Use of PAAs in Institutions

In an attempt to simplify the conceptual complexities of PAAs, a select number of themes are included with life case studies. It is my hope that such an approach will enable readers to better internalize some of what has been accomplished and relate these accomplishments to their respective and unique themes.

Health

Data analytics are used extensively to predict the resource requirements for hospitals. At Texas Hospital, predictive analytics algorithms have been used to enable reduction of its 30-day rate of readmission due to heart failure (Vijayan, & Ravikumar, 2014). The data used to conduct the analysis are the admission number of patients who are readmitted and those having heart failure in the past months. The most commonly used method is a computer program that can be written using Java, JavaScript, or C in which an algorithm is created to establish a regression equation that can be used to predict future readmission rates. The independent variable is the number of patients with heart failures while the dependent variable is the number of readmissions in the past months. The resulting output provides a value of regression equation that can be used in combination with the current number of heart failure patients to predict future readmission rates.

At the Harris Methodist Hospital outside Dallas, predictive analytics algorithms are used to conduct scans on medical records to establish the most suitable care that can result in an improvement in patient outcomes. The algorithm accounts for a number of data characteristics such as blood pressure and the amount of glucose in blood to act as an identifier of patients who are at risk of experiencing heart failure (Alkhatib, Talaei-Khoei & Ghapanchi, 2016). The algorithm creates a 30-day risk score representing the likely heart failure incidence. This enables physicians to focus on patients who need to be provided with intensive care. The commonly used programming languages are Python and PHP. The risk score is determined by creating an algorithm that measures the p-value using a computer program. A particular level of significance is used to determine whether there is a likelihood of heart failure. The input variables are the amount of glucose in blood and blood pressure. The output of the analytic program is the level of significance, which may be 0.05 or any set value by the hospital. Patients whose values fall within the significance value are at risk of heart failure and effectiveness of treatment measures should be improved in promoting their health (Milovic & Milovic, 2012). An algorithm is created that measures multiple regressions in which two independent variables are used; amount of glucose in blood and blood pressure. The resulting regression equation in a computer program contains the sections for input of the independent variables. The program is run and a regression value provided is used to predict the possibility of heart failure in a patient.

Problem statement

It has been necessary to determine methods of identifying patients who are at risk of heart failure with less human involvement. The existence of machine languages such as Java, Javascript, and Python has provided the opportunity for practitioners at Harris Methodist Hospital in Dallas to develop a machine learning algorithm that enables distinction of patients at risk of heart failure in order to provide them with more intensive treatment.

Intervention strategy

The intervention includes the creation of a computer program based on machine learning languages in which the practitioners record patients' data and calculate the relationship between the values of blood glucose level and blood pressure to heart failure. This is where a notification is provided to the practitioners when blood pressure or blood glucose levels reaches a particular value.

Process

The process involved the installation of the machine learning languages into the systems at Harris Methodist Hospital, coding and testing of programs using sample patient values, training the employees to use the program, and its commission for use in identifying patients at risk of heart failure.

Algorithm design

The design of the algorithm was achieved by complying with the framework shown in Figure 13.4.

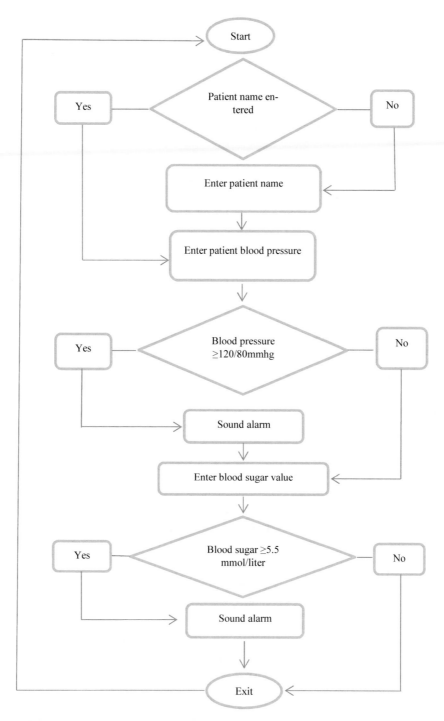

Figure 13.4: Algorithmic framework for testing patients at risk of heart failure

Source: Obermeyer & Emanuel (2016)

Pre-implementation testing

Before the actual implementation of the algorithm, it is tested by adding the value of blood pressures and blood glucose levels of patients to determine whether it is able to sound an alarm when the values are higher than the maximum amounts. The program is also debugged by removing syntax errors and misspelled words in order to improve its readability.

Final implementation

The final implementation is the integration of the machine learning language in the diagnosis of patients who are at risk of heart failure. The implementation involves authorizing the use of the software in the organization as well as training the personnel involved in patient care to examine patients who are at risk of heart failure.

Lessons learned

Machine learning algorithms can be created to enable healthcare professionals to make accurate decisions during the diagnosis of patients such as identifying those who are at risk of heart failure. The effectiveness of the program is determined by the nature of the machine language used, the competence of the personnel, and the dedication of the staff involved in monitoring blood sugar levels and blood pressure as determinants of heart failure.

Challenges

The major challenges that are likely to be encountered in the use of the program are the lack of staff motivation, difficulty in debugging due to failure to locate errors in coding, failure of organizations to allocate enough resources, and the practice of using machine learning language to diagnose patients for risks of heart failure.

Education

Many learning institutions have used predictive analytics to predict future performances by applying past performance scores of students in their institutions. At Southern Methodist University, an associate provost has contributed to student data management practices by applying predictive analytics algorithms that combine the grades attained by students in the past years to predict their performances in the future (Mishra & Silakari, 2012).

The analysis performed involves entering the raw data into the package and following the procedure of regression analysis. The preliminary result of the regression is a regression value that is related to the current performance of the student and is a factor that enables prediction of future performance. The final outcome is a standardized coefficient that acts as a predictor of the performance of a student in future tests based on the present performance.

Problem statement

The need to achieve an accurate prediction of the future performance of students at the Southern Methodist University (based on their present performances) is unquestionable. The use of a machine learning (ML) program is regarded as the most suitable approach for achieving this objective.

Intervention strategy

The intervention strategy that has been recommended is the use of an ML algorithm that calculates the regression value for the students' scores, which can be used to predict their performances in the next academic periods. The recommended statistical package is GNU PSPP, which has features that enable calculation of statistical measures such as simple linear regression, multiple linear regression, cluster analysis, and reliability analysis (Thakar, 2015).

Process

The process involved was the installation of the GNU PSP application into the computer system followed by the design of the machine codes that return particular values of performance when information is input. The computer program will be composed of input points and the points of making decisions regarding the required outputs.

Algorithm design

The design of the algorithm will take place immediately after the installation of the GNU PSP computer application. The design involves the use of computer decision frameworks such as the flowchart shown in Figure 13.5.

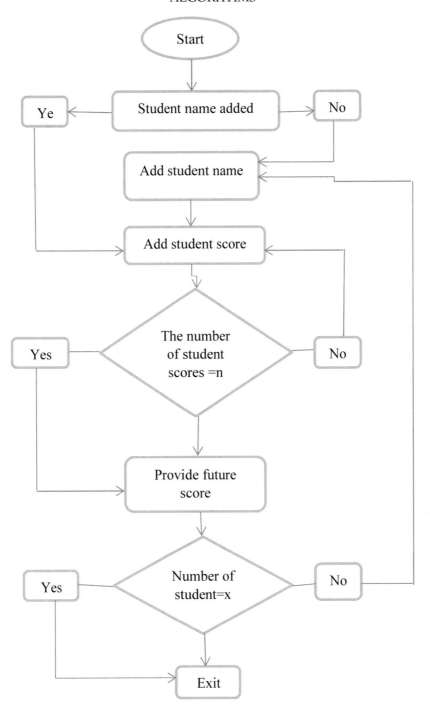

Figure 13.5: Design of the algorithm for prediction of future student's performances

Source: Soumya & Deepika (2016)

Pre-implementation testing

During the pre-implementation stage, the program is tested to determine whether there are any errors. Debugging is done to correct syntax errors and factors contributing to the failure of the program are examined. The ability of the program to be used in a particular system is tested.

Final implementation

The program is authorized for use in predicting the future academic performance of students in an institution in which it is destined to be used (Karkhanis, & Dumbre, 2015). The staff are trained to apply the program during the entry of students' previous performances. They also trained on the skills of interpreting the results of the program.

Lessons learned

The lessons learned from the program are that it is possible to design an effective program if the desired outcome is established. The programmer also needs to have the relevant knowledge including the steps for writing a machine code containing greater details. When a program for predicting future performances is created, it provides an approximate future performance of a student so that potential low performances can be mitigated.

Challenges

The challenges that are likely to be encountered during the design of the computer program are the omission of particular procedures that enable analysis of the inputs to provide the accurate prediction of future outcomes. A challenge is also likely to occur in the debugging stage when the source of the error cannot be located.

Agriculture

AgDNA intends to solve the issue of excess nitrogen by implementing the PAAs concept, in which nitrogen requirements are optimally matched with site-specific conditions in the field, thus reducing the likelihood of the occurrence of high amounts of nitrogen in the atmosphere. The company has integrated next-generation cloud computing technology and techniques for big data analysis, soil characteristics analysis, and climate data as information that enables understanding the nature of a farming field and its suitability for crop production (Kaur, Gulati & Kundra, 2014). These inputs are then combined using the most recent precision nitrogen management (PNM) frameworks to provide a prediction of the required amounts of nitrogen. The methodology used is the creation of a computer program in which the characteristics of the soil are compared to the amount of nitrogen in order to determine whether there is significance in the relationship. The statistical measure used in the analysis is the p-value, which measures the level of significance of the relationship between various soil characteristics and the amount of nitrogen. The software used in the computation of the relationship is JavasScript, which is cloud computing software that enables the creation of programs for regression analyses. The analysis involves the input of the amount of nitrogen and the corresponding soil characteristics such as soil type, colour, moisture content, and soil texture. The preliminary results are the p-values in which the values greater than the set significance value are soil types that have higher amounts of nitrogen that need to be regulated (Arumugam, 2017).

Business: marketing

Business application of PAAs occurs at the New York Times (NYT) as a means of improving its business and operational model. Predictive analytics models have been created that enable subscription to the organization's social media sites and other business decisions. According to a report by Chris Wilgins in a Predictive Analytics conference, predictive analytics is used to influence customers (Soumya & Deepika, 2016). The NYT uses natural language processing as a means of increasing reader engagement so that the most beneficial types of articles can be sold. The software used is C program, in which an algorithm is developed that enables recognition of words such as adjectives used by customers to demonstrate their satisfaction. The software also has a subprogram, which enables the creation of a decision tree that matches the natural languages used by customers to make a particular decision. The preliminary result of the program is a tree diagram, which matches the natural language used by customers and the decisions that need to be taken to promote the sales of the NYT products.

Business: transportation

Virgin Atlantic uses predictive analytics algorithms to determine the prices of tickets according to the likelihood of travel demands by customers (Chitra & Subashini, 2013). The statistical packages used are either MATLAB or SPSS, which have features that enable the calculation of statistical measures such as regression analysis, multiple regression analyses, correlation analyses, and the T-test. The methodology used is the input of the raw data such as prices of tickets and the corresponding number of customers who board flights in a specified period such as a month or a year. The statistical measures conducted include regression analysis and significance analyses. The preliminary regression value is used as a measure of the relationship between independent variables (price) and the dependent variable (number of customers). A final prediction of future demand in ticket sales is established by the use of the regression coefficient to predict the likely number of customers.

Sports

A commonly used predictive analytic model in sports is Sports Performance Platform (SPP) from Microsoft, which incorporates an ML and AI in the creation of algorithms used to make decisions regarding the performance of athletes. This application provides solutions for the locker room, performance lab, and has an algorithm that enables prevention of injuries, making decisions pertaining to games, and changing training schemes to improve the performances of athletes (Razali, Mustapha, Yatim & Ab Aziz, 2017). An example of a sports club that uses PAAs is Midtjylland, a Danish club that was on the brink of bankruptcy but improved to nearly winning a championship title. The club made changes to the steering approach by implementing analytical procedures in which experts conducted an analysis of each player twice a month to obtain information that addressed the player's training needs. The experts also provided the coach with information such as when to change the game plan in accordance with the in-game statistics. Information from analytical models was used to recommend new players (Maszczyk et al., 2014). The programming software used for the analysis of the players was SPP. The methodology used was the creation of an algorithm that enabled input of player behaviours such as the number of passes, distances covered, number of touches of the ball, and the resulting team performance such as the number of wins, draws, and losses. The algorithm creation methodology also involved the creation of a code that measured the regression between the variables. The preliminary results were the raw player data in the computer program and the team's performance in the past matches. The final outcome was the regression value, which showed the relationship between each player's characteristics and the team's performance. This value is important in making decisions such as whether to substitute a player in order to improve the performance of the club.

Social media

Social networking companies such as Facebook have been using predictive analytics algorithms that enable updates regarding a brand to be available to the user after a product has been "liked". Therefore, users are able to see posts, which improve their engagement rates with their individual networks such as posts that their friends have engaged with (Pippal, Batra, Krishna, Gupta, & Arora, 2014). The programming language used is

JavaScript due to its cloud computing feature and the ability to make changes to an already existing algorithm. The methodology used is the creation of an algorithm that enables the site to link a liked product to a user's page. The process includes the statistical analysis of a decision tree in which the website is automatically coded to link a "liked" product to the user's page. The final outcome is a user experience in which when a person likes a product, the updates regarding the product appear on their page in the future. This implies that Facebook will promote the ability of marketers to promote social engagement with customers.

Manufacturing

In manufacturing companies, machine-learning algorithms have been used to understand the machine problems that are likely to be encountered in order to apply preventive practices to keep the supply chain operational. At Georgia Institute of Technology, machine learning algorithms provide the opportunity to promote forecasting the likelihood of machine failures, thus, enabling the technicians to perform maintenance practices (Bastos, Lopes, & Pires, 2014). The machine learning language used is a C program with capabilities for creating codes that enable calculation of statistical tests such as regression analyses, linear regression, and multiple regressions. The methodology used is the creation of a computer algorithm in which past intervals of failures is added. The data are the failure times (the dependent variable) and the time interval (independent variable). A sub-program is created that enables the calculation of simple regression analysis, which establishes the relationship between machine failure times and the time interval. The preliminary results are the input values of failures of the machines against time interval. The outcome of the analysis is a regression coefficient, which can be multiplied by the current failure frequency to determine the next likelihood of the machine's failure. This ML algorithm has been applied in the performance of regular maintenance tasks on lathes, grinders, saws, and gears.

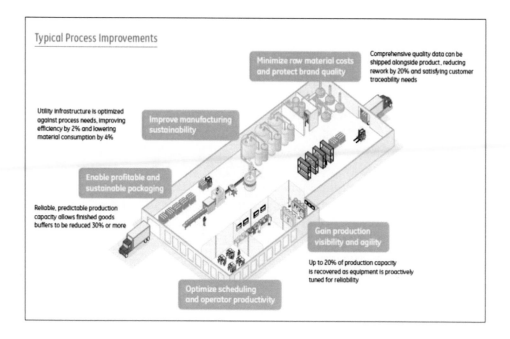

Figure 13.6: Summary of the improvements made at General Electric
Source: Bastos, Lopes & Pires (2014)

Government institutions

In the United Kingdom (UK), the Ministry of Defense uses machine learning algorithms to explore and organize public documents. This is achieved by creating algorithms that enable the identification of documents depending on their subjects and conducts the analysis of information for the purpose of finding patterns and anomalies in data systems (Vijayan & Ravikumar, 2014). The algorithms are also implemented in the detection of fraudulent activities, transactions, or activities of any public official for personal gain. The algorithms have been effective in the detection of activities such as money laundering, the creation of counterfeit trade items or the duplication of business documents. The processes include the installation of machine learning languages into the systems of the organizations, the creation of computer programs, testing, and implementation (Assunção et al., 2015). The inputs are information regarding future activities such as the attempt to change the content of documents in order to achieve personal objectives or defraud the government. The program is capable of providing information about the perpetrators of the acts and insights on characteristics that can be used to trace them.

Crowdsourcing

Bugcrowd Inc. uses crowdsourcing, in cooperation with Fortune 500 companies such as MasterCard Incorporation, to identify vulnerabilities that may be used by hackers to infringe on their infrastructure. This is achieved by the use of a machine learning language called a bug bounty program, which enables the engagement of the cybersecurity community, providing them with monetary rewards for their contribution to the resolution of the vulnerabilities (Purcell, 2014). A major advantage associated with the company is the lack of a requirement for evaluation of claims of cyber threats using the crowd-sourced information to determine the areas of security where greater attention should be placed. Crowdsourcing also involves the use of application programming interfaces (APIs), a tool for software development that integrates the sourced data into the current workflows or reports of business security analyses. The process involves the selection of a suitable programming language such as Python and installing it in the organization's system (El Deen & Solayman, 2015). Professionals in machine code development develop machine codes that enable the recording of information from a number of sources. The output is a list of sources of information containing cybersecurity information that is usable for improving the organization's databases.

International Development Programs That Use PAAs

From a geopolitical perspective, I have also included case studies on themes that are universally applicable with specific emphasis on select themes that significantly contribute in making the world a better place and hence promoting a better quality of life.

Natural disaster programs

The concept of predictive analytic algorithms has been implemented in the analysis of big data regarding past natural disasters and used to predict future incidences (Danjuma & Osofisan, 2015). An example of an incident that provided data for fighting natural disasters is the earthquake that occurred in Haiti in 2010. Crowdsourcing has been used to obtain real-time images of disasters such as earthquakes while big data approaches in artificial intelligence (AI) have been used to determine meanings in messages such as SMS that were generated during the occurrence of natural disasters.

The processes involved the installation of machine learning language followed by the creation of an algorithm that enables the performance of mathematical analyses such as regression analysis and providing the output that can be interpreted to estimate the likelihood of occurrence of a similar incident such as another earthquake in the future (Arumugam, 2017). The analytical procedures performed involve the input of information pertaining to disasters such as the magnitude of an earthquake, time of occurrence, and region into the machine language. The machine language performs an analysis of mathematical processes such as linear regression and multiple regressions to provide statistical coefficients that can be used to predict future disasters.

Poverty eradication program

Predictive analytics have been used by the World Bank (WB) in poverty eradication initiatives such as the collection of information of affected areas, the analysis of the number of people who need relief services, and the relationship between their status with infectious diseases. This is in accordance with the WB objective of eradicating poverty by the year 2050. Countries conduct household surveys and provide WB with information used to classify the population according to the level of poverty (Vijayan & Ravikumar, 2014).

The processes involve the creation of a machine language that enables input of raw data such as the economic statuses of families. Data from statistical offices in various countries are input into the machine learning language that has been designed in a customized fashion to enable the stratification of families according to their gender, age, income levels, geographical location, race, or culture. The program has commands that enable the quick calculation of statistical measures such as linear regression or multiple regressions to provide coefficients that enable the prediction of poverty levels in the future (Purcell, 2014). The machine learning language has also been designed in a manner that enables the transfer of data from mobile phones to the program for analysis. This program has been implemented to measure the economic status of people in Togo, Tanzania, and Tajikistan to provide outputs that enable prediction of poverty status in the future. A similar program has been used by the WB in the measurement of the movements of nomadic people in Somalia to predict future migration patterns.

Programming Software

Turn-key programming model

A turn-key program (TKP) is one that is developed according to specifications because the owner has specified all the functional requirements. A

TKP has the primary advantage of enabling the user to establish a program budget, inputs, and outputs in a scheduled manner. Turn-key programs do not provide easy flexibility in the management of changes and other features requested by the programmer.

In house programming model

In in-house programming, a program is developed by the IT department of the company rather than an outside company (Kaur, Gulati & Kundra, 2014). An example of in-house programming is Google's software development, which is done using its machines that are located in various parts of the computer network system.

Outsourcing programming model

Outsourcing programming is the process in which a computer program is written by a third party and generally external institutions on a consulting basis. It is a more advantageous method of programming because an organization reduces the cost of undertaking a particular project. It is also a means of ensuring time-saving in the development of computer programs because it tends to be less time-consuming when a number of experts are assigned to complete program development. The risks and challenges involved in outsourcing are confidentiality, limited supervision, possible tardiness and service-provider loyalty.

Programming Languages, Architecture Development, Platform, Interfaces

Java

Java is a major programming language used in building server-side programs for video games and apps in mobile phones. It is also popular in the creation of programs for operation on Android-based platforms. Java incorporates both compilation and interpretation techniques (Bastos, Lopes & Pires, 2014). Java compiler is used to convert a source code into bytes. Java Virtual Machine (JVM) performs an interpretation of the bytecode and the creation of a code that can be executed when the program is run. Java is highly recommended during the creation of web server programs, web commerce applications such as electronic trading systems, scientific applications, and enterprise databases.

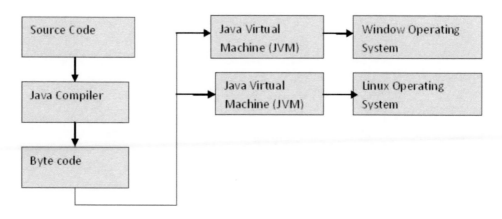

Figure 13.7: A mapping of Java programming language architecture
Source: Bastos, Lopes & Pires (2014)

Python

Python is an object-oriented programming language that is popular due to its simple and readable syntax. It is easy to learn and uses simple language for program coding. For instance, if the computer is required to write something, the command "print" is used. Python makes use of the concept of dynamic typing, reference counting, and detection of garbage in order to facilitate memory management (Mishra & Silakari, 2012). It uses similar expressions to other programming languages such as C and Java.

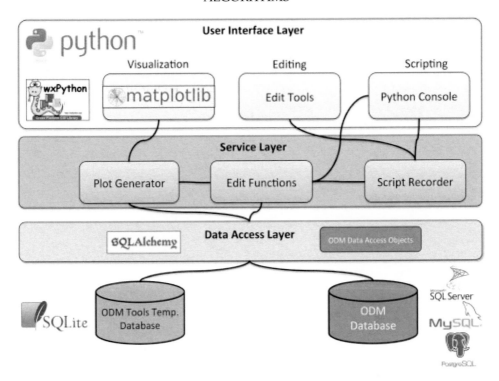

Figure 13.8: Architecture of Python programming language
Source: Mishra & Silakari (2012)

C language

C is a compiler program that can be used to translate functions, declarations, and definitions into files that are executable. It has a simpler command procedure and performs less programming tasks compared with other languages used in programming such as Python or Java. Executable files are created by the compiler translating source code into executable codes independently. It does not remember the defined variables while performing file processing (Purcell, 2014). This implies that a variable cannot be used if it has undergone previous declaration in the same file. C is similar to Java in functions such as loops and conditionals, but the former is simpler in other aspects, such as the structure of data definitions.

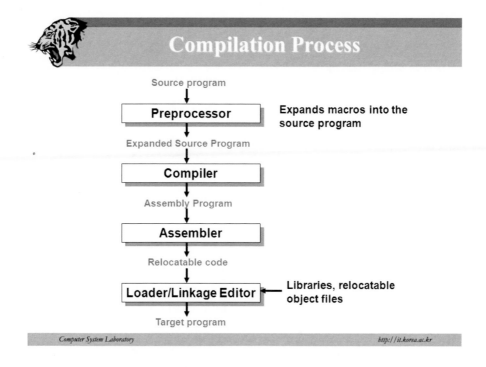

Figure 13.9: Compiler architecture of a C program
Source: Purcell (2014)

Algorithm Development: Examples of Algorithms

Brute force algorithms

Brute force algorithms enable enumeration of all integers from 1 to n and establish whether each number is divisible by n to obtain a whole number. With this type of algorithm, direct computation is performed based on a problem statement to be resolved and the corresponding concepts (Gera & Goel, 2015). The search phase for the text can be done randomly. It is an algorithm that is commonly used in the solution of problems such as sorting, searching, and binomial expansion.

Simple recursive algorithm

A recursive (self-executing) algorithm is one that uses smaller input values and applies simple operations to them in order to obtain the result. It applies the principle of solving a problem by dividing it into smaller versions, which can then be solved by the use of recursive algorithms. If a function is represented recursively, the corresponding recursive algorithm for the computation of its members is a mirror of the definition.

Backtracking algorithms

A backtracking algorithm is an algorithm that is used to find solutions to computational problems such as conditional problems. The process of programming starts with a particular move out of a number of alternatives (Suarjaya, 2012). If it is possible to reach a solution using the selected move, the solution is printed; otherwise, the program backtracks and selects another move to try.

Randomized algorithms

Randomized algorithms use the concept of randomness to determine the task to be performed anywhere in the algorithm. Their preferred use is for the analysis of expectation of worst cases, in which all likely values of the random variables are considered and the corresponding time by a possible value is evaluated.

Dynamic programming algorithms

Dynamic programming is the process where algorithms are created for breaking down a problem into a number of sub-programs. These problems are solved just once and the result is stored so that when a similar problem occurs in the future, a solution is looked up amongst the stored solutions (Gera & Goel, 2015). This basically involves creating a program that memorizes the results of a particular state and using it to solve a sub-problem.

Highlights

This chapter has reviewed and analyzed contemporary documentation pertaining to the use of PAAs, the processes involved in their development, their application in the computation of mathematical procedures, such as linear regression and multiple regression, and prediction of future outcomes. The stages in which PAAs undergo until the outcome is achieved include problem statement, intervention strategy formulation, processes, algorithm design, program development, pilot testing, pre-implementation testing, the analysis of lessons learned, and examination of the challenges encountered.

The concept of PAAs has been used in most machine-learning languages to develop computer programs that provide an output, which enables understanding future events in healthcare, education, manufacturing, governance, and natural calamities such as earthquakes or poverty levels. In healthcare practice, it has been possible to develop a PAA that uses blood sugar levels and blood pressure to predict the patients who are at risk of heart failure so that intervention measures can be implemented. In educational institutions, PAAs have been developed that enable the input of the student's performance in the present period to predict future performances in various fields of specialization. In agriculture, big data PAAs have been used to formulate soil characteristics in the future based on the current characteristics such as soil moisture content, the amount of nitrogen in the soil, and the amount of salts. The output has been used, for example, as a guide on the measures that can be taken to reduce the amount of nitrogen in the soil. Other areas where PAAs have been used are player performance prediction in sports, sales predictions in businesses, predictions of unauthorized acts in government departments, and crowdsourcing to promote organizational cybersecurity.

Summary

The euphoria created by the advent and exponential evolution of predictive analytics seems to have left many stakeholders in awe. From every level of business to different institutional categories, the best and optimal performance seems to be in sight with no establishment being left behind.

While the positive outcomes achieved so far continue to escalate, institutions at large need to take one step backwards to do some stocktaking. This process involves asking critical and provocative questions, including: Are we doing the right thing? How evidence-based are our strategies? Are they sustainable? How reliable are our data sets? Is client data adequately protected from potential cybercriminals? Have all the ethical concerns been adequately addressed? What is the gold standard?

If PAAs' dynamics are any indication, the learning curve is bound to be long, steep, and daunting. One major reason for this possibility is the growing complexities of managing data and the institutions involved in processing them. There is also the challenge of establishing a diverse team of experts involved in developing problem solutions. Members of such a complementary group serve as an invaluable backbone to any potential success. The problems are complex, ranging from good quality data to the nuances that accompany risks and assumptions of selecting and applying the appropriate algorithms.

As already indicated elsewhere in this chapter, good quality data is *sine qua non* to any successful analysis (quantitative and qualitative). Mark Twain's characterization of lies, "lies, damned lies and statistics," should always serve as a compelling reminder that the information generated from data through the machine learning (ML) process is only as useful as the quality of data used. Having and using the appropriate and reliable piece of information is a catalyst for making informed decisions. PAAs are no exception! ML processes continue to gauge significant amounts of data. This data is transformed through the ML process to predictive outcomes (information) used in making informed decisions. ML's propensities to process big data sets have made cloud computing an inevitable requirement. The arrival of quantum computers (QC) has made the transformation process faster, reliable, and more efficient. These QCs, which have miniaturized the binary digit (bit), have moved computing to a higher level. According to an IBM definition, "Quantum computers, on the other hand, are based on qubits, which operate according to two key principles of quantum physics: superposition and entanglement. Superposition means that each qubit can represent both a 1 and a 0 at the same time." Access to good quality data is one way of optimizing the utilization of these QCs.

In one of my series of lectures given to graduate students at the University of the West Indies in Kingston, Jamaica, a student wanted to know why program managers firmly believe that in any strategic framework — "logframe" for example — outputs (and their indicators) always contribute to outcomes, especially given the potential for misleading and unreliable results reported at the output level.

In my response, I agreed with the student while elaborating on the data collection and reporting vulnerabilities, especially in environments where very little appreciation is given to data that are subsequently converted to information. I explained the trade-offs that managers and other stakeholders are faced with. I described what it takes to address issues like these, including conducting a control study. I further shared an anecdote with the group; an experience I had conducting a program evaluation for a UN agency. In this case, the agency had spent 4.5 million dollars over a three-year period on national capacity strengthening. The participants, who were medical health workers, were trained both nationally and internationally. This was identified as one of the output indicators that contributed to a corresponding relevant indicator — improved quality of health services — at the outcome result level. During the evaluation assignment, I followed up (something that was never done after training), and as it turned out, most of those who benefitted from the training had moved on; some changed ministries, others had left the country, and some had even changed professions! Obviously, any planning decisions made using that training report would undoubtedly be erroneous, misleading, and deceptive at best.

It is quite conceivable that the evolving, inclusive, and streamlining dynamic of PAAs will continue to have positive and unquestionable consequences on how programs are managed. The myriad implications are unfathomable with synergies that collectively yield both intended and unintended outcomes. If current thematic applications are any indications, introducing analytics in any intervention will continue to be a win-win initiative.

While different institutions condition their interventions towards their respective strategies, the ultimate outcome is improved productivity and optimization of resource (human, financial, and material) utilization. There is also the human (quality of life) dimension that can revolutionize, reverse, and mitigate certain nuances that affect our wellbeing. For example, academic institutions now apply some models for improving student performance. By using historical data these institutions are able to identify vulnerable students, counsel them on an individual basis, and enable them to set more achievable objectives based on their academic performance with respect to the average group standing. The ultimate outcomes demonstrate counterfactuals that are obvious. And the results have been quite impressive. Some students in some cases have even encouraged themselves to become their own agents of change.

There is also gradually and increasingly, an inclusive element of analytics that continues to encourage and involve members of different community populations: crowdsourcing. This strategy has mushroomed and generated an astounding dynamic amongst communities. It remains to be seen to what extent the strategy will contribute to improving people's quality of life.

In general, business institutions are ahead of the curve with marketing as one of the trailblazers. The competition remains extensive and brutal.

Appendix I: Inventory of BBUC's Working Computers as of 16 July 2013

No.	OFFICE	LAPTOP	DESKTOP
1	Computer lab	-	40
2	Principal	01	-
3	University secretary	01	01
4	Post graduate	01	01
5	Secretary to administration	-	01
6	TAD	-	01
7	HOD business	01	01
8	Head of Music	-	01
9	Procurement	-	01
10	Academic registrar	01	01
11	AR/Reception	-	01
12	AR/Exams	-	01
13	AR/Records	-	01
14	AR/Admissions	-	01
15	Management Accountant	-	01
16	Bursar	01	01
17	Cashier	-	01
18	Financial Accountant	-	01
19	Accountants Assistant	-	01
20	Deputy Principal	01	-
21	Guild	01	01
22	Secretary to Departments	-	01
23	PRA	01	-
24	Masscom Mini-lab	-	05
25	Librarian	-	01
26	Kitchen	-	01
27	Chaplain	01	-
28	University Nurse	-	01
29	Server	-	01
TOTAL		**10**	**69**

Total number of laptops: 10
Total number of desktops: 69
Number of laptops connected to internet: 08

313

Number of desktop connected to internet: 61

Total number of computers: 79

Software: Ubuntu 11.10 (2CDs)-Linux, Windows 7 (1CD), Windows
Server 2003 Enterprise (1CD), Office 2007 (1CD)

Appendix II: Post-Installation Report

Power supply problems:	Need to deploy new powerful backup UPS for server room or Inverters if possible.
What are they used for?	The computers are used for student training and for information searching on the internet and access of e-resources (electronic journals) while the computers in offices are used to perform office work.
How often are they used?	The table above indicates where the computers are located by office and the student teaching/internet lab. They are used almost on a daily basis except on Sunday when our offices and labs are not open.
	The MassCom and the BBA Labs are purely practical labs for communication and computerized accounting students respectively.
Who provides technical support?	Our network Administrator and the Computer Lab Assistant offer technical support but for technical issues beyond their capacity we get tech support from UCU Mukono University ICT Services staff.
Internet connections:	We have internet connection of bandwidth 2mbps, which we connected this week, otherwise we have been on a 512kbps bandwidth. This is not the ideal given the number of students and staff that we serve but this too is costly for us to pay for given that we have to pay $630 every month.

Some power supply problems:	We have unstable power in Kabale and this has caused us to lose some computers due to high voltage. A strong power back up or a bigger standby generator than the one we have would help the problem. Currently we have a 32KVa generator, which serves part of the College when the national grid is off.
How long have we had computers?	Some of these computers we have had since 2005 while others came in 2008. Most of these have been donations from friends of BBUC from the USA, UK, and University of Copenhagen Denmark. However, the College has been purchasing few computers, especially those that we use in our offices.
	Seven laptops were bought this year and are still new. The offices where they are used are indicated in the table above.
	One laptop in the office of the Deputy Principal was received as a used donation from the consignment from the University of Copenhagen while the one in the office of the Principal was bought in 2008.
	Other than the Computer Lab computers, which run on Linux (Ubuntu), some offices are running on MS Windows 2003 and just a few on MS Windows 7.
	We have had our server since 2005 and it is currently very old and unable to handle much of the work, especially the Library Management Software and OPAC.

We have not been able to upgrade to new software because of the cost of licenses and also our computers are very old/outdated to hold such software as MS Windows 7 or 8. This is why we have resorted to using open source software. However, this too releases upgrades that we cannot install because they would be too heavy for our old computers.

Prepared by Sadres Twinomugisha

Head of Library and ICT Services

Appendix III: Post-Implementation Report

REPORT TO MR. BONGS LAINJO ON COMPUTER LAPTOPS TO BBUC

Dear Mr. Bongs,

Greetings in the Name of our Lord and Savior Jesus!

We thank you for the generous donation of 15 laptop computers to Bishop Barham University College.

All 15 computers are in very good working condition since the time we received them, and are serving us in training our students.

BBUC has been training students in the BSc. Information Technology, Business Computing, Computer Education for Secondary School Teachers and Basic Computing skills.

In September 2015, we shall have our third in-take and our pioneer students will join their final year of study at BBUC. Each year, the College recruits new students and in the coming academic year we have projected receiving 500 new students. This will further increase our numbers but reduce the student-computer ratio.

The following students have been trained under the listed programs:

1. The B.Sc. Information Technology program currently has a total number of 22 students (9 in Year I and 13 in Year II) who have been trained;

2. Under the Basic Computing course, over 1,000 students have been trained;

3. 160 students have been trained in Business computing; and

4. 10 students have been trained in Computer Education for Secondary School Teachers.

In total 1,192 students have been trained.

A computer lab has been prepared to cater for this program. This is a teaching and learning computer lab. The space planned for in this room is to host 100 students in one sitting with a student-computer ratio of 1:1. This computer lab has been networked and connected to the campus local area network as well as the internet to facilitate research. It has been furnished with the necessary furniture, i.e., tables and chairs. The available computers have been marked (engraved) with BBUC/UCU logos and the College name, and locked onto the desks to prevent them from being stolen. A whiteboard has been provided for use by the lecturer to protect the computers from chalk dust.

The laptops have been a great resource especially, considering that our students come from very poor families who have difficulty in raising the required university fees, but also cannot afford to buy their children computers to facilitate their course. This donation was timely and as a college we are very grateful.

BSc. Information Technology is a highly practical skills-based program and students undertaking this program must have access to and interact with a computer for optimum learning.

Prepared by Sadres Twinomugisha

Head of Library and ICT Services

Appendix IV: RAPSYS – Summary of Maldives Case Study

Background

Maldives has made significant progress when it comes to improving access to maternal health and family planning within the last few decades. For example, the country has substantially expanded delivery of care and access to care and also improved antenatal coverage, skilled birth attendance, infertility treatment, and adolescent sexual and reproductive health (ASRH) services. The development and use of various national standards and guidelines have also been witnessed. All these have contributed to significant reductions in maternal mortality, infant mortality, and fertility. Since 1984, various family-planning services have been offered in the country, some of which include CoCs Progesterone only pills, injectables, IUD, Norplant, male condoms, and male and female sterilization, all sponsored by UNFPA. A National Reproductive Health Strategy was developed in 2004 as part of efforts to streamline government policies concerning reproductive health.

Ongoing UNFPA Assistance

Under the UNFPA Country Programme III, the Department of Public Health and the Ministry are currently involved in implementing the RH Quality of Care Project from 2003-2007, which focuses on RHCS issues, particularly family planning. The project involves the development of logistics guidelines, development of a national RH strategy and procurement of all free contraceptives and RH commodities. The project has five atolls in addition to the capital. Through the project, UNFPA and the Public Health Department procure free contraceptives and other RH commodities including drugs, consumables and the relevant equipment. The project facilitates training in RHCS according to the developed guidelines. The five atoll areas are strengthened, as they are the basic areas of focus. The project also lays emphasis on advocacy, which is meant to complement the ongoing work in the QoC project. The Thematic Trust Funding extra funding will be highly essential in meeting other atolls.

Challenges Remaining

There are a number of key challenges that require further reinforcement, some of which include the high level of anemia malnutrition amongst women — particularly pregnant women — the continuing high unmet need of FP, and low use of male participation in RH and family planning (FP). The other challenges include discontinuation of contraceptives, inadequate postnatal care, limited availability of services for management of other elements of RH care including STI management, infertility management, voluntary counselling and testing, reproductive organ cancers, and meeting the sexual and RH needs of adolescents, especially unmarried adolescents.

RHCS Assessment

The RHCS assessment of the situation in the country revealed significant gaps in a number of areas namely demand, access, capacity building, advocacy, supervision, procurement, and utilisation. Achievements are graphically summarized in Figure 1.

RHCS Assessment

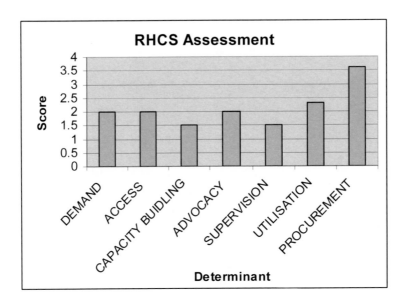

Figure 1

Scores: 1=inadequate, 2=moderate, 3=adequate, 4=substantial, 5=significant

Demand

The gaps related to demand that were identified include the overall low demand for contraceptives, limited targeting of specific demand creation initiatives for vulnerable groups, and poor outreach to dropouts and potential users.

Access

The gaps associated with access include limited access through private outlets (including hotels and the other outlets), weak technical capacity for condom promotion, and marketing campaigns

Capacity building

The gaps identified under capacity building include limited local/national capacity for training, limitations in funding and a lack of a comprehensive staff development plan, high turn-over, skill and work mismatch in filling positions, limited means for establishing systematic mechanisms for regular refreshers.

Advocacy

Under advocacy, the key gaps identified include limited information dissemination on RH issues for political and religious leaders, undeveloped mechanisms for ongoing advocacy, and lobbying for support of political and religious leaders for RH/FP.

Supervision

In supervision, gaps included insufficient systematic supervision, benchmarks and targets not always utilised, limited feedback mechanism, underdeveloped standards/guidelines for supervision, checklist needs to cover supervision, and logistics issues in supervision such as high transportation costs.

Utilisation

Gaps related to utilization included high unmet needs for contraceptives and limited awareness regarding STI prevention and dual protection.

Procurement

The gaps identified under procurement included limited capabilities in quality assurance, costing and budgeting to be undertaking by Government and weak quality assurance.

RHCS action plan

It is observable that the country has made achievements in securing, stabilizing and making the RHCS program sustainable. The UNFPA has played a significant role in assisting the program. The RH project has also gained commodities from the national budget line created by the government. Under the current RH program, an exit strategy has also been established; the government will have to gradually utilize the national budget line in the procurement of contraceptives and reduce reliance on the UNFPA to secure RHCS. The national strategy and the coordinating committee will oversee the implementation of the major strategies and activities in the RH program inclusive of those in the proposal. Based on the RHCS assessment, the country proposal focuses on two basic determinants and three crosscutting determinants. In order of priority these are:

1. **Demand:** In demand, the proposed RHCS action plan and strategies include strengthening awareness of and demand for RH/FP services amongst adolescents; educating young people on RH/FP, including HIV/STI; building capacity of service providers for quality RH/FP services; and promotion of services.

2. **Access:** To address the RHS gaps related to access, the action plan involve strengthening capacities for the promotion of condom use through the media and other means and building partnerships with the private sector to increase availability of contraceptives.

3. **Capacity Building:** The planned strategies of addressing capacity-building related gaps include strengthening the capacity for training at the national level, international training for the Programme Manager and logistics officers, and developing and implementing a staff development plan.

4. **Advocacy:** To reduce advocacy-related gaps, the planned actions include strengthening the dialogue and discussions between MoH and religious leaders, preparing and disseminating user-friendly information on RH/FP issues to political and religious leaders, and building links and partnerships with the media to advocate on behalf of RH/FP issues.

5. **Supervision:** The plan to address supervision-related gaps include developing national standards and guidelines, reforming the management process, and strengthening decentralisation.

6. **Utilisation:** The planned strategies for addressing utilisation RHCS gaps include increasing awareness amongst young people on condom use for dual protection (FP and disease prevention), promoting FP information and services with special emphasis on IUD/male methods, and supporting the local NGOs to participate in RH/FP programs.

7. **Procurement:** The RHCS action plan for addressing procurement gaps includes building national capacities and leadership for projections, forecasting costing and budgeting, liaising MPND/MOH to develop long- and medium-term forecasting and costing (activity), and strengthening national guidelines for contraceptive logistics.

Monitoring and Evaluation

The implementation of the strategies and the planned activities will be monitored by the RH coordinating committee, which was established under the RH strategy. Specifically, the monitoring of the activities will be performed by the Department of Public Health. The Department is already performing oversight roles in the Quality of Care project in the major areas of focus. Any other new initiated activity will thus be under the Department for evaluation of their progress. The findings will then be reported to the overall committee of the UNFPA on the QoC project. The regional hospitals will be designated the responsibility of day-to-day supervision in strengthening its decentralization. A framework has been developed to monitor and evaluate the project. This framework is a qualitative assessment matrix containing the determinants, the level of achievements, possible gaps, and the strategies for the various measures. The core determinants are basically demand, access, capacity building, advocacy, supervision, utilization, and procurement.

Total Budget Requirements

The budget is based on the costs of each determinant and sums up to US$156,050.

Appendix V: PRISM Guidelines – Intra-group Screening Process

Program Indicator Screening Matrix (PRISM)
Intra-Working Group Guidelines

Group name:
Group moderator:
Group rapporteur:
Results level: goal, outcome, output
Thematics are: RH, PDS, GDR

Background

During the most recent mid term review, an assessment of the current country program was made. Key recommendations were made including the realignment of certain interventions and the fine-tuning of objectives (results).

Task

Each group is given a number of output indicators — the level at which UNFPA is accountable (one of its pillars). If these indicators are well-defined and accomplished during the program implementation, they will contribute to either the outcome or the goal. The task of each group, therefore, will be to further refine the output indicators through a screening process using the PRISM provided. PRISM is a matrix of indicators and selection criteria, that if used judiciously, can substantially minimize redundant indicators and, as a result, yield more constructive deliverables and contribute significantly to higher-level results.

Output

At the end of each group work, the following results will be presented:

- Number and type of indicators by criterion unanimously recommended by the group.
- Number and type of indicators by criterion with discordant (indicate number in favour and number against) views.
- Number and type of indicators (overall) unanimously recommended for implementation.
- Number and type of indicators (overall) with discordant (indicate a number in favour and a number against) views.

A follow up action plan of how the performance of the recommended indicators and lessons learned will be periodically monitored by each group.

Appendix VI: PRISM Guidelines – Inter-group Screening Process

Program Indicator Screening Matrix (PRISM)
Inter-Working Group Guidelines

Group name:
Group moderator:
Group rapporteur:
Results level: goal, outcome, output
Thematic area:

Background

During the most recent mid-term review, an assessment of the current country program was made. Key recommendations were made including the realignment of certain interventions and the fine-tuning of objectives (results).

Task

Each group is given a number of output indicators — the level at which UNFPA is accountable (one of its pillars). If these indicators are well-defined and accomplished during program implementation, they will contribute to either the outcome or the goal. The task of each group, therefore, will be to further refine the output indicators through a screening process using the program indicator screening matrix (PRISM) provided. PRISM is a matrix of indicators and selection criteria that if used judiciously can substantially minimize redundant indicators and, as a result, yield more constructive deliverables and contribute significantly to higher-level results.

Output

At the end of each group work, the following results will be presented:

- Number and type of indicators by criterion unanimously recommended by the group.
- Number and type of indicators by criterion with discordant (indicate number in favour and number against) views.
- Number and type of indicators (overall) unanimously recommended for implementation.
- Number and type of indicators (overall) with discordant (indicate number in favour and number against) views.

A follow-up action plan of how the performance of the recommended indicators will be periodically monitored and lessons learned by each group.

Appendix VII: Case Study – Sustainable Development Goal (SDG)

GOAL 3: Good Health and Well-being

B) Quality Basic Services – M&E matrix

Outcomes/ Outputs	Indicator(s) and Baselines	Sources of Verification	Risks and Assumptions
UNDAF Outcome B: Socially excluded and economically marginalized groups have increased access to improved quality basic services	**Indicator B.1:** % of birth attended by skilled birth attendants **Baseline B.1**: 20% (DHS 2006) **Indicator B.2:** School survival rate to grade 5 **Baseline B.2**: Girls 77%, Boys 83% **Indicator B.3:** % Terai Dalits and Janajati households having toilet facilities **Baseline B.3**: 27% (TPAMF 2005)	HMIS EMIS Survey	Delivery of basic services awarded high priority by gov. Continued commitment by gov. to reduce disparities Continued support by donors Political instability and insecurity
CP Outcome B.1: Socially excluded and economically marginalized groups increasingly utilize and participate in the management of basic	**Indicator B.1.1:** Primary school net enrollment rate **Baseline B.1.1:** 87% (Flash 1 report 2063-MOES)	EMIS Annual Report of the Federation of Water	Poor and socially excluded willing to participate Social inclusion wider

B) Quality Basic Services – M&E matrix

Outcomes/ Outputs	Indicator(s) and Baselines	Sources of Verification	Risks and Assumptions
services, including education and health services, and water and sanitation facilities.	**Indicator B.1.2:** No of Water User's Committees having proportional representation. **Baseline B.1.2:** Not yet available	and Sanitation User's - Nepal HMIS based analysis	accepted in society
	Indicator B.1.3: % marginalized children immunized against DPT3 and measles **Baseline B.1.3:** 68%, 82%, 87%, 91%, 94% for lowest to highest wealth quintile (DHS 2006)		
CP Output B.1.1: Socially excluded and economically marginalized groups are trained and mechanisms put in place to ensure participation in planning and management of basic services.	**Indicator B.1.1.1:** % of Districts AIDS Committees with participation of PLWHAs. **Baseline B.1.1.1**: Unknown **Indicator B.1.1.2:** Social and gender composition of School Management Committees **Baseline B.1.1.2:** 17% female, 10% Dalits, 3% Janajatis (TRSE 2006)	UNAIDS reports TRSE District reports/ UNFPA reports	

B) Quality Basic Services – M&E matrix

Outcomes/ Outputs	Indicator(s) and Baselines	Sources of Verification	Risks and Assumptions
	Indicator B.1.1.3: % represent-tation of fe-males and Dalits in Health Management Committees in se-lected VDCs	Annual Report of the Federation of Water and Sanitation User's - Nepal	
	Baseline B.1.1.3: Verifiable but not cur-rently available	Survey/ monitoring report	
	Indicator B.1.1.4: Number of Water User's Committee members from so-cially excluded groups trained in se-lected districts	WFP reports	
	Baseline B.1.1.4: Not yet available		
	Indicator B.1.1.5: % increase of socially excluded in leadership positions in		
	Baseline: B.1.1.5: --		
	Indicator B.1.1.6: % of women and so-cially excluded in leadership positions in Food Management Committees		

B) Quality Basic Services – M&E matrix

Outcomes/ Outputs	Indicator(s) and Baselines	Sources of Verification	Risks and Assumptions
	Baseline: B.1.1.6: will be available early 2008.		
CP Output B.1.2: Socially excluded and economically marginalised households in selected districts will have increased awareness, knowledge, skills and resources to access education, build proper sanitation facilities and practice proper hygiene and environmental sanitation.	**Indicator B.1.2.1:** Number of girls receiving oil from the Girls Incentive Program in selected districts **Baseline: B.1.2.1:** Will be available early 2008.	WFP reports Monitoring Reports	
	Indicator B.1.2.2: No. of disadvantaged VDCs with face to face promotion campaigns on hand washing with soap initiated. **Baseline B.1.2.2:** 33 VDCs (depends on selected districts)	WFP reports	
	Indicator B.1.2.3: Number of children receiving food for education in selected districts **Baseline: B.1.2.3:** Will be available early 2008.	UNFPA reports	

B) Quality Basic Services – M&E matrix

Outcomes/ Outputs	Indicator(s) and Baselines	Sources of Verification	Risks and Assumptions
	Indicator B.1.2.4: No. of adolescent receiving adolescent sexual and reproductive health education both n school and out of school		
	Baseline B.1.2.4: (depends on selected districts)		
CP Output B.1.3: Selected communities, particularly socially excluded and economically marginalized groups, will have enhanced knowledge, skills and resources for improved nutrition, home-based healthcare and health seeking behaviour.	**Indicator B.1.3.1:** % Exclusive breastfeeding in infants < 6 months in selected areas	DHS 2006, Surveys	
	Baseline B.1.3.1: (depends on selected areas)	HMIS	
	Indicator B.1.3.2: % Pregnant women taking iron/folate	MoHP reports	
	Baseline B.1.3.2: (depends on selected areas)		
	Indicator B.1.3.3: % Expected pneumonia cases in children under 5 treated	Surveys	
	Baseline B.1.3.3: (depends on selected areas)		

B) Quality Basic Services – M&E matrix

Outcomes/ Outputs	Indicator(s) and Baselines	Sources of Verification	Risks and Assumptions
		MOH/ UNAIDS reports	
	Indicator B.1.3.4: % under-weight amongst children under 5 in selected areas		
	Baseline B.1.3.4: (depends on selected areas)		
	Indicator B.1.3.5 % of most at risk populations with increased knowledge of HIV prevention		
	Baselines: FSW: 85%; MSM:22%; IDU:78%		
CP Outcome B.2:	**Indicator B.2.1:** % increase in DDC budget	Gov. reports	Elected bodies in place
Local government and line agencies more effectively mobilize and manage resources, and deliver services	**Baseline B.2.1:** UNDP to fill	Gov. reports	Sufficient human resources available in the districts
	Indicator B.2.2: Utilization rate of DDC development budget allocation		
	Baseline B.2.2: UNDP to fill	Gov. reports	
	Indicator B.2.3: Performance based budget allocation for government		

B) Quality Basic Services – M&E matrix

Outcomes/ Outputs	Indicator(s) and Baselines	Sources of Verification	Risks and Assumptions
	development block grants to DDCs rolled out in all 75 districts and annual assessments conducted.	NCASC reports	
	Baseline B2.3: Government development block grants are not performance based		
	Indicator B.2.4: Number of district AIDS plans implemented		
	Baseline B.2.4: 24		
CP Output B.2.1:	**Indicator B.2.1.1:** % teachers in all school types fully trained	EMIS	
Existing human resources in education and health facilities, and community workers and volunteers are trained to provide basic services in selected districts.	**Baseline B.2.1.1:** Female: 57%, Male 59% Linda to find Caste and Ethnicity		
		MoHP reports	
	Indicator B.2.1.2: % FCHVs trained on post natal care in selected districts		
	Baseline B.2.1.2: 0%	MoHP reports	
	Indicator B.2.1.3: Number of health workers trained to be skilled birth		

B) Quality Basic Services – M&E matrix

Outcomes/ Outputs	Indicator(s) and Baselines	Sources of Verification	Risks and Assumptions
	attendants in selected districts		
	Baseline B.2.1.3: To be finalized after districts selected		
	Indicator B.2.1.4: Number of caregivers trained on home based care for HIV/AIDS		
	Baseline B.2.1.4: 1,200		
CP Output B.2.2: District public health and education offices are provided with increased skills and resources to plan, implement, supervise, monitor, and ensure quality health and education interventions.	**Indicator B.2.2.1:** Number of districts with district supervisors trained on integrated health supervision **Baseline B.2.2.1:** Unknown **Indicator B.2.2.2.** Number of districts with computerized program and financial data management **Baseline B.2.2.2:** Unknown	MoHP reports Monitoring Reports	
CP Output B.2.3:	**Indicator B.2.3.1:** Most at-risk	NCASC/UNAIDS Annual Reports	

B) Quality Basic Services – M&E matrix

Outcomes/ Outputs	Indicator(s) and Baselines	Sources of Verification	Risks and Assumptions
Basic package of HIV prevention, care and support for most-at-risk populations and other vulnerable groups is included in District AIDS Plans, and re-sources allocated and services pro-vided in selected districts.	population reached with targeted HIV prevention **Baseline B.2.3.1:** FSW 57-85%, MSM: 22-36%, IDUs: 15%	NCASC/UNAIDS Annual Reports	
	Indicator B.2.3.2: Pregnant women re-ceiving test results and post-test counsel-ling **Baseline B.2.3.2:** 18% (in 7 sites)	NASC report	
	Indicator B.2.3.3: Number of VCT sites established and opera-tional **Baseline B.2.3.3:** 63		
CP Output B.2.4: Local bodies with enhanced skills to establish Public Private Partner-ships and involve NGOs/CBOs in the delivery of basic services and social mobilisation	**Indicator B.2.4.1:** Number of local bod-ies receiving capacity building on public-private partnerships **Baseline B.2.4.1:** 10 municipalities **Indicator B.2.4.2:** Number of new NGO/CBO partner-ships established in targeted districts	District reports District reports	

B) Quality Basic Services – M&E matrix

Outcomes/ Outputs	Indicator(s) and Baselines	Sources of Verification	Risks and Assumptions
	Baseline B.2.4.2: Unknown		
CP Output B.2.5: Local bodies have the knowledge, skills, and increased resources for participatory and inclusive planning, implementation, transparent budgeting, public financial management, and effective monitoring.	**Indicator B.2.5.1:** Number of inclusive and participatory planning meetings, public hearings an social audits held in targeted districts **Baseline B.2.5.1**: No systematic participatory planning and public hearings	Minutes Annual Report of the Federation of Water and Sanitation User's – Nepal	
	Indicator B.2.5.2: Number of District Water User's Federations participating in the development of the District Annual Plans. **Baseline B.2.5.2**: 0	Government assessment reports	
	Indicator B.2.5.3: Number of DDCs getting 20% performance reward to their government development block grants following the national MC/PM assessments **Baseline B.2.5.3**: Baseline assessment	Government assessment reports	

B) Quality Basic Services – M&E matrix

Outcomes/ Outputs	Indicator(s) and Baselines	Sources of Verification	Risks and Assumptions
	will be performed in April 2007		
	Indicator B 2.5.4: Number of DDCs and municipalities where client surveys (e.g. citizen's reports cards) has been conducted.		
	Baseline B 2.5.4: Number of such surveys conducted so far		
CP Outcome B.3: Line ministries and Ministry of Local Development have structures, policies, and programs to support decentralized, quality service delivery that is pro-poor and inclusive.	**Indicator B.3.1:** Mechanism for budget support to decentralization established **Baseline B.3.1:** No such mechanism today	Gov. reports MoHP report	Government funds allocated specifically target socially excluded and poor
	Indicator B.3.2: Number of districts implementing the free healthcare service guideline **Baseline B.3.2:** 0 districts	MoES/Donor documents	Government policies support decentralization External development partners willing to work within a SWAp
	Indicator B.3.3: School Sector Wide Reform is finalized and adopted	MoHP documents	

B) Quality Basic Services – M&E matrix

Outcomes/ Outputs	Indicator(s) and Baselines	Sources of Verification	Risks and Assumptions
	Baseline B.3.3:		
	Indicator B.3.4: Decentralization framework operationalized for the health sector		
	Baseline B.3.4: Not available		
CP Output B.3.1: Community-based healthcare strategies and packages for children including neonates, nutrition, ante-natal and post-natal care, most-at-risk adolescents, and vulnerable children are developed, piloted, and expanded to selected districts.	**Indicator B.3.1.1:** Number of households receiving nutrition support in targeted districts **Baseline B.3.1.1:** ?? **Indicator B.3.1.2:** Number of districts implementing a neonatal health package. **Baseline B.3.1.2:** 0% **Indicator B.3.1.3:** % of most at risk populations, PLWHAs, OVCs and their families receiving treatment, care and support services **Baseline B.3.1.3:** Unknown **Indicator B.3.1.4:** Number of facilities	WFP report MoHP report Monitoring reports Monitoring reports	

B) Quality Basic Services – M&E matrix

Outcomes/ Outputs	Indicator(s) and Baselines	Sources of Verification	Risks and Assumptions
	providing at least 4 types of family planning methods in selected districts		
	Baseline B.3.1.4: To be defined on selection of districts		
CP Output B.3.2: Policy changes and restructuring to support decentralization, programme coordination and sector-wide approaches are recommended and endorsed.	**Indicator B.3.2.1:** Endorsed study on restructuring of DWSS and policy reform is available **Baseline B.3.2.1**: No study to date **Indicator B.3.2.2:** Mechanisms for local government basket funding and/or sector wide approach on decentralization developed **Baseline B.3.2.2:** This is not existing today	Gov documents Gov documents	
CP Output B.3.3: Education policies and curriculum developed and reviewed to ensure social and gender	**Indicator B.3.3.1:** Revised gender responsive and inclusive curriculum exists **Baseline B.3.3.1:** Partly	MoES documents Gov documents	

B) Quality Basic Services – M&E matrix

Outcomes/ Outputs	Indicator(s) and Baselines	Sources of Verification	Risks and Assumptions
responsiveness and relevance.	**Indicator B.3.3.2:** Number of policies developed or revised to promote social and gender responsiveness	UNFPA reports	
	Baseline B.3.3.2: Adolescent Sexual and Reproductive Health curriculum integrated in formal and non-formal education		
CP Output B.3.4: Government's management information systems are providing disaggregated data by age, sex, ethnicity, caste, and economic status for evidenced based planning, monitoring, and equitable resource allocation.	**Indicator B.3.4.1:** Use of the EMIS to allocate education budget to low coverage areas	MoES/FMR	
	Baseline B.3.4.1: Not systematically done	Gov MIS CBS	
	Indicator B.3.4.2: Data for above output indicators available from gov systems by age, sex, ethnicity, caste, and economic status where relevant		
	Baseline B.3.4.2: Partly		

Source: Nepal Government National Program, 2014.

End Notes

[i] Debt relief for heavily indebted and underdeveloped developing countries was the subject in the1990s of a campaign by a broad coalition of development NGOs, faith-based organizations and others, under the banner of Jubilee 2000. This campaign includes the demonstrations at the 1998 G8 meeting in Birmingham, which was successful in pushing debt relief onto the agenda of Western governments and international organizations such as the International Monetary Fund (IMF) and World Bank. The Heavily Indebted Poor Countries (HIPC) initiative was ultimately launched to provide systematic debt relief for the poorest countries, whilst trying to ensure the money would be spent on poverty reduction. The stringent requirements of the structural adjustment reforms, the HIPC program has been stipulated (conditionalities) are similar to those often attached to the IMF and World Bank loans. This sometimes includes the privatization of public utilities such as water and electricity. To qualify for irrevocable debt relief, countries must also maintain macroeconomic stability and implement a "Poverty Reduction Strategy" satisfactorily for at least one year. Under the goal of reducing inflation, some countries have been pressured to reduce spending in health and education sectors. The Multilateral Debt Relief Initiative (MDRI) is an extension of HIPC. MDRI was agreed following the G8's Gleneagles meeting in July 2005. It offers 100% cancellation of multilateral debts owed by HIPC countries to the World Bank, IMF, and the African Development Bank.

[ii] "International migrants" refers to people who sought or obtained jobs outside their own countries, which is not the same as economic migrants and refugees.

[iii] SWAps are represented in the basic principles of program-based approaches (PBAs), which must form 66% of aid from signatories to the Paris Declaration on Aid Effectiveness.

[iv] Interview about the effectiveness of development cooperation with Brian Atwood, the Director of OECD

[v] Winrock International aims to empower the disadvantaged, increase economic opportunity, and sustain natural resources.

[vi] Winrock International is a non-profit organization that works with people in the United States and around the world to empower the disadvantaged, increase economic opportunity, and sustain natural resources.

[vii] http://www.transparency.org/topic/detail/humanitarian_assistance

[viii] When it comes to basic sanitation, Nepal lags behind all the other nations of South Asia as well as most other developing countries. It is worth reviewing the following reference as a follow up to this discussion as it deals importantly with the subject of corruption and reflects what a group of MIT students

(©2003 Hillary Green, Saik-ChoonPoh and Amanda Richards) contributed to the overall discussion concerning strategic development projects in urban settings and on the prevalence of corruption. See http://web.mit.edu/watsan/Docs/Stdent%20Reports/Nepal/NepalGroupReport2 003-Wastewater.pdf. A second reference is included to provide insight into how the problem of sewage and wastewater management identified may be dealt with in the contemporary situation. http://www.adb.org/sites/default/files/linked-documents/43524-014-nep-earfab.pdf.

[ix] The disenchantment among staff members continued to compromise productivity: an observation confirmed by some members during discussions with the team

[x] Funding Agency Statistics.

[xi] Adjustments were made for two outliers: one in 2009 (115 days) and one in 2010 (159 days). In each case, the average figure excluding these cases was calculated and assigned to these outliers.

References

Ababa, A. (2010, September) *Growth and Transformation Plan (GTP) 2010/11–2014/15.*
http://www.ethiopians.com/Ethiopia_GTP_2015.pdf

Abrefa Busia, K. (1961, January 4) *The Prospects for Democracy in Africa. London: Speech at the 18th Christmas Holiday Lectures, Council for Education in World Citizenship.*
http://home.comcast.net/~amaah/writings/prospects-democracy-africa-lecture.html

Action Against Hunger. (2015) *Ethiopia.*
http://www.actionagainsthunger.org/countries/africa/ethiopia

Action Aid. (2011, September) *Real Aid: Ending Aid Dependency.*
http://www.actionaid.org/sites/files/actionaid/real_aid_3.pdf

ADB. (2011) *Development Coordination. Power Sector Rehabilitation Project RRP KGZ 44198.*
http://www.adb.org/sites/default/files/linked-documents/44198-013-kgz-dc.pdf

ADB. (2012, August).*Kyrgyz Republic Country Assistance Program Evaluation: Evolving Transition to a Market Economy.*
http://www.oecd.org/countries/kyrgyzstan/adb.pdf

Agriculture Nepal. (2011, November 20) *Nepal: Priorities for Agriculture and Rural Development.*
http://nepalagricultureinfo.blogspot.com/2011/11/nepal-priorities-for-agriculture-and_20.html

Agriculture Projects Services Centre and John Mellor Associates. (1995) *Nepal Agriculture Perspective Plan.*
http://lib.icimod.org/record/4168/files/APROSC%20Nepalagricultureperspectiveplan630AGN.pdf

Akugizibwe, P. (2012, June 11) *Has Democracy Brought Blind Hope to Africa? This Is Africa Presents.* http://thisisafrica.me/thisisafrica-presents/detail/19498/Has-democracy-brought-blind-hope-to-Africa

Aldenderfer, Mark S. and Blashfield, Roger K. (1984) *Cluster Analysis.* Beverly Hills, CA: Sage

Alkhatib, M., Talaei-Khoei, A., & Ghapanchi, A. (2016). Analysis of research in healthcare data analytics. *arXiv preprint arXiv:1606.01354.*

Allen, J. (2015) *Online privacy and hacking.* Retrieved from https://www.overdrive.com/search?q=D7CAB6D6-20D6-4CA8-BADE-E49E132FE12C

Allen, W., Bosch, O., Gibson, R., & Jopp, A. (1998) Co-learning our way to sustainability: An integrated and community-based research approach to support natural resource management decision-making. In El-Swaify, S. A. and Yakowitz, D. S. (eds.) *Multiple objective decision making for land, water and environmental management.* US: Lewis Publishers.

Alsharnouby, M., Alaca, F. and Chiasson, S. (2015) 'Why phishing still works: User strategies.

Alt, F., Fu, M., & Golden, B. (2006). *Perspectives in Operations Research: Papers in Honor of Saul Gass' 80th Birthday.* New York: Springer Science.

Aly WO (2015) A Framework for Results Based Management to The Public Sector in Egypt: Challenges and Opportunities. *Journal of Public Administration and Governance,* v. 5, no. 4, pp. Pages 23-45.

American Society of Heating, Refrigerating and Air-conditioning Engineers (1986) *Computer-based Monitoring and Controls for Energy/Cost Effectiveness.* Atlanta, GA: American Society of Heating, Refrigerating and Air Conditioning Engineers.

Amoroso, E. (2012) *Cyber attacks: protecting national infrastructure.* Elsevier.

Anderson (2018) Framework of decision tree used by Aurora Health Care.

Andrus, David Ray (2006) *An Analysis of the Accounting Methods Used by Small-volume Home Builders* :Brigham Young University Department of Technology.

Anning, H. (2009) Case Study: Bond University Mirvac School of Sustainable Development Building, Gold Coast, Australia. Journal of Green Building, 4(4): 39–54.

Announcements on Market Value: Capital Market Reactions for Breached Firms and Internet Security Developers', *International Journal of Electronic Commerce*, 9(1), pp. 69–104. doi: 10.1.1.85.3407.

Applegate, S. (2015) Cyber Conflict: Disruption and Exploitation in the Digital Age. In S. Applegate, *Current and Emerging Trends in Cyber Operations* (pp. 19-36). Springer.

Archibald, R. D., Di Filippo, I., & Di Filippo, D. (2012) *The Six-Phase Comprehensive Project Life Cycle Model Including the Project Incubation/Feasibility Phase and the Post-Project Evaluation Phase.* http://www.iil.com/downloads/Archibald_Di_Filippo_Comprehens ivePLCModel_FINAL.pdf

Arumugam, A. (2017) A predictive modeling approach for improving paddy crop productivity using data mining techniques. *Turkish Journal of Electrical Engineering & Computer Sciences*, 25(6), 4777-4787.

Asprey, D. (2012) The state of cloud computing security in Asia. https://www.trendmicro.de/cloud-content/us/pdfs/about/white-papers/wp_state-of-cloud-computing-security-in-asia.pdf

Assunção, M. D., Calheiros, R. N., Bianchi, S., Netto, M. A., & Buyya, R. (2015) Big Data computing and clouds: Trends and future directions. *Journal of Parallel and Distributed Computing*, 79, 3-15.

Automatica, 79, pp. 42–51. doi: 10.1016/j.automatica.2017.01.031.

Awadallah, E. A., & Allam, A. (2015) A critique of the balanced scorecard as a performance measurement tool. *International Journal of Business and Social Science*, 6(7), 91-99.

Baker, N. (2011, December).The Ferghana Valley: A Soviet Legacy faced with Climate Change. ICE Case Studies. No. 252. http://www1.american.edu/ted/ICE/ferghana.html

Balls, A. (2015) *Corrupt Governments Receive No Less Foreign Aid. The National Bureau of Economic Research.* http://www.nber.org/digest/nov99/w7108.html

Bastos, P., Lopes, I., & Pires, L. C. M. (2014) Application of data mining in a maintenance system for failure prediction. *Safety, Reliability and Risk Analysis: Beyond the Horizon: 22nd European Safety and Reliability*, 1, 933-940.

Battle, C. (2009) Essentials of Public Health Biology: *A Guide for the Study of Pathophysiology*. London: Jones and Bartlett Publishers.

Bebbington, J., Brown, J., & Frame, B. (2007) Accounting technologies and sustainability assessment models. *Ecological Economics, 61*: 224–236.

Behn, R. (2000) *Rethinking Democratic Accountability*. Washington, DC: Brookings Institute.

Bennett, John G (2003) A Stytem for Collecting Data on Observer Preferences in the Field Using Personal Data Assistants. CA: Ft. Belvoir Defense Technical Information Center.

Bester, A. (2016) *Results-based management in the United Nations development system: Progress and challenges*. United Nations Department of Economic and Social Affairs, Quadrennial Comprehensive Policy Review. http://www.un.org/esa/coordination/pdf/rbm_report_10_july.pdf

Besterfield, D., et al. (2011) *Total Quality Management 3rd Edition.* India Binding House.

Bhargava, N., Sharma, G., Bhargava, R., & Mathuria, M. (2013) Decision tree analysis on j48 algorithm for data mining. *Proceedings of International Journal of Advanced Research in Computer Science and Software Engineering, 3*(6).

Bickman, Leonard and Rog, Debra J. (1998) *Handbook of Applied Social Research Methods.* Thousand Oaks CA: Sage.

Binnendijk, A. (2000) *Results-based Management in the Development Cooperation Agencies: A Review of Experience.* Paper prepared for OECD/DAC Working Party on Aid Evaluation.

Birdsall, N., Savedoff, W. D., Mahgoub, A., & Vybomy, K. (2011) *Cash on Delivery. A new approach to foreign aid.* Washington, D.C.: Center for Global Development.

Birger, S. (2011). *GIGA-Mapping: Visualization for complexity and systems thinking in design.* Paper presented at NORDES 2011, 30 May 2011.

Boch-Isaacson, J. (2001). *Half-a-Century of Development: The History of U.S. Assistance to Nepal 1951–2001*.United States Agency for International Development.

Bodea, C. N., C. Elmas, A. Tănăsescu, M. Dascălu. (2010). An ontological-based model for competences in sustainable development projects: A case study for project's commercial activities. *Economic Interferences, 12*(27): 177–189.

Boslaugh, Sarah (2005) *An Intermediate Guide to SPSS Programming.* Thousand Oaks, CA: Sage.

Bossler, A., & Burruss, G. (2011) The general theory of crime and computer hacking: Low self-control hackers. *Corporate hacking and technology-driven crime: Social dynamics and implications,* 38-67.

Box, George E.P., Hunter, William Gordon and Hunter, Stuart J. (1978) *Statistics for Experimenters: An introduction to design, data analysis and model building.* New York: NY: Wiley.

Brennan, K. (2015) *Making Global Institutions Work.* Oxon, OX: Routledge.

Brenner, S. (2010) *Cybercrime: criminal threats from cyberspace.* ABC-CLIO.

Briassoulis, H. (2001) Sustainable development and its indicators: Through a (Planner's) glass darkly. *Journal of Environmental Planning and Management,* 44(3), 409–427.

Broughton, R. (2011) *Quality Orientation Guide: Your Personal Guide to Business Success. Business Excellence-The Way Business Should Be Done. Quality Assurance Solutions.* http://www.quality-assurance-solutions.com/support-files/quality_orientation_guide.pdf

Brown, L. D. (2008). *Creating Credibility: Legitimacy and Accountability for Transnational Civil Society.* Sterling, VA: Kumarian Press.

Bruns, A., & Liang, Y. E. (2012) Tools and methods for capturing Twitter data during natural disasters. *First Monday, 17*(4).

Cabral, L. (2010) 2011. *Sector-based approaches in agriculture from expensive experiment to genuine impact.* London: Overseas Development Institute (ODI).

Campbell, B. M. (2017) Responding to global change: A theory of change approach to making agricultural research for development outcome-based. *Agricultural Systems, 152,* 145-153.

CARE. (2012, July 16) *CARE's Response in the Horn of Africa.* http://www.care-international.org/news/stories-and-blogs/emergency-response/horn-of-africa-cares-response-to-food-crisis.aspx

Carlsson, J., Somolekae, G., & van de Walle, N. (1997) *Foreign Aid in Africa. Learning from country experiences.* http://www.diva-portal.org/smash/get/diva2:272899/FULLTEXT01.pdf

Carpenter, C. (2004).*Real World Project Management.*

Carvalho, M. M., & Rabechini, R. Jr. (2011) *Fundamentosem Gestão de Projetos: Construindo competências paragerenciar projetos: teoria e casos*, 3rd ed. São Paulo: Atlas, 422p.

Cashell, B., Jackson, W., Jickling, M., & Webel, B. (2004) The economic impact of cyber-attacks. *Congressional Research Service Documents, CRS RL32331 (Washington DC).*

Cavusoglu, H., Mishra, B. and Raghunathan, S. (2004) *'The Effect of Internet Security Breach.*

CGD. (2015) *Cash on Delivery Aid.* http://www.cgdev.org/initiative/cash-delivery-aid

Chapagain, D. (2013, February 1–2) *Operations Research in Post Modern Era: Apple-pie with Ice-cream.* http://www.dineshchapagain.com.np/admin/files/OR%20in%20Post%20Modern%20Era_Apple%20Pie%20with%20Ice%20Cream.pdf

Charles, D., Gabriel, M., & Furukawa, M. F. (2013). Adoption of electronic health record systems among US non-federal acute care hospitals: 2008–2013. *ONC data brief, 9*, 1-9.

Chelst, K., & Canbolat, Y. B. (2012) *Value-Added Decision Making for Managers.* Boca Raton: CRC Press.

Chen, M., Mao, S., & Liu, Y. (2014) Big data: A survey. *Mobile Networks and Applications, 19*(2), 171–209.

Chiasson, M., Reddy, M., Kaplan, B., & Davidson, E. (2007) Expanding multi-disciplinary approaches to healthcare information technologies: what does information systems offer medical informatics?. *International journal of medical informatics*, *76*, S89-S97.

Chitra, K., & Subashini, B. (2013) Data mining techniques and its applications in banking sector. *International Journal of Emerging Technology and Advanced Engineering*, *3*(8), 219-226.

Chu, W. et al. (2013) *Protect sensitive sites from phishing attacks using features extractable from inaccessible phishing URLs.* IEEE International Conference on Communications.

CIDA. (2004) *Ethiopia. Country Development Programming Framework. Let Us Work Together for Ethiopia's Sustainable Development.* http://www.acdi-cida.gc.ca/inet/images.nsf/vLUImages/Ethiopia/$file/Ethiopia-en.pdf

CIDA. (2007, December) *Executive Report on the Evaluation of the CIDA Industrial Cooperation (CIDA-INC) Program.* http://www.oecd.org/derec/canada/CIDA-Industrial-Cooperation-Program.pdf

CIDA. (2009) Results-based Management. In K. R. Hope (Ed.) Managing the Public Sector in Kenya: Reform and Transformation for Improved Performance. *Journal of Public Administration and Governance*. 2012. 2(4), pp. 128–143.

CIDA. (2011a, March 16) *Project profile: Food Assistance in Nepal — World Food Programme 2010–2011.* http://www.acdi-cida.gc.ca/cidaweb/cpo.nsf/projEn/M013437001

CIDA. (2011b, May) *Canada's Aid Effectiveness Agenda. Securing the Future of Children and Youth.* http://www.acdi-cida.gc.ca/INET/IMAGES.NSF/vLUImages/Youth-and-Children/$file/ChildrenAndYouth3fold-EN.pdf

CIDA. (2012a) *CIDA's Aid Effectiveness Action Plan (2009–2012).* http://www.acdi-cida.gc.ca/INET/IMAGES.NSF/vLUImages/About_CIDA/$file/AI DEFFECTIVENESS_ACTIONPLAN_2009-12-e.pdf

CIDA. (2012b) *CIDA Learns. Lessons from Evaluations. Annual Report 2011–2012.*

http://reliefweb.int/sites/reliefweb.int/files/resources/CIDA-learns-eng%20(1).pdf

Cisco. (2016) The zettabyte era: Trends and analysis. www.cisco.com/c/en/us/solutions/collateral/service-provider/visual-networking-index-vni/vni-hyperconnectivity-wp.html

Clark, H. (2012, July 9) *Remarks on Corruption at the ECOSOC 2012 High Level Segment. UNDP.* http://www.undp.org/content/undp/en/home/presscenter/speeches/2012/07/09/helen-clark-opening-remarks-at-the-ecosoc-2012-high-level-segment/

Cochran, William G. (1977) *Sampling Techniques.* New York, NY: Wiley.

Cole, R. 2005. Building environmental assessment methods: redefining intentions and roles. Building Research and Information, 33(5): 455–467.

Cooperation. Office of Evaluation and Strategic Planning, UNDP.

Cowley, Paula, J. and Whiting, Mark A. (1986) *Managing Data Analysis Through Save-states.* Computer Science and Statistics: Proceedings of the 17th Symposium on the Interface, 121-127. New York, NY: North Holland.

Craven, B., & Islam, S. (2006) *Operations Research Methods: Related Production, Distribution, and Inventory Management Applications.* Hyderabad: The ICFAI University Press.

John W. Creswell (2014) Research Design, Qualitative, Quantitative and Mixed Methods Approaches, Sage Publications 2014.

Cross, N. (2011) *Design thinking: Understanding how designers think and work.* Berg.

Cuddy, Colleen (2005) *Using PDAs in Libraries: A how-to manual.* New York, NY: Neal.

Cullen, R. (2008) *The poverty of corrupt nations.* Toronto, ON: Dundurn Press.

D'Amato, A., Henderson, S., & Florence, S. (2009) *Corporate Social Responsibility and Sustainable Business. A Guide to Leadership Tasks and Functions*. North Carolina: CCL Press.

Daly, Leslie E. and Bourke, Geoffrey J. (2000) *Interpretation and Uses of Medical Statistics* 5th edition. Oxford, Malden, MA: Blackwell Science

Danjuma, K., & Osofisan, A. O. (2015) Evaluation of predictive data mining algorithms in Erythemato-Squamous disease diagnosis. *arXiv preprint arXiv:1501.00607*.

Darling-Hammond, L. (2010, October 1) *What We Can Learn from Finland's Successful School Reform.* http://www.nea.org/home/40991.htm

de Mendoza, A. (2010) *Monitoring and Evaluation Framework* (2010-2013): Fund for Gender Equality.

De Vos, M. (2015, June 19) A first glimpse into Finland's aid cuts. DevEx. https://www.devex.com/news/a-first-glimpse-into-finland-s-aid-cuts-86381

de Waal, A. (1991) *Evil Days: Thirty Years of War and Famine in Ethiopia.* London: Human Rights Watch.

Deakin, M., Huovila, P., Rao, S., Sunikkamand, V. R. (2002) The assessment of sustainable urban development. *Building Research and Information, 30*(2): 95–108.

Delaney, J. (2014) *Construction Program Management.* Boca Raton, FL: CRC Press.

DFAE. (2012, March 8) *More responsibility for the recipients.* https://www.dfae.admin.ch/deza/en/home/news/press-releases-articles-speeches.html/content/deza/en/meta/news/2012/8/3/verantwortung

DFATD. (2014, February 6) *2011–2012 Departmental Performance Report.* http://www.international.gc.ca/department-ministere/plans/dpr-rmr/dev_dpr-rmr_1112.aspx?lang=eng

DFATD. (2015). *Ethiopia.* http://www.international.gc.ca/development-developpement/countries-pays/ethiopia-ethiopie.aspx?lang=eng

Diakonia (no date). *Planned Advocacy Assessment Tool: a Tool for Assessing Your Organization's Strengths and Weaknesses in Planning Advocacy Activities.*

Diamond, J. (2005). *Establishing a performance management framework for the government* (No. 5-50). International Monetary Fund.

Difference. 2005 Development Cooperation Report. Vol. 7. No. 1 2006 49-54.

digital freedoms', in Beyond WikiLeaks: Implications for the Future of Communications, Journalism and Society, pp. 146–165. doi: 10.1057/9781137275745.

Dillon, R., Pate-Cornell, E., & Guikema, S. (2003) Programmatic risk analysis for critical engineering systems under tight resource constraints. *Operation Research*, 51(3), p. 354.

Dinsmore, P., & Cabanis-Brewin, J. (2011) *The AMA Handbook of Project Management,* 3rd ed. New York: AMACOM Books.

Dobre, C. (Ed.). (2014) *Big data and internet of things: A roadmap for smart environments.* Springer International Publishing.

Downey, M. (1998) Making GPRA Work for Your Agency. The Public Manager, Fall, 27(3): 18.

Easterly, W. (2002, March) *The Cartel of Good Intentions: Bureaucracy versus markets in foreign aid. WORKING PAPER NUMBER 4.* http://www.cgdev.org/files/2786_file_cgd_wp004_rev.pdf

Edwards, M., & Hulme, D. (2002) *Non-governmental organisations: Performance and accountability beyond the magic bullet.* London: Earthscan Publications Ltd.

El Deen, M. A., & Solayman, M. M. (2015) Maximizing Strategic Performance Results: Adopting Balanced Scorecards and BI Tools. *International Journal of Computer Applications*, *117*(10).

El-Haram, M., Walton, J. S., Horner, R. M. W., Hardcastle, C., Price, A., Bebbington, J., Thomson, C., & Atkin-Wright, T. (2007) Development of an integrated sustainability assessment toolkit. Proceedings of the International Conference on Whole Life Urban Sustainability and its Assessment, Glasgow. https://download.sue-mot.org/Conference-2007/Papers/El-Haram.pdf

REFERENCES

Elahi, Ata and Elahi Mehran (2006) *Data, Network, and Internet Communications Technology*. Clifton Park, NY: Thomson Delmar Learning.

Elkington, J. (1998) *Cannibals with forks: The triple bottom line of 21st century business*. Gabriola Island, BC: New Society Publishers.

Embassy of Ethiopia. (2015) *Sustainable Development and Poverty Reduction Strategy*. http://www.ethioembassy.org.uk/about_us/sustainable_development.htm

Engelhardt, M. E. (2001) *Modeling Patterns in Data Using Linear and Related Models*. http://www.osti.gov

Engle, Mary (1993) *Internet Connections: A librarian's guide to dial-up access and use.* Chicago, IL: Library and Information Technology Association.

Epstein, J., & Olsen, T. (1996). Lessons Learned by State and Local Governments. The Public Manager, Fall, 41-44.

Eriksson, P., & Kovalainen, A. (2008) *Qualitative Methods in Business Research*. London: SAGE Publications Ltd., London.

Eskerod, P., Huemann, M. (2013) *Sustainable development and project stakeholder management: What standards say*, International Journal of Managing Projects in Business 6(1), 2013.

European Commission. (n.d.). Understanding and monitoring the cost-determining factors of infrastructure projects: A user's guide. http://ec.europa.eu/regional_policy/sources/docgener/evaluation/pdf/5_full_en.pdf

FAO. (2014) *Ethiopia country programming framework*. Food and Agriculture Organization of the United Nations. Office of the FAO Representative to Ethiopia, Addis Ababa. http://www.fao.org/3/a-aq402e.pdf

Farrell, G. (2009) *Results-Based Monitoring and Evaluation at the Commonwealth of Learning - A Handbook*, Vancouver, Canada.

FBI-Internet Crime centre (2012) *2013 Internet Crime Report, FBI*.

357

FBI-Internet Crime centre (2013) *2014 Internet Crime Report, FBI.*

FBI-Internet Crime centre (2014) *2013 Internet Crime Report, FBI.*

FBI-Internet Crime centre (2015) *2014 Internet Crime Report, FBI.*

FBI-Internet Crime centre (2016) *2015 Internet Crime Report, FBI.*

FBI-Internet Crime centre (2017) *2016 Internet Crime Report, FBI.*

Feng, S. and Tesi, P. (2017) *Resilient control under Denial-of-Service: Robust design,*

Fernández-Alemán, J. L., Señor, I. C., Lozoya, P. Á. O., & Toval, A. (2013) Security and privacy in electronic health records: A systematic literature review. *Journal of biomedical informatics, 46*(3), 541-562.

Fernández-Sánchez, G., & Rodríguez-López, F. (2010) A methodology to identify sustainability indicators in construction project management: Application to infrastructure projects in Spain. Ecological Indicators, 10(6): 1193–1201.

Field, Andy P. (2005) *Discovering Statistics Using SPSS* 2nd edition. Thousand Oaks, CA: Sage.

Fleiss, Joseph L. (1981) *Statistical Methods for Rates and Proportions* 2nd edition. New York, NY: Wiley.

Flint, M. (2002). *Easier Said Than Done: A Review of Results-Based Management in Multilateral Development Institutions.* London: UK Department for International Development (DFID).

Folscher, A. (2007). *Local Fiscal Discipline: Fiscal Prudence, Transparency, and Accountability. World Bank Working Papers. Chapter 3.*

for combating phishing attacks', *International Journal of Human Computer Studies,* 82, pp. 69–82. doi: 10.1016/j.ijhcs.2015.05.005.

Foster, M. (2000) *New approaches to development cooperation: What can we learn from experience with implementing sector wide approaches?* Working paper 140, Centre for Aid and Public Expenditure. London: Overseas Development Institute.

Fox, James Allen and Tracy, Paul E. (1986) *Randomized Response: A method for sensitive surveys.* Beverly Hills, CA: Sage.

Francis, Ivor (1979) *A Comparative Review of Statistical Software*. New York, NY: North Holland.

Francis, Ivor (1981) *Statistical Software: A comparative review.* New York, NY: North Holland.

Freedman, L. (2013) *Strategy*. Oxford University Press.

Friess, P. (2013*) Internet of things: Converging technologies for smart environments and integrated ecosystems*. River Publishers.

from inaccessible phishing URLs', in *IEEE International Conference on Communications*, pp. 1990–1994. doi: 10.1109/ICC.2013.6654816.

Frost & Sullivan. (2016) Big data and cloud computing win spot as key growth engines in the Latin American it industry, says Frost & Sullivan. www.frost.com/news/press-releases/big-data-and-cloud-computing-win-spot-key-growth-engines-latin-american-it-industry-says-frost-sullivan/

Fruhlinger, J. (2017) *What is a cyber attack? Recent examples show disturbing trends* | CSO.

Fry, Donna M. (1986) *Air Force Internal Control Systems: A proposal for improvement.* CA: Ft. Belvoir Defense Technical Information Center

Funds for NGOs. (2008, June 20). *Swiss Agency for Development and Cooperation, The (SDC).* http://www.fundsforngos.org/bilateral-funds-for-ngos/the-swiss-agency-funding-support-to-ngos/

Furnell, S., & Warren, M. (1999) Computer hacking and cyber terrorism: The real threats in the new millennium? *Computers & Security, 18*(1), 28-34.

Gal-Or, E., & Ghose, A. (2004) The economic consequences of sharing security information. In E. Gal-Or, & A. Ghose, *Economics of information security* (pp. 95-104). Springer.

Gambrel, B. (2012) *Microsoft Project 2010.* Hoboken, NJ: John Wiley & Sons.

Ganas, S. (2009) Data mining and predictive modeling with excel 2007. In *Casualty Actuarial Society E-Forum, Spring 2010.*

Gandhi, R., Sharma, A., Mahoney, W., Sousan, W., Zhu, Q., & Laplante, P. (2011) Dimensions of cyber-attacks: Cultural, social, economic, and political. *IEEE Technology and Society Magazine, 30*(1), 28-38.

Gao, S., Li, L., Li, W., Janowicz, K., & Zhang, Y. (2014) Constructing gazetteers from volunteered big geo-data based on Hadoop. *Computers, Environment and Urban Systems.*

GAO. (1997). *Foreign assistance USAID's reengineering at overseas missions. GAO/NSIAD-97-194.* Washington, DC: GAO.

GAO. (2007). *Foreign Assistance. Enhanced coordination and better methods to assess the results.* GAO.

Gera, M., & Goel, S. (2015) Data mining-techniques, methods and algorithms: A review on tools and their validity. *International Journal of Computer Applications, 113*(18).

Gianni, D; D'Ambrogio, A; and Tolk, A, eds. (4 December 2014). *Modeling and Simulation-Based Systems Engineering Handbook.*

Gibson, J., & Boisvert, B. (1997) Data-Driven Performance: Accountability, Business Planning and Performance Measurement in Government. The Conference Board of Canada, 207-97.

Gido, J., & Clements, J.P. (2012). *Successful Project Management,* 5th ed. Mason, OH: South-Western Cengage Learning.

Gimenez, C., Sierra, V., & Rodon, J. (2012) Sustainable operations: Their impact on the triple bottom line. International Journal of Production Economics, 140(1): 149–159.

Goel, V. and Perlroth, N. (2016) "Yahoo Says 1 Billion User Accounts Were Hacked", The New York Times.

Golinelli, G.M. (2010), Viable Systems Approach – Governing Business Dynamics, Kluwer/CEDAM, Padova.

Good, Phillip, I. (2005) *Resampling Methods: A practical guide to data analysis* 3rd edition. Berlin, Germany: Boston Basel Berlin Birkhauser.

Gotev, G. (2015, June 10) *Finland slashes development aid by 43%.*
http://www.euractiv.com/sections/development-policy/finland-slashes-development-aid-43-315280

Gragnolati, M., Lindelöw, M., Couttolenc, B., & World Bank,. (2016) *Twenty years of health system reform in Brazil: An assessment of the Sistema Unico de Saude.*

Griffiths, J., Maggs, H., & George, E. (2007) *Stakeholder involvement.* Background paper prepared for the WHO/WEF Joint Event on Preventing Noncommunicable Diseases in the Workplace (Dalian/China, September 2007). http://www.who.int/dietphysicalactivity/griffiths-stakeholder-involvement.pdf

Groot, R., & Molen, P. (2000) *Workshop on capacity building in land administration for development countries: final report.* ITC: The Netherlands.

Grover, Rajiv and Vriens, Marco (2006) *The Handbook of Marketing Research: Uses, misuses and future advances.* Thousand Oaks, CA: Sage.

Gujarati, Damodar N. and Porter, Dawn C. (2009) *Basic Econometrics* 5th edition. Boston MA: McGraw-Hill Irwin.

Gustafsson, J., & Salo, A. (2005) Contingent portfolio programming for the management of risky projects. *Operation Research*, 53(6), pp. 95–946.

Hansen, Morris H. (1953) *Sample Survey Methods and Theory.* New York, NY:Wiley.

Hansen, Morris H., Hurwitz, William N., Madow, William G. (1953) *Theory.* New York, NY: Wiley.

Hassani, H., & Silva, E. S. (2015) Forecasting with big data: A review. *Annals of Data Science*, 2(1), 5-19.

Hatch, J. & Cunliffe, L. (2006) *Organization Theory*, 2nd edition. Oxford: Oxford University, Press.

Haugan, G. (2013). Sustainable Program Management. CRC Press.13.978-1-4665-7516-5.

Helal, Abdelsalam A. (1999) *Any Time, Anywhere Computing: Mobile computing concepts and technology.* Boston, MA: Kluwer Academic.

Heldman, K. (2005) *Project Manager's Spotlight on Risk Management.* Alameda, CA: Sybex Inc.

Henkel, Ramon E. (1976) *Tests of Significance.* Beverly Hills CA: Sage.

Hildebrand, David K., Laing, James D. and Rosenthal, Howard (1977) *Analysis of Ordinal Data.* Beverly Hills, CA: Sage.

Hintz A. (2013) *Dimensions of Modern Freedom of Expression: WikiLeaks, Policy Hacking, and Digital Freedoms.* In: Brevini B., Hintz A., McCurdy P. (eds) Beyond WikiLeaks. Palgrave Macmillan, London.

Holt, T., & Lampke, E. (2010) Exploring stolen data markets online: products and market forces. *Criminal Justice Studies, 23*(1), 33-50.

Houghton, Katherine, Jean (1994) *Applications of Christian Faith Development Theories by the Chief Student Affairs Officers of the Christian College Coalition.* Teachers College, Columbia University http://pocketknowledge.tc.columbia.edu

how-to guide. *Washington, DC: Independent Evaluation Group, World Bank.*

http://www.geoinform.ru/?an=gng2009-all-en

http://www.us-cert.gov/ncas/tips/st04-015

https://pdf.ic3.gov/2012_IC3Report.pdf

https://pdf.ic3.gov/2013_IC3Report.pdf

https://pdf.ic3.gov/2014_IC3Report.pdf

https://pdf.ic3.gov/2015_ic3report.pdf

https://www.idtheftcenter.org/images/breach/2016/DataBreachReport_2016.pdf

https://www.idtheftcenter.org/images/breach/DataBreachReports_2015.pdf

https://www.le-vpn.com/history-cyber-crime-origin-evolution (Accessed: 16 January 2018).

Hutchings, A. (2014) Crime from the keyboard: organised cybercrime, co-offending, initiation and knowledge transmission. *Crime, Law and Social Change, 62*(1), 1-20.

ICSU, ISSC. (2015) *Review of Targets for the Sustainable Development Goals: The Science Perspective.* http://www.icsu.org/publications/reports-and-reviews/review-of-targets-for-the-sustainable-development-goals-the-science-perspective-2015/SDG-Report.pdf

IDC (2012) *Vertical IT and Communication Survey*

IFAD. (2002) *Managing for Impact in Rural Development: A Guide for Project M&E.* Rome: IFAD, Office of Evaluation and Studies. www.ifad.org/evaluation.

IMF. (2006, January) *The Federal Democratic Republic of Ethiopia: Poverty Reduction Strategy Paper — 2003/2004 Annual Progress Report. IMF County Report No. 06/27.* http://www.preventionweb.net/files/9337_ethiopia.pdf

IMF. (2012, December) *Nepal. 2012 Article IV Consultation.* https://www.imf.org/external/pubs/ft/scr/2012/cr12326.pdf

In Lee, C. E., & In Satku, K. (2016) *Singapore's health care system: What 50 years have achieved.* Singapore; Hackensack, NJ: World Scientific Publishing Co. Pte. Ltd.

Index Mundi. (2014) *Nepal Demographics Profile 2014.* http://www.indexmundi.com/nepal/demographics_profile.html

Infotech@Aerospace 2012. doi: 10.2514/6.2012-2438.

Iovan, S., & Iovan, A.-A. (2017) From Cyber threats to cybe crime. *Journal of Information system and operations management*, 425-434.

IRIN News. (2006, February 7) *ETHIOPIA: Struggling to end food aid dependency.* http://www.irinnews.org/report/58056/ethiopia-struggling-to-end-food-aid-dependency

Itell, J. (1998) Where Are They Now? - Performance Measurement Pioneers Offer Lessons from the Long, Hard Road. *The New Public Innovator*, 11-17.

ITRC (2013) *2012 breach report,* ITRC.

ITRC (2014) *2013 breach report,* ITRC.

ITRC (2015) *2014 breach report,* ITRC.

ITRC (2016) *2015 breach report,* ITRC.

ITRC (2017) *2016 breach report,* ITRC.

Jarvis, L., Macdonald, S., & Nouri, L. (2014) The cyberterrorism threat: Findings from a survey of researchers. *Studies in Conflict & Terrorism, 37*(1), 68-90.

Jean, I. (2012, January/February). *Closing the Loop. Systemic feedback mechanisms in international assistance efforts.* http://www.interaction.org/sites/default/files/MD_JanFeb_2012.pdf

Jewkes, Y. (2013) *Crime online.* Routledge.

Johnson, J. A., & Stoskopf, C. H. (2016) *Comparative health systems: Global perspectives.* Sudbury, Mass.: Jones and Bartlett Publishers.

Jones, B., 2006. Trying harder: Developing a new sustainable strategy for the UK. *Natural Resources Forum, 30*(2): 124–135.

Journal, 20(1), pp. 58–64. doi: 10.1080/19393555.2010.544705.

Kalton, Graham (1983) *Introduction to Survey Sampling.* Beverly Hills CA: Sage

Karkhanis, S. P., & Dumbre, S. S. (2015) A Study of Application of Data Mining and Analytics in Education Domain. *International Journal of Computer Applications, 120*(22).

Karl, W. and Gervais, A. (2016) 'Ethereum Eclipse Attacks', *doi.org,* pp. 1–7. doi: 10.3929/ethz-

Kaur, M., Gulati, H., & Kundra, H. (2014) Data mining in Agriculture on crop price prediction: Techniques and Applications. *International Journal of Computer Applications, 99*(12), 1-2.

Keeling, Kellie B. and Pavur, Robert J. (2006) A Comparative Study of the Reliability of Nine Statistical Software Packages. *Computational Statistics and Data Analysis* Volume 51 Issue 8 May 2007 pp 3811-3831.

REFERENCES

Kendrick, T. (2015) *Identifying and managing project risk: Essential tools for failure-proofing your project,* 3rd ed. New York: AMACOM.

Kettl, F. (1997) The Global Revolution in Public Management: Driving Themes, Missing Links, Policy Analysis and Management, 16(3): 446-462.

Khalil, I. M., Khreishah, A., & Azeem, M. (2014). Cloud computing security: A survey. *Computers, 3*(1), 1–35.

Khan, N., Yaqoob, I., Hashem, I. A. T., Inayat, Z., Ali, M., Kamaleldin, W., ... & Gani, A. (2014). Big data: survey, technologies, opportunities, and challenges. *The Scientific World Journal, 2014.*

Kiechel, W (2010) *The Lords of Strategy.* Harvard Business Press.

Kim, A. *et al.* (2012) 'Cyber Attack Vulnerabilities Analysis for Unmanned Aerial Vehicles'.

Kinkade, N., Jolla, L., & Lim, K. (2015) *Dota 2 win prediction.* Technical Report. tech. rep., University of California San Diego.

Kish, Leslie (1965) *Survey Sampling.* New York, NY: J. Wiley.

Kissi, E. (2006) *Revolution and Genocide in Ethiopia and Cambodia.* Oxford: Lexington Books.

Korf, B., & Raeymaekers, T. (2013) *Violence on the Margins: States, Conflict, and Borderlands.* Palgrave Macmillan.

Kusek, Z. & Rist, R. (2004) *Ten Steps to a Results-Based Monitoring and Evaluation.*

Kvint, V. (2015) Strategy for the Global Market: Theory and practical applications.

Kwak, Y., & Anbari, F. (2009). Analyzing project management research: Perspectives from top management journals. *International Journal of Project Management*, 27(2009), pp. 435–446.

Labuschagne, C., Brent, A. C., & Van Erck, R. P. G. (2005). Assessing the sustainability performances of industries. Journal of Cleaner Production, 13(4): 373–385.

Lainjo, B. (2015) Monitoring & Evaluation: Data Management Systems, Published Book.

Lainjo, B. (2017) How big data, cloud and analytics (BCA) have transformed information technology. Unpublished paper.

Lainjo, B. (2013) *Program Indicator Screening Matrix* (PRISM): *A Composite Score Framework. Canadian Evaluation Society* (CES) Conference Toronto, Canada.

Lamb, Richard Lawrence (2008) *Review of the Efficacy of SAS Curriculum Pathways on Student Understanding Chemistry.* NC: North Carolina State University.

Lancaster, C. (2007) Foreign Aid: Diplomacy, Development, Domestic Politics. Chicago: The University of Chicago.

Lawrie, G., Kalff, D., & Andersen, H. (2005) *Balanced scorecard and results based management: Convergent performance management systems.* Maidenhead, UK: 2GC. Retrieved August 1, 2007, from http://www.2gc.co.uk/pdf/2GC-C060130.pdf

Le VPN (2017) *Where Does Cyber Crime Come From? History of Cyber Crime.*

Lee, Frank E., Horn, Frank W. and Meyer, Bruce L. (1973) *ABC of the Telephone.* Chicago, IL: Lee's ABC of the Telephone.

Leech, Nancy L., Barrett, Karen Caplovitz and Morgan, George A. (2008) *SPSS for Intermediate Statistics: Use and interpretation.* 3rd edition. New York, NY: L. Erlbaum Assoc.

Li, J., & Narayanan, R. M. (2004) Integrated spectral and spatial information mining in remote sensing imagery. *IEEE Transactions on Geoscience and Remote Sensing, 42*(3), 673–685.

Lloyd, Robert C. (2004) *Quality Health Care: A guide to developing and using indicators.* Sudbury, MA: Jones and Barlett.

Loukas, G. (2015) 'Cyber-Physical Attack Steps', in *Cyber-Physical Attacks*, pp. 145–179.

Loveland, T. R., Reed, B. C., Brown, J. F., Ohlen, D. O., Zhu, Z., Yang, L. W. M. J., & Merchant, J. W. (2000). Development of a global land cover characteristics database and IGBP DISCover from 1 km AVHRR data. *International Journal of Remote Sensing, 21*(6–7), 1303–1330. doi:10.1080/014311600210191.

Loveland, T., Merchant, J., Brown, J., & Ohlen, D. (1991). Development of a land-cover characteristics database for the conterminous U. S. *Photogrammetric engineering and remote sensing, 57*(11), 1453–1463.

Lu, S., Li, R. M., Tjhi, W. C., Lee, K. K., Wang, L., Li, X., & Ma, D. (2011, November). A framework for cloud-based large-scale data analytics and visualization: Case study on multiscale climate data. *Proceedings of the 3^(rd) International Conference on Cloud Computing Technology and Science* (CloudCom 2011) (pp. 618–622). IEEE.

Mandal, S. K. (2017) Performance Analysis Of Data Mining Algorithms For Breast Cancer Cell Detection Using Naïve Bayes, Logistic Regression and Decision Tree. *International Journal Of Engineering And Computer Science, 6*(2).

Martens, M. L., Brones, F., & Carvalho, M. M. (2013) Lacunas e tendênciasnaliteratura de sustentabilidade no gerenciamento de projetos: umarevisãosistemáticamesclandobibliometria e análise de conteúdo. *Revista de Gestão e Projetos, 4*(1): 165–195.

Maszczyk, A., Gołaś, A., Pietraszewski, P., Roczniok, R., Zając, A., & Stanula, A. (2014) Application of neural and regression models in sports results prediction. *Procedia-Social and Behavioral Sciences, 117*, 482-487.

Mayne, J. (2007) Best practices in Results-Based Management: A Review of Experience – *A report for the United Nations Secretariat, Volume 1*: Main Report, July 2007.

McDowell, M. (2009) *Understanding Denial-of-Service Attacks, Security Tip*.

MCEC. (n.d.). *Introduction to project management*. Manfield Community Education Centre. http://www.mansfield.vic.gov.au/Libraries/Community_Developm ent/Intro_to_Project_Management_Manual.sflb.ashx

McGuire, M., & Dowling, S. (2013) Cyber crime: A review of the evidence. *Summary of key findings and implications. Home Office Research report, 75.*

McKinlay, M. (2008) *Where is project management running to?* Keynote speech, International Project Management Association, World Congress, Rome, Italy.

McLaughlin, K. L. (2011) 'Cyber attack! is a counter attack warranted?', *Information Security.*

Meier, W. (2003) Results-based management: Towards a common understanding among development cooperation agencies, Discussion Paper (Ver. 5.0).

Mekelburg, Alexander (2005) *Ergonimic, Adaptable Keyboard for Fast Data Entry on Mobile Computing Devices.* Massachusetts Institute of Technology, Dept. of Mechanical Engineering.

Melamchi. (2015) *MWSP: Project Financing Plan.* http://www.melamchiwater.gov.np/about-us/melamchi-ws-project/project-financing/

Method, F., Ayele, T., Bonner, C., Horn, N., Meshesha, A., & Abiche, T. (2010, July 20) *Impact assessment of USAID's education program in Ethiopia. 1994–2009. USAID.* https://www.usaid.gov/sites/default/files/documents/1860/Impact%20Assessment%20of%20USAID's%20Education%20Program%20in%20Ethiopia%201994-2009.pdf

Michener, W. K., & Jones, M. B. (2012) Ecoinformatics: Supporting ecology as a data-intensive science. *Trends in ecology & evolution, 27*(2), 85–93.

Miles, Matthew B. and Huberman, A. M. (1994) *Qualitative Data Analysis: An expanded sourcebook.* Thousand Oaks, CA: Sage Publications.

Milovic, B., & Milovic, M. (2012) Prediction and decision making in health care using data mining. *Kuwait Chapter of the Arabian Journal of Business and Management Review, 1*(12), 126.

Ministry for Foreign Affairs of Finland. (n.d.). *Finland's Development Cooperation.* http://www.evropa.gov.rs/Documents/Entity/DACU/Development%20Partners/238/Documents/1033/perusesite_en.pdf

Ministry of Public Health, Thailand. (2016) *Public Health Statistics*. Bangkok: Ministry of Public Health.

Mishra, N., & Silakari, S. (2012). Predictive analytics: a survey, trends, applications, oppurtunities & challenges. *International Journal of Computer Science and Information Technologies*, 3(3), 4434-4438.

Mole, R. (1987). *Basic Business Analysis and Operations Research.* Norfolk: Butterworth & Co.

Moore, R. (2010) *Cybercrime: Investigating high-technology computer crime.* Routledge.

Morfaw, J. (2011) *Project Sustainability: A Comprehensive Guide to Sustaining Projects.* IN, USA: iUniverse.

Morgan, George; Griego, Orlando V. and Gloeckner, Gene (2000) *SPSS for Windows: An introduction to use and interpretation in research.* Mahwah, NJ: Lawrence Erlbaum Assoc. Inc.

Morris, P., & Pinto, J. K. (2007) *The Wiley Guide to Project Control.* New Jersey: John Wiley & Sons Inc. Available at:http://as.wiley.com/WileyCDA/WileyTitle/productCd-0471233021.html

Morris, R. (2010) Computer hacking and the techniques of neutralization: An empirical assessment.

Moynihan, D. P. (2006) 'Managing for Results in State Government: Evaluating a Decade of Reform', *Public Administration Review* 66(1): 77 – 89

Mulder, J., & Brent, A. C. (2006) Selection of Sustainable Rural Agriculture Projects in South Africa: Case Studies in the LandCare Programme. Engineering and Technology, 28(2): 55–84.

Muller, K. E., Smith, J. and Christiansen, D. H. (1981) *Rules We Followed and Wish We Had Followed in Managing Datasets, Programs and Printouts* Proceedings of the SAS Users Group International Conference, Volume 6, 401-405. Cary, NC: SAS Institute, Inc.

Multidimensional Strategic Concept. Long Range Planning Journal, 34(2001): 699–725.

Neuhaus, G. (2012, March 8) *More Responsibility for the Recipients. Interview with J. Brian Atwood, Director of the OECD Development Committee.* https://www.dfae.admin.ch/deza/en/home/news/press-releases-articles-speeches.html/content/deza/en/meta/news/2012/8/3/verantwortung

New York Times', *New York Times*, pp. 7–11. Available at: https://www.nytimes.com/2017/09/07/business/equifax-cyberattack.html?_r=1.

NHS Choice. (2015). *HPV vaccine.* http://www.nhs.uk/conditions/vaccinations/pages/hpv-human-papillomavirus-vaccine.aspx

Nigel Simister. (2011) Results-based management, INTRAC.

Norman, R. (2002) Managing through Measurement or Meaning? Lessons from Experience with New Zealand's Public-Sector Performance Management Systems. *International Review of Administrative Sciences 68*: 619–628.

Norval, Glenn D. (1977) *Cohort Analysis.* Beverly Hills, CA: Sage.

Obermeyer, Z., & Emanuel, E. J. (2016) Predicting the future—big data, machine learning, and clinical medicine. *The New England journal of medicine, 375*(13), 1216.

ODI. (2011). *Progress in Implementing the Paris Declaration.* http://www.odi.org/sites/odi.org.uk/files/odi-assets/events-presentations/953.pdf

OECD (1997) In Search of Results: Performance Management Practices, Paris, France.

OECD. (1998) *Development Co-operation Reviews Development Co-operation Reviews: Canada 1998. No. 26.* Danvers, MA: OECD.

OECD. (2005/2008).*The Paris Declaration on Aid Effectiveness and the Accra Agenda for Action.* http://www.oecd.org/dac/effectiveness/34428351.pdf

OECD. (2006) *Aid Effectiveness: Three Good Reasons Why the Paris Declaration Will Make a Difference. 2005 Development*

Cooperation Report. Vol. 7. No. 1, pp. 49–54.
http://www.oecd.org/development/effectiveness/36364587.pdf

OECD. (2008) OECD Working Party on Aid Effectiveness. Aid Effectiveness: A Progress Report on Implementing the Paris Declaration. Chapter 3: Ownership. OECD Publications.

OECD. (2011a) *The Busan Partnership for Effective Development Co-operation.* 1 December 2011.
http://www.oecd.org/development/effectiveness/49650173.pdf

OECD. (2011b) *Aid Effectiveness 2011: Progress in Implementing the Paris Declaration.* Better Aid, OECD Publishing.
doi:10.1787/9789264125780-en

OECD. (2011c) *Reaching Our Development Goals: Why Does Aid Effectiveness Matter?*
https://www.oecd.org/development/effectiveness/40987004.pdf

OECD. (2012) *Better Aid Effectiveness 2011 Progress in Implementing the Paris Declaration.* OECD Publishing.

OECD/DAC: *Evaluation Criteria.* Available at:
www.oecd.org//dac/Evaluation/htm/evalcrit.htm

OECD/WORKING PARTY ON AID EVALUATION (2001): Glossary of Terms in *Evaluation and Results-Based Management.* Available at: www.oecd.org/dac/htm/glossary.htm

ohjelmiston avulla, Tampereen yliopisto, Matematiikan, tilastotieteen ja filosofian laitos, B53.

Online. Available at: https://www.csoonline.com/article/3237324/cyber-attacks-espionage/what-is-a-cyber-attack-recent-examples-show-disturbing-trends.html (Accessed: 15 January 2018).

Organisation for Economic Co-operation and Development. (2016). *OECD Reviews of Health Systems: Mexico 2016.* Paris: OECD Publishing.

Organization for Economic Co-operation and Development, OECD (1997). *In Search of Results: Performance Management Practices,* Paris, France.

Orr, T. (2008). *Privacy and hacking.* New York: Rosen Central.

Oza, N., Karppinen, K., & Savola, R. (2010, November). User experience and security in the cloud: An empirical study in the Finnish cloud consortium. *Proceedings of the 2nd International Conference on Cloud Computing Technology and Science* (CloudCom 2010) (pp. 621–628). IEEE.

Padhy, N., & Panigrahi, R. (2012) Data Mining: A prediction Technique for the workers in the PR Department of Orissa (Block and Panchayat). *arXiv preprint arXiv:1211.5724.*

Pan American Health Organization. (2017) *PAHO's policy on research for health: PAHO research for health policy approved during the 61st Session of the Directing Council of 2009.* Washington, D.C.: Pan American Health Organization.

Parker, Richard A. and Rea, Louis M. (1992) *Designing and Conducting Survey Research: A comprehensive guide* 2nd edition. San Francisco, CA: Jossey-Bass.

Pate, Anthony, M. and Fridell, Lorie, A. (1994) Police Use of Force (United States) Official Reports, Citizen Complaints, and Legal consequences, 1991-1992. Ann Arbor, MI: Inter-university Consortium for Political and Social Research http://dx.doi.org.

Pedhazur, Elazar J. and Schmelkin, Liora Pedhazur (1991) *Measurement, Design, Analysis.* Hillsdale, NJ: Lawrence Erlbaum Assoc.

Percivall, G. (2010) The application of open standards to enhance the interoperability of geoscience information. *International Journal of Digital Earth*, *3*(S1), 4–30.

Perlroth, N. (2017) "Equifax Says Cyberattack May Have Affected 143 Million Customers", The New York Times.

Perry, C. (2013). Machine learning and conflict prediction: a use case.

Pippal, S., Batra, L., Krishna, A., Gupta, H., & Arora, K. (2014). Data mining in social networking sites: A social media mining approach to generate effective business strategies. *International Journal of Innovations & Advancement in Computer Science*, *3*(1).

Platteau, J.-P. (2003, May). Community-Based Development in the Context of Within Group Heterogeneity. Paper presented to the Annual Bank Conference on Development Economics, Bangalore.

http://siteresources.worldbank.org/INTPUBSERV/Resources/platte
au2.pdf

Plavgo, I., Kibur, M., Bitew, M., Gebreselassie, T., Matsuda, Y., &
Pearson, R. (2013, August).*Multidimensional Child Deprivation
Trend Analysis in Ethiopia.* Available
at:http://www.unicef.org/ethiopia/Multidimensinal_child_deprivati
on_Trend_Analysis_in_Ethiopia.pdf

Plummer, J. (2012) *Diagnosing Corruption in Ethiopia: Perceptions,
Realities, and the Way Forward for Key Sectors.* World Bank.

Poate, D. (1997). Measuring & Managing Results: Lessons for
Development.

Politt, C. & Bouckaert, G. (2011) *Public Management Reform: A
Comparative Analysis - New Public Management*, Governance,
and the Neo-Weberian State. Third edition. Oxford: Oxford
University Press.

Pompa, C. (2012). Literature Review on enterprise mentoring. EPS-
PEAKS

Portney, Leslie Gross and Watkins, Mary P. (2000) *Foundations of
Clinical Research.* Upper Saddle River, NJ: Prentice Hall.

Poulsen, K., & Summerer, E. (2015) *Kingpin : how one hacker took over
the billion-dollar cybercrime underground.* Retrieved from
http://search.ebscohost.com/login.aspx?direct=true&scope=site&d
b=nlebk&db=nlabk&AN=953512

Pritchard, C. (2014) *The Project Management Communications Toolkit,*
2nd ed. Norwood, MA: Artech House.

Purcell, B. M. (2014) Big data using cloud computing. *Journal of
Technology Research*, 5, 1.

Quality Assurance Solutions. (n.d.). *What is the Definition of TQM?*
http://www.quality-assurance-solutions.com/definition-of-
TQM.html

Radio Free Europe/Radio Liberty. (2013, May 31) *Questioning The
Environmental Cost of Kyrgyzstan's Kumtor Gold Mine.*
http://www.rferl.org/content/kyrgyzstan-kumtor-gold-mine-
environmental-/25003485.html

Rahmato, D., Pankhurst, A., & van Uffelen, J.-G. (2013) *Food Security, Safety Nets and Social Protection in Ethiopia.* Addis Ababa: Forum for Social Studies.

Ramboll (2005) Department of Water Affairs & Forestry, Republic of South Africa. Project Monitoring and Evaluation.

Raven, R. P. J. M., Jolivet, E., Mourik, R. M., & Feenstra, Y. C. F. J. (2009). ESTEEM: Managing societal acceptance in new energy projects. *Technological Forecasting and Social Change, 76*(7): 963–977.

Raynor, Jared, Peter York and Shao-Chee Sim (2009). *What Makes an Effective Advocacy Organization?* A Framework for Determining Advocacy Capacity. TCC Group for the California Endowment.

Razali, N., Mustapha, A., Yatim, F. A., & Ab Aziz, R. (2017, August). Predicting Player Position for Talent Identification in Association Football. In *IOP Conference Series: Materials Science and Engineering* (Vol. 226, No. 1, p. 012087). IOP Publishing.

Reed, D., & McConnachie, J. (2002). *The rough guide to Nepal,* 5th ed. London: Rough Guides.

RESPONSE, p. 57. doi: 10.5437/08953608X5403011.

Rick, T. (2011, March 13) *How to hold people accountable: Performance management.* [Blog]. https://www.torbenrick.eu/blog/performance-management/how-to-hold-people-accountable/

Ridley, J. (n.d.). *Total Quality Management and Internal Auditing.* Available at:http://www.financepractitioner.com/contentFiles/QF02/h16mupqe/17/0/total-quality-management-and-internal-auditing.pdf

Rimikis, Antonios M. (2008) <u>A Lightweight TwiddleNet Portal</u>. CA: Ft. Belvoir Defense Technical Information Center.

Roberts, D., & Khattri, N. (2012). Designing a results framework for achieving results: a how-to guide.

Robertson, Alberta Lee (1980) *The Identification of the Competencies Needed by Vocational Supervisors as Perceived by Vocational Supervisors, Principals, and Teachers in Georgia's Comprehensive High Schools*. GA: Georgia State University.

Robichaud, L. B., & Anantatmula, V. S. (2011). Greening project management practices for sustainable construction. *Journal of Management in Engineering, 27*(1), 48–57.

Roche, S., 2014. Geographic information science I: Why does a smart city need to be spatially enabled? *Progress in Human Geography, 38*(5), 703–711.

Rose, K. (2005). *Project Quality Management: Why, What and How.* J. Ross Publishing Inc. pp. 41–43. http://www.azkhan.de/documents/Project%20Quality%20Management%20-%20Why,%20What%20And%20How.pdf

Rubin, R. (2006) *Demonstrating Results: Using Outcome Measurement in Your Library.* American Library Association.

Rumelt, R. P. (2011) *Good Strategy/Bad Strategy.* Crown Business.

Rural Poverty Portal. (n.d.). *Rural poverty in Ethiopia.* http://www.ruralpovertyportal.org/country/home/tags/ethiopia

Ryan, Gery W. and Bernard, H. Russell (1994) *Handbook of Qualitative Research* 2nd edition. Thousand Oaks, CA: Sage

Sahlberg, P. (2009) Educational Change in Finland. In A. Hargreaves & A. Lieberman (Eds.), *Second international handbook of educational change* (pp. 323–348). Springer Netherlands.

Salkind, Neil J. and Rasmussen, Kirstin (2007) *Encyclopaedia of Measurement and Statistics.* Thousand Oaks, CA: Sage.

Sanghera, P. (2008) *Fundamentals of Effective Program Management: A Process Approach Based on the Global Standard.* US: J. Ross Publishing.

Sapkota, C. (2015, July 1). *Final take on economic and poverty impact of Nepal earthquake.* http://blogs.adb.org/blog/final-take-economic-and-poverty-impact-nepal-earthquake.

Sara & Todd, (2016) Cloud Utilization by users (2012-2016).

Savage, K., Coogan, P. and Lau, H. (2015) 'The Evolution of Ransomware', *SECURITY.*

Savitz, A. W. (2006) *The triple bottom line: How today's best-run companies are achieving economic, social and environmental success — and how you can too*, 1st ed. San Francisco, CA: John Willey & Sons.

Schaffer, Joanne (1987) Procedure for Solving the Data-editing Problem with Both Continuous and Discrete Data Types *Naval Research Logistics* Volume 34, pp 879-890 New York, NY: Wiley.

Schwalbe, K. (2010) *Information Technology Project Management.* Boston, MA: Course Technology Cengage Learning. p. 106, p. 198, pp. 295–296.

Security, 2017(8), pp. 5–7. doi: 10.1016/S1361-3723(17)30068-4.

Sellamna, N., & Gebremedhin, A. (2015, February). *A new dynamic for community service in Ethiopian higher education. Policy Brief 1/2015.*

Semenov, A., Romov, P., Korolev, S., Yashkov, D., & Neklyudov, K. (2016, April). Performance of machine learning algorithms in predicting game outcome from drafts in dota 2. In *International Conference on Analysis of Images, Social Networks and Texts* (pp. 26-37). Springer, Cham.

Shachak, A., & Reis, S. (2009) The impact of electronic medical records on patient–doctor communication during consultation: a narrative literature review. *Journal of evaluation in clinical practice, 15*(4), 641-649.

Shah, A. (2014, September 28) *Foreign Aid for Development Assistance.* http://www.globalissues.org/print/article/35

Shapiro, J. (2001) *Monitoring and Evaluation.* CIVICUS: World Alliance for Citizen.

Sharma, S. (2006) *Introductory Operation Research.* New Delhi: Discovery Publishing House.

Shenhar, A. (2011) Meeting time, cost, and moneymaking goals with Strategic Project Leadership®. *Why is Project Management Weak? The Art and Science of Project Management*. PMI Global Congress Proceeding.

Shenhar, A., & Dvir, D. (2007) Reinventing project management: the diamond approach to successful growth and innovation. Harvard Business School Press.

Shenhar, A., Dvir, D., Levy, O., & Maltz, A. C. (2001) Project Success: A Should Know. <Online> Available at http://datascientistinsights.com .accessed on 02 June 2014

Silvius, A. J. G. (2010) Report workshop 2, IMPA Expert seminar survival and sustainability as challenges for projects, Zurich.

Silvius, A. J. G. (2013) Sustainability in Project Management Processes. In A. J. G. Silvius & J. Tharp (Eds.), *Sustainability Integration for Effective Project Management* (Chapter 4, pp.58–75). Hershey, PA: IGI Global Publishing.

Singh, R. K., Murty, H. R., Gupta, S. K., Dikshit, A. K. (2012) An overview of sustainability assessment methodologies. *Ecological Indicators, 15*(1): 281–299.

Singh, V. K., Uddin, A., & Pinto, D. (2015) Computer science research: The top 100 institutions in India and in the world. *Scientometrics, 104*(2), 529–553.

Sirkeci, I., Cohen, J., & Ratha, D. (2012) *Migration and remittances during the global financial crisis and beyond.* Washington, DC: The World Bank.

Smyth, G. (2017) 'Using data virtualisation to detect an insider breach', *Computer Fraud and Security,* Vol. 2017, Issue 8.

Snail, S. (2009) Cyber Crime in South Africa–Hacking, cracking, and other unlawful online activities. *Journal of Information, Law and Technology, 1*, 2001-2009.

Solheim, A., Ragazzon, R., Pedan, D., Chernov, E., Kulbachnuy, P., Sveinsen, A., Faschevsky, S., & Usmanov, T. (2012) *Energy Audit at Talco–Aluminum Company in Tajikistan. Energy Audit Report.* http://www.worldbank.org/content/dam/Worldbank/document/tj-talco-energy-audit-report-executive-summary.pdf

Soumya, S. B., & Deepika, N. (2016) Data Mining With Predictive Analytics for Financial Applications. *International Journal of Scientific Engineering and Applied Science, 1*, 310-317.

Stanoevska-Slabeva, K., Wozniak, T., & Ristol, S. (Eds.). (2009). *Grid and cloud computing: A business perspective on technology and applications*. Springer Science & Business Media.

Stefanovska, L., & Soklevski, T. (2014) Benefits of Using Balanced Scorecard in Strategic and Operational Planning. *Universal Journal of Management, 2*(4), 165-171.

Stuart, B., Sarow, M. and Stuart, L. (2007) *Integrated Business Communication: In a Global Marketplace*. West Sussex, England: John Wiley & Sons.

Suarjaya, I. M. A. D. (2012) A new algorithm for data compression optimization. *arXiv preprint arXiv:1209.1045*.

Sudman, Seymour (1976) *Applied Sampling*. New York, NY: Academic Press.

Sustainable Development Knowledge Platform. (2009). *Decisions by Topic: Rural Development. Commission on Sustainable Development. E/CN.17/2009/19.* https://sustainabledevelopment.un.org/index.php?menu=1263

Sweeney, G., Despota, K., & Lindner, S. (2013). *Global corruption Report: Education. Transparency International.* https://www.transparency.de/fileadmin/pdfs/Wissen/Korruptionsin dices/Global_Corruption_Report_2013__Education.pdf

System. Washington, DC: World Bank.

Szent-Ivanyi, B., & Lightfoot, S. (2015). *New Europe's New Development Aid.* NEW YORK: Routledge.

Taking IT Global. (2015). *German Agency for Technical Cooperation (GTZ).* http://orgs.tigweb.org/german-agency-for-technical-cooperation-gtz

Tavares, L. (2002). A review of the contribution of Operational Research to Project Management. *European Journal of Operational Research*, 136(1): 1–18. http://www.researchgate.net/publication/223092551_A_review_of _the_contribution_of_Operational_Research_to_Project_Managem ent

Taylor, R., Fritsch, E., & Liederbach, J. (2014). *Digital crime and digital terrorism.* Prentice Hall Press.

Thakar, P. (2015). Performance analysis and prediction in educational data mining: A research travelogue. *arXiv preprint arXiv:1509.05176.*

The Guardian (UK). Available at: https://www.theguardian.com/technology/2016/dec/14/yahoo-hack-security-of-one-billion-accounts-breached.

The New York Times. Available at: http://www.nytimes.com/2016/12/14/technology/yahoo-hack.html%5Cnhttp://www.nytimes.com/2016/12/14/technology/yahoo-hack.html?_r=0.

Thielman, S. (2016) Yahoo hack: 1bn accounts compromised by biggest data breach in history, The Guardian.

Thirty, M. (2010) *Program Management.* Surrey: Gower Publishing.

Thomas, E. H., & Galambos, N. (2004). What satisfies students? Mining student-opinion data with regression and decision tree analysis. *Research in Higher Education, 45*(3), 251-269.

Thompson, Steven K. (1992) *Sampling.* New York, NY: Wiley.

Thomson, C. S., El-Haram, M. A., & Emmanuel, R. (2011). Mapping sustainability assessment with the project life cycle. *Proceedings of the ICE: Engineering Sustainability, 164*(2): 143–157.

Thornton, P. K., Schuetz, T., Förch, W., Cramer, L., Abreu, D., Vermeulen, S., & Tomar, R. (2009). COMMERCIAL OPERATIONS MANAGEMENT: Process and Technology to Support Commercial Activities. New Delhi: Global India Publications Pvt. Ltd.

Tomlinson, B., & Foster, P. (2004, September). *At the table or in the kitchen? CIDA's new aid strategies, developing country owners and donor conditionality.* Canadian Council for International Co-operation. Halifax Initiative, Briefing Paper. http://www.ccic.ca/_files/en/what_we_do/002_aid_2004-09_at_the_table.pdf

Turlea, C., Roman, T. D., & Constantinescu, D. G. (2010). The project management and the need for sustainable development. *Metalurgia Internacional, 15*(3): 121–125.

Turner, R. (2014). *Handbook of Project-Based Management,* 4th ed. London: McGraw Hill.

U.S. Department of State. (2010). Leading Through Civilian Power, U.S. Department of State, Quadrennial Diplomacy and Development Review.

UNC. (2010). *Panning for Gold: the Kumtor Mine in the Kyrgyz Republic.* http://www.unc.edu/courses/2010spring/econ/560/002/kumtor.html

UNDP (2007). *Evaluation of Results Based Management at UNDP: Achieving Results*, Evaluation Office, UNDP: New York.

UNDP. (2011, December 8). *Anti-Corruption.* http://www.undp.org/content/undp/en/home/ourwork/democraticgovernance/focus_areas/focus_anti-corruption.html

UNDP. (2012, July 9). *Helen Clark: Remarks on Corruption at the ECOSOC 2012 High Level Segment.* http://www.undp.org/content/undp/en/home/presscenter/speeches/2012/07/09/helen-clark-opening-remarks-at-the-ecosoc-2012-high-level-segment/

UNDP. (n.d.). *Anti-Corruption.* http://www.undp.org/content/undp/en/home/ourwork/democraticgovernance/focus_areas/focus_anti-corruption.html

UNESCO, Bureau of Strategic Planning (2010). *Results-Based Programming, Management and Monitoring (RBM) approach as applied at UNESCO- Guiding Principles, UNESCO* Paris, France.

UNFCCC. (2015) *Technology Transfer Framework: Enabling Environment.* http://unfccc.int/ttclear/templates/render_cms_page?TTF_home

UNFPA. (2014) "Prioritizing sexual and reproductive health will save millions of lives," report.

UNICEF. (2011) *Country Office Portal. Annual Report 2011 for Nepal, ROSA.* http://www.unicef.org/about/annualreport/files/Nepal_COAR_2011.pdf

UNICEF. (2013). *Nepal.*
http://www.unicef.org/infobycountry/nepal_nepal_statistics.html

United Nations. (2011) *Guiding Principles on Business and Human Rights.*

United States.; National Aeronautics and Space Administration (1991) Pre-Magellan Radar and Gravity Data Radar Sets for Venus, the Moon, Mercury, Mars, and Earth, Together with Gravity Data Derived from Tracking the Pioneer-Venus Orbiter and the Mars Viking Orbiters. Washington DC: United States.; National Aeronautics and Space Administration.

USAID, *Centre for Development Information and Evaluation.* <Online> available at: www.dec.org/usaid_eval/

USAID. (2014, July) *Nepal: Nutrition Profile.*
https://www.usaid.gov/sites/default/files/documents/1864/USAID-Nepal_NCP.pdf

USAID. (2015a). Food Assistance Fact Sheet: Ethiopia. 23 June 2015.
https://www.usaid.gov/ethiopia/food-assistance

USAID. (2015b). *USAID History.* 28 May 2015.
https://www.usaid.gov/who-we-are/usaid-history

Vahamaki, M., Schmidt, M. & Molander, J. 2011, *Review: results based management in development cooperation,* Riksbanken Jubileumsfond, Stockholm.

Vanek, V. W., Ayers, P., Charney, P., Kraft, M., Mitchell, R., Plogsted, S., & Kent, S. (2016). Follow-up survey on functionality of nutrition documentation and ordering nutrition therapy in currently available electronic health record systems. *Nutrition in Clinical Practice, 31*(3), 401-415.

Vifell, A. C., & L. Soneryd. (2012) Organizing matters: How "the social dimension" gets lost in sustainability projects. *Sustainable Development, 20*(1): 18–27.

Vijayan, V., & Ravikumar, A. (2014). Study of data mining algorithms for prediction and diagnosis of diabetes mellitus. *International journal of computer applications, 95*(17).

Walters, R. (2014) Cyber attacks on US companies in 2014. *The Heritage Foundation, 4289*, 1-5.

Wang, X. (2010) *Performance Analysis for Public and Nonprofit Organizations.* London: Jones and Bartlett Publishers.

WFP (2014) *Monitoring & Evaluation Guidelines: Reporting on M&E Data and Information for EMOPs and PRROs.* Available at: www.wfp.org

Williams, Bill (1978) *A Sampler on Sampling.* New York, NY: Wiley.

Wilson, A. (2012) *Masters of War: History's Greatest Strategic Thinkers.* The Teaching Company.

Wilson, C. (2008). Botnets, cybercrime, and cyberterrorism: Vulnerabilities and policy issues for congress. LIBRARY OF CONGRESS WASHINGTON DC CONGRESSIONAL RESEARCH SERVICE.

Winrock. (2008, January) *Innovations.* http://newsletter.winrock.org/200801/

Winrock. (2015) *Winrock International in Nepal.* http://winrock.org.np/winrock-international-in-nepal-27.html

Wit, A. (1988) Measurement of project success. *Project Management, 6*(3): 164–170.

Woldehanna, T. (2004, May 30) *The Experiences of Measuring and Monitoring Poverty in Ethiopia. For the inaugural meeting of the Poverty Analysis and Data Initiative (PADI) held on May 6–8 2004 in Mombasa, Kenya.* http://www.heart-intl.net/HEART/110105/TheExperiencesofMeasuring.pdf

World Bank. (2012a) *Inclusive Green Growth: The Pathway to Sustainable Development.* World Bank Publications.

World Bank. (2012b) *Strengthening Governance: Tackling Corruption. The World Bank Group's Updated Strategy and Implementation.* 6 March 2012. http://siteresources.worldbank.org/PUBLICSECTORANDGOVER NANCE/Resources/285741-1326816182754/GACStrategyImplementationPlan.pdf

REFERENCES

World Bank. (2015a) *Migration and Remittances: Recent Developments and Outlook.* 13 April 2015.
http://siteresources.worldbank.org/INTPROSPECTS/Resources/334934-1288990760745/MigrationandDevelopmentBrief24.pdf

World Bank. (2015b) *Economic Overview: Ethiopia.* 5 April 2015.
http://www.worldbank.org/en/country/ethiopia/overview

World Bank. (2015c) *Overview: Nepal.* 19 June 2015.
http://www.worldbank.org/en/country/nepal/overview

World Food Program. (2015) *Overview: Nepal.*
https://www.wfp.org/node/3532/3043/276156

www.idtheftcenter.org/images/breach/ITRC_Breach_Report_2013.pdf

www.idtheftcenter.org/images/breach/ITRC_Breach_Report_2013.pdf

www.idtheftcenter.org/images/breach/ITRCBreachStatsReportSummary2014.pdf

www.statista.com, 2016. *Forecast: global data center IP traffic 2012-2020, by type.*

Xiaohu, W., Lele, W., & Nianfeng, L. (2012) An application of decision tree based on id3. *Physics Procedia, 25,* 1017-1021.

Yadav, S. K., & Pal, S. (2012). Data mining: A prediction for performance improvement of engineering students using classification. *arXiv preprint arXiv:1203.3832.*

Yar, M. (2013) Cybercrime and society. Sage.

Young Lives in Ethiopia. (2012, December).*Improving Education Quality, Equity and Access in Ethiopia: Findings from the Young Lives School Component.*
http://www.younglives.org.uk/publications/PP/improving-education-quality-equity-and-access-in-ethiopia/yl-ethiopia-pb1-education

Young, J. (2006) *Peasant Revolution in Ethiopia: The Tigray People's Liberation Front, 1975–1991.* Cambridge: University Press.

Zizlavsky, O. (2014) The balanced scorecard: Innovative performance measurement and management control system. *Journal of technology management & innovation, 9*(3), 210-	222.

About the Author

Bongs Lainjo, MASc, Engineering, is an RBM systems consultant with expertise in program evaluation. Bongs is a former UN Senior Advisor of Program Management, Reproductive Health Commodity Security (RHCS) and Evaluation. Prior to that, he worked for USAID as a Logistics and Management Information Systems Advisor (LISA). He also served as COP/Senior Data Management Advisor for Columbia University after spending close to a decade teaching as a professor at a number of Canadian academic institutions.

Bongs has worked in several countries in Africa, Asia, Pacific Island Countries, Canada, and the U.S.

Some of his activities include authoring *Monitoring and Evaluation: Data Management Systems*, serving as a member of the Scientific Committee, Burgundy School of Business (Dijon, France), guest lecturer, University of West Indies, (Kingston, Jamaica) and developing and implementing thematic peer-reviewed models. These frameworks include the Program Indicator System Matrix (PRISM), the RHCS Analysis and Planning System (RAPSYS), and the Sustainable Program Management: Hierarchical Causal System. He is also a monitoring and evaluation (M&E) expert who has developed systems, survey protocols, and training manuals and conducted workshops for UN staff and partners, various evaluation missions, and M&E assignments in USAID-funded projects, including reviewing Program Management Plans (PMPs). He also served as a Front Line Supply Chain Advisor in Sri Lanka, Maldives, and Indonesia during the tsunami in 2004.

His many peer-reviewed papers have been presented at international conferences in Bogota (Colombia), Lyon (France), Port of Spain (Trinidad and Tobago), Kingston (Jamaica), Bali (Indonesia), Dhaka (Bangladesh), Rio de Janeiro (Brazil), Nairobi (Kenya), Bangkok (Thailand), Singapore, (Singapore), Toronto (Canada), Montreal (Canada), San Antonio (USA), Shanghai (China), Valetta (Malta), Hanoi, Ho Chi Minh City (Vietnam), Casablanca (Morocco), U. of Mauritius, (Mauritius), Kampala (Uganda), Colombo (Sri Lanka), Ouagadougou (Burkina Faso), and Yokohama (Japan).

WWW.BSUIRU.WORDPRESS.COM

Index

INDEX